This programmatic socio-rhetorical investigation approaches the Epistle of James as an instance of written deliberative rhetoric, and it seeks to ascertain the social texture of James 2.5, a rhetorical performance of language that in other contexts is explicitly attributed to Jesus. Utilizing the conventions of Greco-Roman rhetoric, Dr. Wachob successively probes the inner texture, the intertexture, the social and cultural texture, and the ideological implications of the rhetoric in James 2.1–13. He analyzes James' activation of antecedent texts in the LXX, common conceptions and topics in the broader culture, and also sayings in the Jesus tradition. He concludes that James emanates from the same milieu as the pre-Matthean Sermon on the Mount and shows James 2.5 to be an artful performance of the principal beatitude in that early epitome of Jesus' teachings.

WESLEY HIRAM WACHOB is Senior Minister, Ashland Place United Methodist Church, Mobile, Alabama. He studied at the Candler School of Theology and did his doctoral work at the University of Chicago and at Emory University. Dr. Wachob's publications include contributions to *The Anchor Bible Dictionary* and *Authenticating the Words of Jesus*.

SOCIETY FOR NEW TESTAMENT STUDIES

MONOGRAPH SERIES

General Editor: Richard Bauckham

106

THE VOICE OF JESUS IN THE SOCIAL RHETORIC OF JAMES

The voice of Jesus in the social rhetoric of James

WESLEY HIRAM WACHOB

CAMBRIDGE
UNIVERSITY PRESS

PUBLISHED BY THE PRESS SYNDICATE OF THE UNIVERSITY OF CAMBRIDGE
The Pitt Building, Trumpington Street, Cambridge, United Kingdom

CAMBRIDGE UNIVERSITY PRESS
The Edinburgh Building, Cambridge CB2 2RU, UK
http://www.cup.cam.ac.uk
40 West 20th Street, New York NY 10011–4211, USA
http://www.cup.org
10 Stamford Road, Oakleigh, Melbourne 3166, Australia

First published 2000

Printed in the United Kingdom at the University Press, Cambridge

Typeset in 10/12pt Times   [CE]

A catalogue record for this book is available from the British Library

Library of Congress cataloguing in publication data

Wachob, Wesley Hiram.
The voice of Jesus in the social rhetoric of James / Wesley Hiram Wachob.
    p.   cm. – (Society for New Testament Studies monograph series; 106.)
Includes bibliographical references and indexes.
ISBN 0 521 66069 6 (hardback)
1. Bible. N.T. James II, 1–13 – Socio-rhetorical criticism.
I. Title. II. Series: Monograph series (Society for New Testament
Studies); 106.
BS2785.2.W33   1999
227'.9106–dc21   99–19542   CIP

ISBN 0 521 66069 6 hardback

CONTENTS

ACKNOWLEDGMENTS

This monograph first appeared as a Ph.D. dissertation (Wachob, 1993) written in Emory University. I wish to thank Professor Richard Bauckham, editor of the Monograph series, for his kindness and expeditious handling of my manuscript. To both Professor Margaret Thrall, the previous editor of the series, and to the anonymous reader of my work, I offer my thanks for helpful comments and suggestions. I am grateful to the Syndicate of Cambridge University Press, and Mr. Kevin Taylor, the Senior Commissioning Editor (Religious Studies), for publishing my research.

Many thanks are due to Professor Vernon K. Robbins (Emory University), who served as the director for my dissertation. With his wise counsel and enthusiasm for learning, he has broadened my vision and enriched my life. I am also grateful to Professor Hans Dieter Betz (University of Chicago), who encouraged me to make the question of the relationship between the Epistle of James and the Sermon on the Mount the subject of my research. Appreciation is also due to the Reverend Dr. Kenneth F. Morris (Erskine Theological Seminary), who introduced me to the Greek text of James, almost twenty-five years ago.

Others of my teachers to whom I owe special recognition are, of the University of Chicago, Professor Robert M. Grant and (the late) Mr. David J. Wilmot; and of Emory University, Professors Fred B. Craddock, Robert Detweiler, John H. Hayes, Carl R. Holladay, and Luke Timothy Johnson, who, with Vernon Robbins, formed my doctoral committee. I am especially pleased and honored that Professor Luke Johnson could make use of my research in his excellent (1995) commentary on James.

I am also truly fortunate to have friends like Charles Dean, Trent Foley, John Hipp, Mitch Houston, Volkmar Latossek, Phil Lavender, Mark Ledbetter, Russ Sisson, Judd Stinson, and Ron

Thomas. Their concern for me and for my work has been a source of inspiration.

Above all, I am thankful to my wife, Deborah, and to our children, Wesley and Katherine, for their love and support. To them this book is dedicated.

SOURCES AND ABBREVIATIONS

AARAS	American Academy of Religion Academy Series
AASF	*Annales Academiae Scientiarum Fennicae*
AB	Anchor Bible
AnBib	Analecta biblica
ANRW	*Aufstieg und Niedergang der römischen Welt*
ASNU	Acta seminarii neotestamentici upsaliensis
ATR	*Anglican Theological Review*
BAGD	Baur-Arndt-Gingrich-Danker, *Greek-English Lexicon of the New Testament*
BDF	Blass-Debrunner-Funk, *Greek Grammar of the New Testament*
BETL	Bibliotheca ephemeridum theologicarum lovaniensium
BFCT	Beiträge zur Förderung christlicher Theologie
BGU	Aegyptische Urkunden aus den Staatlichen Museen zu Berlin Griechische Urkunden
BHTh	Beitrage zur historischen Theologie
Bib	*Biblica*
BJRL	*Bulletin of the John Rylands University Library of Manchester*
BSac	*Bibliotheca Sacra*
BT	*The Bible Translator*
BZNW	Beihefte zur ZNW
CBQ	*Catholic Biblical Quarterly*
CBQMS	Catholic Biblical Quarterly Monograph Series
CJ	*Classical Journal*
CNT	Commentaire du Nouveau Testament
ConNT	Coniectanea Neotestamentica
CQ	*Church Quarterly*
CRINT	Compendia rerum iudaicarum ad novum testamentum
Ebib	Etudes bibliques
EDNT	*Balz-Schneider, Exegetical Dictionary of the NT*

ETS	*Erfurter theologische Studien*
EvQ	*Evangelical Quarterly*
EvT	*Evangelische Theologie*
Exp	*The Expositor*
ExpT	*Expository Times*
FB	Forschung zur Bibel
FFNT	Foundations and Facets: New Testament
FOTL	The Forms of the Old Testament Literature
FRLANT	Forschungen zur Religion und Literatur des Alten und Neuen Testaments
GNT	Grundrisse zum Neuen Testament
HeyJ	*Heythrop Journal*
HNTC	*Harper's New Testament Commentaries*
HSCP	*Harvard Studies in Classical Philology*
HTKNT	*Herders theologische Kommentar zum Neuen Testament*
HTR	*Harvard Theological Review*
HUT	*Hermeneutische Untersuchungen zur Theologie*
IB	*Interpreter's Bible*
ICC	International Critical Commentary
IDB	*Buttrick, Interpreter's Dictionary of the Bible*
IDBSup	*Supplementary volume to IDB*
Int	*Interpretation*
JAAR	*Journal of the American Academy of Religion*
JBL	*Journal of Biblical Literature*
JHS	*Journal of Hellenic Studies*
JR	*Journal of Religion*
JRH	*Journal of Religious History*
JSNT	*Journal for the Study of the New Testament*
JSNTSup	*Journal for the Study of the New Testament – Supplement Series*
JSOT	*Journal for the Study of the Old Testament*
JSOTSup	*Journal for the Study of the Old Testament – Supplement Series*
JSS	*Journal of Semitic Studies*
JTS	*Journal of Theological Studies*
KD	*Kerygma und Dogma*
LB	*Linguistica Biblica*
LCL	Loeb Classical Library
LSJ	Liddell and Scott, *A Greek-English Lexicon,* rev. by H. Jones
LPLG	G. W. H. Lampe, *A Patristic Greek Lexicon*

LTP	*Laval théologique et philosophique*
MaTS	*Marburger Theologische Studien*
MM	J. H. Moulton and G. Milligan, *The Vocabulary of the Greek Testament*
Neot	*Neotestamentica*
NHS	Nag Hammadi Studies
NICNT	New International Commentary on the New Testament
NIGTC	The New International Greek Testament Commentary
NKZ	*Neue kirchliche Zeitschrift*
NovT	*Novum Testamentum*
NovTSup	*Novum Testamentum, Supplements*
NTD	Das Neue Testament Deutsch
NTS	*New Testament Studies*
OBT	Overtures to Biblical Theology
OCD	*Oxford Classical Dictionary*
OGIS	W. Dittenberger, *Orientis Gracci Inscriptiones Selectae I–II*
PTMS	Pittsburgh Theological Monograph Series
PW	Pauly-Wissowa, *Real-Encyclopädie der classischen Altertumswissenschaft*
RelSRev	*Religious Studies Review*
ResQ	*Restoration Quarterly*
RHR	*Revue de l'historie des religions*
SBL	Society of Biblical Literature
SBLDS	Society of Biblical Literature Dissertation Series
SBLMS	Society of Biblical Literature Monograph Series
SBLSBS	Society of Biblical Literature Sources for Biblical Study
SBLSP	Society of Biblical Literature Seminar Papers
SBLTT	Society of Biblical Literature Texts and Translations
SBS	Stuttgarter Bibelstudien
SCHNT	Studia ad corpus hellenisticum novi testamenti
SE	*Studia Evangelica*
SKKNT	Stuttgarter kleiner Kommentar: Neues Testament
SNTSMS	Society for New Testament Studies Monograph Series
ST	*Studia theologica*
SUNT	*Studien zur Umwelt des Neuen Testaments*
SVF	H. von Arnim, *Stoicorum Veterum Fragmenta*
SVTP	Studia in Veteris Testamenti pseudepigrapha
TBA	Tübinger Beiträge zur Altertumswissenschaft
TBl	*Theologische Blätter*

TDNT	Kittel-Friedrich, *Theological Dictionary of the New Testament*
TDOT	Botterweck-Ringgren, *Theological Dictionary of the Old Testament*
ThExh	Theologische Existenz heute
TLZ	*Theologische Literaturzeitung*
TSK	*Theologische Studien und Kritiken*
TU	Texte und Untersuchungen
TZ	*Theologische Zeitschrift*
WMANT	Wissenschaftliche Monographien zum Alten und Neuen Testament
WUNT	Wissenschaftliche Untersuchungen zum Neuen Testament
ZKT	*Zeitschrift für katholische Theologie*
ZKWKL	*Zeitschrift für kirchliche Wissenschaft und kirchliches Leben*
ZNW	*Zeitschrift für die neutestamentliche Wissenschaft*
ZTK	*Zeitschrift für Theologie und Kirche*

Abbreviations of ancient sources follow, with minor modification, the standard of *OCD* (1970, pp. ix–xxii); *TDNT* I.xvi–lx; and *JBL* 107,3 (1988), pp. 579–96. Abbreviations of text-critical notes follow Nestle-Atland, *Novum Testamentum Graece*, 26th edn (see below, Bibliography); for explanations, see K. and B. Aland (1987).

1

INTRODUCTION

This investigation concerns itself with the socio-rhetorical function of an apparent allusion to a saying of Jesus in the Epistle of James. It approaches James as an instance of written rhetorical discourse, a text that seeks to modify the social thought and behavior of its addressees. It presupposes a broad scholarly consensus, according to which the text appropriates a tradition of Jesus' sayings, and it seeks to ascertain the social texture of one particular allusion to a saying of Jesus in James 2.5 by a rhetorical analysis according to Greco-Roman conventions.

The reasons for choosing James 2.5 are significant. First, practically all previous investigations that give serious attention to James' use of Jesus tradition identify James 2.5 as an important allusion to a saying of Jesus (Deppe, 1989, pp. 89–91, 237–38). Second, this verse occurs in a unified argument (James 2.1–13) which is one of the three rhetorical units that, in the opinion of the scholarly majority, have the greatest potential for disclosing the thought, piety, and style of the text (Dibelius, 1975, pp. 1, 38–45, 47–50). Third, we shall see that James 2.1–13 displays a definite pattern of argumentation that evinces Greco-Roman rhetorical strategies. Fourth, James 2.5 addresses a social issue, conflict between the rich and the poor, which is not only a principal theme in James, occupying almost a quarter of the entire text (James 1.9–11; 2.1–13; 2.15–16; and 4.13–5.6),[1] but is also a moral issue of social significance in the Jesus tradition and in much of early Christian literature.[2]

---

[1] Apparently James' energetic interest in the "poor and rich" became a prominent feature in NT scholarship with Kern (1835). Almost a century later, in 1921, Dibelius would say: "What is stressed most [in James] is the *piety of the Poor*, and the accompanying opposition to the rich" (1975, p. 48). See also Mußner (1987, pp. 76–84); Rustler (1952); Boggan (1982); and Maynard-Reid (1987).

[2] The literature on this is voluminous; see esp. Dibelius (1975, pp. 39–45, and the bibliography). Also, Keck (1965; 1966); Bammel (1968); Hauck (1968); Hauck and Kasch (1968); Dupont (1969); Grundmann (1972); Finley (1973); Kelly (1973);

The purpose of this chapter is to introduce the thesis that guides our inquiry, along with the method of analysis it employs, and to explain further its scope and goal. To do this, we shall address the issue of the relation between James' epistolary format and its rhetoric. Then, presupposing that James makes use of Jesus tradition, we shall discuss its allusions to Jesus' sayings as an aspect of its strategy of persuasion. Then, we shall give attention to the relation between rhetoric and its social function as a means of setting the stage for the investigation that follows. Finally, we shall provide an overview of the intended progression of our inquiry.

The Epistle of James and rhetoric

James presents itself as an early Christian letter (1.1).[3] As such it is, according to ancient epistolary theory, "a substitute for oral communication and could function in almost as many ways as a speech" (Aune, 1987, p. 158; Demetrius *De elocutione* 223–24; Malherbe, 1988, pp. 1–14). From a rhetorical perspective, James is also intentional discourse: it has "a message to convey" and seeks "to persuade an audience to believe it [the message] or to believe it more profoundly" (G. A. Kennedy, 1984, p. 3).[4]

Whereas distinctively literary-critical studies of James focus primarily on the question of what the text is,[5] this study is an exercise in rhetorical criticism, which is

> that mode of internal criticism which considers the interactions between the work, the author, and the audience. As

Hengel (1974b); L. T. Johnson (1979; 1981); Nickelsburg (1977); Countryman (1980); Maier (1980); Saller (1982); Osiek (1983); Borg (1984); Eisenstadt and Roniger (1984); Horsley and Hanson (1985); Garnsey and Saller (1987); Hollenbach (1987); Horsley (1987); Malina (1987); and Moxnes (1988).

[3] For the purposes of this investigation, ancient letters are considered according to three customary categories: diplomatic, documentary, and literary letters. These are viewed as general, non-rigid, often overlapping classifications, and they are readily conducive to subdivision and/or supplementation by other epistolary typologies, both ancient and modern. On this, see esp. White (1986) and Aune (1987). On ancient letter typologies, see Pseudo-Demetrius (in V. Weichert, 1910), and Pseudo-Libanius (in R. Forester, 1927). The latter are conveniently collected and translated in Malherbe (1988). See also the excellent typology of six epistolary types by Stowers (1986a).

[4] On rhetorical discourse as the "embodiment of an intention," see Sloan (1947). About the implications of this for the NT, see Mack (1990, esp. pp. 9–48).

[5] On the differences between rhetorical and literary criticism, and the ways in which they complement each other, see Bryant (1973, pp. 3–43); Sloan (1947); G. A. Kennedy (1984, pp. 3–5); and Mack (1990, pp. 93–102).

> such it is interested in the *product*, the *process*, and the *effect*, of linguistic activity, whether of the imaginative kind or the utilitarian kind . . . it regards the work not so much as an object of contemplation but as an artistically structured instrument for communication. It is more interested in a literary work for what it *does* than for what it is.[6]
>
> (Corbett, 1969, p. xxii)

Therefore, the function of James, what the text does or rather what it intends to do, shall be our primary concern.

The functional approach to discourse belongs, traditionally and preeminently, to rhetoric (Bryant, 1973, p. 27). So, when Stanley Stowers (1986a, p. 15) says that NT letters should be thought of more "in terms of the actions that people performed by means of them," than as "the communication of information," he expresses a view that is characteristic of rhetoric (as do Meeks, 1983, p. 7; and Malherbe, 1977, p. 50). And this perspective clearly coheres with ancient epistolary theory; for example, the letter handbooks of Pseudo-Demetrius and Pseudo-Libanius list, respectively, twenty-one and forty-one "functional" styles for letters. These are *not actual letter types*, as Koskenniemi (1956, p. 62) correctly observes, *but* rather the *appropriate styles and tones* that could be chosen depending upon both the circumstances involved in writing a letter and the "function" the writer intended to perform through the letter (see White, 1986, p. 190; Aune, 1987, pp. 158–225; and Malherbe, 1992). Moreover, because rhetorical discourse is "an instrument of communication and influence on others" (Perelman and Olbrechts-Tyteca, 1969, p. 513), its inherent social aspect lends itself to an instrumental purpose: the exploration of the intended social function of the discourse.[7] Rhetorical analysis can help us to discover the latent intent in James' rhetoric and to understand how that intent is transmitted to its audience (G. A. Kennedy, 1984, p. 12).

An awareness of the relation that exists between James' epistolary format or genre and its rhetoric is, according to George Kennedy, "not a crucial factor in understanding how rhetoric actually works" in James' argumentative units (1984, p. 32). On the other hand, it may "contribute to an understanding of [James']

[6] Also see Corbett (1971); Bryant (1973, pp. 27–42); Hudson (1923); Wichelns (in Bryant, 1958, pp. 5–42); and Ericson (in Murphy, 1983, pp. 127–36).
[7] On the social function and/or effect of rhetorical discourse, see Corbett (1971, pp. 3–4, 14–15, 31–44); Halliday (1978, pp. 36–58); Wuellner (1987); and esp. Mack and Robbins (1989).

rhetorical situation" (pp. 30–36), especially the audience the text evokes and the presence of various features in the text (p. 31). Consequently, we shall return to this issue when we focus on the rhetorical situation. At this point, however, it is advantageous to spotlight the difficulties involved in classifying James as an ancient letter, to state our position regarding this matter, and to clarify why a rhetorical approach to James is appropriate for our inquiry.

Modern scholarship remains divided over the possibility of assessing James as a letter. On the one hand, seminal literary and form-critical analyses (e.g., Deissmann, 1901, pp. 52–55; and Dibelius, 1975, pp. 1–11) have rightly pointed out that James does not appear to be a "real" letter, that is, a confidential communication in response to a specific epistolary situation.

The classification of letters into two fundamental types: (1) "true"/"real" letters, that are private and conversational (such as the authentic letters of Paul, and 2–3 John), and (2) "literary" letters or "epistles," that are public and artistic (such as 1–2 Timothy, Titus, Hebrews, James, 1–2 Peter, and Jude) harks back to the pioneering epistolary investigations of Deissmann (1927, pp. 233–45). He argued (1901, p. 4) that the "essential character" of a letter is not to be found in its form, external appearance, or contents, but in "the purpose which it serves: confidential personal conversation between persons separated by distance."

Supporting the view that James is not a "real" letter is the observation that apart from the prescript (1.1) James either suppresses or lacks the epistolary framework and conventions that are customary in the common letter tradition, which includes ancient diplomatic and documentary letters. Diplomatic (royal, negotial, or official) letters are generally defined as those written from a government or military representative to others in an official capacity (Exler, 1923, p. 23), and include royal benefactions and concessions (Welles, 1934; Aune, 1987, pp. 164–65; see Demetr. *Eloc.* 234; Ps.-Lib. 76; and Jul. Vict. *Ars Rhetorica* 27).[8] Documentary (nonliterary or private) letters, to which belong most of the extant nonliterary papyri from Egypt, comprise the largest class of ancient letters and represent the common letter tradition. This

---

[8] Apparently letter writing began with official injunctions; in time, however, due to the popularity of personal letters, official letters began to reflect the common letter tradition in both form and style. On this see White (1986, pp. 191–93, 218; 1988, pp. 86–87), who draws on Stirewalt ("A Survey of Uses of Letter-Writing in Hellenistic and Jewish Communities through the New Testament Period").

category comprises letters of recommendation, petitions/requests, invitations, instructions/orders, legal contracts, memoranda, and family or friendly letters (Stowers, 1986a, pp. 17–26; Aune, 1987, pp. 162–64; and esp. White, 1986; 1981b).[9]

Noting James' aphoristic character, the hortatory tone of much of its content, and its diverse, conventional subject matter which seems to lack a dominant theme and to evince no specific historical location, the scholarly trend has been to view James as a loosely arranged collection of sayings and brief essays or treatises that is merely framed by an epistolary prescript.[10]

Recent studies in ancient epistolography, on the other hand, support the long-held possibility of assessing James as a letter.[11] First, they stress the fact that in antiquity the letter was not only the most popular genre; it was also, due to its incredible elasticity, the most variously used of any literary form (White, 1988; Stowers, 1986a, pp. 15–47). Literary variation was one of the hallmarks of the Greco-Roman world, and motifs, themes, and constituent elements of other genres were frequently subsumed within an epistolary frame and function (Norden, 1983, vol. II, p. 492; Kroll, 1924, pp. 202–24). In other words, practically any text could be addressed, *and could function*, as a letter (Aune, 1987, p. 158; Bauckham, 1988). Further, based on the unequivocal variety in both the form and function of ancient letters, scholars now consistently assert that the customary manner of classifying such letters is deficient in both its terminological distinctions and perspectives.[12] In this light, James' perceived incongruities with the common letter

[9] Documentary letters share a number of conventions, themes, and motifs with early Christian letters, especially Paul's; and, since Deissmann, they have dominated the comparative study of NT letters and have largely determined scholarly assessments of early Christian literature (see Schubert, 1939a; 1939b; and Doty, 1973; cf. Koskenniemi, 1956, pp. 18–53). Klaus Berger (1984c, pp. 1327–40), however, rightly criticizes this approach as too narrow, and proposes that ancient philosophical letters of instruction are more appropriate for comparisons with NT letters.

[10] This is Dibelius' view (1975, pp. 1–11). On epistolary conventions as framing devices, see Aune (1987, pp. 167–70).

[11] For earlier assessments of James as a literary letter, see Deissmann (1901, p. 4) and Ropes (1916, pp. 6–18).

[12] Deissmann's terminology: "real" and "non-real," "private" and "public," and "specific" and "general" is ultimately misleading. For example, some "epistles" are also "real" letters, and some "real" letters imply a "general," rather than a "specific," epistolary setting. On this see Aune (1987, pp. 160–61); Bauckham (1988, pp. 471–73); and K. Berger (1984c, pp. 1327–63). Cf. also Hackforth and Rees (1970); Levens (1970); Dahl (1976); Doty (1969; 1973, pp. 4–19, 23–27); Thraede (1970, pp. 1–4).

tradition are hardly sufficient to preclude its classification as a letter (K. Berger, 1984c; Baasland, 1988). Therefore, while emphasizing that James is not a common, private letter, many hold that it is a type of "literary" letter.

The working definition of the "literary" letter employed in this research is provided by David Aune (1987, p. 165): "Literary letters are those that were preserved and transmitted through literary channels and were valued either as epistolary models, as examples of literary artistry, or as vignettes into earlier lives and manners"; he lists the following varieties: letters of recommendation; letter-essays; philosophical letters; novelistic letters; imaginative letters; embedded letters; letters as framing devices; and letter collections (pp. 165–70; see also White, 1981a, pp. 5–6; Thraede, 1970, pp. 17–77; and Traub, 1955).

In comparing James' prescript and contents – which suggest a general "circular," that is, a letter for several communities – with other ancient letters, numerous scholars underscore its similarities with the Jewish encyclical (see Baasland, 1988; Dahl, 1976; Meeks, 1986, p. 121; and Ropes, 1916, pp. 127–28).[13] The latter was a type of letter used for many different administrative and religious purposes. See, for example, the three Aramaic Gamaliel letters (from the Tannaitic period) that are addressed to three regional groups of Diaspora Jews (*y. Sanh.* 18d; *b. Sanh.* 18d; *t. Sanh.* 2.5); the two festal encyclicals in 2 Maccabees (ca. 180–161 BCE): 2 Maccabees 1.1–9 (with a Hebrew prescript), and 2 Maccabees 1.10–2.18 (with a Greek prescript); a prophetic encyclical (ca. 125 CE) in the *Paraleipomena of Jeremiah* 6.19–25. Moreover, embedded in *2 Baruch* is the Letter of Baruch (originally in Hebrew; ca. 100 CE): an unrecorded copy (cf. 77.17–19), described as "a letter of doctrine and a roll of hope" (77.12), was apparently addressed to "our brothers in Babylon" (i.e., "the two-and-one-half tribes in Babylon"); another copy (cf. 78.1–86.3) is addressed to "the nine-and-a-half tribes across the river Euphrates" (texts and discussions of the latter are conveniently found in Pardee, 1982). And this type of letter definitely influenced early Christian letter writing: 1–2 Peter, Jude, and the embedded letter in Acts 15.23–29 evince characteristics of the Jewish encyclical (see also the references to apparent encyclicals in Acts 9.1 and 28.21).

---

[13] On the "circular" letter, see Koester (1982, vol. II, p. 157); Aune (1987, p. 159); Ropes (1916, pp. 6–7, 40–43); and White (1988, p. 101).

In addition, James' distinctive character as a direct address or summons and its use of "sententious maxims" (γνωμολογία) and "exhortations" (προτροπαί) move the discourse away from the conversational tone, style, and content of the common private letter toward that of an address or speech.[14] For, "a letter is designed to be the heart's good wishes in brief; it is the exposition of a simple subject in simple terms. Its beauty consists in the expression of friendship and the many proverbs (παροιμίαι) which it contains . . . But the man who utters sentientious maxims (γνωμολογῶν) and exhortations (προτρεπόμενος) seems to be no longer talking familiarly in a letter but to be speaking *ex cathedra*" (Demetr. *Eloc.* 231b–232). Thus, Baasland (1988, p. 3653) correctly says, "Der Jak. ist aber . . . kein Freundschaftsbrief, auch kein Empfehlungs- oder informativer Privatbrief. Eher haben wir es mit einem Bittbrief oder mit '*Orders and Instructions*' in Briefform zu tun" ("The letter of James is however . . . neither a letter of friendship, nor even a letter of recommendation nor an informative private letter. Rather we have to place it with a letter of supplication or with 'Orders and Instructions' in the form of a letter" (cf. K. Berger, 1984c, pp. 1328–29; White and Kensinger, 1976, pp. 79–91).

While this kind of language appears to indicate a measurable distinction for determining the type of letter that James is (Stowers, 1984), it is also extremely important in gauging the social meaning and function that it intends (Mack, 1990, p. 24). For example, speaking from the sociolinguistic perspective, and stressing "the social meaning of language," M. A. K. Halliday (1978, p. 50) reminds us that: "the whole of the mood system in grammar, the distinction between indicative and imperative, and within indicative, between declarative and interrogative . . . is not referential at all; it is purely interpersonal, concerned with the social-interactional function of language. It is the speaker taking on a certain role in the speech situation." This also befits the official disposition of the encyclical. Further, James' concern with moral advice and social issues corresponds significantly with ancient letter-essays[15]

---

[14] Baasland (1988, p. 3650) correctly argues that James distinguishes itself among NT letters as a direct summons to its hearers.

[15] Ropes (1916, pp. 127–28); Doty (1973, pp. 7–8, 15); Kümmel (1975, p. 408). On letter-essays see Aune (1987, pp. 165–67); Stirewalt (1991); Malherbe (1986); Arrighetti (1973); Cicero, *The Letters to His Friends*; Canik (1967); Coleman (1974); Betz (1978); Fiore (1986).

and philosophical letters,[16] both of which, incidentally, could also display a remarkably limited use of epistolary convention (Aune, 1987, pp. 167–70).

Letter-essays and philosophical letters (συγγράμματα) are literary letters (see the epistolary theorist Ps.-Lib. 50). While family or friendly letters, "especially when expressed in a cultivated manner," were deemed by the Greek and Latin rhetoricians "as the most authentic form of correspondence" (White, 1986, p. 218), G. A. Kennedy points out that most writers (including Quintilian, Cicero, and Dionysius of Halicarnassus) apparently regarded letters "as either subliterary or perhaps more accurately as attaining what literary qualities they have by imitation of one of the three literary genres [oratory, historiography, and the philosophical dialogue]" (1984, pp. 30–31; see Dion. Hal. *Comp.* in W. R. Roberts, 1910, pp. 137–51).

The evidence, then, does seem to suggest that within the vast field of ancient epistolography James may have a place as a type of "literary" letter.[17] For now, therefore, we may tentatively approach James as something of a moral address in the form of an encyclical.

The overlap between letters and rhetoric

Contemporary scholarship increasingly emphasizes the often over-looked fact that, while epistolary theory and rhetoric were not integrated in antiquity, letter writing, at least by the first century BCE, was nonetheless significantly influenced by classical rhetoric, "the theory of persuasion or argumentation."[18] Rhetoric was in a real sense the dominant culture of the Greco-Roman world: "[it] defined the technology of discourse customary for all who participated [therein]" (Mack, 1990, p. 30; G. A. Kennedy, 1984, p. 5; and Kinneavy, 1987, pp. 56–101).

As the core subject in formal education, rhetoric was evidently

[16] On philosophical letters, see Aune (1987, pp. 167–68); and Malherbe (1986; 1987; 1989a; 1992); also *Stoicorum Veterum Fragmenta*; Attridge (1976); K. Berger (1984c, pp. 1328–29); Betz (1961; 1972; 1975a; 1978; 1979); Lutz (1947); Mussies (1972); and O'Neil (1977).

[17] Thus, Laws (1980, p. 6); Davids (1982, p. 24; 1988, p. 3627); Baasland (1988, pp. 3649–55). Also see Francis (1970, p. 126) who argues that "in form" James is a "secondary" letter, i.e., it lacks situational immediacy, but "in treatment of [its] subject matter" it is a "literary" letter.

[18] Perelman and Olbrechts-Tyteca (1969); Mack (1990, pp. 19–21); G. A. Kennedy (1984, pp. 3, 12); Betz (1972; 1975b; 1986); Wuellner (1976; 1978a; 1979; 1986; 1987).

introduced at the secondary level of the Hellenistic school, when
students, in their "first exercises" (*progymnasmata*), were taught to
read and analyze literature for its rhetorical principles and
practice.[19] "One of the results of this merger of literature and
rhetoric" was that besides oral discourse, literary composition,
including letters, "began to reflect studied attention to rhetorical
principles."[20]

While it is possible that letter writing may also have been
introduced at the secondary level in Hellenistic education, A. J.
Malherbe (1988, p. 7) rightly concludes that the evidence is insufficient to make this claim.[21] On the one hand, Theon's *Progymnasmata*, the earliest extant textbook of "preliminary exercises" (ca.
mid- or late first century CE),[22] mentions letters in the exercise on
προσωποποιΐα ("speech-in-character"; Butts, 1987, pp. 444–64).
On the other hand, as Malherbe (1988, p. 7) emphasizes, letters are
mentioned here not for learning how to write letters, "but to
develop facility in adopting various kinds of style." In other words,
προσωποποιΐα involves "writing or giving a speech whch reflects
the character of another person" (Butts, 1987, p. 460). Moreover,
letter writing receives no attention in the earliest surviving rhetorical handbooks (G. A. Kennedy, 1963, pp. 52–79; Malherbe,

[19] Marrou (1956); M. L. Clarke (1971); see D. L. Clark (1957, pp. 61–66,
177–212, 266–76); Bonner (1977, pp. 250–76, 380–92); G. A. Kennedy (1963,
pp. 268–73; 1972, pp. 316, 614–16, 619–20; and 1980, pp. 34–35, 41–160); Hock
and O'Neil (1986, esp. pp. 9–22, and 51–56 notes 46–138); Butts (1987); Mack
(1990, pp. 25–31); Mack and Robbins (1989).
[20] Mack (1990, p. 30; also 1984); and esp. Mack and Robbins (1989). Among the
many scholars who detect the influence of rhetoric in early Christian literature are
Church (1978); Jewett (1982); Fiore (1986); and Conley (1987).
[21] See Malherbe's theory that a handbook such as *Bologna Pyprus* 5 (a third- or
fourth- century CE collection of eleven samples of letters without any introductory
descriptions as to their letter-type and evincing no interest in epistolographical
theory) may have been used at this elementary level (1988, pp. 4–6, 10; 44–57). Cf.
also Rabe (1909); O'Neil's "Discussion of Preliminary Exercises of *Marcus Fabius
Quintilianus*" (in Hock and O'Neil, 1986, pp. 113–49); Colson and Whitaker (1919
and 1921).
[22] Apparently, *progymnasmata* were in use already in the first century BCE
(Bonner, 1977, p. 250; Hock and O'Neil, 1986, p. 10; Mack and Robbins, 1989,
p. 33). Apart from Theon's (Walz, vol. I, pp. 137–262; Spengel, vol. II, pp. 57–130;
and Butts, 1987, which is the most recent critical edition), the three most important
progymnasmata are: (1) Hermogenes' *Progymnasmata* (second century CE; Rabe,
vol. VI, pp. 1–27); an English translation is provided by Baldwin (1928 [1959],
pp. 23–38). (2) Aphthonius' *Progymnasmata* (fourth century CE; Rabe, vol. x);
English trans. Nadeau (1952). (3) The *Progymnasmata* of Nicolaus of Myra (fifth
century CE; in Felten, 1913). There is no English translation of the latter.

1988, pp. 2, 8 note 11); in fact, its earliest mention in a rhetorical treatise (mid-third to first century BCE) belongs to Demetrius *De elocutione* (223–25).[23]

Incidentally, epistolary handbooks, such as Pseudo-Demetrius' Τύποι Ἐπιστολικοί (first century BCE to 200 CE) and Pseudo-Libanius' Ἐπιστολιμαῖοι Χαρακτῆρες (fourth–sixth centuries CE) do not appear to have belonged to this stage in the curriculum. Their narrow concern with epistolography, their rigor in classification, and the rhetorical theory they presuppose combine to suggest that these handbooks were most probably used in the training of professional letter writers.[24] Therefore, despite the difficulty of assessing the relation of these two handbooks both to formal education and to the discussion of epistolary theory in general, the frequent violations of letter theory in the actual practice of letter writing leads J. L. White (1988, p. 190) to conclude: "One thing is certain. There was never a full integration of the practice and the theory."[25]

In sum, the judgment of G. A. Kennedy (1983, pp. 70–73) reflects the evidence well: on the one hand, letter writing in antiquity remained on the fringes of formal education;[26] on the other, the influence of rhetoric on both oral (conversations and speeches) and written discourse is undeniable (1984, pp. 8–12, 86–87; 1980, p. 111). One of the dominant cultural contexts for early Christian letters was Greco-Roman rhetoric.

Thus, in this investigation the fundamental approach to James proceeds according to Greco-Roman rhetorical conventions: the statements in this "literary" letter will be interpreted by their

[23] G. A. Kennedy (1984, p. 86; see also 1963, pp. 284–90). Cf. Grube (1965, pp. 110–21); and Roberts' introduction to Demetr. *De eloc.* (1953, pp. 257–93). This disquisition is most probably incorrectly ascribed to Demetrius of Phaleron (Kennedy, 1963, p. 286). Julius Victor, a minor Latin rhetorician (fourth century CE), provides the earliest mention of letter writing "as part of the *ars rhetorica*" (Malherbe, 1988, p. 3; Halm, 1863). Yet it was not until the Middle Ages that "the rhetorical art of letter writing" (i.e., the *dictamen*), became "a major development within the discipline of rhetoric" (Kennedy, 1980, pp. 185, 186–87).

[24] Malherbe (1988, p. 7). Whether the instructors of professional letter writers were also teachers of rhetoric (as Malherbe supposes) or civil servants who were experienced letter writers (as G. A. Kennedy suggests, 1983, pp. 70–73), the epistolary handbooks clearly evince the influence of rhetorical theory.

[25] Cf. Hack (1916); Allen (1972–73). On epistolary theory, in addition to Malherbe (1988), see Koskenniemi (1956, pp. 18–53) and Thraede (1970, pp. 17–77).

[26] This is noted in Malherbe (1988, p. 11 note 62).

rhetorical origin and function.[27] The basic methodology utilized for our rhetorical analysis is proposed by G. A. Kennedy (1984, pp. 33–38);[28] it consists of five interrelated steps: delimiting the rhetorical unit; analyzing the rhetorical situation; determining the species of the rhetoric, the question and the stasis; analyzing the invention, arrangement, and style; and evaluating the rhetoric. As a matter of course, it applies insights derived from investigations of Hellenistic handbooks, textbooks, and treatises on rhetoric. Moreover, wherever possible, the effort to integrate rhetorical theory and epistolary theory will be made.

James as rhetorical discourse

The high literary quality and rhetorical character of James are readily acknowledged by most scholars.[29] Dibelius' assessments are representative; he concludes that James is composed "in relatively *polished* Greek," and that the vocabulary and the grammar reveal "a certain linguistic cultivation." He notes the presence of Semitic influences or Biblicisms, but rightly argues that these are "not contrary to Greek usage." He finds that while James contains a considerable amount of traditional material, the discussion is arranged mostly in obvious groupings in a comparatively uniform "linguistic dress." And he concludes that the speech and style of James, its distinctive syntactic preferences, and its feeling for rhythm and emphasis demonstrate its "*rhetorical character*" (Dibelius, 1975, pp. 34–38).

In addition to the rhetorical features mentioned above, which clearly move the discourse away from a common private letter toward that of an address or speech,[30] analyses of James detect the

[27] See Bryant (1973, p. 35). Further, as G. A. Kennedy (1984, p. 33) suggests, it is from the rhetoric of smaller units in James that we can perhaps better understand the rhetoric of the whole.

[28] An excellent example of this method's viability is D. F. Watson's (1988) *Invention, Arrangement, and Style: Rhetorical Criticism of Jude and 2 Peter.*

[29] Mayor (1892 [1990], pp. ccxl–ccxlv); Ropes (1916, pp. 25–27); Chaine (1927, pp. xci–civ); Schlatter (1956, pp. 77–84); Wuellner (1978a, pp. 7–11, 62–63); and Baasland (1988, pp. 3650–62).

[30] Baasland (1988, p. 3653): "Am besten kann man jedoch den Jak als eine Rede, die Bitte und Befehle/Anweisungen enthält, charakterisieren, die später als Brief publiziert wurde, wie schon die ἐπιστολαὶ Δημοσθένους die Reden des großen Rhetors wiedergeben. Die Briefform ist deshalb nicht vorschnell als eine Fiktion abzutun, was ein bestimmtes Konzept des Privatbriefes voraussetzen würde" (as do Dibelius, 1975; and Deissmann, 1927; though Deissmann, pp. 242–43, did regard James as a "literary letter"). On James as "a speech," see also Wuellner (1978a).

influence of rhetoric in the following:[31] alliteration and assonance
(James 1.2; 3.2, 5, 6, 8, 17; 4.1); rhyme (1.6, 14; 2.12; 4.8); parechesis
(1.24, 25; 3.6, 7, 17); word plays and paronomasia (1.1, 2; 2.4, 13,
20; 3.17, 18; 4.14); rhythm (1.2, 13, 20; 2.8, 9, 15, 18; 3.3, 5, 8, 14;
4.4; 5.10–11); hexameter (1.17); anaphora (4.11; 5.7–8); epiphora
(3.7–8; 4.11, 14); anadiplosis (1.3–4; 1.19–20; 1.26–27); *gradatio*
(1.3–4, 15); parallelism (3.6–7; 5.2–3, 5); chiasmus (1.19–21,
22–25; 3.13–18; 5.7–8); *inclusio* (1.2–4 and 12; 1.17 and 27; 2.14
and 26); a remarkable similarity in the length of the argumentative
units;[32] asyndeton (1.19, 27; 2.13; 3.15,17; 4.2; 5.6);[33] antithesis
(1.4, 5–8, 9–11, 13–15, 26–27, and *passim*); pleonasm (3.7);
synonymia (1.5, 25; 3.15; 4.19); *digressio* (2.14–26); analogy and
example (2.2–4, 15–16, 21–24, 25–26; 3.7; 5.7); *comparatio* (1.6,
10–11, 23–24; 3.3–4); metaphor (3.2, 6); personification (1.15; 2.13;
4.11; 5.14); irony (1.9–10; 2.19; 5.5); metonymy (1.1); rhetorical
questions (2.2–4, 5, 6b, 7, 14a, 14b, 15–16, 20, 21, 25; 3.11, 12, 13a;
4.1a, 1b, 4a, 5–6a, 12);[34] exclamation (3.10b); apostrophe (4.1, 4,
13; 5.1); imaginary dialogue (2.18); and invectives (2.20; 4.4).

In the terminology of Greco-Roman rhetoric, James generally
exhibits the characteristics of symbouleutic or deliberative discourse.[35] Such discourse seeks to make an effective difference in a
given social history by using exhortation (προτροπή) and dissuasion (ἀποτροπή) to persuade its addressees to take a particular
course of action in the future (Arist. *Rhet.* 1.3.3–9).[36]

[31] With few exceptions, however, analyses that have detected the influence of
rhetoric have failed to address the social significance of rhetorical performance. On
this issue, see Wuellner (1986; 1987) and Robbins (1984).
[32] 1.1–12 = 9 sentences; 1.13–27 = 12 sentences; 2.1–13 = 12 sentences; 2.14–26
= 13 sentences; 3.1–18 = 18 sentences; 4.1–12 = 15 sentences; 4.13–5.6 = 11
sentences; 5.7–20 = 14 sentences. Cf. Wuellner (1978a, p. 36).
[33] Schlatter counts 79 instances (1956, p. 84).
[34] The RSV adds James 4.14b; 5.13a, 13c, 14a.
[35] This is the conclusion of K. Berger (1984a, p. 147; cf. 1984b, pp. 457–61
section 71); Baasland (1982; 1988); and Wuellner (1978a). For example, James may
be divided into eight (argumentative) sections (1.1–12; 1.13–27; 2.1–13; 2.14–26;
3.1–18; 4.1–12; 4.13–5.6; 5.7–20); each section is characterized by exhortation and
dissuasion that concerns thought and action of social consequence in reference to the
future or the present. Cf. Shepherd's (1956) eight subdivisions of James.
[36] συμβουλευτικόν (Arist. *Rhet.* 1.3.3); συμβουλή (*Rhet.* 1.3.3; 1.3.9); δημηγορ-
ικόν ([*Rhet. Al.*] 1.1421b.8); δημηγορία ([*Rhet. Al.*] 1.1421b.13); *deliberativus* (*Rhet.
Her.* 1.2.2; Cic. *Inv. Rhet.* 1.5.7; 2.51.155–58.176; *De Or.* 2.81.333–83.340; Quint.
Inst. 2.4.24–25; 2.21.23; 3.3.14; 3.4.9,14–15; *deliberatio* (*Inv. Rhet.* 1.9.12; Quint.
Inst. 3.8.10; *Rhet. Her.* 3.2–5. In the LCL, see Aristotle, *Ars Rhetorica*, 1926;
Rhetorica ad Alexandrum, 1965; *Rhetorica ad Herennium*, 1954; Cicero, *De Inven-
tione, De Optimo Genere Oratorum, Topica*, 1949; *De Oratore*, Books I–II, 1942; *De*

Approaching James in this way, however, requires an awareness of a certain artificiality that exists in classifying rhetoric by different species. Quintilian tells us: "it is quite certain that all the most eminent authorities among ancient writers, following Aristotle . . . have been content with the threefold division of rhetoric [i.e., epideictic, deliberative, and forensic]" (3.4.1).[37] Although Quintilian is himself an adherent of this view (3.4.1), firmly believes that the adoption of the threefold division is "the safest and most rational course" (3.4.12), and contends that "there is nothing that may not come up for treatment by one of these three kinds of rhetoric" (2.21.23), he marvels that "a subject of such great variety" is restricted "to such narrow bounds" (3.4.4).[38] Further, in thinking about the subjects which are treated by each respective division of rhetoric, he notes that in any one discourse "all three kinds rely on the mutual assistance of the other" (3.4.16; see Mack, 1990, pp. 34–35; and G. A. Kennedy, 1984, pp. 18–20). He observes that in epideictic discourses one treats both judicial and deliberative topics, like justice and expediency, respectively; that in deliberative discourses an epideictic topic like honor may be incorporated; and that it is rare not to find something of both deliberative and epideictic in a judicial case (3.14.16). In other words, the classifications of rhetorical species are heuristic, not definitive (see Perelman, 1982, pp. 9–20).

The importance of the latter observation is perhaps especially

Oratore, Book III and *De Partitione Oratoria*, 1942; and Quintilian, *Institutio Oratia*, 1920. Also Lausberg (1967, vol. I, sections 224–38); J. Martin (1974, pp. 167–76, 356–420); and G. A. Kennedy (1963, pp. 203–06; 1972, pp. 18–21).

[37] According to Aristotle (*Rhet.* 1.3.3) there are three species of rhetoric (1.3.3): symbouleutic (συμβουλευτικόν), judicial (δικανικόν), and epideictic (ἐπιδεικτικόν), which distinguished according to their (A) divisions, (B) times, and (C) ends are as follows. (I) Symbouleutic or deliberative rhetoric (A) is characterized by exhortation and dissuasion (προτροπή and ἀποτροπή, 1.3.1), (B) refers mainly to the future (1.3.4) but on occasion to the present (1.6.1 and 8.7); and (C) has as its end the expedient or harmful (1.3.5); "all other considerations, such as justice and injustice, honor and disgrace, are included as accessory in reference to this" (1.3.5). (II) Judicial rhetoric (A) is divided into accusation and defense (κατηγορία and ἀπολογία, 1.3.1), (B) refers to the past (1.3.4), and (C) has as its end the just or the unjust (1.3.5), and "all other considerations are included as accessory" (1.3.5). (III) Epideictic rhetoric (A) concerns the subjects of praise and blame (ἔπαινος and ψόγος, 1.3.3), (B) refers "most appropriately" to the present but may recall the past or anticipate the future (1.3.4); and (C) has as its end the honorable or disgraceful, and to these "all other considerations" are referred (1.3.5).

[38] This complaint is frequently heard in both ancient and modern discussions; e.g., Cic. *De Or.* 2.10.43–12.54; 2.15.62–16.70; Stowers (1986a, pp. 51–52, 91–94); and Aune (1987, pp. 198–99).

pertinent with reference to James on account of its large hortatory content. Because exhortation is a subject that appears to transcend the classifications of rhetorical species and is not systematically treated by the rhetoricians, it may be perceived as particularly troublesome for rhetorical criticism. On the other hand, because exhortation appears so pervasively in the writings of certain moral philosophers, there is considerable discussion of it. According to Seneca (*Ep*. 94.39), exhortation (*adhortatio*) is really a type of advice (*monitio*).[39] This at least suggests its affinity with deliberative or advisory rhetoric. In addition, Seneca equates "advice by precept" (*praeceptiva*) – which he names as the "third department" of philosophy[40] – with παραινετική, an adjective which generally qualifies a statement as "hortatory" or "advisory" (see LSJ, *s.v.* παραινετικός.). It is noteworthy, however, that there are problems with Seneca's "apologetic" usage of *praeceptiva*.[41] For one thing, it is strictly philosophical and not rhetorical or grammatical (Dihle, 1973); it is used technically with reference to Posidonius' moral philosophy (*Ep*. 95.65). Moreover, E. N. O'Neil has pointed out that this "apologetic" usage is questionable. On the one hand, Seneca "gives the Latin word a sense that is outside its normal range of meaning" (Hock and O'Neil, 1986, p. 124);[42] on the other, παραινετική "appears nowhere in the fragments of Posidonius collected by L. Edelstein and I. F. Kidd (*Posidonius: The Fragments* [Cambridge, 1972])" (Hock and O'Neil, 1986, p. 141 note 27). O'Neil concludes that this is perhaps an indication that the word "paraenetic" had a technical use in both philosophy and rhetoric (p. 124).[43]

[39] Other types of advice, according to Seneca (*Ep*. 94.39), include: consolation (*consolatio*), warning (*dissuasio*), reproving (*obiurgatio*), and praising (*laudatio*). See Seneca, *Epistulae Morales* (LCL, 3 vols., 1917; 1920; 1925).

[40] See *Ep*. 94.48; cf. 94.1 and *Ep*. 89. Concerning the *pars praeceptiva* of philosophy, Seneca writes to Lucilius: "You keep asking me to explain without postponement a topic which I once remarked should be put off until the proper time, and to inform you by letter whether this department of philosophy which the Greeks call *paraenetic*, and we Romans call the 'preceptorial' ['*praeceptivam*'], is enough to give us perfect wisdom" (*Ep*. 95.1; cf. also 95.34, and Appendix A, in *Epistulae Morales*, vol. III, pp. 451–52).

[41] See the discussion in Hock and O'Neil (1986, pp. 123–24; and also pp. 140–41 note 26).

[42] O'Neil notes: "*The Oxford Latin Dictionary s.v. praeceptio* fails to include this meaning and lists Seneca's passage under the meaning 'the inculcation of rules, instructions'" (p. 141 note 28).

[43] On the differentiation between προτρεπτική and παραινετική, see chapter 2, below.

Another problem of usage with respect to παραινετική is raised by the epistolary theorist Pseudo-Libanius, who would differentiate the paraenetic letter (λόγος παραινετικός) or letter of exhortation from the symbouleutic or advisory letter (λόγος συμβουλευτικός; see Ps.-Lib. 5, in Malherbe, 1988, pp. 68–69). For Pseudo-Libanius the essential difference between paraenesis and advice is that advice admits a counter-statement, while paraenesis does not. Again, this distinction does not derive from rhetorical theory, but is ideological or philosophical.[44] From the point of view of rhetoric (or argument), every statement theoretically admits a counter-statement and is thus subject to debate.[45] Moreover, Pseudo-Libanius' *distinction* between exhortation and advice does not cohere with the conceptions of symbouleutic rhetoric in Aristotle (*Rhet.* 1.3.3), the *Rhetorica ad Alexandrum* (1.1421b.8–2.1425b.35), Cicero (*Inv.* 1.5.7; 2.51.155–58.176; *De Or.* 1.31.141; 2.81.333–83.340), the *Rhetorica ad Herennium* (1.2.2; 3.2.1–5.9), Quintilian (2.21.23; 3.3.14; 3.4.15), or Syrianus (Walz, vol. vii, p. 763), nor even with the earlier epistolary handbook of Pseudo-Demetrius.

On the one hand, Pseudo-Demetrius has no reference to the paraenetic letter; on the other, his definition of the letter of advice, as one in which "by offering our own judgment [opinion or advice, γνώμην] we exhort [προτρέπωμεν] (someone to) something or dissuade [ἀποτρέπωμεν] (him) from something" (Ps.-Demetr. 11, in Malherbe, 1988, pp. 36–37) is a rather straightforward example of what the rhetoricians call symbouleutic or advisory rhetoric. Furthermore, Pseudo-Libanius' definition of paraenesis is itself also the rhetoricians' definition of advisory rhetoric: "the paraenetic style is that in which we exhort [παραινοῦμεν] someone by urging

[44] This point is also made by Perdue (1990). Ps.-Libanius' epistolary handbook dates from the fourth to the sixth centuries CE, a period in which there was a conscious rapprochement between philosophy and rhetoric. The rigorous distinctions between paraenesis and advice made by Ps.-Libanius possibly derive from that discussion. Perhaps an investigation that focuses on the philosophical understanding of paraenesis and its relationship to rhetorical theory during that later period could provide some clarification of this issue.

[45] "Because rhetoric was understood as debate, with two sides to every issue, it was natural for the Greeks to distinguish two contrastive subtypes for each of the three species of rhetoric. These were designated in terms of the overall mode of argumentation that characterized each one . . . In actual practice, however, a given speech might contain all six forms of argumentation at given junctures, depending on the circumstances" (Mack, 1990, p. 34). On the other hand, one of the fundamental reasons some philosophers denounced rhetoricians was that some sophists enthusiastically cherished the ability and willingness to argue both for and against any issue.

[προτρέποντες] him to pursue something or to avoid something. Paraenesis is divided into two parts, persuasion [προτροπήν] and dissuasion [ἀποτροπήν]" (Ps.-Lib. 5; cf. Arist. *Rhet.* 1.3.3, 5–6). Thus, while it is possible in certain cases – from a philosophical point of view – to differentiate paraenesis from advice, it is, as S. Stowers notes (1986a, pp. 91–94), practically very difficult to do; and, as a rule, it is not a great issue for the rhetoricians.

Stowers (1986a, p. 93) also points out "a closely related question," namely, "whether paraenesis or exhortation in general belongs to deliberative (that is, advising) rhetoric or to epideictic rhetoric (the occasional rhetoric of praise and blame)." And he rightly observes, as mentioned above, that exhortation transcends rhetorical categories, inasmuch as it is found in both of the latter species (pp. 51–53, 91–94). According to G. A. Kennedy (1984, p. 146; see pp. 145–47), however, "exhortation (or paraenesis) is one of the two forms of deliberative rhetoric, the other being dissuasion (Quint. 3.4.9)."[46] This is further corroborated by Quintilian, who says: "Arguments such as the following belong in the main to the hortative [*hortativum*] department of oratory: – 'Virtue brings renown, therefore it should be pursued; but the pursuit of pleasure brings ill-repute, therefore it should be shunned'" (5.10.83). H. Lausberg (1973, vol. II, p. 717 section 1244; vol. I, p. 210 section 381; see also sections 61.2, and 224–38) also agrees with this and concludes that the *hortativum genus* is the *genus deliberativum*. Moreover, G. A. Kennedy's and Lausberg's view coheres with J. Martin's summary of advisory rhetoric (1974, pp. 167–76).

According to the rhetoricians, the fact that paraenesis is incorporated within epideictic discourse need not invalidate exhortation's fundamental rhetorical categorization as symbouleutic, any more than the presence of praise in a symbouleutic discourse invalidates its fundamental categorization as epideictic (*Rhet. Al.*

[46] Quint. (3.4.9) refers to Anaximenes (see [*Rh. Al.*] 1.1421b.7–23), equates *hortandi* and *dehortandi* with προτρεπτικόν and ἀποτρεπτικόν, respectively, and argues that they are "clearly deliberative." Cf. Aune (1987, p. 199): "The two basic forms of deliberative rhetoric, persuasion [protreptic or exhortation] and dissuasion, included not only advice but also most of the features associated with moral and religious exhortation: encouragement, admonition, comfort, warning, and rebuke." In antiquity the terms παραίνεσις and προτροπή are familiar as synonyms (cf. Burgess, 1902, esp. pp. 229–34). Despite this, some scholars have pressed for an (artificial and patently) technical distinction between these terms. This matter will be taken up in chapter 2.

1.1427b.31–34; cf. Cic. *De Or*. 2.82.333–83.336; and G. A. Kennedy, 1980, pp. 167–76). Further, the presence of exhortation or praise in a discourse does not automatically determine its rhetorical species. What does determine the species is the overall context in which the exhortation or praise occurs. Thus, for hortatory statements, G. A. Kennedy maintains that the issue is whether the exhortations "inculcate belief without calling for action, in which case they are epideictic, or [whether] they exhort the recipient[s] to a particular course of action, in which case they are deliberative" (1984, p. 147).

Consequently, in our analysis of James we will treat exhortation and advice as interchangeable. This seems to reflect the predominant, familiar usage of the terms in the ancient sources. Similarly, the analysis will presuppose that exhortation (paraenesis or protropē) and advice belong primarily to deliberative rhetoric, though they are by no means limited to it. Again, this appears to be the predominant understanding in the rhetorical theory of both the Greco-Roman world and the most eminent contemporary historians of classical rhetoric.

James' allusions to sayings of Jesus and rhetorical theory

One of the most fascinating features of James' rhetorical discourse is its use of Jesus tradition, namely, its numerous allusions to sayings of Jesus. In "Der geschichtliche Ort des Jakobusbriefes," G. Kittel (1942, p. 84) asserts: "Es gibt keine Schrift des NT außer den Evangelien, die so mit Anklängen an Herrnworte gespickt ist wie er" ("There is no other writing of the NT outside the Gospels, which is so enhanced with echoes to the Lord's words as is James").[47] Though there is much speculation and debate about the origin, form, and content of the tradition known to James, there is a broad, scholarly consensus that this document reflects a widespread terminological, material, and religio-historical appropriation of a tradition of Jesus' sayings in its discourse.[48] The text at no time attributes a saying to Jesus; rather, it alludes to sayings that

---

[47] See also Kittel (1950/1, pp. 54–112, esp. pp. 83–109). For criticism of Kittel's historical conclusions about James, see Aland (1944) and Lohse (1957); cf. also von Campenhausen (1972, pp. 103–46, esp. 118–22).

[48] On the similarity of James' sayings and those of Jesus, see esp. Dibelius (1975, pp. 28–29).

other Christian texts attribute to Jesus. In other words, this discourse attributes the wise sayings of Jesus[49] to "James, a servant of God and of the Lord Jesus Christ" (1.1).[50]

From a rhetorical perspective, the echoes of or allusions[51] to Jesus' sayings are an important aspect of that part of persuasion the rhetoricians called invention (εὕρεσις, *inventio*). The art of rhetoric, according to Aristotle, is "the faculty of discovering the possible means of persuasion on any subject" (*Rhet.* 1.2.1), and this art consists of five parts: invention, arrangement, style, memory, and delivery.[52] Of the five parts, invention is the most important.[53] Invention refers to the process of finding and selecting the "proofs" (πίστεις; ἐπιχειρήματα) that, *from the speaker's point of view*, would make a convincing argument for the audience.[54] The process includes determining the species of rhetoric, the question or cause in the debate, and the stasis or main points at issue.[55] This means that invention is primarily conceptual or ideational and only

[49] That James is a wisdom document is clearly the consensus among NT scholars; see Dibelius (1975, pp. 1–57); Meyer (1930); Thyen (1957), Lohse (1957), Gertner (1962); Reicke (1964); Ward (1966b); Kürzdörfer (1966); Luck (1967; 1971; 1984); Halson (1968); Thomas (1968); Kirk (1969); Francis (1970); Poehlmann (1974); Hoppe (1977); Wanke (1977); Davids (1982); Baasland (1982); Popkes (1986).

[50] I hold that James is a pseudonymous, Jewish-Christian letter. The "James" to whom the letter is attributed is most probably James, the brother of Jesus. See chapter 6, pages 201–02.

[51] "The technique of allusion assumes: (1) an established literary tradition as a source of value; (2) an audience sharing the tradition with the poet; (3) an echo of sufficiently familiar yet distinctive elements; and (4) a fusion of the echo with the elements in the new context . . . It usually requires a close poet–audience relationship, a social emphasis in literature, a community of knowledge, and a prizing of literary tradition" (Preminger, 1974, p. 18, as quoted in W. G. E. Watson, 1984, p. 300). See chapter 4, below, pages 114–16.

[52] Cic. *Inv. Rhet.* 1.7.9; *De Or.* 1.31.142; *Rhet. Her.* 1.2.3; Quint. 3.3.1. See G. A. Kennedy (1984, pp. 12–14, 15–30); D. F. Watson (1988, pp. 18–27). Of the five parts of rhetoric, only invention, arrangement, and style have immediate pertinence to our study; memory and delivery will not be discussed, inasmuch as they concern oral discourse.

[53] The first two books of Aristotle's *Rhetoric* deal with invention (see G. A. Kennedy, 1963, pp. 87–103). Cicero says that invention "is the most important of all the divisions, and above all is used in every kind of pleading" (*Inv. Rhet.* 1.7.9; cf. Quint. 3.3.1–6). See Lausberg (1973, vol. I, sections 260–442); J. Martin (1974, pp. 15–210); and Perelman (1982, pp. 3–4).

[54] G. A. Kennedy (1973, pp. 87–103); D. F. Watson (1988, pp. 19–27); Lausberg (1973, vol. I, sections 350–426); J. Martin (1974, pp. 97–135).

[55] G. A. Kennedy (1984, pp. 16–20, 36–37, 147); D. F. Watson (1988, pp. 12–18); Lausberg (1973, vol. I, sections 66–138); J. Martin (1974, pp. 15–28). See Quint. 3.10.1–3; 3.5.4–18; 3.6.63–82; and Nadeau (1964).

secondarily linguistic: it "deals with the planning of a discourse and the arguments to be used in it" (G. A. Kennedy, 1984, p. 13).[56]

To understand invention in rhetorical theory and practice, one should recall that rhetorical "proofs" are of two kinds. The first kind are extrinsic (ἄτεχνοι) to the art of rhetoric, such as laws, witnesses, contracts, tortures, and oaths (Arist. *Rhet.* 1.2.2; 1.15.1–33; Quint. 5.1.1–7.37). These proofs evoke authority "from outside" the immediate context. The second kind are intrinsic (ἔντεχνοι) to rhetoric, being drawn from the case in question (Arist. *Rhet.* 1.2.2; Quint. 5.8.1–14.35). These intrinsic proofs inhere in the three universal factors of the rhetorical or argumentative situation: the speaker, the audience, and the speech itself. According to Aristotle (*Rhet.* 1.2.3), these factors are respectively the sources of the three modes of intrinsic or "artistic" proof: *ethos*, which concerns the character and credibility of the speaker (*Rhet.* 1.2.4; 1.8.6; 2.1–17; 3.7.6; 3.16.8–9; Quint. 6.2.8–19); *pathos*, which concerns the mood and emotions of the audience (*Rhet.* 1.2.5; 2.1–17.6; 3.7.1–7; 3.17.8; *adfectus*, Quint. 6.2.20–36; 8.3.1–6); and *logos*, which concerns the reasoning and argumentation in the discourse (*Rhet.* 1.2.6–22; Quint. 5.8.1–10.19). Moreover, argument has two forms: deductive proof or the enthymeme (*Rhet.* 1.2.8, 13–18; 2.22–26), and inductive proof or example (*Rhet.* 1.2.8, 13; 2.20.1–9; Quint. 5.11.1–44). Finally, in constructing arguments, the speaker or writer has recourse to both the common and specific topics (τόποι), that is, "places" where it is possible to find arguments or lists of arguments and argumentative techniques (Arist. *Rhet.* 1.2.21–22; 2.18.3–19.27; 2.23–24; and *Topica*; Cic. *Top.* 2.8; Quint. 5.10.20).[57]

Of particular importance for our purposes is the form of inductive proof called "judgments" (κρίσεις) or recourses to ancient authorities.[58] In judicial contexts, judgments usually refer

---

[56] The classical understanding – that rhetoric is primarily conceptual and secondarily linguistic – is apparently forgotten or ignored by scholars who typically reduce rhetoric to literary style "or elocution, the study of ornate forms of language" (on this, see Perelman, 1982, pp. xvii–xviii; 3–4; cf. G. A. Kennedy, 1984, p. 3; Wuellner, 1987, esp. pp. 450–54). The conceptual basis of rhetorical behavior is, however, fundamental (see Baldwin, 1924 [1959], p. 43).

[57] On rhetorical proofs and topics, see G. A. Kennedy (1984, pp. 14–18, 20–23, 49–51, 56–61, 103–06, 118–38; 1963, pp. 88–103); D. F. Watson (1988, p. 19–27); Lausberg (1973, vol. I, sections 257, 351–426); J. Martin (1974, pp. 97–135, 155–56, 158–66); Mack (1990, pp. 35–41); Conley (1984); Robbins (1985a); and Wuellner (1978b).

[58] See Mack and Robbins (1989, pp. 38–39, 53–55).

to legal precedents, but "in philosophical, educational, and ethical environments of thought," as Vernon K. Robbins points out, "judgments can have a much wider reference" (Mack and Robbins, 1989, p. 28). This coheres with Quintilian's view that judgments include "the opinion of nations, peoples, philosophers, distinguished citizens, or illustrious poets," as well as "common sayings," "popular beliefs," and "supernatural evidence" (5.11.36, 37, 42–44).[59] So, while generally presented as either a primary or supporting argument, "a well-known saying in the culture may function as a *judgment* about some aspect of life and its challenges" (Mack and Robbins, 1989, p. 28). Therefore, Robbins stresses that while "some early Christian literature uses quotations or allusions from scripture as judgments . . . sayings of Jesus appear to be the primary resource for judgments about life and its responsibilities in the Synoptic traditon" (p. 29).

Against this background, then, the sayings of Jesus to which James alludes appear to manipulate a tradition that is a widespread social possession of early Christians.[60] By making statements that have an intertexture that resonates with sayings that circulate throughout early Christianity as sayings of Jesus, the text relocates judgments traditionally attributed to Jesus by attributing them to James. These statements, then, are neither haphazard nor mechanical appropriations of tradition, as Dibelius and others have argued. They manipulate tradition in a specific way that has social ramifications for traditions about Jesus, James, and early Christianity. Most of all, however, this manipulation of tradition provides clues to the social location of the thought that manifests itself in the discourse of James (see Rohrbaugh, 1987; and Robbins, 1991a).

James' rhetorical discourse and its social function

To argue that the discourse in James intends to evoke a social response in the thought and behavior of its addressees and that it offers clues to the social environment or location of thought that stands behind and in the discourse, is merely to lay claim to understandings that are elemental in the classical conception and

---

[59] Cf. Hermog. *Prog.* (8,7 Rabe). See D. F. Watson (1988, pp. 22–23); Lausberg (1973, vol. I, section 426); and J. Martin (1974, pp. 111, 126).

[60] On the sayings of Jesus and their character as a social possession, see Kelber (1981, esp. pp. 1–43).

formulation of rhetoric.[61] According to that tradition, rhetorical discourse is situationally or contextually specific: it "comes into being *in* the situation, to *affect* the situation, and to *alter* the situation" through language (Bryant, 1973, p. 36). Further, the situation necessarily involves not only the discourse, but its speaker/writer and its audience (Bitzer, 1968). Thus conceived, argumentative discourse is an interpersonal response to preexistent or emerging conditions; it is the use of language in an avowedly social mission (Bryant, 1973, pp. 24–43, esp. 31–32; G. A. Kennedy, 1984, p. 3).

This view of rhetoric departs from the typical, truncated conception of rhetoric as mainly "stylistics," or the "artistry of textual disposition and structure." It reclaims the classical position, which holds that rhetorical discourse is inherently social discourse designed to produce social effects (Mack, 1990, pp. 9–17). Therefore, "rhetorical criticism leads us away from a traditional message- or content-oriented reading of Scripture to a reading which generates and strengthens ever-deepening personal, social, and cultural values" (Wuellner, 1987, p. 461).

Rhetoricians stress that rhetorical discourse "must reveal its context or situation" (Sloan, 1947; Halliday, 1978, pp. 1–58, 154–92, 211–35). This does not mean that a particular discourse is a map of the author's mind, nor does it hold that a rhetorical analysis of a text will disclose the historical situation that engendered it.[62] Thus Wuellner (1987, pp. 450, 456) emphasizes that the "context" or "situation" which argumentative discourse reveals is not the "historical context or literary tradition or genre or the

[61] Arist. *Rhet.* 1.3.3–9; Cic. *Inv. Rhet.* 1.5.1–7; *Rhet. Her.* 1.2.1–3; Quint. 2.15; 2.21.20–24. G. A. Kennedy (1984, pp. 3–38); Mack (1990); Mack and Robbins (1989); Wuellner (1987); Perelman and Olbrechts-Tyteca (1971, pp. 411–59); and esp. Perelman (1963). Cf. Bryant (1973, pp. 3–43).

[62] As is well known, the historical location of James is a notoriously difficult and debated problem (see the discussion in chapter 2, below). In no way do I maintain that my investigation will disclose the historical location of James. The rhetorical situation is not the same thing as the historical or social setting of the author or addressee (on this see Britton, 1981; McGuire, 1982; Lausberg, 1967, pp. 21–23). Whereas the historical critic focuses on the issues of when, where, why, by whom, and to whom, to reconstruct the past, "the rhetorical critic looks foremost for the premises of a text as appeal or argument" (Wuellner, 1987, p. 456). This does not mean that the rhetorical situation and the historical situation are without similarity and unconnected; theoretically, it is possible that "reconstructions of the implications uncovered in the investigation of a rhetorical situation" may complement other methods in the effort to locate the socio-historical setting of a text (see Mack, 1990, p. 24).

generic *Sitz im Leben*" of the text. Rather it is what G. A. Kennedy (1984, pp. 34–35), following L. Bitzer (1968), refers to as the rhetorical or argumentative situation: "that complex of persons, events, objects, and relations presenting an actual or potential exigence which calls for a particular discourse." Wuellner, following T. O. Sloan (1947, pp. 802–3), defines it as the "attitudinizing conventions, precepts that condition (both the writer's *and* the reader's) stance toward experience, knowledge, tradition, language, and other people," and further notes that it "can also come close to being synonymous with what K. Burke and others call the 'ideology' of, or in, literature" (1987, p. 450).[63]

Extremely important for our purposes is the fact that a rhetorical situation is inevitably a social context; rhetoric is after all social discourse and distinctively deals with interpersonal relations.[64] Within such a context James seeks to constrain the thought and behavior of its audience; it intends a social function. Moreover, to get inside this discourse, to probe the social implications of its rhetorical situation, "to describe its elements, their interrelations, their potential interactions, and form," should provide clues to the social location of the thought that manifests itself in the discourse, and the potential social function of the discourse in its argumentative situation (Bryant, 1973, pp. 35, 36–43).

The classical understanding of rhetorical discourse works well for the interpretation of James. As we shall see, the text appears to be fundamentally deliberative rhetoric. It is perhaps the most directly socially oriented text in the New Testament; it is thoroughly ethical in its outlook.[65] This inquiry specifically focuses on one facet of James' rhetoric, the social function of the relocation of a saying of Jesus in James 2.5.

The present investigation

The thesis that guides this study, therefore, may be stated as follows: the Epistle of James is a deliberative discourse in the guise

[63] See Burke (1978, pp. 401–16). The rhetorical situation is a "semiotic construct," i.e., "an edifice of meanings"; cf. Halliday (1978, pp. 1–5, 9–11).

[64] Sloan (1947, pp. 798–99). This is a basic presupposition for Mack (1990) and also for Wuellner (1987).

[65] On the social orientation of James, see Souček (1958); esp. Ward (1966b); Burchard (1980). "The epistle of James is the most consistently ethical document in the New Testament" (Laws, 1980, p. 27). Cf. Schulz (1987, pp. 647–57); Schrage (1988, pp. 9, 10, 279–93); and Schrage and Balz (1980, pp. 5–59).

of a letter that uses sayings of Jesus to persuade an audience to think and act in ways that have significant social consequence. The test case for this hypothesis is James 2.5: a rhetorical performance of language that in other contexts is explicitly attributed to Jesus – a saying attributed to James that concerns the conflict between the rich and the poor, a social issue that is pivotal in the discourse of the epistle.

In our next chapter, we shall review the historical, literary, and theological problems that have surrounded the interpretation of James. In particular, we shall look at Martin Dibelius' solution to these problems. Since his solution is based on an extremely questionable conception of "paraenesis," an issue of importance that we have already broached, we shall look into the historical, literary, and theological aspects of that issue. Then, building on the research of Dibelius, we shall briefly look at specific, recent investigations that return to "rhetoric" as a method for interpreting the writings of the New Testament. On this basis, we shall turn to our rhetorical analysis of the "internal dynamics" of James 2.1–13.

In chapter 3, we shall begin our discussion of the "internal dynamics" of the rhetoric in James 2.1–13, according to Greco-Roman rhetorical conventions. In particular, we shall look at the invention, arrangement, and style of this argument and discuss its inner texture.

We shall continue to discuss the "inner dynamics" of James 2.1–13 in chapter 4, focusing specifically on the "intertexture" of the unit. Because James 2.5 uses language that Q^{Matt} 5.3, Q^{Luke} 6.20b, Polycarp, *Phil.* 2.3, and *Gos. Thom.* 54 attribute to Jesus, we shall also concentrate on the intertexture of these rhetorical performances, as we seek to locate the socio-ideologically located voice in James 2.5.

The "internal dynamics" of our unit, as these are expressed in its "social and cultural texture," will be the focus in chapter 5. There we shall establish the rhetorical situation that evoked this argument, and determine its question, stasis, and species of rhetoric. Then, we shall probe the social implications of certain cultural scripts that are at play in the rhetoric, and address the kind of "social" and "cultural" rhetoric that James 2.1–13 is. Finally, drawing on the results of our discussion of the "internal dynamics" (that is, the "inner texture," "intertexture," and the "social and cultural texture") of our unit, we shall determine the socio-rhetorical function of the allusion to a saying of Jesus in James 2.5.

We shall conclude our investigation in chapter 6 by asking several questions about the "ideological implications" of the rhetoric in James 2.1–13 and by summarizing the course of our investigation.

2

THE HISTORY OF RESEARCH AND THE PRESENT INVESTIGATION

Introduction

The purpose of this chapter is to review the history of research on the Epistle of James and to locate the present study with respect to both past and current scholarly investigations. First, we shall discuss some of the historical, theological, and literary problems surrounding James, and the ways in which scholarship dealt with these issues up to the publication of Martin Dibelius' commentary. Second, because Dibelius' conclusions have dominated Jamesian scholarship for more than seventy years and remain today the most influential assessment of James, we shall focus on his research. We shall concentrate on his use of the so-called "genre," paraenesis. Finally, we shall build on this previous scholarship as we look at more recent research which suggests rhetorical criticism as a promising method for the investigation and interpretation of James.

The Epistle of James as a problem

The history of research on the Epistle of James reveals that it is not a popular document; it is in fact maligned and neglected (Adamson, 1989, p. x; Davids, 1982, p. 1; L. T. Johnson, 1986, p. 453; Laws, 1980, pp. 1–2; and Popkes, 1986, p. 9). When James is studied, it is seldom read on its own terms (L. T. Johnson, 1985, pp. 166–69, 178–79). Instead scholars tend to approach the text by focusing obsessively upon one of two areas: either they concentrate on issues related to the letter's historical setting, which as a rule is reduced to the question of its relationship with Paul, or they grapple with difficulties involving its literary aspects. The research suggests that the letter is one of the most difficult texts of the New Testament to locate historically, theologically, and literarily (Baasland, 1982, p. 119). Consequently, scholars customarily refer to the Epistle of

James as an unsolved "riddle." This has come into vogue since the excellent study of Meyer (1930; see, e.g., Adamson, 1989, p. vii; Baasland, 1988, p. 3646; Popkes, 1986, p. 14; and Wuellner, 1978a, p. 5). A brief summary of James' history in research will make this clear and also set the stage for the present inquiry.

James as a historical problem

From the early church to the present, the Epistle of James appears to have been a historical problem.[1] While scholars continue to debate the possibility that the letter is echoed in 1 Peter, *1 Clement*, and *Hermas*,[2] the first certain references to it by a Christian writer belong to Origen, writing in Alexandria in the early third century (Grant, 1963, p. 220. Cf. Ropes, 1916, pp. 86–87, 92–94; Mußner, 1987, pp. 38–39). Origen quotes James frequently, considers the author an apostle, probably the Lord's brother, and, while implying that there is elsewhere reservation concerning its authenticity, he definitely accepts James as scripture and includes it in his New Testament.[3] Also from the third century, perhaps even prior to Origen, the pseudo-Clementine tractate, *De virginitate* 1.11.4, quotes James; thus it is plausible that James was at that time also regarded as scripture in southern Syria or Palestine (Dibelius, 1975, pp. 51–52; Ropes, 1916, pp. 51–52; Mußner, 1987, p. 39; and Adamson, 1989, p. 161. But see the objection and discussion in Meyer, 1930, pp. 33–34 note 8). Some scholars have speculated that perhaps Origen discovered the letter when he was in Caesarea

[1] Adamson (1989, pp. ix–xv, 147–66); Cantinat (1973, pp. 44–54); Dibelius (1975, pp. 51–61); Grant (1963, pp. 219–23); Kümmel (1975, pp. 405–07, 411–14); Laws (1980, pp. 6–26, 32–42); Mayor (1892 [1990], pp. 19–102, 152–95); Mußner (1987, pp. 33–47); Ropes (1916, pp. 43–115); Vielhauer (1975, pp. 568–71, 578–80); Zahn (1909, vol. I, pp. 123–51).

[2] For representative lists and discussions of the parallels between James and these writings see: Mayor (1892 [1990], pp. lxx–lxxi, lxxiv–lxxviii, cii–cvii, clxi–clxv, clxvii, clxxix–clxxx, clxxxix–cxcii); Spitta (1896, vol. II, pp. 183–202, 230–36, 382–91); Zahn (1909, vol. I, pp. 123–36); Ropes (1916, pp. 22–23, 87–90); Dibelius (1975, pp. 30–33); Meyer (1930, pp. 59–82); Schlatter (1956, pp. 67–73); Mußner (1987, pp. 33–38); Laws (1980, pp. 18–26); Davids (1982, pp. 8–11, 26–28; 1988, pp. 3632–35); Carrington (1940, pp. 23–31, esp. p. 28); Seitz (1944; 1947; 1957; 1959); Wolverton (1956); Wifstrand (1948); Young (1948); Selwyn (1955 [1981], pp. 365–466, esp. pp. 462–66); and Deppe (1989).

[3] For lists and discussions of Origen's references to James, see Mayor (1892 [1990], pp. lxxxi–lxxxii, clxx–clxxi); Ropes (1916, pp. 92–94); Dibelius (1975, p. 52); Mußner (1987, pp. 38–39); Adamson (1989, pp. 156–57) and Metzger (1987, pp. 138–41).

and returned with it to Alexandria (Barnett, 1962; Ropes, 1916, pp. 1, 42, 51–52; Adamson, 1989, pp. 160–61). In any case, by the time of Origen's death (254 CE), the traditional position on the authorship and date of James was circulating in the East (Ropes, 1916, pp. 44, 86–87, 92–94; Dibelius, 1975, pp. 51–52; Adamson, 1989, pp. 156–58).

The evidence suggests that it was through the influence of Alexandria that James was first admitted into the canon among the Greeks, a process that was probably complete by the time of Eusebius' history (ca. 324 CE; Ropes, 1916, pp. 86–87. P[23] and P[20] also attest to James' use in Egypt in the third century; see Dibelius, 1975, pp. 52, 57). Eusebius himself (*Hist. eccl.* 2.23.24–25; 3.25.3) follows Origen in accepting the letter as an apostolic writing by the Lord's brother, but he states that there were some churches that did not recognize it as scripture (Dibelius, 1975, p. 52; and Mußner, 1987, p. 40). This statement, as J. H. Ropes (1916, pp. 44, 94) points out, is most likely a reference to the then current status of the epistle among the Syrian and Latin churches.

The earliest knowledge of the epistle in a Latin translation comes from around 350 CE, and the earliest quotation of it by a Latin author comes from Hilary of Poitiers (356–58 CE; *On the Trinity* IV.8; *Migne, PL.X*.101; cited in Adamson, 1989, pp. 150–51). The form of the quotation, however, suggests that Hilary was not using a Latin text but was most likely translating from a Greek text (Ropes, 1916, p. 101; Mußner, 1987, pp. 41, 55 section 9.4; and Adamson, 1989, pp. 149–50). It was not until the end of the fourth century, at the councils of Hippo (393 CE) and Carthage (397 and 419 CE), that James was officially recognized in the West (Barnett, 1962, pp. 794–95; Ropes, 1916, pp. 102–03; Davids, 1982, p. 7), and here the influence of both Jerome and Augustine was crucial (Mußner, 1987, p. 41; Adamson, 1989, p. 151). The often quoted statement of Jerome (*De vir. ill.* [*On Famous Men*] 2: "James, who is called the Lord's brother . . . wrote only one Epistle, which is reckoned among the seven Catholic Epistles, and even this is claimed by some to have been published by some one else under his name, and gradually, as time went on, to have gained in authority") is, according to Ropes (1916, pp. 44, 52), a paraphrase of Eusebius' statements and in no way suggests that Jerome knew more about James than did Eusebius. Evidently Augustine's acceptance of James came with his adoption of Jerome's canon (*De doctrina christiana* [*On Christian Doctrine*] 2.8.13). He quotes James frequently, and wrote a commentary on it, which unfortunately is lost (Ropes, 1916, p. 102; Dibelius, 1975, p. 53 note 204; Mußner, 1987, pp. 41–42; Adamson, 1989, pp. 150–51; and Bergauer, 1962).

In Syria James was not officially accepted as scripture before its translation as part of the Peshitta in the early years of the fifth century (Ropes, 1916, pp. 96–100; Dibelius, 1975, p. 51). Although there were certainly a number of church leaders in Western Syria who had used and accepted the letter prior to this time, it is also true that in Eastern Syria as late as the sixth century not a few theologians rejected all of the Catholic Epistles as scripture (Mußner, 1987, pp. 39–41; Adamson, 1989, pp. 152–62; see Siker, 1987). Strong doubts about James' authenticity seem to have existed from the beginning.[4]

Basically there are two different historical assessments of the Epistle of James, and these stand as opposite extremes in the discussion.[5] One theory, which is supported by an increasing number of scholars,[6] asserts that the letter is early, perhaps the earliest document in the NT (ca. 40–62 CE).[7] Here the prescript (1.1) is taken literally: the purported author is James the Just,[8] who writes from Jerusalem to Jewish Christians who have scattered after Stephen's death (cf. Acts 8.1; see Geyser, 1975, esp.

[4] Dibelius (1975, pp. 51–61); Ropes (1916, pp. 74–109); Adamson (1989, pp. 147–66); Grant (1963; also 1965, pp. 155, 167, 171–79, 182–87); Kümmel (1975, pp. 403–16); and Vielhauer (1975, pp. 567–80).

[5] For this observation and the following discussion of the various historical assessments of James, I am dependent on Ropes (1916, pp. 46, 59–74) and especially Childs (1984, pp. 431–35). Cf. Davids (1982, pp. 2–21).

[6] As advocates of this position, Childs (1984) refers to Mayor (1892 [1990], cxliv–ccv); Zahn (1909, vol. I, pp. 73–151); and Kittel (1942). According to Lüdemann (1989, p. 286 note 1), scholars who more recently have adopted this position are: Mußner (1987, pp. 1–10); Wuellner (1978a, p. 38); and Stuhlmacher (1979, pp. 234–35). To these may be added Adamson (1989, pp. 3–52, 425–31, 481–88; cf. 1976, pp. 18–19, 49–52, 59, 105–06); and Hartin (1991, pp. 237–40). For a more extensive list, see Pratscher (1987, p. 209 note 3). Davids (1982, p. 4) provides a larger, though incomplete, list of twentieth-century scholarly views on the authorship and date of James.

[7] Massebieau (1895) and Spitta (1896) argued that James is a Jewish text from a period prior to James the Just. Elliott-Binns (1956, pp. 51–52) held that James was a very early Jewish-Christian text, but was not written by the Lord's brother. Among those who support the traditional opinion on James' authorship there is division: some argue that James wrote the letter early in his career; e.g., Mayor (1892 [1990], p. cl) and Kittel (1942, p. 71). Others date it to the final years of James' life; e.g. Parry (1903, pp. 99–100) and Tasker (1957, pp. 31–32). On this see Davids (1982, pp. 3–5).

[8] On James the Just, see Ropes (1916, pp. 53–74); Ward (1973; 1993). And see esp. Pratscher (1987, pp. 209–21).

pp. 28–29). As evidence supporting this position scholars stress the letter's lack of reference to Paul's letters, its eschatological fervor, and "close continuity with the pre-literary synoptic tradition of the teaching of Jesus and the Jewish wisdom traditions" (Childs, 1984, p. 434. On the close continuity between James and the Jesus tradition, see esp. Davids, 1985).

The second theory, which is now the majority opinion, holds that James is pseudonymous,[9] that its provenance is other than Jerusalem,[10] and that it was written at a later date (70–130 CE; see Davids, 1982, p. 4). Evidence for this hypothesis includes arguments that the period reflected in James is after the fall of Jerusalem (70 CE); that its Greek is too good, and its obvious use of rhetorical conventions too advanced, for James the Just; that its familiarity is with the LXX rather than the Hebrew Bible; that its "paraenetic style reflects the history of transmission of Christian teaching which finds its closest parallels in 1 Peter and in the *Didache*, rather than in direct, personal remembrances"; that the portrait of James in Acts and Galatians lacks harmony with James' content; and, that its late appearance and acceptance by the early church does not cohere with a text written by "the brother of the Lord" (Childs, 1984, pp. 434, 435).

An additional hypothesis, recently championed by P. H. Davids (1982, p. 22.), provides a compromise solution that has genuine merit: traditions from James the Just (40 CE and the Jerusalem Council) were redacted and augmented in and for a later period (between 55–65 or possibly 75–85 CE) by a Jewish Christian. Prior to Davids there were others who, in one form or another, suggested that our letter is a post-Jamesian document that makes use of earlier traditions emanating from Jerusalem and James the Just

[9] Among those who contend that James is pseudonymous are: Ropes (1916, pp. 47–48); Dibelius (1975, pp. 18–19); Moffatt (1928, p. 1); Meyer (1930, p. 306); Goodspeed (1937a, p. 293); Elliott-Binns (1956, pp. 47–48); Reicke (1964, p. 4); Laws (1982, pp. 38–42); Schrage and Balz (1980, 10–11); Vielhauer (1975, pp. 578–80); Kümmel (1975, pp. 411–14); Lüdemann (1989, p. 140); Vouga (1984, p. 18). Others are mentioned in Dibelius (1975, p. 19 note 51); Davids (1982, p. 4); and Pratscher (1987, p. 209 note 2).

[10] Dibelius argued that James is paraenesis from "liberated Diaspora Judaism," and its provenance cannot be fixed (Dibelius, 1975, p. 47). Ropes (1916, p. 49) suggested some town in Palestine, perhaps Caesarea. Weiss (1937, vol. ii, p. 751) opted for a Syrian provenance; Goodspeed (1937b, p. 295) and Hartin (1991, p. 240) nominated Antioch. Rome has been hypothesized by Reicke (1964, p. 6) and Laws (1982, pp. 25–26). And Egypt (Alexandria perhaps) has had its share of supporters too; see H. A. A. Kennedy (1911).

(Oesterley, 1910, vol. IV, p. 408; Burkitt, 1924, pp. 69–70; W. L. Knox, 1945. Also see Marxsen, 1968, pp. 224–32, esp. p. 228). Currently, there is no scholarly consensus on the historical setting of James (Childs, 1984, p. 435. See Pearson, 1989, pp. 371–76, 387–88, and esp. Popkes, 1986, pp. 9–52. Also Baasland, 1988, pp. 3646–49, and Davids, 1982, pp. 1–61; and 1988).

James as a theological problem

A review of the earliest interpretations of the Epistle of James in the Alexandrian School and the Latin Fathers suggests that the principal issue was its theological theme.[11] The letter was rather dogmatically classified as moralistic instruction (Baasland, 1988, p. 3647; Lachmann, 1949). Augustine's view of James, as well as his interpretation of 2.14–26, which differentiates between works before and after justification, appears to have been authoritative for almost a millennium (see Harnack's illuminating remarks on Augustine, in Dibelius, 1975, p. 53 note 204). The Augustinian synthesis, however, was broken by Luther (cf. Kawerau, 1889, and Schmidt-Clausing, 1969. For the argument that Luther misunderstood Augustine, see Lachmann, 1949; Baasland, 1988, p. 3647).

Luther's argument against James was fundamentally a religious argument.[12] He contended that the epistle fails to show Christ, that compared to the Gospel according to John, 1 John, Romans, Galatians, Ephesians, and 1 Peter, "it is really an epistle of straw . . . for it has nothing of the nature of the gospel about it" (*Luther's Works*, vol. XXXV, p. 362). Its content he considered to be hardly Christian: "it does not once mention the Passion, the resurrection, or the Spirit of Christ." Moreover, he concluded that the letter "is flatly against St. Paul and all the rest of the Scripture in ascribing justification to works" (*Luther's Works*, vol. XXXV, p. 396). With

---

[11] Here I am indebted to the excellent discussion in Baasland (1988).

[12] Dibelius (1975, p. 56 note 229) reminds us that in Luther's "lecture on the Letter to the Romans in 1515/16 [ed. Ficker, vol. I, part 2, pp. 84–85] he still treats Paul and James as though they are in harmony: Paul is speaking of 'works of the Law', James is speaking of 'works of faith'." During this period, therefore, it appears that "Luther seems not to have thought so critically about the letter." In the Leipzig Debate, however, James was used against Luther; in defense, Luther criticized James: "The style of that epistle is far beneath the apostolic majesty, nor does it compare in any way with that of Paul" (quoted in Dibelius, 1975, p. 54 note 6, from the *Resolutiones super propositionibus Lipsiae disputatis* in *D. Martin Luthers Werke: Kritische Gesamtausgabe*, vol. II [Weimar: Böhlau, 1884], p. 425). Cf. Mitton (1966, p. 221).

Luther, therefore, the question of "faith and/or works" became the main issue in the discussion, and James 2.14–26 the focus. Because he understood it to support the law and to contain many good sayings, Luther did not support an outright rejection of the Epistle of James. Yet he was emphatically opposed to granting the letter full apostolicity (*Luther's Works*, vol. xxxv, pp. 395, 397 note 55).

Although Luther's views were representative of most of the older German Protestants, there were others, like Melancthon, who tried to harmonize James and Paul, arguing that the former contends not against Paul but against a dead faith (Ropes, 1916, pp. 107–08; Dibelius, 1975, p. 56. Cf. Baasland, 1988, p. 3647). It was this opinion, and not Luther's, that found expression in the *Formula of Concord*. Outside Germany, Luther's negative assessments of James' place in theology received less approbation. The epistle was regularly accepted as sacred scripture, though its authorship was contested. Zwingli, Calvin, Beza, and Knox were among the many who accepted James (see the discussion in Ropes, 1916, pp. 108–09, which is repeated in Adamson, 1989, pp. 164–65).

Throughout most of the seventeenth and eighteenth centuries, this situation continued, but with the rise of the Tübingen School in the nineteenth century Luther's views began to predominate (Baasland, 1988, p. 3647). The letter of James was perceived as promoting a legalistic understanding of Christianity in fundamental opposition to Paul's gospel of freedom from the law; the question of James' origin became exceedingly significant. Representative of this approach is F. H. Kern, who regarded James "als Ausdruck einer ebionitisch-judenchristlichen Frömmigkeit, deren antipaulinische Tendenz deutlich ist" ("as an expression of Ebionite-Jewish-Christian piety, in which an anti-Pauline tendency is clear"; Baasland, 1988, pp. 3647–48). In 1835, Kern argued against the letter's authenticity on the basis of its good Greek, its character, and world of thought. Three years later, however, in his commentary, *Der Brief Jakobus*, he contended for its authenticity (see Dibelius, 1975, p. 57 notes 239–40). Furthermore, especially important for our purposes is Baasland's observation that it was Kern who brought the theme "poor–rich" into prominence in Jamesian research (1988, p. 3648 note 11). This theme, along with that of "testing and endurance" (Fry, 1978) and "Christian wisdom" (Hoppe, 1977), has become the principal rival of "faith and/or works" as the main theme in the letter of James (Baasland, 1988, p. 3647. See Dibelius, 1975, esp. pp. 39–45; Mußner, 1987, pp. 76–84; Vielhauer, 1975, pp. 576–77). In his unpublished dissertation, "Thema und Disposition des Jakobusbriefes: Eine formkritische Studie" (Vienna), Rustler (1952) argued that the organizing theme of the entire letter is to be found in a social problem, the conflict between the rich and the poor.[13] Finally, it must be noted that both Luther's formulation of the theological problem and his criticisms of James from a Pauline perspective remain compelling today; in fact, James-viewed-through-Paul is (lamentably) still the norm (L. T. Johnson, 1985, p. 166; 1986, esp. pp. 453–63; and B. A. Pearson, 1989, pp. 371–76, 387–404).

James as a literary problem

The Epistle of James as a literary problem has long occupied a significant place in scholarly discussion. Here also Luther's views remain extremely influential. Besides his religious and theological arguments against the epistle, Luther maintained that James is literarily dependent on 1 Peter, and stylistically "chaotic": "there is no order or method in the epistle" (*Luther's Works*, vol. XXXV, p. 397; LIV, p. 425; see Dibelius, 1975, pp. 54–56). This low opinion of James' style, that it lacks "apostolic majesty" and is beneath Paul's,[14] is rightly traced back to the earlier literary judgments of Erasmus, who was dependent on Jerome (Ropes, 1916, p. 104). For example, concluding his commentary on James, Erasmus wrote: "For neither does it [James] seem to bear anywhere that apostolic majesty and dignity, nor the large number of Hebraisms one would expect from James, who was bishop of Jerusalem" (*Opera Omnia*, vol. VI; Leiden: Vander, 1705; repr. London: Gregg Press, 1962, col. 1038, as quoted in Dibelius, 1975, p. 54 note 216). On the other hand, Luther's disparaging remarks about James' lack of arrangement have ignited a debate that has continued to burn its way through centuries of research and into the present (Beck, 1973, 10–14).

One of the ways in which the Renaissance interest in history

[13] For criticism – not of the importance of the "poor–rich" theme but – of Rustler's schematization of the letter, see Dibelius (1975, p. 6 note 22) and Mußner (1987, pp. 57–58).

[14] Cardinal Cajetan, Luther's opponent, also knew the opinions of Jerome and, like Luther, was influenced by Erasmus' opinions of James' language and style. Cajetan quibbled about "the secular form of the letter's greeting" and argued that its authorship was uncertain; see Dibelius (1975, p. 56), Ropes (1916, p. 105), Adamson (1989, p. 164), and their respective notes.

manifested itself was in the humanist concern for sources (Kümmel, 1972, pp. 20–39). This is profoundly evident in the Reformation period in the literary judgments that Erasmus, Cajetan, Luther, and their followers pronounced on James. Doubts about James' authenticity as well as questions about its value in theology and doctrine tended to give way to "a stricter doctrine of inspiration" (Ropes, 1916, pp. 107–08). The turning-point among the Protestants was probably the *Formula of Concord* (Kawerau, 1889, p. 369). In similar fashion the Council of Trent (8 April 1546) superseded the critical views of scholars like Cajetan and declared James to be apostolic and sacred scripture (Ropes, 1916, p. 105; cf. Dibelius, 1975, p. 56). In the latter half of the sixteenth century, and throughout the seventeenth, this concern expressed itself in further explorations of the text of the New Testament (Kümmel, 1972, pp. 40–50). Along with the discoveries of contradictions in the text and historical problems with the canon, debates arose about the roles of reason and faith (and the tradition of the church) in evaluating these discrepancies (pp. 51–73). With the enthusiasm spawned by the Enlightenment the eighteenth century gave serious attention to these literary problems, and this in turn prompted forays into primitive Christianity and its world of thought (pp. 74–97). Thus we begin to find source-critical investigations of James, like those of G. C. Storr (1797) and J. D. Schulze (1802), that produced tables of James' literary parallels with other literature (see Baasland, 1988, p. 3648).

In the nineteenth century, Jamesian research passed through three stages, and each is marked by this literary, or more correctly source-critical, concern.[15] According to Dibelius (1975, p. 56) the first stage in the modern critical study of James began in 1826 with W. M. L. de Wette. He denied the authenticity of the letter, arguing that the Lord's brother would have been incapable of composing and writing in such fluent Greek. The kernel of this criticism, as we have seen above, was already raised in the sixteenth century by Erasmus. It was reiterated by Luther (Dibelius, p. 54 note 217), and has been emphasized by many scholars since de Wette (see the

---

[15] The division of Jamesian research in the nineteenth century into three stages belongs to Dibelius (Dibelius, 1975, pp. 56–57). Interestingly, Adamson (1989, pp. x–xi) observes that these stages "correspond to similar stages in the modern study of Jewish Christianity": first, from the Tübingen School in the 1830s; second, from the *Religionsgeschichtliche Schule* in the 1880s; and third, from the discoveries of the Qumran Scrolls (1947) and the Nag Hammadi library in the 1950s.

list in Adamson, 1989, p. 35 note 1). The second stage began in 1831 with F. C. Baur and his followers in the Tübingen School (Dibelius, 1975, p. 57 note 241). Here James was understood to be a pseudepigraphic work of the second century which synthesized Jewish and Christian views, and was anti-Pauline, and even anti-gnostic.[16] The third stage is marked by the studies of L. Massebieau (1895) and F. Spitta (1896), who independently espoused the view that the letter was a Christian revision of an originally Jewish document (Dibelius, 1975, p. 57).[17]

In the latter part of the nineteenth, as well as in the early twentieth, century important studies of James' language, style, and arrangement appear. Among these, the investigations of H. J. Cladder, J. B. Mayor, and J. H. Ropes are especially significant.

Cladder (1904a; 1904b) contended for a thematic pattern in James' arrangement and he also discussed James' use of poetic strophes. His influence is felt in A. Schlatter's (1932) compelling study of the characteristics of James' linguistic usage, and particularly in his observations of James' poetic resemblance to the Psalms and the wisdom literature (see Schlatter, 1956, pp. 77–84, 99; cf. Mußner, 1987, p. 26 note 5; and Baasland, 1988, p. 3648). On the other hand, some fifty years prior to Cladder, E. Pfeiffer (1850) became the first scholar to oppose Schleiermacher and W. M. L. de Wette and to argue for a logical order in James, adducing James 1.19 as the key to the letter's arrangement (see Beck, 1973, p. 16).[18]

J. B. Mayor's (1892 [1990]) massive commentary on James re-

---

[16] Literary parallels that had been drawn up by earlier scholars, like Storr (1797) and Schulze (1802), were now analyzed traditio-historically for information about James' origin and historical placement. For a discussion of various, earlier arguments that James belongs to the second century, see Mayor (1892 [1990], pp. clxxviii–cxciii). And for the view that James is anti-gnostic, see Schwegler (1846, p. 442); Schammberger (1936); and Schoeps (1949, pp. 343–49).

[17] Meyer (1930, pp. 240–347) followed Massebieau's and Spitta's idea of a Jewish *Grundschrift* for James; likewise Hartmann (1942); Easton (1957, pp. 10–11); and Thyen (1956, pp. 14–16). Davids (1982, p. 5 note 11) has noted that Bultmann (1955, pp. 143, 163) also accepted the possibility that James was originally a Jewish text. For a discussion and refutation of Massebieau and Spitta, see Mayor (1892 [1990], pp. cxcii–ccv); Ropes (1916, pp. 32–33); and Dibelius (1975, esp. pp. 21–23, 66, 126).

[18] Among the many others who have found some intentional progression of thought or arrangement in James, Dibelius (1975, p. 6 note 22) mentions Tielemann (1894); Parry (1903); B. Weiss (1904); and Rustler (1952). To these should be added Beker (1950, p. 37) who finds in James a twelve-part instructional pattern corresponding to Genesis 49; Gertner (1962) who posits Psalm 12 as the basis for James' arrangement; and Beck (1973) who holds for an arrangement based on two Qumran Documents, *Manual of Discipline* (1QS) and *Rule of the Congregation* (1QSa).

mains one of the best. Its extensive sections on the language, grammar, and style of James (see chapters 8–10, and pp. ccvi–cclxviii) are unsurpassed. Further, it offers a wealth of comparative material and is a valuable resource for the history of Jamesian scholarship, especially in the nineteenth century.

J. H. Ropes (1916) provides excellent presentations of James' ideas, historical background, and the history of interpretation. His remarks about the diatribe, protrepticus, and paraenesis (pp. 10–16, 18) are particularly significant. And his discussions of James' language (pp. 27–43) and literary relationships (pp. 18–24) are remarkable.

The year 1921, however, stands as a watershed in Jamesian research: Martin Dibelius' commentary on James was published. In this monumental study, the historical, theological, and literary problems associated with the letter of James received a treatment that has remained dominant for the last seventy years. On the one hand, Dibelius drew together the wealth of comparative research done by Mayor and Ropes, and augmented it with his own vast knowledge of the Greco-Roman world. On the other hand, as a pioneer in form-criticism, he approached the text in an atomistic fashion that seemed to give depth and precision to the theological and literary judgments Luther had made four hundred years earlier.[19] Furthermore, Dibelius so persuasively discussed the genre, form, and origin of the materials in James that his assessments have seemed to many the final word.[20] All subsequent

[19] See Dibelius' "Foreword to the Seventeenth German Edition" of the Meyer commentary series, dated September 1920 (in Dibelius, 1975, pp. xi–xii). On Dibelius' interpretation of James, see the assessment of Koester in the "Foreword" to the Hermeneia volume (1975, pp. ix–x). On the commentary's uniqueness, consider the views of H. Greeven, particularly for Dibelius' use of "the form-critical methodology" and the "Analyses" which precede each section of the commentary (1975, pp. xiii). Also cf. Ward (1966), and the incisive comments about "paraenesis" as a literary genre in L. T. Johnson (1985, pp. 166–83). On Dibelius' life's work, see Kümmel (1965).

[20] The scholarly investigation of James' genre and form belongs properly to the twentieth century. Although Dibelius' (1975, pp. 1–61) argument for "paraenesis" as James's genre has been predominant, there is no scholarly consensus on this matter. The hypotheses are numerous and varied; for example, Ropes (1916, pp. 2–18) argues that James is a protreptic text, a diatribe. Francis (1970) approaches James as a "literary" letter or "epistle." Thyen (1956, p. 16) classifies James as a "homily" (see Adamson, 199, p. 110 note 47, for others who hold this view). Halson (1968) regards James as a collection of catechetical wisdom material. Lohse (1957) calls it an enchiridion of Christian ethics, while Gertner (1962) and Schille (1977) prefer a "tractate."

scholarly research on James is judged with reference to Martin Dibelius.[21]

Martin Dibelius and the present situation in Jamesian research

Notwithstanding the fact of Dibelius' enormous importance in Jamesian studies, or the vitality of many of his assessments, the present situation in the research suggests that some of his most cherished presuppositions and conclusions are no longer acceptable. Before addressing this matter, however, it is necessary to rehearse the results of Dibelius' investigation of James.

Dibelius concluded that the letter of James is composed primarily of sayings materials of two broad divisions. The first division consists of aphorisms, variously labeled as traditional sayings, admonitions, instructions, and proverbial rules (James 1.2, 4, 5, 17, 22, 23; 2.5; 3.12; 4.4, 11–12; 5.2, 10, 19). The second division is made up of longer discourses, which Dibelius further partitioned into three groupings. First, there are three "*treatises*" (*Abhandlungen*) that form "the core of the writing": James 2.1–13 on partiality; 2.14–26 on faith and works; and 3.1–12 on the tongue. Second, there are three "*series of sayings*" (*Spruchreihen*) that are characterized by the brief or expanded saying: James 1.2–18 on temptations; 1.19–27 on hearing and doing; and 5.7–20 on various themes. Third, there are two "*groups of sayings*" (*Spruchgruppen*): James 3.13–4.12 against contentiousness, and 4.13–5.6 against worldly-minded merchants and rich people; "there are both smaller, self-contained units (3.13–17; 4.1–6; 4.13–16) but also less unified texts (4.7–12) and even isolated sayings (3.18 and 4.17)" (see Dibelius, 1975, p. 1; and the respective "Analyses" in the commentary).

Extremely noteworthy is Dibelius' observation of a "three-fold similarity" between the sayings of Jesus in Q and the sayings in James; namely, a similarity in the form, style, and general

---

[21] For a general overview of Jamesian research since Dibelius the reader should consult the introductions of Kümmel (1975), Vielhauer (1975), and Childs (1984), and the commentaries by Mußner (1987), Adamson (1976), Laws (1980), Davids (1982), and Popkes (1986). In addition, the review articles by Davids (1988) and Pearson (1989) provide fine summaries of the scholarship between World War II and 1986. Adamson (1989) includes references to much of the work done since then. Also see the 12th edn. of Dibelius (1984, esp. pp. 311–22) for newer literature.

convictions of their sayings. He also argued that both the sayings of Jesus and the sayings of James have the same intention, they "were collected for a paraenetic purpose" (Dibelius, 1975, p. 28). Thus, Dibelius treated both Q and the Epistle of James under the rubric of paraenesis (for an incisive discussion of this see Kloppenborg, 1984, and 1987a, pp. 1–40, esp. 16–18; cf. Dibelius, [1935] 1971, pp. 233–65, and 1975, pp. 1–11).

Dibelius held paraenesis to be a literary genre that he defined as "a text which strings together admonitions of general ethical content" (1975, pp. 3, 5, 11). He listed the following as the most distinctive features of the genre: eclecticism; lack of continuity or thoughtful progression; merely external (catchword) connection between admonitions; repetition of the same motifs in different places; and the lack of a single situation into which all the admonitions will fit (pp. 5, 6, 11). On the basis of its genre classification, he concluded that James is devoid of theology, and that it lacks an identifiable historical context (pp. 21–26). Recent research, however, has found that both Dibelius' conception of paraenesis and his treatment of Q and James under this rubric are highly problematic.

Paraenesis and kerygma: a theological problem

In *From Tradition to Gospel*, Dibelius ([1935] 1971, p. 14) argued that "all tradition about Jesus' evolved out of early Christian sermons or preaching. He held that missionary purpose was the motive for, and preaching the means of, transmitting the sayings of Jesus (p. 13; see pp. 9–36). The "heart of the Christian tradition," he emphasized, was not located in sayings of Jesus; "that position was reserved for the kerygma" (Kloppenborg, 1987a, p. 16; Dibelius, [1935] 1971, pp. 15–23). The kerygma Dibelius perceived to be the (Pauline) proclamation of an eschatological event: the salvific death and resurrection of Jesus (Koester, 1990, p. 51; Dibelius, [1935] 1971, pp. 17, 23, 25, 230, 244). Dibelius observed that this kerygma plays no part in Q, and because Q shows no trace of a development toward narrative, that is, the story of the Passion and Easter, he hypothesized that the law governing the development of Jesus' sayings must have been different from the law that controlled the development of the narrative tradition (pp. 23–28, 237, 244–46). The "sayings of Jesus' in view here are not the "paradigms" (pp. 37–69), that is, sayings "which constituted either the kernel or goal of the story"; rather they are "exhortations" (pp. 233–65), "loosely connected sayings" or "isolated sayings, especially proverbs, metaphors and commandments" (p. 27).

Dibelius' impression of the "different law" that constrained the development and transmission of the Jesus tradition was based on his understanding of the role that Jesus' sayings appear to play in the so-called "paraenetic" sections of Paul's letters (Dibelius, [1935] 1971, pp. 238–42). He observed that Paul confines his use of Jesus' sayings to distinct hortatory sections that frequently conclude his letters. Further, he found that these hortatory sections of Paul's letters are characteristically loose, unconnected, and aphoristic in style, and that their content is general, lacks specificity, and shows no immediate relation to the historical situation at hand. He judged that these hortatory sections lack the charm and individuality of those sections in which the apostle treats of religious and theological concerns, like the kerygma and christology. In fact, except in 1 Thessalonians 4.15–17, Dibelius discovered that Paul does not use Jesus' sayings for religious and theological purposes, neither "to support a Christological demonstration, nor to give an authentic reference for the plan of redemption" (p. 241). Instead, Paul utilizes sayings of Jesus alongside other hortatory material that is the common property of the Hellenistic world as rules for everyday life (pp. 240–42). Further, because this material is common and not unique to Paul, Dibelius said that "one would do well not to overestimate the author's part in the development of thought in the writing" (1975, p. 5). Thus he emphasized that the hortatory sections of Paul's letters cannot be used to discover "the theoretic foundation of the ethics of the Apostle" (Dibelius, [1935] 1971, p. 239). He maintained that they contain practically no "'theology' at all, and quite certainly [not] the theology of Paul" (Dibelius, 1975, p. 21). The materials in these sections, he argued, grow out of "didactic habit" and the need for moral instruction. Dibelius concluded, therefore, that the sayings of Jesus in Paul's letters were collected for paraenetic purposes and were incidental to the proclamation of the kerygma (Dibelius, [1935] 1971, pp. 238–39).

This judgment about Paul's use of the sayings of Jesus Dibelius then transferred to Q, which, for him, was merely "a stratum" without independence and theology (Dibelius, [1935] 1971, p. 235). Despite the fact that Q does not refer directly to the kerygma, he presupposed the kerygma's presence and dominance in Q. So, Q was Christian halakah, a paraenetical supplement to the kerygma (1971, pp. 28, 238). In this fashion Dibelius determined that the sayings of Jesus in Q belong in the category of paraenesis; they were collected and used as in Paul's letters: not kerygmatically but paraenetically, not as proclamation but as catechetical instruction (1975, p. 3).

Q research, however, has come not only to question this assessment, but to argue against it (Kloppenborg, 1987a, pp. 1–40). Scholars like Hans Dieter Betz (1985), Helmut Koester (1990), and John S. Kloppenborg (1987a) suggest that in early Christianity there were Christians who did not find the significance of Jesus in (the Pauline proclamation of) his death, burial, and resurrection (1 Cor. 15.3–7). Instead some Christians appear to have found the "turning point of the ages" in Jesus' words and deeds. For these Christians "the sayings of Jesus actually constituted the message of salvation upon which they based their faith" (Koester, 1990, p. 159).

For example, in his *Essays on the Sermon on the Mount*, Betz has argued that the Sermon on the Mount (= SM) "represents a pre-Matthean composition of a redactional nature" (1985, p. 19), in which "the primitive Christian kerygma of the death and resurrection plays no role" (p. 92). The SM "derives from a Jewish-Christian group in which law and gospel are strongly intertwined" (p. 35); "in the SM, Jesus is regarded as the authoritative teacher and interpreter of the Jewish Torah" (p. 91). "According to the SM, Jesus' authority depends upon that of the Torah, though naturally in accord with his particular interpretation" of it (p. 92). "The Torah taught by Jesus is nothing less than the way revealed by God which corresponds to his kingdom and which leads one into it ([Matt] 7.13–14)" (p. 95).

Moreover, as Koester (1990, p. 171) has correctly observed, "the author of this epistle [James] and the redactor of Q who produced the Sermon on the Mount belong to the same Jewish-Christian milieu; both share the decision that the followers of Jesus belong to law-abiding Israel and that fulfillment of the law, though without any emphasis upon circumcision and ritual law, is the appropriate interpretation of the teachings of Jesus."

If these scholars are correct in arguing that for some early Christians the sayings of Jesus constituted the message of salvation, and I think that they are correct, then Dibelius' view of the so-called paraenetic tradition, including both its origin and significance, needs radical reassessment. One of the subsidiary goals of this research is to participate in this endeavor.

Paraenesis and literature: a literary problem

Also in Dibelius' view of the development of the Jesus tradition was the idea that the people who stand behind this material were merely collectors and transmitters of a sacred tradition ([1935] 1971, p. 3; [1936] 1979, pp. 15–20). The corollary to this is that the transmitters were not authors who had their own designs on the material and its media of communication. As collectors – apart from simply arranging and grouping the material on the basis of its themes, or merely connecting it formally by catchwords, or perhaps occasionally ordering it on the basis of logical associations – they tended to pass the tradition along, rarely altering it, and then only to adapt it to changes and needs of everyday life. Therefore, Dibelius argued that we are not dealing with a "purely literary process"; instead we are dealing with *Kleinliteratur* (Kloppenborg, 1987a, pp. 1–8). Thus he emphasized that the transmitters of the Jesus tradition were "unlettered people" who lacked both the capacity and inclination for "a true literary activity" (Dibelius, [1935] 1971, p. 9).

But just as Q research has argued against allowing Dibelius' historico-religious and theological presuppositions about the kerygma to predetermine the role and place of Jesus sayings in nascent Christianity, it has also joined with literary studies and rhetorical investigations to challenge the romantic view of the authors of the New Testament as basically simple uneducated folk lacking both literary abilities and interests (Petersen, 1978; Mack, 1990). For example, Burton Mack and Vernon Robbins (1989, pp. 1–29) have shown that, because Dibelius (and Bultmann) either overlooked or purposefully ignored the dominance of rhetoric in the Hellenistic period, some of their venerable categories, like "apophthegm," "paradigm" – and, as I propose to show, even "paraenesis" – are inadequately informed.[22] Conse-

---

[22] Dibelius ([1935] 1971, pp. 233–65) classified the Jesus tradition as (1) narrative material and (2) paraenesis. The narrative material he placed into five groups: paradigms, tales, legends, myths, and the passion narrative. And, among the sayings of Jesus, he formally distinguished six groups: maxims (= proverbs, sayings, gnomes), metaphor, parabolic narrative, prophetic call (= beatitude, woe, eschatological preaching), short commandment, and extended commandment (with a basis, promise or threat). Bultmann (1963, pp. 11, 69) held that the Jesus tradition may be

quently, some of the assured results of their investigations require reassessment.

Paraenesis: a literary genre or mode of persuasion?: a historical problem

As was mentioned in the previous chapter, it is only recently, and largely under the influence of studies in ancient rhetoric and epistolary theory, that New Testament scholarship has begun to focus seriously on the subject of paraenesis (Aune, 1987, p. 191; Perdue and Gammie, 1990a). Besides the problems just discussed, research has raised fundamental questions about Dibelius' conception of paraenesis as a literary genre. And this is of primary significance for at least two reasons. First of all, Dibelius' commentary on James is an effort to understand the epistle as an example of the genre "paraenesis": "to explicate the problems of the letter in terms of the particular presuppositions of this paraenesis, the way in which it is transmitted, and the way in which it combines Christian, Jewish, and Hellenistic elements" (Dibelius, 1975, pp. xi, xii–xiii). Second, it is quite apparent that most New Testament scholars owe their understanding of paraenesis to Dibelius, either directly or as his views have been refracted through subsequent studies. For example, Vielhauer's (1975, esp. pp. 49–57, 69, 120–21, 280–91, 567–80; see his index, *s.v.*, p. 808) discussion of paraenesis is basically a rehearsal of Dibelius' views.

Where did Dibelius get his understanding of paraenesis? The noun παραίνεσις does not occur in the text of the NT. The verb παραινέω occurs only *twice*: Acts 27.9 and 27.22, and in both instances it has the sense of "to advise," "to urge," or "to exhort." In either case, the verb παρακαλέω (which occurs 109 times in the NT) could have been used; cf. Acts 27.33, 34, and Dionysius of Halicarnassus, *Isoc.* 10. The terms παρακαλέω and παραινέω (as well as προτροπέω and συμβουλεύω) were customarily employed as interchangeable terms for "to exhort" and "to advise" (see LSJ, *s.v.* παραίνεσις, παραινέω, παρακαλέω, παράκλησις, προτρέπω,

form-critically divided into two major types, apophthegms (= pronouncement stories) and dominical sayings (= sayings of the Lord). Primarily on the basis of content, and partly due to form, he divided the latter category into three groups: (1) sayings or *logia* in the narrower sense (= wisdom sayings); (2) prophetic and apocalyptic sayings; and (3) laws and community regulations. In each of the latter groups he also listed (another group) the "I-sayings." See Conzelmann and Lindemann (1988, pp. 65–82).

and συμβουλεύω; cf. also νουθεσία, ὁρμάω, and σωφρονισμός).[23]
Primarily, Dibelius appears to have depended on two excellent
investigations: Paul Wendland's (1905) "Die Rede an Demonikos,"
and especially Rudolf Vetschera's (1911–12) *Zur griechischen Paränese* (see Dibelius, 1975, p. 2 note 12). Both Wendland and
Vetschera held paraenesis to be a literary genre, and for this
impression they were heavily indebted to Paulus Hartlich's (1889)
dissertation, *De exhortationum* (προτρεπτικῶν) *a Graecis Romanisque sciptarum historia et indole.*

Wendland's study traced the development of the prose protreptic
out of advisory and didactic gnomic poetry (Jaeger, 1948, p. 56
note 1). He held that Isocrates' political exhortations *To Nicocles*
and *Nicocles* are "the oldest preserved paraeneses," but because
they principally concern politics, Wendland recommended that *To
Demonicus* provides "a better example of the average type of
paraenesis" (1905, pp. 82–83). His analysis of the latter texts
mentioned practically all of the characteristic features of paraenesis
that Dibelius emphasizes: its gnomic quality, loosely connected
thoughts, lack of strict arrangement, abrupt transitions between
sentences, and repetition.

Hartlich's study was the fundamental investigation of the form
of the λόγος προτρεπτικός (Gaiser, 1959, p. 25 note 23). Largely
on the basis of the use of the terms προτρεπτικὸς λόγος and
παραίνεσις in Pseudo-Isocrates' exhortation *To Demonicus* 3–5,
the gnomic style employed in that discourse, and Seneca's reference
(in *Epistle* 95.65; cf. 95.1) to the use of "precepts" in Posidonius'
philosophy, Hartlich argued that paraenetic discourse and protreptic discourse were "formally" distinct genres. He defined protreptic speech as mainly "sayings" (*verba*) which, if closely
connected and arranged, constitute a vital exhortation or encoura-
ging address (Hartlich, 1889, pp. 221–22). Paraenesis, however, he
regarded not as pure exhortation but as advice by precept.[24]

[23] The variant reading in Luke 3.18 is of particular interest: the text employs
παρακαλῶν for John the Baptist's "exhortations" in preaching the "good news to
the people"; Cantabrigiensis (05) replaces παρακαλῶν with παραινῶν. On the one
hand, this reflects the familiar interchangeable usage and understanding of these
terms; on the other, it raises a question about the arguments of Dibelius (and others)
that the "preaching of the gospel" (εὐαγγελίζω) and the giving of exhortations
(παρακαλέω/παραινέω) are two neatly separated matters. See Furnish (1968,
pp. 259–62, 272–74).

[24] "Παραίνεσις non est exhortatio, sed ut Senecae verbo (ep. 95,65) praeceptio. In
paraenesi dantur ὑποθῆκαι ὡς χρὴ ζῆν (Isocr. or. II,3); orator in ea non adhortatur,
sed monet, suadet, praecipit. Itaque paraenesis propius attinet ad γένος συμβουλευ-

Vetschera (1911–12, p. 5) accepted Hartlich's "formal" distinction but was quick to add that a mere examination of the external forms of protreptic and paraenetic discourse is insufficient to determine the essence of either one. To accomplish that, he argued, one also must consider the contents and goals of the discourses in question. In essence, then, Vetschera's study tried not only to refine and strengthen Hartlich's "formal" distinction between paraenesis and protrepsis, but to show that the latter were "materially" distinct as well. Vetschera focused specifically on Pseudo-Isocrates' *To Demonicus*, and Isocrates' *To Nicocles* and *Nicocles*, and compared them with other protreptic pieces like those in Iamblichus and that from Emperor Manuel Palaeologus to his son John (ca. 1400 CE). He concluded that, while both kinds of exhortation share common conceptions and strive for virtue as their chief goal, the paraenetic discourse "übertrifft den Protrepticus an Vielseitigkeit des Inhalts" ("surpasses the protrepsis in the versatility of its content"; Vetschera, 1911–12, p. 6).[25] On the one hand, protreptic discourse "ermahnt zur Philosophie oder Rhetorik oder sonst einer Kenntnis und durch diese zur ἀρετή" ("exhorts to philosophy or rhetoric or as a rule to a knowledge and by this to ἀρετή"); on the other, paraenesis seeks to lead one on to virtue by providing "eine Sammlung von Vorschriften für das Verhalten in allen möglichen Lebenslagen" ("a collection of prescriptions for behavior in every possible life-situation"; p. 6). Vetschera defines paraenesis as "ein Literaturzeugnis, das nach seiner Anlage und seinem Zwecke eine Sammlung von Vorschriften darstellt, die sich durchwegs auf die

τικόν, ut recte statuit Ammonius de diff. verb. 132: παραίνεσίς ἐστι συμβουλὴ ἀντίρρησιν οὐκ ἐπιδεχομένη διὰ τὸ ἐξ αὐτῆς λεγόμενον πάντως ὁμολεγεῖσθαι ἀγαθόν, ὡς εἴ τις παραινέσει σωφρονεῖν, ὅσπερ ἐστὶν ὡμολογημένον ἀγαθόν" (Hartlich, 1889, p. 222). Of interest here is that Ammonius says nothing about the "form" of paraenesis whatsoever. Instead, paraenesis is equated with "συμβουλή" (advice, counsel, deliberation) that does not admit rebuttal, since it persuades toward a commonly agreed upon good. Cf. Ps.-Libanius' definition of the "paraenetic letter" where he disagrees with some (like Ammonius, Ps.-Demetrius) who understand paraenesis as συμβουλή (in Malherbe, 1988, pp. 68–69). It should also be remembered that the rhetors always understood συμβουλή as inherently positive and negative, i.e., it not only persuaded toward something; it also dissuaded from something. Moreover, the literature reveals that the "commonly agreed upon good" was a matter not uncommonly debated. "Rebuttal" (ἀντίρρησις) was one of the "preliminary exercises" that students learned; see Theon, I,200–01 (Butts, 1987, pp. 120–21), as well as Butts' "Introduction" (esp. pp. 17–19).

[25] This distinction "by content" is the one most emphasized by Fiore (1986) in his excellent study, *The Function of Personal Example in the Socratic and Pastoral Epistles*.

praktische Lebensführung beziehen, bestimmt, die, die es angeht, zu fördern und zur Tugend zu führen" ("a literary production, that according to its construction and its goal constitutes a collection of prescriptions, which without exception refers to the practical conduct of life, [and] determines what this concerns in order to encourage and lead one on to virtue"; p. 7).

From these investigations, Martin Dibelius learned of paraenesis. In turn, he has taught us that paraenesis is a distinctive literary genre, one that has both a definite form and content (1975, pp. 2–3 note 12). Moreover, emphasizing the form and origin of the materials in paraenesis, he has trained us to read James as basically disconnected sentences (L. T. Johnson, 1985, pp. 166–68); and accentuating the letter's traditional character, Dibelius has implanted within us the idea that it contains little thought, and thus, little or no distinctive function (Furnish, 1968, pp. 259–62). Is this correct?

Theodore C. Burgess' (1902) outstanding investigation, "Epideictic Literature," appears to have gone unnoticed by Wendland, Vetschera, and Dibelius. This is unfortunate. For, despite the fact that some of Burgess' conclusions about epideictic oratory now appear anachronistic,[26] his expansive reading of the primary texts provided the basis for what seems to be a broader view and more commensurate assessment of protrepsis and paraenesis. It is interesting and helpful to note here that Burgess' understanding of the history of epideictic depended heavily on Richard Volkmann's exposition in *Die Rhetorik der Griechen und Römer in systematischer Übersicht* ([1885] 1987, esp. pp. 314–61), which, notwithstanding its excellence and systematical thoroughness, has "very little historical perspective" (G. A. Kennedy, 1963, p. 10 note 7). Consequently, Volkmann's conceptions of epideictic offer "more information from Menander Rhetor and the second sophistic than from the practices of the fourth century B.C." (Chase, 1961, p. 56). Thus, with a similar lack of historical perspective, Burgess would have us view Aristotle's *Protrepticus* and Isocrates' protreptic discourse *To Nicocles* as epideictic set pieces. This I think is incorrect, for, as Werner Jaeger (1948, esp. pp. 54–60) demonstrated long ago, Aristotle's *Protrepticus* was in form "a *logos symbouleutikos* imi-

---

[26] For example, Burgess would have us believe – incorrectly – that the category of epideictic oratory was as large and as viable in the works of Isocrates (436–338 BCE) as it was in commentaries of Menander Rhetor (3rd cent. CE). For a more accurate historical assessment, see esp. Russell and Wilson (1981, pp. xi–xlvi).

tating Isocrates ['*protreptic*' discourse *To Nicocles*]" (see Jaeger, 1939, vol. III, p. 308 note 3; and also pp. 84–105, 307–12). Just as Isocrates exhorted the Cyprian prince Nicocles, so Aristotle exhorted the Cyprian prince Themison; their fundamental difference consistsin the fact that Aristotle's παραίνεσις or προτροπή is toward Plato's paideia, and not toward Isocrates' understanding of philosophy. Given Aristotle's own definition of epideictic rhetoric (*Rhet.* 1.3.3–5) and his particular conception of its goal (*Rhet.* 1.3.5) it is, to say the least, rather difficult to hold that he would have perceived his *Protrepticus* as an epideictic discourse, as Burgess and others suggest. Aristotle uses the functions of praise and blame, but he uses them deliberatively to persuade Themison to think and act in accord with Platonic life and philosophy (see Jaeger, 1948, p. 82).

Although Hartlich knew that the overwhelming majority of ancient authors used the terms protrepsis and paraenesis as interchangeable terms for exhortation, on the basis of Pseudo-Isocrates and Seneca he made the "formal" differentiation between protrepsis and paraenesis into an established rule. Burgess correctly pointed out that this was an overstatement of the evidence. He judged that, while Hartlich's "formal" differentiation between paraenesis and protrepsis states "a true distinction," it also "gives an impression of uniformity in the use of these words which is not warranted by the usage of the Greek authors" (Burgess, 1902, p. 229 note 2).

Prior to Vetschera, Burgess' discussion showed that, given certain presuppositions, the differentiation between protrepsis and paraenesis on the basis of "content" can be maintained (Burgess, 1902, p. 230; the "content" distinction is emphasized by Fiore, 1986, p. 41). On the other hand, but to a greater extent than Vetschera, Burgess made it equally clear that the "content" distinction was anything but the established norm (see esp. pp. 231–33). Moreover, he found that even among the relatively few ancient authors who did distinguish paraenesis from protrepsis there was frequent and unmistakable inconsistency (p. 230). For example, Burgess (p. 232) showed that in Iamblichus' *Protrepticus* the terms are not only used interchangeably; they are used in such fashion as to allow for the presence of paraenesis *within* protreptic.[27] Simi-

---

[27] Cf. Vetschera (1911–12, pp. 6–7) who deals with this under the rubric of matters held in common by both protrepsis and paraenesis.

larly, Burgess found that Plato himself uses the terms interchangeably, as do the historians (Herodotus, Thucydides, and Dionysius of Halicarnassus), and also Menander Rhetor. He observed that Herodotus appears to use προτρέπω "but once (I, 31,1), and there it means 'admonish by example', for which παραινῶ might be used" (p. 232). And what Burgess observed about the "formal" and "material" differentiations between protrepsis and paraenesis other scholars have recently confirmed.

Abraham Malherbe has repeatedly warned against conceptions of paraenesis that are too narrow (see 1986, esp. pp. 65–67, 80, 82, 93, 124–29, 136, 138, 145, 154; and 1989, pp. 49–66).[28] For example, Malherbe (1986, p. 121) calls attention to the fact that "Clement of Alexandria differentiated between protrepsis and paraenesis (*Pedagogue* 1.1)." But he quickly cautions us that both before and after Clement, there were writers who used the terms interchangeably. As evidence of this, Malherbe adduces texts by Pseudo-Justin (third century) and Ennodius (fifth century). What is interesting about those texts is that they are in their authors' views paraenetic writings: Pseudo-Justin's *Paraenetic Address to the Greeks*, and Ennodius' *Paraenesis didascalia*. The contents of both writings, however, are precisely what Vetschera would have us label protreptic discourse. Differentiating between protrepsis and paraenesis on the basis of "content" was obviously not the established rule.

Stanley Stowers has recently suggested a third possible distinction between paraenesis and protrepsis, one "relative to the audience's disposition toward the new life" (Stowers, 1986a, p. 92). Werner Jaeger reminds us that προτρεπτικοὶ λόγοι, as advertisements for the philosophical way, implied a change of life and consequently may be called conversion literature (Jaeger, 1961,

---

[28] L. G. Perdue, (1981, esp. pp. 242–46), offers an excellent, general discussion of Malherbe's views of paraenesis. He agrees (p. 241 note 2) with Malherbe that Dibelius' literary and form-critical definition of paraenesis is too narrow. In addition, he pointedly raises questions about the "social settings" and "social functions" of paraenesis (pp. 247–56). While L. T. Johnson (1983, p. 329 note 9) believes that "it is misleading to think of paraenesis as a genre (*Gattung*) as Dibelius did," he finds that Perdue's "attempts to fit this supposed genre to various social settings and social functions in a mechanical fashion" are "all the more disastrous." In my opinion, Johnson is correct that paraenesis is *not* a genre, and I concur with his judgment that "mechanically" fitting hortatory statements to social settings and functions is disastrous. But I also agree with Perdue that the social settings and functions of hortatory material are issues that can and must be addressed. Although Perdue still (incorrectly) views paraenesis as a genre, he has made some valuable contributions in the effort to address the "social dimensions" of hortatory speech (see esp. Perdue, 1990; Perdue and Gammie, 1990).

p. 25; and 1939, vol. II, pp. 295–300; on conversion to philosophy, see Nock, 1933, pp. 164–86; and Marrou, 1956, pp. 206–16). Stowers picks this up and correctly argues that Aristotle's *Protrepticus* is conversion literature. Then, Stowers labels Isocrates' *To Nicocles* as paraenesis, and suggests that it is not "conversion" literature but "confirmation" literature, not an exhortation to "turn" to a new life, but an exhortation to continue in the way of conventional cultural values (Stowers, 1986a, pp. 91–92).

It is extremely doubtful, however, that Isocrates would have agreed with Stowers' assessment of his work. His own view, Isocrates states rather well: "I maintain also that if you compare me with those who profess 'to turn' [προτρέπειν] men to a life of temperance and justice, you will find that my teaching is more true and profitable than theirs" (*Antidosis* 84). To be sure, the "philosophy" of Isocrates is practical and conventional, and certainly inferior to that of Aristotle – at least in my opinion – but neither my bias nor Aristotle's philosophy is the criterion by which to judge Isocrates' *protrepsis*.

Turning to the New Testament, Stowers demonstrates the criterion of "audience disposition" by saying that Paul's first preaching to the Thessalonians may be called conversion or protreptic discourse; his subsequent letter, 1 Thessalonians, would be paraenetic or confirmation discourse. In any case, however, Stowers hastens to warn us that the terms protrepsis and paraenesis "were used this way only sometimes and not consistently in antiquity" (Stowers, 1986a, pp. 91–92).

It is not without importance that even modern scholars differ in their understanding of protrepsis and paraenesis. For example, Malherbe (1983, pp. 49–50) considers 1 Thessalonians a paraenetic letter; Koester, on the other hand, rejects this definition and labels it a protreptic letter (1975, p. 35).[29] Both Koester and Malherbe are correct.

Recalling Malherbe's observation that Clement of Alexandria differentiated between paraenesis and protrepsis, we should remember that Clement wrote not only an *Exhortation* (Προτρεπτικός) *to the Greeks*, but also an *Exhortation* (Προτρεπτικός) *to Endurance or To the Newly Baptized* (Eusebius, *Eccl. Hist.* 6.13). As the titles of these works plainly suggest Clement of Alexandria did not consider the "audience disposition" to be a very important

---

[29] This is noted in Malherbe (1983, pp. 49–50).

criterion for distinguishing protrepsis and paraenesis. Moreover, if the fragment discovered by P. M. Barnard really is part of Clement's protreptic to the newly baptized, then the (preceptorial) form and (ethical) content appear not to have been overly important distinctions either.[30]

It does appear then that hard and fast distinctions between protrepsis and paraenesis, whether based on form, content, or audience disposition, were anything but the accepted norm and understanding of these terms in the ancient world. What stands out, what is distinctive, is their established interchangeable use as terms for hortatory speech.

What about the genre distinction? Burgess found that the evidence for the προτρεπτικὸς λόγος as a literary genre was better and more frequent than the evidence for assuming that paraenesis was a genre (1902, pp. 229–34; see esp. the information in his note on pp. 230–31). Παραίνεσις, he discovered, had practically no technical definition (pp. 229–32). And this stands in stark contrast to what New Testament scholars have come to believe.

It is helpful to reiterate that the προτρεπτικὸς λόγος, which is so important to philosophy, did not owe its origin to Socrates, Plato, or Aristotle. The προτρεπτικὸς λόγος was first the property of the sophists (Wendland, 1905, p. 81; Jaeger, 1948, p. 55; also see Gaiser, 1959, p. 25). It is also important to remember that the προτρεπτικὸς λόγος grew out of gnomic poetry (Wendland, 1905, pp. 81–82; Jaeger, 1948, pp. 54–56). Thus its original form was neither dialogical nor syllogistic;[31] it was gnomic or preceptive in form. Moreover, whether expressed in dialogical dress or syllogistically or gnomically, the προτρεπτικὸς λόγος was perceived and intended to have a paraenetic function.[32] In other words, its fundamental function was rhetorical: the προτρεπτικὸς λόγος was originally a persuasive or argumentative discourse designed to

[30] *Clement of Alexandria* (*LCL*; 1919, pp. 368–77).

[31] Plato's Socrates offers a dialogical version of the προτρεπτικὸς λόγος in *Euthydemus*; see *Euthydemus* 278E-282D, 288B-307C. Also see Gaiser (1959, pp. 45–50, 137–40, 175–78) and Jaeger (1948, pp. 30, 55, 62–63). Jaeger points out that the protreptic discourse is an "exhortation"; that it is "not a development of the Socratic method," and that it "by no means necessarily demands the dialogue dress" (p. 55).

[32] See Theon III, 1–291 (Butts, 1987, pp. 187–223) on the chreia; and esp. III, 4–21 (Butts, pp. 186–89) on the maxim. For the maxim or γνώμη as principal source of προτροπή, see Walz (vol. II, pp. 291, 297; noted in Burgess, 1902, p. 231). Cf. also Horna (1935, *s.v.* "Gnome, Gnomendichtung, Gnomologien'); and K. Berger (1984c, pp. 1049–74).

attract and win students for the educational program of the sophists (Jaeger, 1948, pp. 54–101). Consequently, the content of such exhortations reflected what the sophists believed.

More than a half-century ago, Werner Jaeger (1948) determined that Aristotle's *Protrepticus* was a devastating attack on sophistic philosophy in general, and on the sophistic philosophy of Isocrates in particular. Jaeger demonstrated that within Iamblichus' *Protrepticus* there are portions of Plato's dialogical protreptic *Euthydemus*, as well as fragments of Aristotle's *Protrepticus*. He further showed that Aristotle's *Protrepticus* draws its content from Plato's paideia, particularly *Euthydemus*; its "form," however, Jaeger demonstrated to be "a symbouleutic discourse" modeled – not on Plato's discourse but – on Isocrates' *protreptic* discourse *To Nicocles* (Jaeger, 1948, p. 55).

This is very significant for us because – apart from Seneca's reference to Posidonius' philosophy (not his rhetoric![33]) – the basic evidence for assuming that paraenesis was an established and distinctive literary genre is the apparent differentiation between them in Pseudo-Isocrates' *To Demonicus*. As Jaeger has suggested, the latter discourse was prompted by Aristotle's attack on Isocrates and was written by a follower, probably a student, of Isocrates. In *To Demonicus* 3–5, the writer says that he is not writing a hortatory discourse (παράκλησις = προτρεπτικὸς λόγος[34]) as others have

---

[33] On the questionable nature of Seneca's suspicious usage in *Ep.* 95.65, see Hock and O'Neil (1986, pp. 123–25), and the discussion in chapter 1, above (p. 14).

[34] In *To Demonicus* 3–5 προτρεπτικός and παράκλησις are used synonymously, as are παραίνεσις and συμβουλία. On the basis, then, of an apparent opposition between προτρεπτικός/παράκλησις and παραίνεσις/συμβουλία, some scholars exhort us to believe that προτρεπτικός and παραίνεσις are two distinct genres with different purposes. And we note that Isocrates' *To Nicocles* and *Nicocles* are sometimes brought forward as "paraeneses" rather than protreptic discourses. Likewise we note that Isocrates certainly understands *To Nicocles* as a συμβουλία (6), and like the ancient poets he sees himself as providing paraenetic instruction (43, 46). But it is crucial that Isocrates is unaware of the so-called distinction between paraenesis and protrepsis, for in *To Nicocles* (8) he clearly sees his purpose as "protreptic" (προτροπή). This is further corroborated by his remarks in the *Antidosis* (84), where he describes his teaching in *To Nicocles* (the *Panegyricus*, and *On the Peace*), as "protreptic" discourse: the goal of which is "to turn [προτρέπειν] men to a life of temperance and justice" (cf. also *Antidosis* 86). And see *Antidosis* 87 where he says that these writings, along with others, have won for him both distinction and students. It is not easy to overlook *Nicocles* (12) where he uses the terms παρα-καλέσαι and προτρέψαι synonymously in counting out his "precepts"; cf. *Evagoras* 77. As for the remarks in *To Demonicus* (written by a follower of Isocrates!) about those who compose speeches exhorting to oratory, see Isocrates' remarks in *Antidosis* 275.

done (namely Aristotle!); rather he is writing a moral treatise (παραίνεσις = συμβουλευτικὸς λόγος). On the basis of this statement some scholars have mistakenly argued that Pseudo-Isocrates brings forth a new and distinctive literary genre. But, as Jaeger clearly demonstrated, he does no such thing; and, despite his remarks about those who teach oratory, he neither discounts the "skill" and "cleverness" of the rhetorician in speech, nor does he oppose the use of προτρεπτικοὶ λόγοι by the sophists – indeed, Pseudo-Isocrates is himself a sophist and follower of Isocrates, who, as we all know, wrote προτρεπτικοὶ λόγοι like *To Nicocles* and *Nicocles*. These two gnomic speeches are very good examples of Isocratean "philosophy." Moreover, by design and content they advertise the paideia he taught and the school he represented.

What kind of writing is *To Demonicus* and what does it oppose? Jaeger has shown that it is a "protreptic discourse," written in preceptive form and composed of conventional content. Further, Jaeger (1948, p. 59 notes 1 and 2) has established that what *To Demonicus* really opposes is the use of προτρεπτικοὶ λόγοι to support the logical and dialectical philosophy of Plato. Because deliberative and epideictic rhetoric are very close to each other (see Quint. *Inst.* 3.7.28; cf. also 3.4.11, and *Rhet. Her.* 3.8.15), it is hardly surprising that some (e.g., Volkmann, [1885] 1987, p. 336) have argued that "protreptic discourse" is epideictic and not deliberative rhetoric. Others, like Klaus Berger (1984c, p. 1139; see pp. 1138–45; cf. 1984a, esp. pp. 217–20), while recognizing the closeness of deliberative and epideictic rhetoric and appreciating the reasons for assigning protreptic discourse to epideictic, argue that protreptic discourse, as a mode of persuasion that seeks to convert its addressees to a particular philosophy, is symbouleutic or deliberative rhetoric. This, I think, is correct. Style, even highly polished style, is not the only, nor even the basic, criterion for determining rhetorical genres. There is little doubt that protreptic's origination with the sophists lends it the reputation of rhetoric for show, but, again, it must be asked whether the sophists' goal was merely to have people praise their eloquence and their educational program or to become a part of it. And there is no doubt that after Menander Rhetor and possibly even earlier, protreptic pieces moved increasingly into the epideictic function. But the discourse *To Demonicus* is not epideictic; it is a deliberative response to Aristotle. History, however, has shown quite well that it could not compete with Aristotle's *Protrepticus*; the latter became the model for both philosophers and rhetoricians, as Cicero and Augustine demonstrate (Jaeger, 1948, pp. 62–65).

This brings us back to the extremely important discovery in Burgess' investigation, which New Testament research has only recently begun to realize and emphasize: as a rule, paraenesis and protrepsis are not genre distinctions; they are interchangeable terms for exhortation or hortatory speech. Consequently, distinctions between protrepsis and paraenesis, whether based upon "formal" or "material" criteria, or upon "audience disposition," are comparatively seldom applicable and habitually inconsistent. The actual usage of the terms in antiquity militates against the narrow, precise, and ultimately ideological distinctions – not to mention the spurious hermeneutical conclusions which are based on such distinctions – that some modern scholars have made between the protrepsis and paraenesis. Literary and rhetorical judgments about the ancient texts can and will be made, but they must be made commensurate with (all) the historical evidence that we have.

I reiterate: there is better and greater evidence for προτρεπτικὸς λόγος as a literary genre than there is for παραίνεσις as a literary genre. The debate about προτρεπτικοὶ λόγοι, for which incidentally there is no extant rhetorical treatment as a distinctive form,[35] will surely continue.[36] And certainly among New Testament scholars,

[35] Burgess (1902, p. 220) notes that the προτρεπτικὸς λόγος has "no extant rhetorical treatment as a distinctive form of epideictic oratory." Neither Menander Rhetor (3rd century CE) nor the earlier Dionysius of Halicarnassus (fl. ca. 30 BCE), both of whom were occupied with epideictic oratory, offer treatments of it as a separate category of epideictic. In Menander Rhetor (according to Burgess, pp. 230–31), it is treated "only as a concomitant of some other form of oration." The προτρεπτικὸς λόγος occurs "in the λαλιά," which is "an informal style of demonstrative speech with no fixed rules" (G. A. Kennedy, 1972, p. 637), and in "the προπεμπτικὸς λόγος," a valedictory speech/composition wishing a friend a prosperous journey (see *OCD*, "Propemptikon," p. 886). Concerning Dionysius of Halicarnassus, Burgess (pp. 232–33) notes that the προτρεπτικός is treated only in the "specialized form" of the προτρεπτικὸς ἀθληταῖς (which is "a speech of exhortation before the games"; G. A. Kennedy, 1972, p. 635). On the προτρεπτικὸς ἀθληταῖς, see the following note.

[36] For example, concerning the "speech of exhortation before the games" (προτρεπτικὸς ἀθληταῖς), Burgess (1902, p. 209) observes that it is remarkably close to the "general's oration before battle, urging his army to deeds of valor." Then Burgess asserts that both the "importance and frequence" of the general's speech for epideictic "are greater, and it preserves its identity even more thoroughly, than many of those which have unquestioned recognition and detailed rhetorical presentation" (p. 209). And he makes this assertion despite the fact that the general's speech – like the προτρεπτικὸς λόγος – is not a recognized division of epideictic in either Menander or Dionysius of Halicarnassus (p. 209). The question naturally arises: is the general's speech epideictic rhetoric as Burgess contends? It is not. G. A. Kennedy

where so much has been invested in its highly questionable status as a distinct literary genre, the debate about παραίνεσις will continue. Be that as it may, we propose to follow the established and predominant view among the ancients: παραίνεσις is more correctly understood *not* as a literary genre but as a mode of persuasion or argument, a method of education (thus Jaeger, 1948, pp. 55–56, and G. A. Kennedy, 1984, pp. 145–46).[37]

So, what does this mean with regard to James? I summarize. Paraenesis is an ideologically loaded term, and it is generally employed without the precision that critical historical study mandates (Baasland, 1982, 119). Malherbe and others have made it clear that at the very least Dibelius' understanding of paraenesis is much too narrow. Theodore Burgess has demonstrated that, as a rule, the ancients understood paraenesis to be exhortation, and not a distinct literary genre. Classicists like George A. Kennedy (1984, pp. 145–46) have reminded us that – at least since the time of Aristotle – paraenesis/protrepsis has been accepted as the positive form of symbouleutic or advisory rhetoric. And all of this coheres with Klaus Berger's encyclopedic investigations and it culminates in a definitive judgment about Dibelius' thesis regarding the genre of the Epistle of James: "Von Dibelius' These bleibt daher nicht viel übrig: Jak. is eine symbuleutische Komposition, aber keine Paränese" ("Therefore of Dibelius' thesis nothing much remains: James is a symbouleutic composition, but not a paraenesis" (Berger, 1984a, p. 147).

The return to rhetoric

Despite Dibelius' untenable thesis that the genre of James is paraenesis, as well as his misguided treatment of the sayings of Jesus in Q under the rubric of paraenesis, his analyses contain many valuable insights. As already stated, his recognition that

(1972, p. 18; see pp. 18–20) shows rather easily that the general's speech or *contio* was symbouleutic or deliberative oratory; in fact, it was the "commonest Roman form" of this rhetorical genre. The debate goes on!

[37] L. T. Johnson (1985, p. 167) holds that Dibelius "wrongly identified paraenesis as a genre. It is better described as a mode of ethical teaching which can be fitted to many different literary genres." Malherbe (1986, pp. 121–34) discusses "protrepsis," "paraenesis," and "diatribe" under "styles of exhortation" and he provides sage advice about the use of the terms, whether by the ancients or by modern scholars: "More important than the nomenclature attached to them are their aims and the ways in which they sought to attain them" (p. 121).

James is composed of sayings that have a threefold similarity to the sayings of Jesus in Q is of vital significance to the present inquiry. I propose to build on that observation, but also to correct and refine it on the basis of Greco-Roman rhetorical conventions.

The conception of James (and Q) as written, rhetorical composition moves us far beyond Dibelius. Apart from his typical observations that the language of James evinces a certain linguistic cultivation and rhetorical "style" due to the presence of various rhetorical figures, Dibelius did not pursue the rhetorical dimensions of sayings materials; even less did he consider Greco-Roman rhetoric to be a vital factor for the character and function of this material.

On the other hand, Burton Mack and Vernon Robbins (1989) have demonstrated that the logic and techniques of rhetorical composition can provide insights into the development and transmission of sayings materials that Dibelius' (and Bultmann's) genetic literary-historical approach simply overlooks. For example, Dibelius ignored the differences between oral and written discourse; he simply assumed that the written performance of a saying of Jesus is always something of a scribal reproduction of its oral performance. Also, stressing the form and origin of sayings materials, he failed to realize that a written composition is more than the sum of its parts. In his view the sayings of Jesus and James were basically collections of oral and written traditions: "they both belong to the genre of paraenesis" (Dibelius, 1975, p. 17). Moreover, Dibelius' view of the authors who stand behind James (and Q), as people lacking in literary capabilities and interests, allowed him no reason to engage in a rhetorical analysis that was guided by the information in either the ancient *progymnasmata* or the rhetorical treatises. Thus, he regarded the development of the "core units" or "treatises" in James not as rhetorical compositions but as the sedimentation of tradition, the end product of the evolutionary power in the genre of paraenesis itself. He said: "the three treatises . . . contain nothing other than expansions of paraenetic sayings, either generalizations or specializations . . . [and] are not unrelated in character to the surrounding sayings and groups of sayings" (Dibelius, 1975, p. 3). So, even in these treatises "where the structure and lines of thought were apparently shaped by the author himself," Dibelius maintained that the compositional power inheres predominantly in the developmental forces that reside in the form and content of the paraenetic tradition (1975, p. 5; see the discussion in Petersen, 1978).

In Dibelius' opinion, therefore, the problems of the writer's invention or choice of materials ("eclecticism"), the lack of arrangement or order in the discourse, and its gnomic and repetitive style are determined by the artificial genre paraenesis. What Dibelius ignored is what the ancient *progymnasmata* and rhetorical handbooks emphasize: namely, that the problems of invention, arrangement, and style are the compositional concerns of ancient rhetoric (G. A. Kennedy, 1984; D. F. Watson, 1988; Butts, 1987; Mack, 1990; Mack and Robbins, 1989). Moreover, the ancients appear to have regarded the "rhetorical function" of their discourses as "more important than the nature of the genre as a literary entity" (Wuellner, 1976, p. 132), a fact they clearly demonstrate by modifying literary genres to meet the needs they address (see Betz, 1975b; cf. Wuellner, 1976, pp. 130–31).

"The pervasiveness of rhetorical culture throughout the Mediterranean society during the Hellenistic period" (Robbins, 1991b, p. 159) is a historical fact that New Testament scholars are once again beginning to take seriously. For example, scholars like Wilhelm H. Wuellner and Ernst Baasland have returned to rhetoric to solve some of the riddles associated with the Epistle of James.

Baasland, 1988, p. 3648, reminds us that prior to the decline of rhetoric in the nineteenth century, J. D. Schulze (1802), C. G. Küchler (1818), and C. G. Wilke (1843) had derived insights into James on the basis of ancient rhetoric. Their findings were then supplemented in certain later commentaries (esp. Mayor, 1892 [1990], pp. cxciii–cciv; also Chaine, 1927, p. xci, and Mußner, 1987, pp. 28–30). Further, Baasland notes that, on the basis of his familiarity with rhetoric, J. A. Bengel ([1877] 1981, vol. II, p. 694) provided James with a three-part rhetorical outline:

   I.   Inscription (1.1)
  II.   Exhortation (*adhortatio*)
      A. to patience (1.1–15)
      B. the proposition (*propositio*, 1.16–18; 1.19–21)
         i.   Hearing is to be joined with deeds and words (1.22–2.26)
        ii. Speech is to be modest (3.1–12)
       iii. Wrath and passions are to be restrained (3.13–4.17)
      C. a second exhortation to patience (5.1–18)
 III.   Conclusion (*conclusio*; 5.19–20)

Baasland correctly points out the need for further research in this area.

Wuellner's "Der Jakobusbrief im Licht der Rhetorik und Text-pragmatik" (1978a) drew on "the new rhetoric,"[38] as well as modern semiotic and communications theory, and offered a rhetorical analysis of James that tried to answer the questions of James' genre, train of thought, and the situation of the letter or reader. Wuellner contends that *"ein prozessualer Textbegriff"* ("a processual conception of the text") is more proper than Dibelius' static conception (1978a, pp. 12–13). Historical questions are placed in the background, and textual issues are the primary focus. This approach supports the inventional theory of both ancient and modern rhetoric: the text (or speech) unfolds itself as it is read (or heard), and it functions within a system of pragmatic relations that exists within the text itself (that is, within its "structure of argumentation"), and within the social setting in which it gives and receives meaning (pp. 12–21; see G. A. Kennedy, 1984, pp. 5–6, 146–47; and on the system of pragmatic relations with a text, see Robbins, 1985b). Wuellner concludes that James is a text for application, and that its goal is not didactic or paraenetic but "recruiting, re-claiming" (*werbend, gewinnend*). He argues that James possesses a thoroughly pragmatic, rhetorical conception, and found that its stylistic "peculiarity" (*Eigenart*) corresponds to its intention (1978a, p. 65). Wuellner's (pp. 36–37) basic outline of James appears to be:

    I.   *exordium* (James 1.2–4)
   II. *narratio* (1.5–12)[39]
 III. *argumentatio* (1.13–5.6)
 IV. *peroratio* (5.7–20)

[38] See Perelman and Olbrechts-Tyteca (1971), which is, according to G. A. Kennedy (1984, p. 29), "perhaps the most influential modern treatise on rhetoric". Perelman (1982) is an abbreviated version of this treatise; Perelman (1968) provides an important explanation of his understanding of the relationship between rhetoric and philosophy. For a review of Perelman and Olbrechts-Tyteca, see Kozy (1970).

[39] Baasland's (1988, p. 3655) argument – based on Aristotle *Rhet.* 1414a – that Wuellner's (1978a, pp. 37–41) inclusion of *narratio* as a part of his outline means that Wuellner understands James as an example of judicial or forensic oratory is an overstatement. The mere presence of a narration does not guarantee a forensic or judicial structure, because deliberative oratory may also employ narration; see G. A. Kennedy (1984, p. 24). In fact, Wuellner's conclusions suggest that he understands James to belong primarily to deliberative oratory, as does Baasland (1988, pp. 3655–57). Moreover, Baasland clearly draws insights from Wuellner (1978a), and both of the latter are dependent on K. Berger (1984c).

In "Der Jakobusbrief als Neutestamentliche Weisheitsschrift"
(1982), Baasland finds Dibelius' designation of James' genre as
paraenesis to be useless. He prefers to classify James as *hortatio*,
which, he maintains, is an expansion of the term paraenesis.[40]
Baasland (1982, p. 182) outlines James as follows:

I.   *exordium* (1.2–18)
II. *propositio* (1.19–27)
III. *argumentatio* (in two parts)[41]
     A. *confirmatio* (2.1–3.12)
     B. *confutatio* (3.13–5.6)
IV. *peroratio* (5.7–20)

He suggests that James was read in the community's worship
service, and he believes that it possesses the character of a baptism-
catechesis, though it is more likely a wisdom-instruction (*Weisheits-
belehrung*). In fact, Baasland (1982, pp. 123–25, esp. 124) argues
that James is *the* wisdom book in the NT; he notes that 40 of its 108
verses contain parallels to wisdom literature. And, as most scholars
do, Baasland (pp. 125–27) emphasizes that James is "decidedly
impressed" by the Jesus tradition. He also holds that James'
exhortation confronts an argumentative situation analogous to
Paul's (pp. 127–33).[42]

In "Literarische Form, Thematik und geschichtle Einordnung
des Jakobusbriefes," Baasland (1988) has refined and expanded his
arguments concerning the literary form (or goal of argumentation),
theme, and historical placement of James. He concludes that the
text is a "protreptische Rede weisheitlicher Prägung bestimmt" (a
"protreptic speech in an unequivocal wisdom impress"), or perhaps
better "eine weisheitliche Lehrrede" ("a wisdom-like speech of
instruction") emanating from a Palestinian-Jewish-Christian
milieu; it teaches its addressees that God's order has a future "trotz
allen Leidens, Unheils, der Verfolgungen und Unterdrückung in
der Gegenwart" ("in spite of all the tribulations and disaster in the
persecutions and oppression of the present" [1988, pp. 3655, 3671;
3675–79]).

[40] On *hortatio*, "encouragement; exhortation," see Lausberg (1973, section 381),
who refers to Quint. 5.10.83 and discusses the "hortative department of oratory"
under deliberative rhetoric (in sections 224–38).
[41] Baasland (1982, p. 182) finds that James displays a few features of *argumentatio*, but no trace of *narratio*.
[42] On James' place in NT/biblical theology, see Baasland (1982, pp. 133–34).

More recently, Vernon Robbins (1991b) has explored the various kinds of writing in the Hellenistic period. He calls attention to the fact that "the system of communication that prevailed before print, and during the first stages of print, was called 'rhetoric'" (p. 160). Thus he reminds us that the writings of the New Testament originated in a "rhetorical culture," a culture where oral and written composition interacted with one another and were intimately related (p. 160). In such a culture Theon could argue that the *progymnasmata*, the preliminary exercises through which a student worked in preparation for rhetorical training, were "the foundation stones for every form of writing" (Theon, II, 142–43; Butts, 1987, pp. 154–55). Butts (p. 181 note 36) notes that "This statement is clear evidence that T[heon] understood the *progymnasmata* as providing instruction for literary activity ranging far beyond the technical parameters of rhetoric. Such a claim can be verified only through the investigation of possible links between the literature of antiquity and the content of the *progymnasmata*." And this is precisely what I hope to demonstrate for James 2.1–13.

Referring to such preliminary rhetorical instruction as "progymnastic rhetoric," Robbins (1991b, p. 161) proposes that the phrase "progymnastic composition" be employed "to refer to the writing activities associated with it." Further, he emphasizes that the *progymnasmata* were used in preparation for intensive rhetorical instruction and suggests that "progymnastic composition is the activity that bridges the gap between the kind of rhetorical analysis performed by people like George A. Kennedy . . . and text, source, form, and redaction analysis" (p. 161). And especially important for our research is Robbins' thesis that the form and function of the Jesus tradition, specifically, "sayings" attributed to Jesus, are better understood on the basis of the recitation exercise in the *progymnasmata* than on the basis of a genetic literary-historical model like that used by Dibelius (and Bultmann) (pp. 168–86).

If the author of the Epistle of James was informed by ancient rhetorical conventions, then we should be able to discover this influence in the text. Moreover, if this influence can be shown to exist precisely in those sections of James that Dibelius and subsequent scholarship have claimed are the most revealing of the thought, style, and purpose of the author in view, namely, James' "core sections" or "treatises," then it may be possible for research to show the influence of rhetorical conventions in the other sections of James as well.

In this investigation, however, my goal is not to perform an analysis of James in all its parts, nor to provide an in-depth treatment of its three core sections. That belongs to future research. As already indicated, my immediate interest is the socio-rhetorical function of the saying in James 2.5. Therefore, in the next chapter I shall perform a rhetorical analysis of James 2.1–13. I shall discuss the "internal dynamics" of the unit, as these pertain to its invention, arrangement, and style. I shall show that it is composed according to ancient rhetorical conventions.

3

THE INNER TEXTURE OF JAMES 2.1–13

Introduction

This chapter comprises an exegetical and rhetorical analysis of James 2.1–13. Our primary concern is the "inner texture" of this unit: its form, structure, and argumentative pattern. Utilizing basic strategies of rhetorical criticism, we shall approach the unit from the perspectives of invention, arrangement, and style. In the course of analyzing the unfolding argumentation in this unit we shall show that James 2.1–13 contains a form of the elaboration of a theme or proposition that approximates a complete argument as it is found and displayed in the *progymnasmata* and rhetorical handbooks.

James 2.1–13 is recognized by practically all commentators as a clearly defined rhetorical unit. It has a definite beginning, an admonition that states the theme of the unit (2.1); a middle, in which the theme is elaborated (2.2–11); and a conclusion, or summarizing exhortation (2.12–13).[1] Most commentators have also accepted Dibelius' view that the unit exhibits the characteristics of a *"treatise"* (*Abhandlung*), a unit in which "the ideas are grouped together," "closely connected," and "centered around one theme" (Dibelius, 1975, pp. 124–25; cf. pp. 34–38).

The style of the unit reflects certain features that are common to the diatribe and the sermon (Dibelius, 1975, pp. 38, 125–30). Typical of diatribal style are apostrophe (2.1, 5), vivid and graphic

---

[1] Adamson (1976, pp. 45, 102–20); Baasland (1982, pp. 122–23); K. Berger (1984b, pp. 458–59); Cantinat (1973, pp. 119–37); Davids (1982, pp. 105–19); Dibelius (1975, pp. 121–45); Hoppe (1989, pp. 10–11, 51–62); Kümmel (1975, p. 406); Mayor (1892 [1990], pp. 210–14); Mußner (1987, pp. 114–26); Schlatter (1956, pp. 162–84); Schrage and Balz (1980, pp. 25–29); Chaine (1927, pp. 19, 69–82); Vielhauer (1975, pp. 568, 576–77); Wuellner (1978a, pp. 48–51). Ropes (1916, pp. 4–5, 185–202) finds two units, James 2.1–7 and 2.8–13. Laws (1980, pp. 93–117) also argues for two units but differs with Ropes. She divides the passage into James 2.1–9 and 2.10–13.

examples (2.2–4), and rhetorical questions (2.7–8). From the "sermonic statements" in 2.5–7 on, however, Dibelius says the unit "seems to be less of a diatribe and more of a sermon," though he concedes that it is often difficult to distinguish between these genres (p. 125). In any case, Dibelius and others correctly stress that James is not a diatribe; and, of the three core units in James, Dibelius finds that James 2.1–13 has the fewest diatribal features (p. 125).[2] Its content pertains to the theme of "the faith of our glorious Lord Jesus Christ" and "respect of persons," which is exemplified in the conflicting relations between poor and rich (1975, p. 48; see pages 39–50).[3]

Because the unit resembles a treatise, Dibelius rightly suggests that it has a distinctive importance in the letter of James. For over against the view that James is essentially an eclectic collection of sayings, the one predominant characteristic of which is a lack of continuity of thought, James 2.1–13 demonstrates thoughtful progression (1975, p. 124). In addition to our unit Dibelius finds that James 2.14–26 and 3.1–12 are also treatises. And it is primarily because of these three units, as well as the author's repetition of certain motifs and themes (p. 124), that Dibelius is quick to assert that, despite the apparent lack of thoughtful development in James, the text does indeed possess "an animated and characteristic unity" (pp. 5, 48).

Following Dibelius, then, the significance of James 2.1–13 may be summarized as follows. First of all, it gives some unity and coherence to the letter as a whole. Second, as one of three units that were "apparently shaped by the author himself," it is one of our best sources for understanding the style and thought of the author (Dibelius, 1975, p. 5; Schrage, 1988, p. 281). Third, of James' core units, this one stands alone as the treatise in which the author addresses the particular issue that (Dibelius believes) concerns him most: "the *piety of the Poor*, and the accompanying opposition to the rich and to the world" (1975, p. 48).

---

[2] On the diatribe, see esp. Geffcken (1909, pp. 45–53); for Dibelius' argument (*contra* Ropes, 1916, pp. 6–18) that James "on the whole" is not a diatribe, see Dibelius (1975, p. 2 note 6; and p. 38); cf. Adamson (1989, pp. 103–04); Davids (1982, pp. 12, 23); and Wifstrand (1949, p. 178). On the sermonic features in James, see Wessel (1953, pp. 73–89), who holds that such are also typical of diatribes (pp. 71–112; cited in Davids, 1982, p. 23). For the argument that "sermons" and "homilies" are "interchangeable terms" but not literary genres, see Aune (1987, p. 197); and for doubts about the "diatribe" as a genre classification, see Davids (1982, pp. 12, 23, 58–59).

[3] As already mentioned above (p. 1), almost a quarter of the entire letter deals with some aspect of this particular conflict.

The issues of invention, arrangement, and style – which occupy this chapter – concern the questions of how the author conceives, develops, and verbalizes the argument in James 2.1–13. "Invention" (εὕρεσις, *inventio*) is the conceptual process of devising "the matter, true or plausible, that would make the case convincing" (*Rhet. Her.* 1.2.3). In other words, invention is primarily the location and selection of the "proofs" to be employed in the argument.[4] "Arrangement" (τάξις, *dispositio*) refers to "the ordering and distribution of the matter, making clear the place to which each thing is assigned" (*Rhet. Her.* 1.2.3). "Style" (λέξις, *elocutio*) involves the choice and "adaptation of suitable words and sentences to the matter devised" (*Rhet. Her.* 1.2.3), and it includes the use of tropes as well as "figures" of thought and of speech (σχήματα, *sententiarum exornatio*).[5]

The development of an argument or speech was taught in both the *progymnasmata* and the rhetorical handbooks.[6] This program of study dealt with the inner unity and organization of the speech, as well as the inner logic, structure, and function of its elements (Mack and Robbins, 1989, p. 2). Accordingly, the standard outline for a speech consisted of four parts: an introduction (προοίμιον, *exordium*), a statement of facts (διήγησις, *narratio*), the argumentation (πίστις, *confirmatio*), and a conclusion (ἐπίλογος, *peroratio*) (Mack, 1990, p. 41). While the conventional outline was modeled on the judicial speech,[7] "it was easily accommodated to the

---

[4] For my discussion of invention, see chapter 1 (pp. 18–20), above. Books I and II of Aristotle's *Rhetoric* deal with invention; on which, see esp. G. A. Kennedy (1963, pp. 87–103; 1984, pp. 14–23; and 1991). Also cf. Lausberg (1973, vol. I, sections 260–442); J. Martin (1974, pp. 15–210); and D. F. Watson (1988, pp. 14–20).

[5] On arrangement and style, see G. A. Kennedy (1984, pp. 23–30); Lausberg (1973, vol. I, sections 443–1082); J. Martin (1974, pp. 211–345); and D. F. Watson (1988, pp. 20–26).

[6] On the relationship between the rhetorical handbooks and the *progymnasmata*, see Hock and O'Neil (1986, esp. pp. 10–22). While the *progymnasmata* took students "one step at a time through the skills required for composing the various speeches and the several parts of a speech" (p. 21), the "elaboration exercise" came to be recognized "as the basis for writing one specific rhetorical composition rather than a mere elementary exercise" (p. 163). Cf. also Mack (1990, pp. 31–48).

[7] The judicial speech "provides the fullest conventional structure" (G. A. Kennedy, 1984, p. 23) and could consist of as many as six parts: (1) introduction, (2) statement of facts, (3) proposition, (4) partition, (5) refutation, and (6) conclusion (D. F. Watson, 1988, pp. 20–21). As may be expected, however, there was considerable debate over this matter. See Quint. (3.9.1–5), who says that "most authorities" partitioned the judicial speech into five parts: (1) introduction, (2) statement of facts, (3) proof, (4) refutation, and (5) conclusion (3.9.1).

requirements of the deliberative speech" (p. 42).[8] Eventually, the deliberative speech was "transformed into a standard outline for a 'declamation' and this was variously called a 'thesis', 'the complete argument', or an 'elaboration' " (p. 42).

The "elaboration exercise" (ἐργασία), one of the *progymnasmata*, consisted of making seven or eight statements that correspond in function to the four parts of the standard speech (Mack, 1990, 42). Thus an elaboration comprised the following steps: (1) introduction; (2) proposition; (3) reason or rationale; (4) opposite (contrary); (5) analogy (comparison); (6) example; (7) citation (authority); and (8) conclusion. To be sure, there was variation in the implementation of the pattern. For example, in Hermogenes' *Progymnasmata*, the exercise is used to elaborate a "chreia," which is "a brief statement or action attributed to a person or something analogous to a person" (Mack and Robbins, 1989, p. 11). It consists of eight steps: (1) ἐγκώμιον (encomium; praise); (2) παράφρασις (paraphrase); (3) αἰτία (rationale); (4) κατὰ τὸ ἐναντίον (statement from the opposite or contrary); (5) ἐκ παραβολῆς (statement from analogy); (6) ἐκ παραδείγματος (statement from example); (7) ἐκ κρίσεως (statement from authority); (8) παράκλησις (exhortation).[9] Very similar to the latter is the *tractatio*, the elaboration of a theme, in the *Rhetorica ad Herennium* (4.43.56–58; cf. Hock and O'Neil, 1986, pp. 161, 171 note 53). It comprises seven steps: (1) theme (*res*), (2) reason (*ratio*), (3) restatement of the theme in another form (*pronuntiatum*), (4) contrary (*contrarium*), (5) comparison (*simile*), (6) example (*exemplum*), and (7) conclusion (*conclusio*).[10]

---

[8] According to G. A. Kennedy (1984, p. 24) the usual structure of the deliberative speech consists of four parts: (1) introduction, (2) proposition, (3) proof, and (4) conclusion (cf. Arist. *Rhet.* 3.13). Kennedy further says that "occasionally a narration is employed; when it does occur, it is often after rather than before the proposition" (p. 24).

[9] Walz (vol. i, pp. 21–23). Also see Aphthonius, who follows Hermogenes' list of eight topics for elaborating both a chreia (*Progymnasmata*; Walz, vol. i, pp. 62–67) and also a "hortatory maxim" (γνώμη προτρεπτική; Walz, vol. i, pp. 67–72). While his first five items are identical to Hermogenes', Aphthonius has for item (7) μαρτυρία παλαιῶν (testimony of ancients), and for item (8) ἐπίλογος (epilogue). The latter are, as the examples prove, synonymous with numbers (7) and (8) in Hermogenes.

[10] Cf. *Rhet. Her.* 2.18.28, where the author introduces "the most complete and perfect argument" in five parts: (1) proposition (*propositio*), (2) reason (*ratio*), (3) proof of the reason (*confirmatio*), (4) embellishment (*exornatio*), and (5) the résumé (*conplexio*). Note also that the fourth part, the *exornatio*, could include such arguments as (1) analogy (*simile*), (2) example (*exemplum*), (3) amplification (*amplificatio*), and (4) judgment (*res iudicata*; *Rhet. Her.* 2.29.46); see Mack and Robbins (1989, pp. 56–57).

"At first glance," as Mack (1990, p. 44) observes, the elaboration "appears to be a rather crude stringing together of loosely related items." However, they are anything but that. A closer examination reveals that these seven or eight rhetorical figures are really "shorthand technical designations for various rhetorical tropes and arguments"; furthermore, any one of them "may combine internally a multiple number of rhetorical figures and topics" (Mack and Robbins, 1989, p. 28). Rhetoricians and texts, both ancient and modern, agree and demonstrate that, while the sequence of those figures may vary and one or several of them may be absent in a given case, one or more of them are the necessary ingredients for a complete argument (p. 28).

This pattern was very popular in the ancient world as a guide for progymnastic or rhetorical composition (Mack and Robbins, 1989, p. 28, *passim*). Because James 2.1–13 begins with a theme, rather than with a chreia, I shall use the pattern for elaborating a "theme" and for developing "the complete argument" in the *Rhetorica ad Herennium* (4.43.56–44.56; 2.18.28; 2.29.46). I shall show that James 2.1–13 represents a particular manifestation and adaptation of this pattern; in so doing the particular dimensions of invention, arrangement, and style in our unit will become clear. The Jamesian adaptation produces the following outline:

1.	Theme	2.1
2.	Reason	2.2–4
	(*Probatio*)	2.5–11
3.	Argument from example,	2.5
	a. with opposite	2.6a
	b. and social example	2.6b–7
4.	Argument from judgment, based on the written law, in four parts:	2.8–11
	a. Proposition based on the written law	2.8
	b. Argument from the contrary	2.9
	c. Rationale for judgment based on law	2.10
	d. Confirmation of the rationale with written testimony	2.11
5.	Conclusion	2.12–13

The pattern of argumentation

1   Theme in a statement of apotreptic advice (γνώμη ἀποτρεπτική[11])

James 2.1 Ἀδελφοί μου, μὴ ἐν προσωποληψίαις ἔχετε τὴν πίστιν τοῦ κυρίου ἡμῶν Ἰησοῦ Χριστοῦ τῆς δόξης.

My brothers [and sisters], do not hold the faith of our glorious Lord Jesus Christ with acts of partiality.

This initial admonition introduces the topic for which a sequential argument unfolds in James 2.1–13. In other words, this sentence brings forward "summarily what we intend to prove" (*Rhet. Her.* 2.18.28). In more specific terms, this statement has the function of "hortatory" advice; it is a general statement concerned "with the objects of human actions, and with what should be chosen or avoided with reference to them" (Arist. *Rhet.* 2.21.2). Μὴ ἔχετε should be rendered as an imperative.[12]

Clearly the most difficult problem with the theme is how to translate and interpret τὴν πίστιν τοῦ κυρίου ἡμῶν Ἰησοῦ Χριστοῦ τῆς δόξης. First, there is the delicate, fundamentally grammatical, question of whether τὴν πίστιν followed by the genitive τοῦ κυρίου ἡμῶν Ἰησοῦ Χριστοῦ is an objective genitive that yields the translation "(the) faith *in* Jesus Christ," or a subjective genitive that should be translated "the faith *of* Jesus Christ."

As is well known, πίστις Ἰησοῦ Χριστοῦ formulas play a critical role in Paul's writings. For this reason the debate about such phrases, and the kinds of genitive employed in them, has been largely a discussion in Pauline studies. A majority of scholars are united in understanding the phrase πίστις Ἰησοῦ Χριοστοῦ to mean "faith in Jesus Christ." On the other hand, an increasing number of scholars are now suggesting that this genitive is in almost every instance subjective; thus it refers not to faith placed in Christ, but to Jesus Christ's own faith, especially in the sense of his faith-obedience to God (see esp. Hays, 1983, pp. 170–74; also Howard, 1974, pp. 212–15; 1967, pp. 459–65; and Barth, 1969, pp. 363–70).

[11] On the theme, see *Rhet. Her.* 4.43.56. "What Aristotle calls *gnōmē*, or 'maxim', is in Latin *sententia* (cf. English "sententious"). Literally, *gnōmē* means 'a thought', usually an opinion given as a judgment or advice" (G. A. Kennedy, 1991, p. 182).

[12] As in the AV, RV *text*; RSV; TEV; NEB; not as an indicative, as in the RV *mg.*; WH; Goodspeed; NRSV. See Mayor (1892 [1990], p. 79); Ropes (1916, p. 186) and Dibelius (1975, p. 126 note 9).

To be sure, there is no excuse for allowing Paul's use of such phrases to determine the meaning of James 2.1. Our goal is to understand what James says. Having said that, we note that a majority interpret the phrase in James 2.1 as if the genitive were objective; thus the NRSV translates "do you . . . really believe in our glorious Lord Jesus Christ?" This, I think, is incorrect. The genitive appears to be subjective, and the phrase should be translated "the faith *of* our Lord Jesus Christ."[13] If this is the correct sense of the genitive here, then a satisfactory understanding of what the theme entails would seem to require that we at least allow the possibility that the audience is admonished to hold (ἔχειν) a faith that in quality is like the faith-obedience of Jesus Christ. The verb ἔχειν ("to hold") appears ten times in James (1.4; 2.1, 14 [2x], 17, 18 [2x]; 3.14; 4.2 [2x]). A look at the subjects and objects of ἔχειν shows that every usage is in some way associated with faith, except perhaps those in 3.14 and 4.2. A second look at the latter, however, may disclose that even these dissuasive statements are directed against a (faithless) disobedience to God.

Moreover, there is nothing in the thoroughly theocentric letter of James that plainly suggests a faith *in* Jesus, in the sense of the Pauline kerygma. Salvation in James is fundamentally a matter of faith-obedience to God (see James 2.14, 17, 22, 26; 1.21, 25, 27; 4.12a; 5.19–20). The verb πιστεύειν, "to believe," occurs twice in James and in both instances it is directed toward God: in 2.19 it concerns the belief that God is one; and in 2.23, a citation of Genesis 15.6, it refers to Abraham's faith-obedience to God (cf. James 2.21–24). In Genesis 22.1–19 the call to sacrifice Isaac is a testing of Abraham's faith, a testing of faith that was endured by obedience to God.[14] As we shall see in a later chapter, such an interpretation coheres much better with the fact that the fundamental issue in the argument concerns the definition or essence of "acts of partiality."

The long genitive phrase τοῦ κυρίου ἡμῶν Ἰησοῦ Χριστοῦ τῆς δόξης is no less challenging. Though the concatenation of genitives is understandable, it is frequently argued that τῆς δόξης ("of the

---

[13] D. W. B. Robinson's (1970, p. 79; cited in Hays, 1983, pp. 164, 187) view that the phrase is "broadly adjectival" and means "the (Christian) faith" is certainly satisfactory for James, but only if by "the (Christian) faith" Robinson has in mind what the subjective genitive seems to mean; namely, faith that is of like quality to Jesus Christ's *own* faith, his faith-obedience to God.

[14] The noun πίστις, "faith," occurs 16x in James: with the article 11x (1.3; 2.1, 14, 17, 18[2x], 20, 22[2x], 26; 5.15); without the article 5x (1.6; 2.5, 14, 18, 24).

glory") reads like an unnecessary appendage (Laws, 1980, pp. 94–97).[15] Hence some witnesses (e.g., the minuscule 33 and a few others, including more than one Vulgate manuscript) would emend the text by omitting that genitive. Others would solve the problem by excising ἡμῶν Ἰησοῦ Χριστοῦ, arguing that it is a Christian interpolation in a thoroughly Jewish document (Spitta, 1896, pp. 3–8; Massebieau, 1895, p. 285; and also Meyer, 1930, pp. 118–21). Neither of these solutions is acceptable, however; the textual evidence for omitting τῆς δόξης is significantly inferior to that for including it, and there is simply no textual warrant for excising the reference to "our Jesus Christ." Consequently, one must attempt to understand the text as it stands.

In trying to solve this riddle, scholars have construed τῆς δόξης with practically every substantive in the sentence.[16] Of these attempts, four are promising.[17] First, τῆς δόξης is connected with τὴν πίστιν, either as a genitive of quality, yielding "the glorious faith of our Lord Jesus Christ" (Reicke, 1964, p. 27, p. 65 note 13) or less probably as an objective genitive, meaning "(the) faith in the glory of our Lord Jesus Christ."[18] The connection between these terms is supported and strengthened by the Peshitta and several manuscripts (614, 630, 2495, some Syriac and Sahidic witnesses, and the Bohairic versions).[19] The established text, which is similar

[15] Ward (1966b, pp. 28–32; p. 29) observes that "the use of genitives, one dependent upon another, reflects a Semitic idiom"; for example, Ps. 144.5. For a discussion of James' style as Semitic, see Wifstrand (1948, p. 176) and Beyer (1962, pp. 296–99); cf. Mayor, (1892 [1990], pp. ccvi–cclxviii); Ropes (1916, pp. 24–27); Dibelius (1975, pp. 34–38); Mußner (1987, pp. 26–33); Davids (1982, pp. 57–59); Adamson (1989, pp. 119–46).

[16] For example, Calvin and Erasmus both take τῆς δόξης as a subjective genitive and construe it with ἐν προσωπολημψίαις, "denoting the cause and source" of the latter. This construction is opposed by the word order; see the discussion and references in Mayor (1892 [1990], pp. 79–80).

[17] See the discussion in Mayor (1892 [1990], pp. 79–82); Ropes (1916, pp. 187–88); Dibelius (1975, pp. 127–29); Mußner (1987, p. 116); Adamson (1976, pp. 103–04); and Davids (1982, pp. 106–07).

[18] Dibelius (1975, p. 126 note 16) says this is probably the interpretation intended by the variant reading in the Peshitta. Zahn subscribed to this opinion (1909, vol. I, p. 151; cited in Dibelius, p. 127 note 18).

[19] This transmission of the text, τῆς δόξης τοῦ κυρίου ἡμῶν Ἰησοῦ Χριστοῦ, seems to offer some support for Adamson's (1976, pp. 104–05) proposal that τῆς δόξῆς is modified by ἡμῶν (though Adamson does not mention it!). This construal would effect an interlacing hyperbaton – (τῆς δόξης) τοῦ κυρίου (ἡμῶν) Ἰησοῦ Χριστοῦ – in which τῆς δόξῆς stands forward because it is emphatic. This would allow his desired translation, "in the Lord Jesus Christ, our Glory." Instead, he would emend the text, moving ἡμῶν to the end of the sentence (p. 105). On hyperbata, see Denniston ([1952] 1979, pp. 54–55).

to James 3.3 and Acts 4.33 (Dibelius, 1975, p. 127), also allows the connection between τὴν πίστιν and τῆς δόξης as a striking hyperbaton.[20] On the other hand, most scholars feel that the distance between the terms is too great (Laws, 1980, p. 95).

The second suggestion is that τῆς δόξης modifies κυρίου, and signifies "(the) faith of our *Lord of glory*, Jesus Christ" (cf. 1 Cor. 2.8; *Barn.* 21.9). This view is generally discounted, since it holds that two postpositive genitives, ἡμῶν and τῆς δόξης, modify "the Lord," and such crude Greek is judged too awkward for our author.[21]

Third, τῆς δόξης is taken as standing separate from the preceding phrase, as either a complement or supplement. This view, which is adopted by the RSV and GNB, suggests that τῆς δόξης provides a second title of lordship to Christ: "our Lord Jesus Christ, the Lord of glory." This, however, is simply not what the text says. According to Mayor (1892 [1990], p. 80) it is "without parallel, and is not supported by any of the later commentators"; see also Laws (1980, p. 95). More probable is the recommendation that τῆς δόξης stands in apposition to Ἰησοῦ Χριστοῦ: "the faith of our Lord Jesus, the Glory."[22] Though this is an attractive suggestion, it lacks corroborative evidence. As Davids puts it: "Despite the parallel form in Jn. 14.6 ('the Truth') and its later use by Justin (*Dial.* 128.2), there is no instance of such a title [= *the Glory*] being applied to Jesus at this period of history" (Davids, 1982, p. 106; also Ropes, 1916, p. 188).

Fourth, τῆς δόξης is understood as a genitive of quality that modifies the entire phrase, producing "the faith of our glorious Lord Jesus Christ."[23] Most scholars hold that this suggestion

[20] Admittedly, this would be more palatable if τῆς δόξης were in the accusative case, like τὴν πίστιν; but the author's preference for the qualitative genitive may readily explain the case of the genitive phrase.

[21] Thus Dibelius (1975, p. 127) and Davids (1982, p. 106). According to Brinktrine (1954, p. 42) and Emmerton (1962, pp. 111–17), this awkward Greek can be a Semitic idiom (cf. Ward, 1966b, p. 29). Laws (1980, p. 94) says, "The title 'Lord of Glory' is not in any case so common a title for God in Judaism as to argue its being the natural original reading for the verse" (cf. also Davids, 1982, p. 106).

[22] This was suggested by Bengel ([1877] 1981, vol. II, p. 702); thus, Mayor (1892 [1990], pp. 80–82); Hort (1909, pp. 47–48); Mitton (1966, pp. 82–83); Laws (1980, pp. 95–97).

[23] Laws (1980, p. 95) says that "one would expect a different word order," if this were the intent of the verse; e.g., τὴν τῆς δόξης πίστιν τοῦ κτλ.; or perhaps, τὴν πίστιν τῆς δόξης τοῦ κτλ.

presents the fewest linguistic problems, since it allows the concatenation of genitives and coheres with the use of the genitive of
quality elsewhere in the text (see Ropes, 1916, p. 187; Dibelius,
1975, pp. 127–28; Cantinat, 1973, p. 121; Mußner, 1987, p. 116;
and Davids, 1982, p. 106–07). Still, despite the author's predilec-
tion for the genitive of quality, one may wonder with Mayor (1892
[1990], p. 80) whether such a genitive "would be appended to a
phrase which is already complete in itself."

Because the last proposal seems to our modern sensibilities an
easier appropriation of the established text, I shall prefer it in this
inquiry. Thus, I would translate the theme as follows: "My brothers
[and sisters], do not hold the faith of our glorious Lord Jesus Christ
with acts of partiality." But what does the text mean by "our
glorious Lord Jesus Christ"?

In all its various uses within the New Testament, the term δόξα is
in some fashion related to the basic idea of "honor," "value," and
"reputation." For example, it refers to the splendor of kings and
kingdoms (Luke 4.6 // Matt. 4.8; Luke 12.27 // Matt. 6.29; Rev.
21.24, 26), and is associated with throne motifs (Matt. 19.28; 25.31,
34). It is used synonymously with "honor" (τιμή, Luke 14.10; 1
Cor. 11.15; opp. ἀτιμία, 11.14; cf. 2 Cor. 6.8; 1 Thess. 2.6, 20; Eph.
3.13; Phil. 3.19) and it refers to the heavenly-divine sphere (Acts
7.55).[24] Here, in its only usage in James, it is associated with Jesus
as an honorific designation. Though we may safely assume that it
presupposes the resurrection, James never mentions anything about
the death and resurrection of Jesus. Indeed, apart from his name
being mentioned twice (1.1; 2.1), and the references to "the Lord"
which in themselves "waver between a theological and christological reference" (L. T. Johnson, 1986, p. 457),[25] the only time we
hear of Jesus is in possible allusions to some of his sayings (see
James 2.5).

Because δόξα is used in the LXX to translate the Hebrew term
kābôd ("honor, nobility, glory"; cf. Gen. 31.1; 45.13; Exod. 24.16;

[24] On "δόξα" and "δοξάζω" see LSJ, p. 444; BAGD, pp. 203–04; G. Kittel and
G. von Rad, *TDNT* II.232–55; H. Hegermann, *EDNT* I.344–49.
[25] The term κύριος occurs fourteen times in James: κύριον: 3.9 (of God, the
Father); κύριος: 4.15 (of God or Jesus Messiah?); 5.11 (of God); 5.15 (of God or
Jesus Messiah?); κυρίου 10x: 1.7 (of God); 2.1 (of Jesus Messiah); 5.4 (κυρίου
σαβαώθ; of God); 5.7 and 8 (of the parousia of the Lord: God or Jesus Messiah?);
5.14 ("in the name of the Lord": God or Jesus Messiah?); without the article – 1.1
(of Jesus Messiah); 4.10 (of God or Jesus Messiah?); 5.10, 11 (of God).

Ps. 8.6; 49.16; Isa. 6.3; 16.14; 17.4; 1 Kgs. 3.13; cf. Warmuth, 1983; Schneider, 1972) some scholars would read in James 2.1 a designation of Jesus as the visible manifestation of God's person and power (e.g., Davids, 1982, p. 107, who cites Exod. 14.17–18; Ps. 96.3; Isa. 60.1–2; Ezek. 39.21–22; Zech. 2.5–11). Though this may be its intended sense, caution is necessary because the text gives no further specification as to the exact meaning of the term. Whatever the author's christological conceptions may have been, he gives precious little indication of them.[26] On the other hand, we may note in passing that James' use of δόξα in relation to "Jesus Messiah" coheres rather nicely with other elements that seem to evince a messianic sensibility. For example, the imagery of "the twelve tribes" in the prescript (1.1) brings into focus a symbol that is an important feature in some of the early discussions about the Messiah and his role in the restoration of Israel.[27] Furthermore, scholars remind us that celebrated conceptions of that restoration included the ideas of judgment and the reestablishment of justice as fundamental components, both of which are very prominent elements in our unit and letter (see Horsley, 1987, pp. 199–208).

As a rhetorical topic, "glory" or "reputation" (δόξα) is regarded as an external good (Arist. *Rhet.* 1.5.4), and "a good reputation (εὐδοξία) consists in being considered a man of worth by all, or in possessing something of such a nature that all or most men, or the good, or the men of practical wisdom desire it" (1.5.8). It is related to "honor" (τιμή), another external good which is defined as "a sign [σημεῖον] of the reputation [δόξα] for doing good [εὐεργετικῆς]; and those who have already done good [εὐεργετηκότες, 'benefactors') are justly and above all honored" (Arist. *Rhet.* 1.5.9). Both δόξα and τιμή, then, are advantageous goods; they have intrinsic worth, are desirable, and "are generally accompanied by the possession of those things for which men are honored" (*Rhet.*

---

[26] Observing that James "relies heavily on the Jewish wisdom tradition in its understanding of man and the world," Ward (1976, p. 470) suggests that the author's "Christology may be a wisdom Christology." Cf. Hoppe (1977, pp. 72–78; 1989, pp. 25–28); also Hartin (1991, pp. 89–97, 241–42).

[27] Schürer (1973–87, vol. ΙΙ, pp. 530–31); *Sib. Or.* 2.171; 3.249; Acts 26.7. Mayor (1892 [1990], p. 30) says the "chosen people are still regarded as constituting twelve tribes." Further, there is evidence to suggest that Jesus understood his own mission as part of "a task which would include the restoration of Israel" (E. P. Sanders, 1995, p. 106; see pp. 91–119).

1.6.13; cf. Cicero *Inv. Rhet.* 2.55.166). It should also be remembered that δόξα and τιμή are regarded as component parts of "happiness" (εὐδαιμονία), which is a fundamental subject in deliberative discourse (Arist. *Rhet.* 1.5.4; 1.5.2). While the term εὐδαιμονία does not occur in the NT, the closely related terms χαρά ("joy") and μακάριος ("blessed," "supremely blissful") are frequent, and they are strategically important in James. For example, "joy" is invoked in the prescript (χαίρειν, James 1.1), and is featured in the first admonition of the letter (1.2), and in a call to repentance (4.9); "supreme happiness" (μακάριος) appears in the central proposition of the letter (1.12), and is conspicuous in the first reference to "the perfect law, the law of liberty" (1.25); and the verb μακαρίζω occurs in the first section of the *peroratio* (5.11), where the rhetorical exigence of the letter, namely, "the steadfast endurance of various trials," is repeated (cf. 1.12!).[28] At the very least, then, James' use of δόξα clearly connotes the honor and reputation of Jesus Messiah.[29]

It seems then that the theme of our argument introduces contraries, two incompatible courses of action; one honorable, the other dishonorable. Acts of partiality are contrary to "the faith of our glorious Lord Jesus Christ."[30] Because Jesus Christ is emphatically qualified as honorable, it follows that "his faith" is also honorable. Further, the emphatic location of the topic δόξα, as the final element in a Greek sentence, suggests that it is a fundamental topic in the admonition to which it belongs. Thus we may expect the topic of "glory" or "honor" to play a significant role within the elaboration that follows. In dissuading from "acts of partiality," one may anticipate that the elaboration will attempt to prove that such behavior is "dishonorable."

---

[28] On the relation of χαίρειν and μακάριος, see Arist. *Nic. Eth.* 7.11.2; and for the relation of μακάριος and εὐδαιμονία, see *Nic. Eth.* 1.7.16; 1.12.4.

[29] Here the topic of the "praiseworthy" is apparent. This topic is generally defined as "what produces an honorable remembrance, at the time of the event and afterwards" (*Rhet. Her.* 3.4.7). We may safely assume that "the faith of our glorious Lord Jesus Christ" is here considered "praiseworthy." Further, while the "praiseworthy" was understood to have its source in the "right," both of the latter were understood as components of the larger topic "honor." The latter and its corollary category "security" were subsumed under the topic of "advantage," which is the aim of a deliberative speech. For a general discussion, see *Rhet. Her.* Book 3.

[30] Whatever one may wish to say about the author's understanding of "faith," the letter makes it abundantly clear that "faith" comprises thoughts, words, and deeds (James 2.1–24).

2 Reason (*ratio*) in an argument from comparison (ἐκ παραβολῆς)

James 2.2 ἐὰν γὰρ εἰσέλθῃ εἰς (συναγωγὴν) ὑμῶν ἀνὴρ χρυσοδακτύλιος ἐν ἐσθῆτι λαμπρᾷ, εἰσέλθῃ δὲ καὶ πτωχὸς ἐν ῥυπαρᾷ ἐσθῆτι,

For if there should enter into your synagogue a gold-fingered man in bright clothes, and a poor man in shabby clothes also enters,

James 2.3 (ἐπιβλέψητε δὲ) ἐπὶ τὸν φοροῦντα τὴν ἐσθῆτα τὴν λαμπρὰν καὶ εἴπητε· σὺ κάθου ὧδε καλῶς, καὶ τῳ πτωχῷ εἴπητε· σὺ στῆθι (ἐκεῖ ἢ κάθου) (ὑπὸ) τὸ ὑποπόδιόν (μου),

and you look favorably upon the man wearing the bright clothes and say: "You sit here honorably"; and to the poor man you say: "You stand there or sit by my feet";

James 2.4 (οὐ) διεκρίθητε ἐν ἑαυτοῖς καὶ ἐγένεσθε κριταὶ διαλογισμῶν πονηρῶν;

have you not made distinctions among yourselves and become judges with evil calculations?

The text

For verse 2 the critical apparatus of Nestle–Aland[26] shows that the seventh-century corrector of 01, 02, 025, and the Majority text insert τήν before συναγωγὴν ὑμῶν, while the established text follows the first hand of Codex Sinaiticus, 03, 04, 044, the minuscules 630, 2495, and a few less important witnesses in omitting the article. Without the article "synagogue" may refer to more than one. This is the preferred reading and it coheres better with the sentiment of James as an encyclical. Compare T. Zahn (1909, vol. II, pp. 83, 89, and 94 note 1), who takes the statement as referring to a building.

In verse 3 there are five variant readings: first, καὶ ἐπιβλέψητε (in 01, 02, the Majority text, and part of the Bohairic tradition) is due most probably to "the proliferation of καί" (Dibelius, 1975, p. 130 note 41). Second, in some manuscripts (025, the Majority text, and so forth through the Coptic versions) αὐτῷ is inserted as the indirect object of εἴπητε. The emendation results from the effort to balance the clause with James 2.3e (καὶ τῷ πτωχῷ εἴπητε) where the verb εἴπητε is repeated with its indirect object (τῷ πτωχῷ). The established text is better attested. Third, alternative readings to ἐκεῖ ἢ κάθου, which is preferred, either rearrange the word order (e.g., ἢ κάθου ἐκεῖ, in 02, 945, 1241, 1243, 1739, a few minor witnesses, an Old Latin manuscript, and the Sahidic versions); insert an adverb (ἐκεῖ ἢ κάθου ὧδε, as in [papyrus P[74] apparently] uncials 01, the second hand of 04, 025, the Majority text, the Peshitta, and the Bohairic versions); or insert the adverb and also alter the word order (ὧδε ἢ κάθου ἐκεῖ, as in 365). These variants may be readily explained by analogies to the clause in 2.3d (σὺ κάθου ὧδε καλῶς) as attempts to provide a smoother reading (Dibelius, 1975, p. 131; and Metzger, 1971, pp. 680–81). Fourth, some manuscripts (the second hand of 03, 025, 044, the minuscules 33, 323, 614, 630, and so forth through the Sahidic tradition) insert the preposition ἐπί for ὑπό, suggesting a problem in understanding how one could sit "under a footstool." The usage in the text, however, is not difficult; the phrase is tropical, meaning "on the floor" (Dibelius, 1975, p. 132), or "at the foot of" (cf. ὑπὸ τὸ ὄρος, Exod. 19.17; 24.4; Deut. 4.11; see Mayor, 1892 [1990], p. 84; Ward, 1966b, p. 94). Fifth, after ὑποπόδιον (in 02, 33, an Old Latin version with minor differences, and the Vulgate) μου is replaced with τῶν ποδῶν μου, which is a deliberate reference to LXX Psalm 109.1 (see Mayor, 1892 [1990], p. 85, and Dibelius, 1975, p. 132 note 45). Some scholars have been troubled by the fact that the verb εἴπητε is in the second plural, while the pronominal qualification of "footstool" is in the first singular. But the first singular appears regularly in the LXX phrase τὸ ὑποπόδιόν μου as a reference to God's footstool (Ps. 98.5; 131.7; Isa. 66.1; cf. 1 Clem. 36.5; Barn. 12.10; esp. Matt. 5.35 and cf. James 5.12!), and the usage in James may well be an allusion to such (Ward, 1966b, pp. 94–95; Davids, 1982, p. 109).

In verse 4 the negative interrogative particle οὐ is replaced first, with καὶ οὐ (in 025, and the Majority text); second, with καί (in 322, 323, and a few other witnesses); third, with the rarer and emphatic οὐχί (in 044), which occurs nowhere else in James; and fourth (in the original hand of 03, 1852, and a few other witnesses) it is omitted. Of these variants, the first and second probably arose in assimilation to the use of καί in the previous verses (Dibelius, 1975, pp. 130–31). Reading three is simply an attempt to intensify the indictment implied in the question; and the omission of the particle is probably due to scribal confusion between the final element in James 2.3 and the first element in 2.4, μου – οὐ, respectively (Mayor, 1892 [1990], p. 85 note 1).

The analysis

James 2.2–4 presents the *ratio*, the reason why those who hold the faith of the Lord Jesus Christ should not show partiality. According to the *Rhetorica ad Herennium*, the *ratio* is "a brief explanation" that is "subjoined" to the theme, thus providing its "causal basis" and establishing its truth (2.18.28; cf. 4.53.57).[31] In other words, the rationale provides the "reason" why the initial statement in James 2.1 is, from the speaker's perspective, true or plausible (Mack, 1990, p. 30).

Analysis of the *ratio* shows it to be a complex sentence consisting of fifty-five words that comprise nine clauses. This is one of the longest sentences in James.[32] The clauses are as follows: (1) εἰσέλθῃ εἰς ... λαμπρᾷ; (2) εἰσέλθῃ δὲ ... ἐσθῆτι; (3) ἐπιβλέψητε δὲ ἐπὶ ... (the man); (4) τὸν φοροῦντα τὴν ἐσθῆτα τὴν λαμπρὰν; (5) καὶ εἴπητε; (6) σὺ κάθου ὧδε καλῶς; (7) καὶ τῷ πτωχῷ εἴπητε; (8) σὺ στῆθι ἐκεῖ ἢ κάθου ὑπὸ τὸ ὑποπόδιόν μου; (9) οὐ διεκρίθητε κτλ.[33] The rhetorical figure "transplacement" (*traductio*; *Rhet. Her.* 4.14.20–21) is exploited here in the repetition of: (a) verbs: εἰσέρχεσθαι (clauses 1 and 2), and εἰπεῖν (clauses 5 and 7); (b) substantives: ἐσθής (clauses 1, 2, and 4), and πτωχός (clauses 2 and 7); (c) the adjective λαμπρός (clauses 1 and 4); and (d) the verb κάθου (clauses 6 and 8). The figure "homoeoteleuton" (ὁμοιοτέλευτον; Quint. 9.3.77) marks the end of clauses 5 and 7 (εἴπητε). Also, "paronomasia" (*adnominatio*; *Rhet. Her.* 4.21.29) is evident in the play on διεκρίθητε/κριταί in clause 9. By such figures the comparison is marked with emphasis and refinement.

---

[31] "The term *ratio* in the *ad Herennium* corresponds to the αἰτία (rationale) in Hermogenes' elaboration" (Mack and Robbins, 1989, p. 58).

[32] In Mayor's (1892 [1990], p. cclv) opinion, James 2.2–4 and James 4.13–15 are the "only two sentences in his [James'] Epistle which exceed four lines."

[33] I have have counted the attributive participle, τὸν φοροῦντα (with complements) as a subordinate relative clause; thus the RSV. This is permissible, because an attributive participle (with complements) and a relative clause are agnate constructions (Funk, 1973, sections 773 and 672; Smyth, 1956, sections 2049–50; Goodwin, [1894] 1981, section 1560). On the other hand, one may translate the attributive participle as a substantive qualifed by a participle *phrase*; thus the NRSV. If the latter option is chosen, the sentence will have eight clauses.

The sentence is conditional and interrogative. Introduced by the particle ἐάν (cf. James 2.14, 15, 17; 4.4, 15; 5.15 κἄν, 19), the protasis consists of five subordinate clauses with leading verbs (εἰσέρχεσθαι [2x], ἐπιβλέπειν, and εἰπεῖν [2x]) in the aorist subjunctive; one relative clause formed by an attributive present participle (τὸν φοροῦντα) with complements,[34] and two dependent clauses of direct discourse, which feature three present imperative verbs (καθῆσθαι [2x], and ἱστάναι).[35] Thus the protasis has eight clauses and expresses a supposed or assumed case. The apodosis (verse 4) consists of one compound clause which is marked by the particle οὐ as a question that expects an affirmative answer. The two verbs in the apodosis are in the aorist indicative, and express what follows if the condition is realized (Smyth, 1956, sections 2326 [b], and 1934). Therefore, the sentence presents a future, more vivid, condition: "the speaker clearly desires to be graphic, impressive, emphatic, and to anticipate a future result with the distinctness of the present" (Smyth, 1956, section 2322; see sections 2297, 2321–28).

In rhetorical theory, there are basically three species of "example" that provide the "raw data" for the artistic proofs to be used in arguing a case (Mack, 1990, p. 40; Lausberg, 1973, vol. I, sections 410–26). These are the historical example (παράδειγμα; *exemplum*), the comparison (παραβολή; *similitudo*), and the fable (μῦθος; *fabula*). "The term 'example', as the rhetoricians used it, is meant to refer to a specific person like Demosthenes, Socrates, or Alexander" (Mack and Robbins, 1989, p. 28). Thus in James, the references to Abraham (2.21, 23), Rahab (2.25), Job (5.11), Elijah (5.17) are examples. "Comparisons" could be taken from any of the orders of reality, but customarily they were taken from the

---

[34] This is the only participle in the sentence, and, with complements, it stands as the direct object of ἐπιβλέψητε. James employs the participle seventy-one times. *With the article, twenty-nine times*: the *present participle* occurs 20x (1.5, 6, 12, 21; 2.3, 5, 23; 3.4, 6, 18; 4.1, 11[2x], 12[2x], 13, 14; 5.1, 4, 15); the *aorist participle* occurs 8x (1.25; 2.7, 11, 13; 5.4[2x], 11, 20); and the *perfect participle* occurs 1x (5.4). *Without the article, forty-two times*: the *present participle* occurs 28x (1.3, 4, 5, 6[3x], 13, 14[2x], 15, 17, 22, 23, 26[2x]; 2.9, 12*, 15; 3.4[2x], 6[2x], 15; 4.14, 17; 5.1, 7, 16); the *aorist participle* occurs 10x (1.12, 15, 18, 21, 25[2x]; 2.21, 25[2x]; 5.14); the *perfect participle* occurs 4x (3.1, 9; 4.17; 5.15); the future participle without the article does not occur; instead the periphrastic construction (pres. active participle + the present infinitive) appears in 2.12*. Cf. Mayor (1892 [1990], pp. ccxxxi–ccxxxii).

[35] The verbs ἐπιβλέπειν and καθῆσθαι occur in James only here; εἰσέρχεσθαι and ἱστάναι appear once more, in James 5.4 and 5.9, respectively; and εἰπεῖν occurs an additional three times, 2.11(2x), 16. On James' use of direct and indirect discourse, and conditional sentences, see Mayor (1892 [1990], p. ccxxxiii–ccxxxiv).

natural world or normal social practice. As Mack (1990, p. 40) puts it: they "captured a customary observation about types of people, normal events, and regular natural processes" (Mack and Robbins, 1989, p. 28; *Rhet. Alex.* 1.1422a.25–27; Cic. *Inv. Rhet.* 1.30.47–49; *Rhet. Her.* 2.29.46; and Lausberg, 1973, vol. I, sections 422–25). The "fable," like the analogy or comparison, is an invented proof "taken not from the historical world but from the worlds of nature and social practice"; unlike the analogy or comparison, however, "the fable entertained an imaginative world created by fiction" (Mack, 1990, p. 40).[36]

The example in James 2.2–3 is drawn from the social sphere and is essentially an antithetic comparison (*Rhet. Her.* 4.15.21). Although the two men that are compared are similar in certain respects – both are male; both are litigants expecting justice at the hands of a judicial assembly, and, like those who judge their case, they are members of the elect community – it is their differences rather than their similarities that are emphasized. In fact, as social types, the two men are opposites: one has wealth; the other does not have wealth.

The comparison exploits the topics of "fortune" and "rank" to show that the men belong to different social levels. "Fortune" and "rank" are subtopics under "security," those things that attract (perhaps the author of James would say those things that "lure and entice," 1.14) humans because of some profit or advantage to be derived from them (*Rhet. Her.* 3.2.3; cf. Arist. *Rhet.* 1.3.5). As already mentioned, the first man, bedecked with a gold ring and wearing bright clothes, obviously has status and wealth. The second man is pointedly designated "poor," and the reference to his dirty or shabby clothes both amplifies and confirms his identity and inferior status. In addition, the social example compares the antithetic treatments the men receive at the hands of the judicial assembly. The first man, whose status and wealth are carefully noted (ἐπιβλέπειν) by the judges, is directed to sit "honorably" (καλῶς), while the second man is instructed either to stand or to sit on the floor. These "court instructions," as Ward (1969) has shown, are unambiguous signs of favoritism toward the wealthy man.

Whether the social example in James 2.2–3 refers to an actual or hypothetical case simply cannot be conclusively determined. Be

---

[36] On "proof" (πίστις) in rhetoric, see Lausberg (1973, vol. I, sections 348–430).

that as it may, Sophie Laws has made an important (rhetorical) observation when she says that even if the social example contains caricature and hyperbole, we may reasonably presume that it could not fulfill its function in the discourse unless it had some obvious correspondence to what might have or could have customarily occurred (Laws, 1980, p. 98). Furthermore, if we may accept what cultural anthropologists tell us about the patron–client system that permeated the Greco-Roman world during that period, then the incident envisioned looks typical rather than unusual (Garnsey and Saller, 1987; Saller, 1982; and Malina, 1981; 1986b; and 1987). The issue of favoring the wealthy over the poor in judicial proceedings is, in fact, a conventional subject in ancient sources.

For example, among the topics of "justice" included in Menander Rhetor's epideictic "address" (ὁ προσφωνητικὸς λόγος) to a governor we find: τὸ μὴ πρὸς χάριν μηδὲ πρὸς ἀπέχθειαν κρίνειν τὰς δίκας, τὸ μὴ προτιμᾶν τοὺς εὐπόρους τῶν ἀδυνάτων ("freedom from partiality and from prejudice in giving judicial decisions, equal treatment of rich and poor"; in *Menander Rhetor*, 1981, pp. 166–67). Though the form of the encomium dates from the Byzantine period, the elements or topics are "of proved antiquity" (1981, p. xxxii). This is corroborated by Pseudo-Phocylides (50 BCE–100 CE), sentences 9 and 10: πάντα δίκαια νέμειν, μὴ δὲ κρίσιν ἐς χάριν ἕλκειν. μὴ ῥιψῇς πενίην ἀδίκως, μὴ κρῖνε πρόσωπον ("Always dispense justice and stretch not judgment for a favour. Cast the poor not down unjustly, judge not partially," in van der Horst, 1978, pp. 117–18; see LSJ, *s.v.* "χάρις"; Saller, 1982, pp. 152–53).

Against that background, the comparison in James 2.2–3 is a thoroughly plausible social example that offers what the author holds to be a customary observation about the types of people and events it depicts; thus it coheres with the stated purpose of the *ratio* (*Rhet. Her.* 2.18.28). Further, as an exercise in inductive reasoning, the comparison provides a given case from which the author draws a conclusion about the audience he addresses: "have you not discriminated among yourselves and become judges with evil thoughts?" (James 2.4).

A closer look at this incriminating rhetorical question, which is epideictic in nature, discloses the fact that those who show partiality are making judgments about others; the issue invokes the topic of "justice" (Arist. *Rhet.* 1.9.6,7; cf. *Eth. Nic.* book 5; and δικαιοσύνη in Ps.-Arist. *VV.* 2.6; 5.2. See *Rhet. Her.* 3.2.3; 3.4.3;

Cic. *Inv. Rhet.* 2.53.160–54.162; *Off.* 1.5.15; 1.7.20).[37] On the basis of the deeds (ἐπιβλέψητε . . . καὶ εἴπητε) and words (σὺ κάθου κτλ.; σὺ στῆθι κτλ.) featured in the comparison, the question translates "acts of partiality" (προσωπολημψίαι, James 2.1) as "judgmental actions" (διεκρίθητε . . . κριταὶ) that are character-ized by "evil calculations/motives" (διαλογισμῶν πονηρῶν). This is an interpretive move; the rhetor has focused on the theme in 2.1 (that the faith of the Lord Jesus Christ is incompatible with acts of partiality), and has clarified partialities in terms of action, thought, and quality (διακρίνειν, διαλογισμός, and πονηρός; James 2.4). In so doing, the author restates the theme: an act of partiality is essentially an evil or unjust judging.[38]

It needs to be emphasized (*contra* Dibelius, 1975, pp. 129–30) that the author does not intend this example to function as a mere illustration for the advice in James 2.1; he offers it as proof, as the compelling social basis for what he says (Mack 1990, p. 40). This is also indicated by the causal conjunction γάρ, which introduces the example (Smyth, 1956, section 2810; cf. G. A. Kennedy, 1984, pp. 16–17).[39] In particular, this connective particle unites the theme (2.1) with the main clause of the *ratio* (2.4) and produces an enthymematic structure (see Arist. *Rhet.* 1.2.8–9; cf. Ropes, 1916, p. 188). The reasoning may be reformulated as follows:

Major premise (unstated):	Unjust judgings are incompatible with the faith of our glorious Lord Jesus Christ.
Minor premise:	Acts of partiality are unjust judgings (2.4).
Conclusion:	Acts of partiality are incompatible with the faith of our glorious Lord Jesus Christ (2.1).

At this point, the author has advanced his theme (2.1) by both inductive and deductive argument. First, he has expressed it in a statement of apotreptic advice (2.1); then, subjoining the reason, he has grounded the theme in the social sphere (2.2–3), and translated

[37] Epideictic components in both deliberative and forensic discourse were stan-dard fare and were formally recognized by the rhetoricians; see Nadeau (1952, pp. 376–77).

[38] On the restatement of the theme in elaboration, see *Rhet. Her.* 4.43.56.

[39] Γάρ occurs 15x in James: 1.6, 7, 11, 13, 20, 24; 2.2, 10, 11, 13, 26; 3.2, 7, 16; 4.14.

"acts of partiality" as unjust judgments (2.4). Further, having introduced several topics that are strategic to his argument – in particular, the topics of honor (2.1) and injustice (2.4), and their contraries – he has essentially laid out the case he will attempt to confirm or prove (cf. *Rhet. Her.* 2.18.28).

3   Probatio: argument from example, with opposite and social example

a. Argument from example (ἐκ παραδείγματος):

James 2.5 Ἀκούσατε, ἀδελφοί μου ἀγαπητοί· οὐχ ὁ θεὸς ἐξελέξατο τοὺς πτωχοὺς τῷ κόσμῳ πλουσίους ἐν πίστει καὶ κληρονόμους τῆς βασιλείας ἧς ἐπηγγείλατο τοῖς ἀγαπῶσιν αὐτόν;

Listen, my beloved brothers [and sisters]: Has not God chosen the poor in the world to be rich in faith and heirs of the kingdom which he has promised to those who love him?

b. Statement of the opposite (ἐξ ἐναντίου):[40]

James 2.6a ὑμεῖς δὲ ἠτιμάσατε τὸν πτωχόν.

But you have dishonored the poor.

c. Embellishment of the opposition with argument from social example (ἐκ παραβολῆς):[41]

James 2.6b οὐχ οἱ πλούσιοι καταδυναστεύουσιν ὑμῶν καὶ αὐτοὶ ἕλκουσιν ὑμᾶς εἰς κριτήρια;

Do not the rich oppress you and do they not drag you into courts?

James 2.7 οὐκ αὐτοὶ βλασφημοῦσιν τὸ καλὸν ὄνομα τὸ ἐπικληθὲν ἐφ' ὑμᾶς;

[40] In *Rhet. Her.* (4.43.56), it says that, after refining or expressing "the theme in another form, with or without Reasons; next we can present the Contrary (*contrarium*)," the opposite (ἐκ τοῦ ἐναντίου); cf. 4.44.57. Also see Anaximenes, [*Rh. Al.*] 1.1422a.25–27; Cic. *Top.* 47–49; and Hermog. *Inv.* (Rabe, vol. III, pp. 148–50).

[41] After the argument from the contrary or opposite, in *Rhet. Her.* 4.43.56 comes "a comparison" or social example. "Embellishment (*exornatio*) consists of similes (*similibus*; παραβολῶν; comparisons), examples, amplifications, previous judgments (*rebus iudicatis*; κεκριμένων; κρισέων)" (*Rhet. Her.* 2.29.46). See Mack and Robbins (1989, pp. 56–57).

Do they not blaspheme the honorable name that was pronounced over you?

The text

The attempt to provide a smoother reading for verse 5 explains why some manuscripts (322, 323, a few others, and the Vulgate with minor variations) replace τῷ κόσμῳ with ἐν τῷ κόσμῳ. According to Dibelius (1975, p. 137), replacing τῷ κόσμῳ with τοῦ κόσμου (in the second hand of both 02 and 04, 025, 044, the majority tradition, a Latin codex, probably the Coptic tradition, and Priscillian, + τούτου in 61 and others) may be due to the influence of the Koine texts, perhaps relying on 1 Corinthians 1.27–28. In any case, the established text easily accounts for these variant readings. The alternative reading, substituting ἐπαγγελίας for βασιλείας (in the original hand of 01, and in 02), may find its source in Hebrews 6.17 (cf. 6.12).

In verse 6b some manuscripts (02, apparently the first hand of 04, 614, 630, 1505, 2495, and others, including all the Syriac witnesses) replace the negative particle οὐχ with its emphatic form οὐχί. This is simply an attempt to emphasize the assertion made in the rhetorical question and the affirmative answer it expects; see the alternative reading in James 2.4, mentioned above. Other manuscripts seek a smoother reading by substituting οὐχὶ δέ (papyrus P[74] [apparently]) or οὐχὶ καί (044). The genitive plural ὑμῶν, which stands as the direct object of the verb καταδυναστεύω, is replaced (in papyrus P[74], the original hand of 01, 02, and a few other witnesses) with the accusative plural ὑμᾶς; in the first hand of 623 ὑμῶν is simply omitted. Both the replacement and the omission are emendations based on the fact that ὑμᾶς immediately follows in a coordinated clause as the direct object of the verb ἕλκω. Not only is the established text better, these variants hamper the rhetorical affect of the sentence.

In verse 7 the negative particle οὐκ is replaced by the conjunction καί (in papyrus P[74], 02, 044, 33, 81, 614, 630, 1505, 2495, some others and the Harklean Syriac). This is another attempt to provide the text with a smoother transition between sentences.

The analysis

James 2.5 begins the *probatio* or argumentation proper (Quint. 5.10.8). Analysis of this sentence will show that it functions as a historical example. In chapter 4 we will focus on this particular example (James 2.5) as a Jamesian recitation of a well-known saying of Jesus; here, we will limit the discussion to its function as part of the deliberative argument in James 2.1–13.

This verse begins like the theme (2.1), with the familiar Jamesian vocative "my beloved brothers" (ἀδελφοί μου ἀγαπητοί), an initial indication of its function as the "further development" of the initial statement (2.1) and a "further elaboration" of the social example in 2.2–4 (Dibelius, 1975, p. 137; see p. 38 note 132). This is the third and final usage of ἀδελφοί μου ἀγαπητοί (cf. 1.16, 19), which is the most endearing of the three ways in which the term ἀδελφός is used to address the audience. Here, however, the vocative is preceded by an imperatival verb (ἀκούσατε, "Listen!"; see 1.19; 5.11; cf. ἀκροατής in 1.22, 23, 25; also cf. 5.4). This is customary in James, for in twelve of the fifteen instances where ἀδελφός occurs as a form of direct address (1.2, 16, 19; 2.5, 14; 3.1, 10, 12; 4.11; 5.7, 9, 10), the verb precedes the vocative. In thirteen instances, the verb has an imperatival function (1.2, 16, 19; 2.1, 5; 3.1, 10, 12; 4.11; 5.7, 9, 10, 12). Note that in James 2.5 the vocative ("my beloved brothers") is found in the interior of the sentence, as is customary in Greek; but in 2.1 (and 5.19), it stands as the first element in its clause and is emphatic (Smyth, 1956, section 1285). The only other case in which ἀδελφοί μου precedes the verb is in 5.11, but there the vocative is also in the interior of the sentence.

James 2.5, with twenty-four words and five clauses, is a complex interrogative sentence. The five clauses are: (1) Ἀκούσατε ... ἀγαπητοί; (2) οὐχ ... κόσμῳ; (3) [εἶναι] πλουσίους ... βασιλείας; (4) ἧς ἐπηγγείλατο; (5) τοῖς ἀγαπῶσιν αὐτόν. Clauses (1) and (2) are independent, while the last three are subordinate. Clause (3) is a compound purpose clause; the infinitive εἶναι, which is complementary to the verb ἐξελέξατο in the second clause, is ellipsed (on this, see BAGD, "ἐλέγομαι"; on ellipses in James, see Mayor, 1892 [1990], pp. ccxxxvi–ccxxxvii). Clauses (4) and (5) are relative clauses: the former is introduced by the relative pronoun ἧς, which has been attracted to the (genitive) case of its antecedent βασιλείας; and (5) is formed by the articular present active participle ἀγαπῶσιν (and complement) and stands as the indirect object of the aorist indicative ἐπηγγείλατο. This verse is the second of four rhetorical questions in the unit. While this and the preceding question (2.2–4) concern the poor, the next two (2.6b–7) focus on the rich. All four questions expect an affirmative answer; this one does so apparently on the grounds that what it asserts is already well known by the audience.[42]

As is often the case with verbs of choosing, ἐκλέγεσθαι ("to choose") is used here with ellipsis of the infinitive (εἶναι), and also with double accusatives (πλουσίους and κληρονόμους).[43] Structured in this fashion, James 2.5 is a precedent that discloses several facts about God and the poor that are fundamental to the author's argument. First, God has chosen (ἐξελέξατο) the poor for himself. The verb ἐκλέγειν occurs in the NT always in the middle voice (ἐκλέγεσθαι).[44] Here it functions as an indirect reflexive middle and represents its subject, God, as acting for himself and in his own interests (Smyth, 1956, sections 1713–14; 1719–21; and 1483. See esp. BDF section 316.1). The (aorist middle indicative) form of the verb makes it sufficiently clear that the poor are not chosen because they are poor; that is, their being chosen is not "some sort of compensation for earthly poverty" (Dibelius, 1975, p. 138; Bammel, *TDNT* VI. 890–91). The primary focus of the sentence is God's action for himself. Compare βουληθείς in James 1.18 (Zahn, 1909, vol. I, pp. 88, and esp. p. 99 note 7; Schlatter 1956, p. 168).

Second, God has promised (ἐπηγγείλατο) the kingdom to those who love him. Like ἐξελέξατο, the verb ἐπηγγείλατο ("to promise") is also an aorist middle indicative (cf. James 1.12; Schniewind and Friedrich, *TDNT* II. 576–86), and suggests that God has acted according to his own volition. Here, however, the action is with reference to something that belongs to God, namely, his "kingdom" (see Smyth, 1956, sections 1719; 1721; BDF section 311; cf. BAGD, "ἐπαγγέλλομαι," 1.b; Louw and Nida, vol. I, 33.286). This is the only occurrence of βασιλεία in James (cf. Matt.

---

[42] For other expressions appealing to previous knowledge on the reader's part, see γινώσκειν (James 1.3; 5.20 [in 03, 69, 1505, 2495, a few others, and the Harklean Syriac version]); εἰδέναι (James 1.19; ἴστε, literary Attic, occurs in the NT only here; Eph 5.5; and Heb 12.17; see A. T. Robertson, 1923, pp. 87, 238–39, 319); εἰδότες (James 3.1; cf. 4.17); οὐκ οἴδατε (James 4.4); ὁρᾶν (5.11); ἀκούειν (2.5–7; 5.11); see Mayor (1892 [1990], p. 375); and esp. L. T. Johnson (1985, pp. 170, 180 note 28).

[43] On the usage of ἐκλέγεσθαι with the infinitive, see 1 Chr. 15.2; 28.5; 1 Esdr. 5.1; Acts 15.7; and with ellipsis in Acts 5.31; Rom. 3.25; 8.29; 1 John 4.14. For further references and comment, see Mayor (1892 [1990], p. 86). See Smyth (1956, section 1613); BDF sections 155–58; Robertson (1923, pp. 479–84, esp. 480). Dibelius (1975, p. 138 note 79) correctly observes that πλουσίους and κληρονόμους are not to be construed appositionally.

[44] This is the only occurrence of ἐκλέγεσθαι in James. Elsewhere in the NT 21x: Mark 13.20; Luke 6.13; 9.35; 10.42; 14.7; John 6.70; 13.18; 15.16(2x), 19; Acts 1.2, 24; 6.5; 13.17; 15.7, 22, 25; 1 Cor. 1.27(2x), 28; Eph 1.4. See G. Schrenk, *TDNT* IV.144–92; G. Schrenk and V. Herntrich, *TDNT* IV.194–214.

4.23; 9.35; 13.19; 24.14; 8.12; 13.38; Heb. 11.33; 12.28; Acts 20.25; see K. L. Schmidt, *TDNT* I.574–93, esp. 582). The indirect object of God's promise, τοῖς ἀγαπῶσιν, is here a dative of advantage (Smyth, 1956, section 1481).

Third, inasmuch as God's kingdom is promised to those who love God and "the poor" are chosen by God to be "heirs" (κληρονόμους) of the kingdom of God, the author holds that "the poor" are "those who love God." That is, the chosen and advantaged ones are here referred to in terms of their actions ("love") toward God. This is the only occurrence of κληρονόμος in James (cf. Matt. 5.5; 19.29; 25.34; see W. Foerster and J. Hermann, *TDNT* III.768–85). The phrase τοῖς ἀγαπῶσιν is also featured in the central *propositio* of the letter (James 1.12), where it concerns God's promise of "the crown of life."[45] There the person who endures trial is synonymous with one who loves God and therefore will receive the crown (cf. *1 Clem.* 34.8; 59.3; 1 Cor. 2.9; Rom. 8.28).

Fourth, "the poor" in James does not simply mean the "religious" poor; they are also economically and socially disadvantaged. This is suggested by the dative τῷ κόσμῳ which modifies τοὺς πτωχούς. Here, as Luke Johnson (1985, pp. 172–73) points out, the term κόσμος ("world") is a system of measure or meaning that is distinguishable from and opposed to God's. Moreover, this perspective of the world is consistently maintained in every usage of κόσμος in James (1.27; 2.5; 3.6; 4.4 [2x]).

For example, the term κόσμος first appears in a characterization of "pure religion before God the Father" (James 1.27). That portrayal is made with respect to "the poor" and "the world" in a twofold use of the attributes of action.[46] First, pure religion is (the action) "to visit" orphans and widows ("the poor") in their afflictions. The verb ἐπισκέπτεσθαι denotes an "act of kindness" (Isa. 58.7; Job 22.7; *Test. Jos.* 1; *m. 'Abot* 1.2; see Lachs, 1987,

---

[45] τὸν στέφανον τῆς ζωῆς occurs only here and in Rev. 2.10. Mayor (1892 [1990], p. 359) says it is a genitive of definition (an epexegitical genitive): "the crown which consists in eternal life" (p. 243); also Ropes (1916, p. 152); Mußner (1987, pp. 85–86); Laws (1980, p. 68); and Davids (1982, p. 80). Dibelius (1975, p. 89) agrees that it refers to "the final salvation of the consummation" but, because he (erroneously) views James 1.12 as an isolated saying, connected neither with what precedes nor follows (p. 88), he says that the kind of genitive (quality, content, or apposition) cannot be determined. On James 1.12, as the central *propositio* of the letter, see Wuellner (1978a, pp. 37, 42).

[46] On the "attributes of action," see Cic. *Inv. Rhet.* 1.26.37–43; *Top.* 9.38–10.46; and Nadeau (1952, pp. 390–91).

pp. 394–95) or "one of the works of love" (Deut. 10.18; LXX Ps.
9.35; Isa. 1.17; Ezek. 22.7; Matt. 25.34, 36; *Herm. Sim.* 2.4.3; Beyer,
TDNT vi.603; Dibelius, 1975, p. 121).[47] Second, pure religion is
(the action) "to keep oneself unstained (ἄσπιλος) from the
world."[48] The use of the prepositional phrases παρὰ τῷ θεῷ καὶ
πατρὶ ("before God, the Father") and ἀπὸ τοῦ κόσμου ("from the
world") clearly suggest an opposition between God and the world.
The second occurrence of "world" occurs here in James 2.5. As a
dative of reference τῷ κόσμῳ denotes "the [personification] to
whose judgment or estimate reference is made."[49] The community
is poor to/in the world's point of view: the possessions, power/
ability, and status of those whom God has chosen are "poor"
(Ropes, 1916, p. 193).[50] Therefore for James the poverty of "the
elect poor" cannot be limited to the religious dimension.

The fifth fact we learn from James 2.5 is that God's choice of the

[47] It will be remembered that in the OT the concern for widows and orphans is
included under "covenantal obligations or duties." In rhetoric, "duty" (*pietas*) and
"religion" (*religio*) – key issues in James 1.27 – are subtopics of "justice"; and
"justice" is a topic of "honor" (Cic. *Inv. Rhet.* 2.22.66; 2.53.161).
[48] ἄσπιλος occurs only here in James, and but 3x elsewhere in the NT: 1 Tim.
6.14; 1 Pet. 1.19; 2 Pet. 3.14. See Oepke, *TDNT* i.502; BAGD, *s.v.* As L. T. Johnson
(1985, pp. 172–73) correctly observes, " 'To keep oneself unstained from the world'
(James 1.27), does not mean physical or ritual separation . . . 'World' and 'God' are
opposed as measures of valuation."
[49] Smyth (1956, section 1496); Mayor (1982, p. 244). Ropes (1916, p. 193) calls
this the "dative of reference or "interest"; on the dative of interest, see Smyth (1956,
section 1474). Also opting for the dative of reference are Moulton–Howard–Turner
(1963, vol. iii, p. 238); Robertson (1923, p. 536); Zahn, (1909, vol. i, p. 88); and L. T.
Johnson (1985, p. 172). The dative of reference belongs to the dative case proper,
and stresses the idea of personal relations or interests; it "is not a local case"
(Robertson, 1923, pp. 537; *contra* Maynard-Reid, 1987, p. 62). Mußner (1987,
p. 120) says it is a dative of personal (dis)interest, which would be close to a *dativus
incommodi* (dative of disadvantage). Dibelius (1975, pp. 137, 138) takes it as a
dativus commodi (dative of advantage; but cf. Smyth, 1956, section 1481), and is
followed by Adamson (1976, p. 109 note 60), and Davids (1982, p. 112). Among
those who take it as dative of respect (an instrumental case; cf. BDF section 197;
Smyth, 1956, section 1516) are Schlatter (1956, pp. 169–69, who suggests that the
author should have expressed it as an accusative of respect); Schoeps (1949, p. 350);
Cantinat (1973, p. 126, "pauvres en biens de ce monde"); and Laws (1980, p. 103,
"materially poor").
[50] On dative of reference, Smyth (1956, section 1496) says it "often denotes
the person in whose opinion a statement holds good." Some refer to this as an
"ethical dative" (Zerwick and Grosvenor, 1981, p. 694). Technically, the ethical
dative most often occurs with "the personal pronouns of the first and second
person," and while it treats of the personal interest of the subject or object, it is more
of an emotional reference than one of opinion or estimation. Hence the ethical dative
is often called a "dative of feeling" (Smyth, 1956 section 1486).

poor has a purpose. It is that the poor "before the world" might be "rich in faith." The dative ἐν πίστει is a dative of sphere, and the phrase may be translated "rich in the sphere of faith" (Ropes, 1916, p. 141; similarly, Mayor, 1892 [1990], pp. ccxxviii, 86, 610; Dibelius, 1975, pp. 136, 138; Adamson, 1976, p. 109; and Davids, 1982, p. 111).[51] Compare 1 Timothy 6.17,18; *Herm. Sim.* 2.4. But what does this mean? How would our author explain "rich in the sphere of faith"?

Certainly he understands faith to include both belief and trust in God (αἰτείτω δὲ ἐν πίστει, James 1.6; 2.23), but he makes very clear that it cannot be limited to belief in God (2.19). His fundamental argument is that faith necessarily entails obedience to God (1.22, 25) in both word and deed (2.12). Whatever else we might say, the author is sure that "faith has works" (2.14). To those who would limit "rich in faith" as an internalizing reference, our author would probably respond, "show me your faith apart from your works" (2.18). For instance, just as he grounds the abstract noun προσωπολημψία in a social example that treats of the conflict between rich and poor (2.2–3), he uses, in the next argumentative unit (2.14–26), another social example about the poor (2.14, 15–16) to suggest the kinds of works that should accompany πίστις. Then, he concretizes πίστις in two "historical examples" (παραδείγματα) that recall the "works of mercy" of Abraham and Rahab (2.21–25).[52] Consequently, for our author "being rich in the sphere of faith" could not mean less than possessing the works that cohere with faith (2.17, 26). Moreover, this prosperity "in faith" is viewed by the author as present and palpable, just as is the "wealth" (πλοῦτος, James 5.2) of the rich τῷ κόσμῳ. The poor are chosen by God, for God, that they might be

[51] Mußner (1987, p. 120) agrees with this translation but argues that the case is technically local-instrumental (namely, the dative of respect; cf. BDF section 197). Robertson (1985, section 523.e) argues that the case is neither dative nor instrumental but locative. Hort says the meaning is "rich in virtue of faith," and apparently he understands the case to be the dative of cause (cited in Mayor, 1892 [1990], p. 610). Laws (1980, p. 103) translates, "spiritually rich by virtue of their faith," which seems to agree with Hort, though it is likely that she takes it as a dative of respect.

[52] Ward (1966b, pp. 164–67) is right in suggesting that the reference to Abraham's works is not merely a reference to his willingness to sacrifice Isaac but presupposes his acts of mercy, his hospitality to strangers. Thus, "from the concern that there be no divisive partiality in the community the author proceeds to an exhortation for acts of mercy toward the needy within the community" (p. 200). Cf. Chadwick (1961, p. 281).

rich now in obedience to God and therefore receive the promised reward, God's kingdom.[53]

With this the argument in James 2.5 introduces God as the opposite of the κριταὶ διαλογισμῶν πονηρῶν (2.4). Already in the *narratio*,[54] the author has emphasized that God cannot be associated with "evil" (κακός, 1.13). Moreover, we underscore the fact that the *topoi* used to characterize God in both the *exordium* and the *narratio* are not logically unrelated but are typical in discourses praising a wise and just ruler/judge.[55] That particular conception of God as wise and just ruler/judge runs through the whole of James, and it undergirds the judgment here, allowing it to function as a historical example (παράδειγμα) that opposes the social example in verses 2–3. God, the supremely wise and just ruler/judge, has chosen, and thus honored, the poor (cf. Arist. *Rhet.* 1.5.9); the community's judges, on the other hand, "look upon" (ἐπιβλέπειν) and favor the wealthy over the poor. Further, because the entire letter presupposes a unity of purpose and action for God and the Lord Jesus Christ, this argument presumes a congruence between the faith of the Lord Jesus Christ and God's choice of the poor, and supports the thesis that Jesus' faith and acts of partiality are contrary and incompatible.[56]

The example in James 2.5, then, is basically a "refining" (*expolitio*) of the theme of the argument (*Rhet. Her.* 4.42.54). That is, while it appears to say something new, the example expresses "the theme in another form" (*Rhet. Her.* 4.43.56). Put differently, James

---

[53] As Laws (1980, p. 103) puts it, "there is a promise for the poor, but inasmuch as their pverty is accompanied by faith and the love of God, and as they are chosen in order that it should be so." Similarly, Adamson (1976, p. 109, "Poverty does not guarantee either faith or final salvation") and Ropes (1916, p. 193, "The election of the poor to privileges is not here said to be due to any merit of their poverty, but, in fact, poverty and election coincide").

[54] My tentative outline of James as a rhetorical discourse is as follows: *inscriptio* (1.1); *exordium* (1.2–11); *propositio* (1.12); *narratio* (1.13–27); *argumentatio* (2.1–5.6); *peroratio* (5.7–20). Cf. this with the outlines of J. A. Bengel, Ernst Baasland, and esp. Wilhelm Wuellner, in chapter 2 (pp. 54–56), above.

[55] For example, cf. with the topics of "honor," "justice," and "wisdom" in Menander Rhetor's epideictic "address" (ὁ προσφωνητικὸς λόγος) to a governor (a ruler and judge over his subjects; Russell and Wilson, 1981, pp. 166–67). Though the form of this encomium dates from the Byzantine period, the elements or topics are, as I noted above, "of proved antiquity" (Russell and Wilson, 1981, p. xxxii).

[56] While someone might argue that God's favoring the poor is itself an act of partiality, the logic of the text suggests that such an argument fails to understand what "justice" and "partiality" παρὰ τῷ θεῷ καὶ πατρί are. See James 2.4, 5, 9.

2.5 essentially restates the enthymematic beginning of the argument by capturing and reformulating the reasoning in James 2.1–4. We note also that, from the perspective of invention, the author appears to play on a Jesus-beatitude, reformulating it around certain terms that are key to his persuasive purpose. While we shall deal with this matter in the next chapter when we focus on the "intertexture" of this saying, here we are concerned with James 2.5 as a supporting argument for the theme introduced in 2.1–4.

James 2.5 repeats in a more endearing form (ἀδελφοί μου ἀγαπητοί) the vocative address of the theme (2.1). Then, by the rhetorical figure "transplacement" (*Rhet. Her.* 4.14.20–21), "love," which is introduced in the verbal adjective ἀγαπητός, is reintroduced in the dative participle ἀγαπῶσιν, where the advantage of the beloved addressees is expressed in terms of the attributes of action ("love") of the elect poor toward God. So, the example argues that real wealth – being "rich in faith" – is synonymous with "loving God." While the theme (2.1) speaks of "holding the faith of our glorious Lord Jesus Christ," James 2.5 plays on the presumed unity of purpose and action between the Lord Jesus Christ and God (1.1) and exemplifies this by reminding the addressees of God's behavior (actions) toward the poor. God's action therefore functions as a precedent for the life and responsibilities of the brothers and sisters who "hold Jesus' faith." Thus, while the reasoning in 2.1–4 shows the elect community's "acts of partiality" toward the rich to be a perversion of justice, the restatement of the theme and its rationale in 2.5 proclaims God's actions toward the poor as a just/righteous judgment. Further, it argues that while God's honoring of the poor and Jesus' faith cohere, neither of the latter are what the world considers wise, just, and advantageous. At this point, the author has clearly set forth the principle upon which he differentiates "the poor" and "the rich."

Verses 6–7 embellish the argument from example (2.5). In the context of the statement that God has honored the poor, James 2.6a recycles the theme and rationale (2.1–4) in a statement of the opposite. The two rhetorical questions in 2.6b–7 embellish the opposition stated in 2.6a with a social example (παραβολή) about the rich, and, in so doing, they open "acts of partiality" to other and larger arenas of the community's life.

James 2.6a is the second non-interrogative sentence in the argument. As mentioned, it follows two successive questions about the poor (2.2–4, 5), and is, in turn, followed by two successive questions about the rich (2.6b, 7). With five words and one clause, 2.6a is the briefest and simplest sentence in the unit.

The formal distinctiveness and placement of this statement in the elaboration pattern suggest that it is peculiarly important. Its content reveals that it is one of the most significant statements in both the unit and the whole letter. First, while the interests and concerns of the poor are prominent throughout James (1.9–11, 27; 2.1–13, 15–16; 4.13–5.6), this is the last sentence in which the term πτωχός appears. Second, by employing the denominative verb, "to dishonor" (ἀτιμάζειν), and thus introducing the topic of "dishonor," (ἀτιμία), it levels a value judgment against the elect community (ὑμεῖς).

Here ὑμεῖς, the grammatical subject of the verb ἠτιμάσατε, functions as a vocative. Following 2.1 and 2.5, this is the third instance of direct address in the unit. The particular form of the personal pronoun (ὑμεῖς) occurs only once more, in James 5.8; there it also has vocative force, but follows the verb rather than preceding it as it does in 2.6b. As Ward (1966b, pp. 104–05) has correctly argued, "there is no reason why the 'you' in 2.6, 7 would be understood to be any other than the 'you' in the exhortation in 2.1, in the reproach in 2.4 or in the address of 2.5."

This indictment, an epideictic element, effectively restates the accusation in James 2.4. There the allegation connotes the topic of "injustice," which in rhetorical theory is a subtopic of "honor/ dishonor"; here the whole topic is broached. Thus, it argues that the behavior of the elect community toward the poor man is the conspicuous opposite of God's actions toward the poor in James 2.5. In the latter verse, the verbs ἐκλέγεσθαι and ἐπαγγέλλεσθαι essentially denote that God has honored the poor; on the other hand, both the phrase πλουσίους ἐν πίστει and the participial clause τοῖς ἀγαπῶσιν αὐτόν propose that the poor are those who honor God. Thus, James 2.6a uses the privative contrary of "honor" to accuse the "beloved brothers and sisters" not just of an attitude but of actions toward the poor (members of the community) that are opposed to God's attitude and action toward them.[57] While it bluntly accuses the addressees of dishonoring those whom

---

[57] This is indicated by the adversative particle δέ, which here suggests that the content of James 2.6a is opposed to the content of the previous statement in 2.5. See Smyth (1956, section 2834). Cf. Prov. 14.21; 22.22; and Sir. 10.22. On privative contraries (*privantia*; στεργτικά), see Cic. *Top.* 11.48; cf. *Boethius's De topicis differentiis* (Stump, 1978, pp. 66–67).

88   *The social rhetoric of James*

God has chosen and honored, the invective builds on the comparison in James 2.2–4, and brings to recognition that "the elect poor" have in effect chosen and honored the rich.[58] The linear development of the argument and the topical liaisons it presumes, creates, and amplifies, combine here to make this statement of the opposite a strong support for the thesis proposed (2.1).[59] In other words, the "faith of our glorious/honorable Lord Jesus Christ" is incompatible with acts that *dis*honor the poor whom God has chosen.

The rhetorical questions in 2.6b–7 form a social example about the rich. The sentences, which begin in the same way, are parallel and almost identical in length, are rational arguments. The first question is a compound sentence of eleven words; each of its two coordinate clauses has five words, comprising fourteen and twelve syllables, respectively. Precise or approximate equality measured by number of syllables is the rhetorical figure "parisosis" (παρίσωσις; *Rhet. Her.* 4.20.27).[60] The second question is a complex sentence of ten words in two clauses; the main clause precedes its subordinate clause, which consists of an articular aorist passive participle (τὸ ἐπικληθέν) with complement. The repetition of the negative particle and personal pronouns (οὐχ ... ὑμῶν ... αὐτοὶ ... ὑμᾶς ...; οὐκ αὐτοὶ ... ὑμᾶς;) is the figure "transplacement" (*traductio*); this is a passionate figure and the emphasis is unmistakable (*Rhet. Her.* 4.14.20–21; Denniston, [1952] 1979, pp. 80–81).

Though the term "wisdom" (σοφία) is not mentioned here, the questions certainly appeal to practical wisdom, and they expect an affirmative answer.[61] Conventionally, wisdom, "the knowledge of what is good, what is bad and what is neither good nor bad" (Cic. *Inv. Rhet.* 2.52.160), was considered to be a fundamental topic in deliberative discourse (*Rhet. Her.* 3.2.3). Because wisdom by its very definition was understood to be conducive to the "expedient" and thus to "happiness," an argument from wisdom was a natural

---

58 Such "frankness of speech" is the rhetorical figure *parresia*; see *Rhet. Her.* 4.35.48; and Quint. 9.2.27; 9.3.99. On this topic, see Malherbe (1970 and 1989b).
59 On the conepts of "linearity" and "liaison" in rhetoric, see G. A. Kennedy (1984, pp. 5–6, 146–47), and Perelman (1982, in his "Index," *s.v.* "liaisons").
60 Some rhetoricians distinguish between "isocolon," precise equality, and "parisosis," approximate equality; see Demetr. *Eloc.* 25; and Volkmann ([1885] 1987, p. 82).
61 The distinction between σοφία, "theoretical wisdom," and φρόνησις, "practical reason," is not operative in the NT and early Christian literature. On this see Arist. *Eth. Nic.* 6.5.1–13.8, and J. P. Hershbell's discussion of Plut. *Mor.* 440D-452D (in Betz, 1978, esp. pp. 158–60). Also see U. Wilckens, *TDNT* vii.496–528; G. Bertram, *TDNT* ix.220–35.

topic in any effort to persuade an audience toward advantage or to dissuade them from disadvantage (Arist. *Rhet*. 1.9.13; *Eth. Nic.* 6.12.1–6). Here the topic of wisdom undergirds the author's accusations against the rich. Further, the topics advantage/disadvantage are clearly in view. At the same time, playing upon the fact that God, who is supremely wise and just (cf. James 1.5, 12, 13, 17, 20; 2.5; 3.17–18) has chosen the poor, wisdom suggests that honoring the rich and dishonoring the poor is neither wise nor just but clearly disadvantageous.

The three accusations against "the rich" (οἱ πλούσιοι) are interesting: they oppress (καταδυναστεύουσιν) the elect poor; they drag them into courts (ἕλκουσιν ... εἰς κριτήρια); and they blaspheme (βλασφημοῦσιν) the honorable name which was pronounced over the community. The first two accusations apparently refer to socio-economic injustices perpetrated by the rich against the poor; compare James 5.1–6. While the third allegation against the rich has religious overtones, Ropes (1916, p. 196) correctly says that this does not necessitate the idea of a religious persecution. The reference to the honorable (καλόν) name which was pronounced (ἐπικληθέν) over the community invokes the topic of the "noble/honorable," and reiterates the theme of election (Ward, 1966b, p. 104). In the present context "the honorable name" probably means the name of Jesus, and recollects James 2.1 (cf. Acts 9.15; Pol. *Phil*. 6.3; *Herm. Sim*. 8.10.3; 9.12.4; 9.13.2; Dibelius, 1975, p. 141; Mußner, 1987, p. 122; Davids, 1982, p. 113). And, as others have argued, it is possible that the aorist participle (τὸ ἐπικληθέν) refers to baptism (cf. Acts 2.38; 10.48; cf. *Herm. Sim*. 8.1.1; 8.6.4; Mayor, 1892 [1990], p. 89; Dibelius, 1975, p. 141; Mußner, 1987, pp. 122–23; Laws, 1980, p. 105; Davids, 1982, p. 113). Why the rich "speak against" or "slander" (βλασφημοῦσιν) the name of Jesus is not disclosed.

It should be observed here that the "example" in James 2.6b–7 functions in a way that is typical of social examples that are used as supporting proof for a deliberative thesis. That is, verses 6b–7 expand the understanding of "acts of partiality" in the theme (2.1) and rationale (2.2–4) by referring this behavior to a broader arena of relationships. The theme and rationale, and even the argument from the opposite (2.6a) located "partialities" within the community of "the elect poor"; the social example here finds "unjust judgments" against the (elect) poor in the larger spheres of life, in the socio-economic arena (2.6b) and in the arena of religion (2.7).

With the two questions in James 2.6b–7, the author tries to persuade his audience to recognize that the rich are their enemies. Concomitantly, this move promotes the peculiar identity and solidarity of the elect community against rich outsiders, just as it also establishes the honor and good will of the speaker (Cic. *Inv. Rhet.* 1.16.22). On the other hand, it solicits a change in the community's attitude and behavior. The questions about the rich offer solid support for the prohibition in James 2.1.

4 Argument from judgment, based on the written law, in four parts[62]

a. Proposition based on the written law

James 2.8 Εἰ μέντοι (νόμον τελεῖτε βασιλικὸν) (κατὰ τὴν γραφήν·) *ἀγαπήσεις τὸν πλησίον σου ὡς σεαυτόν*, καλῶς ποιεῖτε·

If you really fulfill the royal law according to the scripture: "You shall love your neighbor as yourself," you do honorably;

b. Argument from the contrary

James 2.9 εἰ δὲ προσωπολημπτεῖτε, ἁμαρτίαν ἐργάζεσθε ἐλεγχόμενοι ὑπὸ τοῦ νόμου ὡς παραβάται.

But if you show partiality, you commit sin and are convicted by the law as transgressors.

The text

In verse 8 the words νόμον τελεῖτε βασιλικόν are rearranged (in 04 and a few other manuscripts) as νόμον βασιλικὸν τελεῖτε; in the minuscule 1241 they are replaced with λόγον Βασιλικὸν λαλεῖτε. The first alternative seeks to avoid the hyperbaton between the noun νόμον and its adjective βασιλικόν; the second alternative, which follows the word order of the previous varaint, retains the

[62] While *Rhet. Her.* 4.43.56 suggests following the argument from comparison or social example with an argument from "historical example," James follows the argument from social example (2.6b–7) with a four-part argument from judgment (2.8–11). See *Rhet. Her.* 2.29.46, where the argument from historical example is followed with an argument from judgment. The pattern of argument was flexible and allowed adaptation.

adjective but substitutes another noun and corresponding verb, and thus appears to be an assimilation to the mention of λόγος in James 1.22, 23 and λαλεῖτε in 2.12. See also Romans 13.9 which introduces the scripture (LXX Lev. 19.18) cited in James 2.8 with the phrase ἐν τῷ λόγῳ τούτῳ (cf. Matt. 22.39).

Some witnesses (322, 323, the Latin Vulgate, more than one Sahidic manuscript, and the Bohairic tradition) replace the citation formula κατὰ τὴν γραφήν with κατὰ τὰς γραφάς. This emendation may be an assimilation to 1 Corinthians 15.3, 4, which features the only other occurrences of κατὰ τὰς γραφάς in the NT, and in that context "James" is mentioned as an apostle (1 Cor. 15.7). The omission of the citation formula (in the first hand of the minuscule 623 and a few others) may be based on the citation attributed to Jesus in Matthew 22.39.

The analysis

Verses 2.8–9 are the first two parts of a four-part argument from judgment in the written law. The following analysis will show that 2.8 continues the elaboration by introducing a key proposition that is based on the written law; verse 9, as we shall see, essentially introduces the contrary of the proposition in verse 8.

That James 2.8 continues the elaboration is clearly indicated by the emphatic conjunction μέντοι ("indeed, really"). The only other emphatic use of μέντοι in the NT occurs in Jude 8; elsewhere, it is used adversatively (John 4.27; 7.13; 12.42; 20.5; 21.4; 2 Tim. 2.19; see Dana and Mantey, 1927, section 233; and BDF section 450.1). Moreover, this conjunction specifically recalls the indictment in verse 2.6a, which, referring to the social examples in 2.2–4 and 2.6b–7, suggests that the elect poor show partiality to the rich. While Dibelius (1975, p. 142) understood μέντοι to refer to verses 6a and 6b–7, he did not see it referring to the social example in 2.2–4. He held that the latter example is "out of the picture" when we reach James 2.5 (p. 135). With that assumption Dibelius errs, for James 2.2–4 is crucial to the entire unit.

The argument here is advanced in the form of a present simple or first class conditional sentence, which assumes the reality of its condition, states it as a fact, and makes a straightforward assertion (Smyth, 1956, section 298; Robertson and Davis, 1985, sections 436–37; cf. BDF section 371.1). The judgment, which is introduced in a substantive clause of direct discourse by the citation formula, κατὰ τὴν γραφήν, is properly a judgment based on the written law. In addition to James 2.8, the term γραφή occurs in 2.23 (ἡ γραφὴ ἡ λέγουσα) and in 4.5 (ἡ γραφὴ λέγει). All three instances are "citation formulas"; James 2.8 quotes Leviticus 19.18; 2.23 cites Genesis 15.6; and the citation in 4.5 is unknown, perhaps extracanonical (see Popkes, 1986, pp. 125–88; esp. his chapter on "Die Bergpredigt-Tradition," pp. 156–76; and Deppe, 1989, pp. 31–54).

The "royal law" (νόμον βασιλικὸν), as Ropes and Dibelius argued, is probably best understood as a reference to the whole law. On the one hand, this is supported by the fact that νόμος is regularly used as a reference to the law as a whole, while ἐντολή ("commandment") is the customary term for a precept of the law. Further, the context seems to corroborate this understanding of νόμος, since James 2.10 expressly addresses the relationship between "the whole law" and "one" of its precepts (Dibelius, 1975, p. 142; Ropes, 1916, p. 198; and see Betz, 1985a, p. 48 note 44, in reference to Matt 5.17, 18; 7.12). Moroever, of the ten times that James uses the term νόμος, not one suggests anything other than the law in its unity and entirety (cf. James 1.25; 2.8, 9, 10, 11, 12; 4.11 [4x]).

Though the translation and interpretation of the adjective βασιλικός is debated (see Dibelius, 1975, pp. 142–43; Adamson, 1976, pp. 114–15; and Ward, 1966b, pp. 134–36), it is most likely correct to render it as "royal." Thus the law is called βασιλικόν "probably not because of its transcending significance but because it is given by the king (of the kingdom [James 2.5], namely, God)."[63] As an "honorific" epithet, signifying the source and status of the whole law, βασιλικός certainly coheres with the references to God in James 2.11 (ὁ εἰπὼν· . . . , εἶπεν; Laws, 1980, pp. 114–15) and in James 4.12a (εἷς ἐστιν ὁ νομοθέτης καὶ κριτής) as the one source and authority behind both the individual commandments (2.11), as well as the law in its entirety (2.10). Ropes (1916, p. 198) argued that the adjective is simply a "decorative epithet," but in the present context it is much more. After the example in James 2.5, which mentions the βασιλεία that God has promised to those who love him, this inventive reference, νόμον βασιλικὸν, suggests both that the law originates with God and that it is also applicable to his kingdom. In other words, God's law is the law of God's kingdom.

---

[63] BAGD, *s.v.*, refers to Dit., Or. 483.1; BGU 820.2; 1074.15; 1 Esdr. 8.24; 2 Macc. 3.13; see MM, *s.v.* Thus also Deissmann (1927, p. 362 note 5); and K. L. Schmidt, *TDNT* I.591.

It follows that those who love God, οἱ κληρονόμοι τῆς βασιλείας (James 2.5), are to fulfill (τελεῖν[64]) the νόμον βασιλικόν.

The logic in James 2.8 is simple and straightforward: if the antecedent is so, then the consequent is so. This kind of argument is, according to Cicero, what ancient logicians and rhetoricians called "first form of conclusion" (*Top.* 13.54), or *modus ponendo tollens* (Hurley, 1985, pp. 266–72). Theon calls this a syllogism, and it is essentially a constructive hypothetical syllogism (in Butts, 1987, pp. 197–98, 235–36). The argument runs: if X is so, then q is so; X is so; therefore, q is so. Moreover, the rhetorical handbooks and *progymnasmata* tirelessly demonstrate that students learned to invent, arrange, linearly amplify, and "work out" such obviously logical arguments with just those *topoi* that they believed were pertinent to their persuasive purposes.

Having said this, we turn to the logic behind the argument adduced in James 2.8. Presumably, the author understands both the antecedent and consequent to be true. In conventional rhetorical fashion he elaborates the consequent in terms of "the noble/ honorable" (τὸ καλόν), which, as we are discovering, is a deliberative topic very important to the letter of James. Here the quality of "honor" is attributed to "fulfilling the royal law," that is, to "loving one's neighbor as oneself."[65] This coheres with the "honorable" or "royal" quality (βασιλικός) of the law itself, just as it also reflects the nobility of the lawgiver (God; James 2.11; 4.12). Further, as James 2.5 suggests, the "rich in faith" who will inherit God's kingdom should be dealt with "honorably."

The ways in which the author employs the topic of the "honorable," especially in his usage of the adverb καλῶς, shows that he is quite aware that "honor" is a variously defined value.[66] For example, in James 2.19 it says, "You believe that God is one; you do honorably (καλῶς). Even the demons believe and shudder." Given the progression of the text, the author allows, at least for the

---

[64] On τελεῖν ("to fulfill"), see G. Delling, *TDNT* VIII.49–87; and the discussion of James 2.10, below.

[65] The "lawful/unlawful" is a topic of "justice/injustice," and both of the latter are topics of "the honorable/dishonorable." Cic. *Inv. Rhet.* 2.53.160.

[66] The term καλῶς ("honorably, well") occurs 3x in James: 2.3, 8, 19. See also καλός ("honorable, good") 3x: 2.7, 3.13; 4.17; and cf. also ἀγαθός ("good") 2x: 1.17; 3.17, and their opposites: κακία ("wickedness, dishonor, shame") 1.21; κακός ("bad, evil, wicked") 2x: 1.13; 3.8; πονηρός ("bad, evil, wicked") 2x: 2.4; 4.16. For the "honorable" see *Rhet. Her.* 3.2.3–4.7.

sake of argument, that one may indeed believe and do that which is really honorable and yet fail to fulfill the royal law. Moreover, given, in James 2.3, the honorable treatment of the wealthy man and the dishonorable treatment of the poor man, the text implies that there may be some who hold as honorable that which is really unjust and evil (2.4). In any case, the reference to the honorable in James 2.8 recalls the behavior in 2.2–3, as well as the previous indictments of such behavior in 2.4, 6a, and now qualifies such actions as the opposite of "loving one's neighbor as oneself."

From this the logic behind the statement in James 2.8 may be stated syllogistically, as follows:

Major premise: People who fulfill the royal law are people who do honorably (καλῶς).
Minor premise: People who love their neighbors as themselves are people who fulfill the royal law.
Conclusion: People who love their neighbors as themselves are people who do honorably.

That this is so will be made even clearer as the elaboration continues.

The judgment in James 2.9 is similar to the one in James 2.8 in several respects. It is a maxim in the form of a present simple or first class conditional sentence: introduced by εἰ, the verb in both its protasis and apodosis is in the indicative mood. It is also a hypothetical syllogism, a logical, "first form of conclusion" argument (Cic. *Top.* 13.54). Utilizing the figures of "epanaphora" and "homoeoteleuton," the successive verses 2.8 and 9 begin with the same word (εἰ/εἰ) and end with similar sounds (ποιεῖτε/παραβάται).[67] Further, each of the two verses has three clauses, and though their clauses are unequal in length – James 2.8 has thirty-five syllables; James 2.9 has thirty-one – their sentences are parisonic.[68] As their conjunctions (μέντοι ... δέ, respectively) suggest the two maxims express a contrast (cf. Ropes, 1916, p. 198) and, structurally speaking, the two clauses in the protasis of James 2.8 are evenly weighted by the two clauses in the apodosis of James

[67] On "epanaphora" (ἐπαναφορά, *repetitio*) see *Rhet. Her.* 4.13.19, and Demetr. *Eloc.* 268, who uses ἀναφορά and ἐπαναφορά synonymously. See Denniston ([1952] 1979, pp. 84–87). On "homoeoteleuton," see Quint. 9.3.77.
[68] Arist. *Rhet.* 3.9.9; [*Rh. Al.*] 27.1435b.39–1436a.1–4; *Rhet. Her.* 4.20.27; cf. Demetr. *Eloc.* 25; and Volkmann ([1885] 1987, p. 82).

2.9, giving the expressed contrast a balanced form. Finally, an examination of the content of these maxims discloses that they are antithetically related; though formally similar to verse 8, James 2.9 is an argument from the opposite.[69]

Adjoining contrary judgments like this is standard procedure in deliberative discourse (Arist. *Rhet.* 1.3.1, προτροπή καὶ ἀποτροπή). According to Aristotle, "this kind of style is pleasing, because contraries are easily understood," especially "when they are placed side by side" (*Rhet.* 3.9.8). In other words, reasoning by contraries leads to immediately obvious conclusions. To paraphrase Aristotle, if some quality is said to belong to a thing, it is confirmed when the opposite quality belongs to things contrary; so, it is denied when the opposite quality does not belong to the things being opposed (Arist. *Rhet.* 2.23.1).

Thus in adducing προσωπολημπτεῖν as the contrary of τελεῖν νόμον βασιλικὸν κατὰ τὴν γραφήν· ἀγαπήσεις τὸν πλησίον σου ὡς σεαυτόν, the logic holds that ἁμαρτίαν ἐργάζεσθαι ἐλεγχόμενοι ὑπὸ τοῦ νόμου ὡς παραβάται, which is predicated of προσω-πολημπτεῖν, cannot be predicated of τελεῖν νόμον βασιλικὸν κατὰ τὴν γραφήν· κτλ. Likewise, ποιεῖν καλῶς, which is the predicate of τελεῖν νόμον βασιλικὸν κατὰ τὴν γραφήν· κτλ. but also the contrary of ἁμαρτίαν ἐργάζεσθαι ἐλεγχόμενοι κτλ., cannot be predicated of προσωπολημπτεῖν.

Juxtaposing two antithetical maxims, both of which are themselves syllogisms, suggests that the maxims function like the premises in an enthymeme. Again, this is rudimentary, for the topic of opposites or contraries was customarily used to construct enthymemes (Cic. *Top.* 13.55).[70] An enthymematic structure normally has a conclusion and a premise. Here, however, we have the premises without their conclusion (see G. A. Kennedy, 1991, p. 298). The explanation, again, is that when reasoning from contraries, especially from juxtaposed contraries, the conclusion is an immediate inference; it is obvious. Therefore, as Cicero says, "one may dispense with the conclusion" (*Inv. Rhet.* 1.40.73). In this case, the immediate inference (the conclusion) is "If you show

[69] On the "parallelism" and "balance" of antithetic cola and clauses, see Adams ([1905] 1950, pp. 347–48).

[70] According to Quintilian (5.10.2), "you will find that a majority are of the opinion that an enthymeme is a conclusion from incompatibles: wherefore Cornificius [*Rhet. Her.* 4.18.25] styles it a *contrarium* or argument from contraries." This is cited in the Loeb edition of *Rhet. Her.* (p. 292 note *b*). Cf. Arist. *Rhet.* 2.23.1.

partiality, you do not fulfill the royal law according to the scripture, 'You shall love your neighbor as yourself.' "[71]

Here we also underscore the maxim's twofold or compound predication of προσωπολημπτεῖν; that is, ὁ προσωπολημπτῶν both "commits sin" and "is convicted by the law as a transgressor." As Peter Davids correctly points out, the second attribution is like an appositive to the first (Davids, 1982, p. 115). There is a reason for this rhetorical expansion. By introducing the second consequent (ἐλεγχόμενοι ὑπὸ τοῦ νόμου ὡς παραβάται) as an adjunct to the first (ἁμαρτίαν ἐργάζεσθε), the maxim sets forth two unlawful and dishonorable attributes of action that the elaboration will later develop and corroborate. On the one hand, the elaboration will argue that in προσωπολημπτεῖν and in ἁμαρτίαν ἐργάζεσθαι one fails to keep the whole law in one of its points or commandments; in particular, one fails to fulfill the love-command. On the other hand, as the juxtaposition of verses 8 and 9 has already made clear, since προσωπολημπτεῖν is "sin," and obviously a failure to fulfill the whole law, the elaboration will argue that ὁ προσωπολημπτῶν is "guilty of all the law."

Here, given the form and content of the maxim in James 2.9, and the way in which it is introduced, we conclude that it is not presented as a judgment (or quotation) from the written law; rather it is adduced as a judgment that is based upon the written scriptural summary of the law cited in James 2.8. To put it differently, James 2.9 is an interpretation of the love-command (see Quint. 7.8.3; cf. 3.6.43).

With the verb προσωπολημπτεῖν ("to show partiality") James 2.9 specifically recalls the thesis in James 2.1, that προσωπολημψίαι ("acts of partiality") are incompatible with Jesus' faith.[72] In so doing, this judgment concomitantly suggests an intimate connection between holding Jesus' faith (2.1) and fulfilling the royal law (2.8), for προσωπολημτεῖν is contrary to both. As with the maxim in James 2.1, here also in James 2.9, the subtopics of honor/ dishonor amplify the statement. For, in maintaining that to show

[71] The apparent argument restated in categorical form is as follows: (Major premise): All who really fulfill the royal law according to the scripture . . . , do honorably; (Minor premise): No one who shows partiality, does honorably; (Conclusion, unstated): No one who shows partiality really fulfills the royal law according to the scripture . . .

[72] The repetition προσωπολημψίας/προσωπολημπτεῖν (2.1,9) is the rhetorical figure "transplacement" (Quint. 9.3.41–42).

partiality is to commit "sin" (ἁμαρτίαν[73]) and "be convicted" (ἐλεγχόμενοι[74]) by the law (ὑπὸ τοῦ νόμου[75]) as a "transgressor" (παραβάτης[76]), the judgment clearly asserts that such behavior is shameful and unlawful.

Let us look more closely at the ways in which James employs these terms. The extremely important noun ἁμαρτία ("sin") occurs seven times. It appears twice in the letter-*confirmatio*: first in 2.9, then in 4.17. The latter occurrences are "linearly" related to its first appearances (twice in 1.15) in the letter-*narratio*, thus recalling and specifically carrying forward the negative consequent of the "trial of faith" (1.3, 12). The "trial of faith" is also reiterated in the three, final, occurrences of ἁμαρτία in the letter-*conclusio* (5.15, 16, 20). Closely related to ἁμαρτία is the the verb ἐργάζεσθαι ("to work, do, perform"), which is used twice: first, in conjunction with δικαιοσύνη (the contrary of ἁμαρτία) in James 1.20; then here in 2.9 with reference to the "law."[77] James employs ἐλέγκειν ("to expose, convict") only here, as an anarthrous present passive participle that concerns the adjuncts and consequence of the action, "you commit sin" (ἁμαρτίαν ἐργάζεσθε; see Mayor, 1892 [1990], p. ccxxxii).[78]

Similarly, as in the social examples of James 2.2–3 and 6b–7, where the topics of advantage/ disadvantage are so conspicuous, they are here, too. Since showing partiality is "committing sin," and earlier we learned that "sin" – the mainspring of which is one's own desire for evil things (1.13–14) – results in death (1.15), the topics in James 2.9 expand the notion that "partialities" manifest "evil calculations" (2.4) and propose that they are deadly

---

[73] See the cognate noun ἁμαρτωλός ("sinner") 2x: James 4.8; 5.20.

[74] This evokes the topics of "shame" (αἰσχύν; Arist. *Rhet.* 2.6) and "dishonor" (περὶ ἀδοξίας; *Rhet.* 2.6.14).

[75] The prepositional phrase ὑπὸ τοῦ νόμου ("by, under the agency of") personifies the "law" as an external agent; see Smyth (1956, section 1698.b note 1; Mayor (1892 [1990], p. ccxxviii). James uses the prep. ὑπό ("by, under") 7x: with the gen. 5x (1.14; 2.9; 3.4 [2x], 6), and 2x with the acc. (2.3; 5.12).

[76] The noun παραβάτης ("transgressor") is infrequent in the NT, occurring only 5x: Paul uses it 3x (Rom. 2.25, 27; Gal. 2.18); it appears in James 2x, only in our unit (2.9, 11). See BAGD, *s.v.* Like the terms ἁμαρτία and ἐλέγκειν, with which James associates it, παραβάτης evokes the topic "shame." See Schneider, *TDNT* v.740–42.

[77] See the cognate nouns ἔργον ("work, deed"; 15x: 1.4, 25; 2.14, 17, 18 (3x), 20, 21, 22 (2x), 24, 25, 26; 3.13) and ἐργάτης ("worker"; 5.4).

[78] Elsewhere in the NT, ἐλέγκειν occurs 16x (Matt 18.15; Luke 3.19; John 3.20a; 8.46; 16.8; Eph. 5.11,13; 1 Tim. 5.20; 2 Tim. 4.2; Tit. 1.9, 13; 2.15; Heb. 12.5; Jude 15; Rev. 3.19). Cf. *Herm Vis.* 1.1.5; Philo *Jos.* 48.

actions that should be avoided. Drawing on the topics of the "unlawful," "shame," and "dishonor," the intent of James 2.9 is clearly related to the negative end of symbouleutic rhetoric, the "harmful" (τὸ βλαβερόν; Arist. *Rhet*. 1.3.5), which is featured in dissuasion.

To know how the topics functioned in rhetorical theory and Hellenistic moral philosophy is to understand James' use of the topics (see L. T. Johnson, 1983; and 1985, p. 168; also Wuellner, 1978b). The logic and topics in James 2.9 are very persuasive support for the thesis in James 2.1.

4 Argument from judgment, based on the written law, in four parts (continued):

c. Rationale for judgment based on the law.

James 2.10 ὅστις γὰρ ὅλον τὸν νόμον τηρήσῃ πταίσῃ δὲ ἐν ἑνί, (γέγονεν πάντων ἔνοχος).

For whoever keeps the whole law but fails in one point has become guilty of all of it.

d. Confirmation of the rationale, using written testimony.

James 2.11 ὁ γὰρ εἰπών· (*μὴ μοιχεύσῃς*, εἶπεν καί· *μὴ φονεύσῃς*)· εἰ δὲ οὐ μοιχεύεις φονεύεις δέ, γέγονας παραβάτης νόμου.

For the one who said: "Do not commit adultery," also said: "Do not commit murder." Now if you do not commit adultery but you do commit murder, you have become a transgressor of the law.

The text

In verse 10 the aorist active subjunctive 3rd singular τηρήσῃ is replaced: first, with the future active indicative τηρήσει (in 025 and the Majority text); second, by τελέσει, the future active indicative of τελεῖν (in 044, 81, 945, 1241, 1739 with negligible variations, 2298, and other witnesses); third, by πληρώσει, the future active indicative of πληροῦν (in 02, several minuscules and other manuscripts); and fourth, by πληρῶσας (the aorist active participle nominative masculine singular) with the τελέσει. All of these emendations are easily explained as arising from the established text. In particular, they are most probably due to ὅστις without ἄν (Dibelius, 1975, p. 144 note 109; see Smyth, 1956, sections 2327, 2339, and 2567b, on the omission of ἄν in the protasis of conditional and conditional relative sentences; cf. Mayor, 1892 [1990], p. 402; and BDF section 380.4).

Next, in similar fashion, several manuscripts (025, 044, the Majority text, and more than one Latin Vulgate manuscript) replace the aorist active subjunctive 3rd singular πταίσῃ for either the future active indicative πταίσει, or the second aorist active subjunctive πέσῃ (in 614 with minor variations, 2495, and a few others). Finally, the words γέγονεν πάντων ἔνοχος are replaced (in the uncial 044) with πάντων ἔνοχος ἔσται. The rearranged word order, the substitution of εἰμί for γίνομαι, as well as the change of tense (from γέγονεν, a perfect active indicative, to ἔσται, a future active indicative) are, like the previous readings, secondary alterations of the established text.

There are four alternative readings for verse 11. First, several witnesses (04, 614, 630, and several other minuscules) read φονεύσῃς . . . μοιχεύσῃς. This variant appears to be an effort to adjust the order of the commandments to that in the Masoretic text (Exod. 20.13, 14, "murder . . . adultery"; cf. Matt. 5.21, 27 [*Sondergut*]; Mark 10.19 // Matt. 19.18; *Did.* 2.2a). Second, the negative particle μή is replaced by οὐ (in 044, 614, 630, 1505, 2464, 2495, and other manuscripts). Third, the second aorist indicative ἐγένου replaces the second perfect indicative γέγονας (in Papyrus[74], 02, and 33). Fourth, (in Papyrus[74] and 02) παραβάτης is replaced by ἀποστάτης, "apostate, rebel," which occurs nowhere in the NT, though knowledge of the term may be presupposed for the use of both ἀποστασία ("rebellion, abandonment") and ἀποστάσιον ("a divorce"). Cf. 2 Maccabees 5.8; Acts 21.21 (see BAGD, *s.v.* ἀποστασία; *LPGL, s.v.*; H. Schlier, *TDNT* I.513–14). All four variant readings are secondary emendations.

The analysis

Verses 10 and 11 are the final two parts of the four-part argument from judgment based on the written law. James 2.10 states the rationale for judgment based on the law; 2.11 then confirms the rationale, corroborating it with written testimony.

Like the judgments in James 2.8–9, verse 10 is a conditional sentence. But whereas verses 8 and 9 present first class conditional sentences, the maxim in James 2.10 is functionally equivalent to a third class condition. This complex relative sentence has thirteen words in two clauses. The protasis (ὅστις γὰρ .. ἐνί) is an indefinite relative clause with a compound predicate of two aorist subjunctive verbs (τηρήσῃ πταίσῃ δὲ); accordingly, it may be resolved into an "if clause," in which the indefinite pronoun ὅστις ("whoever") corresponds to εἴ τις, "if anyone" (Smyth, 1956, section 2560). The apodosis (γέγονεν πάντων ἔνοχος) is marked by a proleptic or futuristic use of a perfect indicative verb (γέγονας). Thus this conditional relative sentence corresponds to a more vivid future conditional sentence. The supposition is viewed as a probable case, and the sentence makes a generalizing assertion or rule (Smyth, 1956, sections 2321–26, esp. 2322). Though the form in which 2.10 is presented is different, the maxim is a syllogistic or "first form of conclusion" argument, as are those in verses 8 and 9.

As the causal conjunction γάρ suggests, James 2.10 provides the reason for the judgment in James 2.9; thus the elaboration moves forward by deduction: verses 9 and 10 form an enthymeme. Verse 10, the broad general rule, is the major premise, verse 9 the conclusion; the minor premise is tacitly assumed. Note that just as verse 8 is the major premise in an enthymeme with verse 9, verse 10 is also the major premise in an enthymeme with verse 9. We may reformulate this enthymeme as follows:

Major premise (2.10):	Whoever keeps the whole law but fails in one point is guilty of (the whole law[79]).
Minor premise (unstated):	If you show partiality, you fail in one point of the law.
Conclusion (2.9):	If you show partiality, you commit sin and are convicted by the law as a transgressor.

[79] On the phrase πάντων ἔνοχος ("of the whole [law]"), see LSJ, *s.v.* "πᾶς." Πάντων is neuter [as is ἐν ἑνί], and the genitive, as in classical Greek, denotes the crime. This is a rhetorical way of saying that he is a transgressor of "the law as a whole . . ., not of all the precepts in it" (Ropes, 1916, pp. 199–200). Πᾶς occurs 12x: James 1.2, 5, 8, 17 (2x), 19, 21; 2.10; 3.7, 16; 4.16; 5.12; on its use, see Mayor (1892 [1990], pp. clxvi–clxvii). The term ἔνοχος ("liable/ subject to, guilty") is used only in 2.10; and εἷς ('one') 3x: 2.10; 2.19; 4.12.

Comparing the structure and content of the major premise with the conclusion shows that failure "in one point" of the law and being "guilty" of the whole law is the parallel equivalent to committing "sin" and being "convicted by the law as a transgressor." Also, it shows that "to commit sin" is functionally equivalent to "failure in one point of the law," and also that "to commit sin and be convicted by the law as a transgressor" is an amplified tautology for "is guilty of the whole law." Consequently, verse 9 could just as easily have read, "If you show partiality, you are guilty of the whole law." Similarly, verse 10 could have read, "Whoever keeps the whole law but fails in one point of it commits sin and is convicted by the law as a transgressor." In each of the latter reformulations the meaning of verses 9 and 10 is unchanged.

Why, then, does the author state these maxims as he does? We have already seen that the maxim in verse 9 is emphatically formulated as the contrary of verse 8, making it obvious that "if you show partiality, you do not fulfill the *royal* (or *whole*) law." The present form of verse 10 is determined by the fact that it serves as the major premise for two logical deductions in the unit. Again, we have seen that, as the general premise of the enthymeme it forms with verse 9, James 2.10 brings out the opposition between "being guilty of the whole law" and "fulfilling the *whole* (*royal*) law." As we shall see momentarily, verse 10 also serves as the major premise of the epicheireme it makes with verse 11.

The maxim in James 2.10 is essentially a judgment based on the law. It states the well-known hermeneutical rule that God's law is a complete whole, the unity of which is derived from the fact that the law-giver is one (cf. James 2.19b and 4.12ab; see Mayor, 1892 [1990], p. 403). In James 2.11 the elaboration will paraphrastically reiterate this conception: ὁ γὰρ εἰπών. κτλ., εἶπεν καί· κτλ. (James 2.11a–d).

The judgment in verse 11 is introduced as the citation of an authority, namely, God, who, in the author's mind, is the one law-giver and judge (James 4.12; on the citation of an "authority," *auctoritas*, see Quint. 5.11.36; Lausberg, 1973, vol. I, section 426). The citation formulas (ὁ εἰπών, εἶπεν καί, apparently rhetorical "periphrasis," *circumitio*, for "God"; Quint. 8.6.59) and the two commandments from the decalogue they introduce indicate that this is also a judgment from the written law, as is James 2.8.

Though the six clauses in James 2.11 are punctuated as one sentence, it is best to approach the verse as two complex sentences. James 2.11a–d features two coordinated independent clauses (2.11a, c), each of which has a subordinate clause of direct narration (2.11b, d). James 2.11e–f is a present simple conditional sentence (εἰ . . .); the protasis features a compound predicate of two present indicative verbs (μοιχεύεις φονεύεις δέ) and in the apodosis the predicate is formed by a second perfect indicative verb (γέγονας). Here, the commandments are cited as "words of God," and this form of citation reminds the audience that all the commandments in the law are God's authoritative words.

Just as the judgment in James 2.10 is marked as the reason for the judgment in James 2.9, this one (James 2.11) is marked by the causal conjunction γάρ as the corroborating basis for 2.10. But here, as was mentioned above, the deductive argument in 2.10–11 is an epicheireme: both the premises and the conclusion are stated.[80] James 2.10 again serves as the major premise; 2.11a–d is the minor premise; and 2.11e–f the conclusion.

The judgment in James 2.11e–f is a present simple conditional sentence, as are verses 8–9. And, like the latter, it is a first form of conclusion argument. James 2.11a–d, on the other hand, is the only judgment in the series (verses 8–11) that is not a conditional sentence. While it artfully reminds the audience that all the commandments in the law come from one authoritative source, it also makes precise two points of the whole law that are particularized in the conclusion (James 2.11e–f). Ward is correct to suggest that the injunctions against "adultery" and "murder" in James 2.11 may not be "chosen at random" but deliberately; "if μοιχεύειν and φονεύειν are read according to their figurative meanings," they are "well chosen and well ordered for the context" (1966b, p. 152; see pp. 149–52).[81] The epicheireme may be reformulated as follows:

Major premise: Whoever keeps the whole law but fails in one
                  point has become guilty of (the whole law).

[80] On the epicheireme, see Quint. 5.10.1–7; 5.14.4; G. A. Kennedy (1984, pp. 17, 90, 148); Lausberg (1973, vol. I, sections 357, 371); J. Martin (1974, pp. 102, 103, 105–6); Volkmann ([1885] 1987, p. 194).

[81] Also sensitive to the figurative use of terminology in James are L. T. Johnson (1985; see pp. 169–70, on μοιχαλίδες [James 4.4]); Mußner (1987, pp. 125–26); and Davids (1982, p. 117). For a different opinion, see Dibelius (1975, p. 147 note 121); and Laws (1980, p. 113).

Minor premise: God [who gave the whole law[82]] said: "Do not
                 commit adultery"; he also said, "Do not kill."
Conclusion: If you do not commit adultery but you do kill,
                 you have become a transgressor of the law (= you
                 have become guilty of the whole law).

Analogous to the enthymeme in James 2.9, 10, we find here that
πταίσῃ δὲ ἐν ἑνί, γέγονεν πάντων ἔνοχος (2.10b–c) is the parallel
equivalent to φονεύεις δέ, γέγονας παραβάτης νόμου (2.11e–f).[83]
Both are functionally equivalent to προσωπολημπτεῖτε, ἁμαρτίαν
ἐργάζεσθε ἐλεγχόμενοι ὑπὸ τοῦ νόμου ὡς παραβάται (2.9), which
is the opposite of James 2.8.

Before turning to the conclusion of the elaboration, let us
summarize the use of the judgments in James 2.8–11. First, these
four verses comprise five complex sentences which advance seven
judgments (five are stated, two are unstated). Second, two of the
judgments are introduced with citational formulas (verses 8 and
11a, c);[84] three are presented without such formulas (verses 9, 10,
11e–f). Third, with the exception of James 2.11a and c, all the
judgments are presented in conditional sentences: three are present
simple conditionals (verses 8, 9, 11e–f); one is a conditional relative
sentence (verse 10). Fourth, four of the judgments are themselves
syllogistic or first form of conclusion arguments (verses 8, 9, 10,
11e–f); one is a declarative sentence (verse 11a–d). Fifth, the
arguments form two enthymemes (verses 8/9; verses 9/10), and one
epicheireme (verses 10/11). Sixth, the two unstated judgments are
the conclusion of the enthymeme in verses 8/9, and the minor
premise of the enthymeme in verses 9/10, respectively. Seventh, while
verse 8 serves as the major premise of the deductive argument in
verses 8/9, verse 10 serves as the major premise in two deductions:
in the enthymeme in verses 9/10, and in the epicheireme in verses
10/11. Eighth, all of the judgments are elaborated by the topics and/
or subtopics of honor/shame and advantage/disadvantage. Finally,

[82] I add this relative clause merely to bring out the implication of the periphrasis
with respect to the major clause. The balanced and compressed form in which James
2.11a–d is presented is much superior to my reformulation.
[83] The term πταίειν ("to fail") occurs 3x: James 2.10; 3.2 (2x); see K. L. Schmidt,
TDNT VI.883–84 It evokes the topic of "shame," as does ἔνοχος' ("guilty");
H. Hanse, *TDNT* II.828; BAGD, *s.v.* ἔνοχος; LSJ, *s.v.*
[84] Note that James 2.11a, c actually contains two judgments; these, however, are
presented as one.

in addition to the straightforward judgment in verse 9, the elaboration has made clear the following facts about "acts of partiality": "If you show partiality you do not fulfill the royal law according to the scripture, 'You shall love your neighbor as yourself' "; "If you show partiality you fail in one point of the whole law (namely, the love-command)." The overall implication of these judgments is unmistakable, "If you show partiality you are guilty of the whole law." This would seem to confirm the thesis in James 2.1.

5   *Conclusio*

James 2.12 Οὕτως λαλεῖτε καὶ οὕτως ποιεῖτε ὡς διὰ νόμου ἐλευθερίας μέλλοντες κρίνεσθαι.

Thus you should speak and thus you should do as those who are to be judged by the law of freedom.

James 2.13 ἡ γὰρ κρίσις ἀνέλεος τῷ μὴ ποιήσαντι ἔλεος· κατακαυχᾶται ἔλεος κρίσεως.

For judgment is without mercy to the one who has not shown mercy; mercy triumphs over judgment.

The text

In verse 12 the papyrus P[74] reads λόγου rather than νόμου. This may be explained as an emendation to the established text where λαλεῖν ("to speak") is one of the two lead verbs in the main clause of James 2.12; cf. also 1.22, 23.

The critical apparatus for verse 13 shows that the accepted reading κατακαυχᾶται, a present middle (deponent) indicative 3rd singular, is replaced (in 02, 33, 81, 323, 945, 1241, the margin of 1739, other manuscripts, and the Sahidic tradition) by the present imperative 3rd singular, κατακαυχάσθω (+ δέ in 02, 33, 81); κατακαυχᾶσθε, a present imperative 2nd plural, is read in the second hand of 04, 1739, and the Peshitta; and κατακαυχᾶται δέ appears in the first corrector of 01, other manuscripts, and a united Latin witness. These variants are secondary attempts to provide a smoother reading to the established text (see Dibelius, 1975, p. 148 note 126).

The analysis

The purpose of the *conclusio* or ἐπίλογος is twofold: first, it repeats (*repetitio*) or recapitulates the main argument; and second, it seeks to arouse emotions (*adfectus*) that favorably dispose the audience to accept the speaker's case.[85]

In "the elaboration exercise," the *conclusio* is typically a summarizing exhortation, and verse 12 corresponds in form and function. The sentence is complex, consisting of two clauses that comprise eleven words. The principal clause, οὕτως λαλεῖτε καὶ οὕτως ποιεῖτε, features compound imperative verbs making the sentence a hortatory maxim (Smyth, 1956, section 2162a). The demonstrative adverb οὕτως refers forward by correlation (ὡς) to the subordinate comparative clause that follows, and, being repeated, οὕτως amplifies and emphasizes the exhortations as earnest and weighty advice. This is the rhetorical figure "epanaphora" (*Rhet. Her.* 4.13.19).

The comparative (ὡς) clause, featuring μέλλοντες with the present passive infinitive κρίνεσθαι, is a periphrastic reference to the future. Ward (1966b, p. 154) is correct that this reference to the future "does not demand an eschatological interpretation"; it stresses the "certainty" of the judgment (Davids, 1982, p. 110). Hence the sense is "as those who are 'certainly' to be judged by the law of freedom" (cf. Smyth, 1956, section 1959). The appeal to emotion is hard to miss, for to remind the community that they will certainly be judged by the law which they are accused of having transgressed certainly evokes the topics of "fear" and "shame" (Arist. *Rhet.* 2.5.1–15). Thus this comparative clause measures qualitatively the judgment διὰ νόμου ἐλευθερίας with respect to the "words" and "deeds" in the principal clause. It suggests that the quality of that judgment corresponds to the quality of one's actions, a suggestion that verse 13 confirms. The compound verbal predicate forms a résumé that signifies all the actions one may perform, and "actions" are indeed what James 2.1–13 discusses. As the *conclusio* to this particular elaboration, the résumé recalls προσωπολημψίαι as "words" and "deeds" (cf. 2.2–4; 2.6a; 2.9) and recapitulates the admonition in James 2.1.

Verse 13 is a complex declarative sentence. The participle clause

---

[85] On the purpose and function of the *conclusio/peroratio* or ἐπίλογος, see G. A. Kennedy (1980, in his index, *s.v.*); Lausberg (1973, vol. I, sections 431–42); Mack and Robbins (1989); J. Martin (1974, pp. 147–66); Volkmann ([1885] 1987, section 27).

τῷ μὴ ποιήσαντι ἔλεος (2.13b) is subordinate to its principal clause, ἡ γὰρ κρίσις ἀνέλεος (2.13a),[86] while the independent clause κατακαυχᾶται ἔλεος κρίσεως (2.13c) is asyndetically juxtaposed to 2.13ab. The asyndeton here is rhetorical: it signals a contrast in thought to the preceding clause, amplifies each idea that follows as distinctive, and manifests heightened emotion (*adfectus*; Smyth, 1956, sections 2165–67; see Quint. 9.3.50). It should be remembered that for these reasons asyndeton is not only common in the *conclusio*; it is regarded as "most appropriate" here (Arist. *Rhet.* 3.19.6).

That the text introduces verse 13 with γάρ, as the rationale for verse 12, and that these successive sentences are parisonical and marked by paromoeosis are clear rhetorical signals that the author intends to relate them. They form an epicheireme, a rational argument.[87]

Before we analyze the epicheireme in James 2.12–13, let us briefly consider the phrase διὰ νόμου ἐλευθερίας ("by the law of freedom," James 2.10). The usage διὰ νόμου promotes the law (of freedom) as the "agent employed to bring about an intended result" (see Smyth, 1956, section 1685.2d).[88] This is the second and last time the text characterizes the law as "the law of freedom." The first instance is found in 1.25, where τὸν τῆς ἐλευθερίας is an attributive reference to νόμον τέλειον ("the perfect law"). There, as the context shows, both of the latter are synonymous expressions for τὸν ἔμφυτον λόγον τὸν δυνάμενον σῶσαι τὰς ψυχὰς ὑμῶν ("the implanted word which is able to save your souls," 1.21; see Ward, 1966b, pp. 127–33; and Dibelius, 1975, p. 116). All of these

---

[86] The verb εἶναι ("to be") is ellipsed here, a simple way of compressing, condensing, and giving force to expression. On this rhetorical figure, see Quint. 9.3.58; BDF sections 127–28; Smyth (1956, section 3022).

[87] For the figure "parisosis" (verse 12 has 11 words, 27 syllables; verse 13 has 11 words, 28 syllables), see *Rhet. Her.* 4.20.27; Arist. *Rhet.* 3.9.9. For "paromoiosis" ("similarity of the final syllables of each clause"), see Arist. *Rhet.* 3.9.9; [*Rh. Al.*] 28.1436a.5.

[88] On the absence of the definite article with νόμος in James 2.12 and 1.25, see BDF section 270; BAGD *s.v.*, and Mayor (1892 [1990], pp. ccxiv–ccxv). The preposition διά occurs once more in James 4.2 (with the infinitive αἰτεῖσθαι). Law's (1980, p. 116) remark, concerning διά with the genitive in James 2:10, that "the law is not here the norm or standard by which they are measured for judgment, for that would require the preposition κατά," may not be wholly correct. Smyth (1956, section 1685.2d) clearly shows that "sometimes there is little difference between" the genitive and accusative cases. Furthermore, is the law here the "agent of action" or the "agent employed" (by an actor, whether God or the community) to bring about an intended result?

expressions, including "the royal law" (2.8), refer to the one law of God, "the whole law" (2.10; cf. Davids, 1982, pp. 114–19).

As stated above, James mentions the term νόμος only ten times; this hardly provides the whole of the author's understanding of the law. Yet there are some things that can be said. For our author, the law is a thoroughly positive entity; he never speaks of it negatively. The law, which certainly contains the decalogue (2.10–11) and can be summarized in the love-command (2.9), is to be obeyed (1.25). Indeed, obeying the law, "the implanted word," leads to salvation (1.21). As Oscar Seitz correctly observes, "To the author of our epistle, νόμος clearly means the 'old' law, the legislation given by Moses, which is ultimately the law of God: 'There is one lawgiver and judge, he who is able to save and destroy'" (1964, p. 485). Further, note that in James 2.1–13 both the summary of the whole law in the love-commandment (2.8) and also the argument for obeying the whole law (2.9–11) are clearly assimilated to holding Jesus' faith. In other words, the law is emphatically "qualified by an understanding of life given by Jesus the Messiah" (1.1; 2.1; L. T. Johnson, 1986, p. 460). And in every case, the author is at pains to bring the law to bear on everyday human life, especially on communal relations (4.11–12; thus, Souček, 1958; and Ward, 1966b).

Let us look more closely at the epicheireme in James 2.12–13. Verse 13 provides the major and minor premises; verse 12 the conclusion. The argument is based on the topic of contraries. In James 2.13a, ἡ γὰρ κρίσις ἀνέλεος is antithetical to the converse statement, κατακαυχᾶται ἔλεος κρίσεως, in 2.13c; and the term "mercy," which appears in all three clauses of verse 13 ([ἀν]έλεος ... ἔλεος ... ἔλεος is a passionate and emphatic use of the rhetorical figure "transplacement"; *Rhet. Her.* 4.14.20–21), is opposed in three ways. First, it is negativized in the alpha privative adjective ἀνέλεος; then, in 2.13b, the clause τῷ μὴ ποιήσαντι ἔλεος states the contrary of ἔλεος in terms of the attributes of action.[89] The third opposition to ἔλεος occurs in 2.13c, where the nouns ἔλεος/κρίσεως are agonistically juxtaposed; this is similar to the structures of antithesis with the verbs τηρήσῃ/πταίσῃ (2.10a) and μοιχεύεις/φονεύεις (2.11e).[90] Notice that the participial clause τῷ

---

[89] The predicate adjective ἀνέλεος ("unmerciful") is *hapax legomenon* in NT, and is not surely attested outside the NT; see MM *s.v.*; and R. Bultmann, *TDNT* III.487.

[90] The repetition κρίσις ... κρίσεως, ποιεῖτε/ποιήσαντι, and κρίνεσθαι/κρίσις is the figure "transplacement" (Quint. 9.3.41–42).

μὴ ποιήσαντι ἔλεος (2.13b) in the dative case uses the generic singular to refer to the class whose attributes of action are presumed to make ἡ κρίσις ἀνέλεος (2.13a) a true statement. James 2.13c (κατακαυχᾶται ἔλεος κρίσεως), on the other hand, is stated without a similarly limiting clause. Nevertheless, a qualifying reference is presumed for 2.13c by both the structure and content of the verse itself. Reasoning from contraries suggests that, since κατακαυχᾶται ἔλεος κρίσεως (2.13c) is clearly antithetical to ἡ κρίσις ἀνέλεος (2.13a), and the latter is presumed true with respect τῷ μὴ ποιήσαντι ἔλεος (2.13b), then the inferred contrary of the latter (2.13b), namely τῷ ποιήσαντι ἔλεος, expresses the class for whom κατακαυχᾶται ἔλεος κρίσεως is true. As we have already discussed, "implication" is typical in arguments from the contrary; moreover, by leaving τῷ ποιήσαντι ἔλεος unstated and abruptly juxtaposing the proverbial statement κατακαυχᾶται ἔλεος κρίσεως (2.13c), the author has artfully compressed his thought, and, as Dibelius judged, has given it "a particularly forceful expression" (Dibelius, 1975, p. 148). If this is correct, then what is implied in the opposition between 2.13a–b and 2.13c may be restated in full, as follows: ἡ γὰρ κρίσις ἀνέλεος τῷ μὴ ποιήσαντι ἔλεος· τῷ ποιήσαντι ἔλεος κατακαυχᾶται ἔλεος κρίσεως. And it will readily be seen that τῷ ποιήσαντι ἔλεος κατακαυχᾶται ἔλεος κρίσεως is essentially the contrapositive of ἡ γὰρ κρίσις ἀνέλεος τῷ μὴ ποιήσαντι ἔλεος.

The (full) epicheireme in verses 12–13 may be reformulated as follows:

Major premise (2.13a–b):	For judgment is without mercy to one who has shown no mercy;
Minor premise (2.13c):	[but for one who has shown mercy,] mercy triumphs over judgment.
Conclusion (2.12):	Thus you should speak and thus you should do as those who are to be judged under the law of freedom.

From this we can see more clearly how the reasons in verse 13, which undergird the exhortation (in verse 12), employ contrary attributes of action with respect to negative (2.12a) and positive (2.13c) judgments.[91] The judgment in view is διὰ νόμου ἐλευθερίας,

[91] On the phrase ποιεῖν ἔλεος, see Mayor (1892 [1990], p. 95); Dibelius (1975, pp. 147–48); Bultmann, *TDNT* III.477–87; H. Braun, *TDNT* VI.458–84; and below. James uses the term ποιεῖν 12x: 2.8, 12, 13, 19; 3.12 (2x), 18; 4.13, 15, 17 (2x); 5.15.

that is, God's judgment (4.12; cf. Ward, 1966b, p. 155); τῷ μὴ ποιήσαντι ἔλεος (and its unstated contrary), both of which are reflected in the verbs λαλεῖτε/ποιεῖτε, are attributes of action belonging to those who are to be judged. To reiterate, the argument holds that the (negative/positive) judgment by the law of liberty is qualitatively determined by the (merciless/merciful) quality of the attributes of one's actions. As the *conclusio* to this particular elaboration, it would be difficult for the addressees to miss the point. Reminding the audience that they will be judged by the law which is fulfilled in the love-commmand, the conclusion argues that "one should show mercy to the poor neighbor/brother."

But why the reference to "mercy" in verse 13? In other words, how is the appeal to mercy in the *adfectus* (2.13) connected with the prohibition against partialities in the theme (2.1)? Dibelius and others have argued there is no real connection. But already we have seen that James 2.12–13 forms a rational argument that concludes the unit. Let us consider briefly, but closely, the thought in and the function of this conclusion.

That the *adfectus* of an argument, which verse 13 is, should mention and seek to arouse the "emotions" (πάθη) of "pity" or "mercy" (ἔλεος) is rudimentary (cf. Lausberg, 1973, vol. I, section 439; cf. sections 433; 1221; 257.3). Indeed, the appeal to emotion is one of the primary goals of the *conclusio* (Arist. *Rhet.* 3.19.1). R. Bultmann (*TDNT* II.478), referring to the *Rhetorica ad Alexandrum* (34.1439b.25, ἐπὶ τόν ἔλεον ἄγειν), notes precisely that ἔλεος "is one of the πάθη that the orator must know how to kindle". Although the Stoics considered it a "weakness," mercy was regularly esteemed as "fitting in the noble," and thus one of the subtopics of "honor/dishonor," and, sometimes it looks more like a virtue than an emotion (for the Stoic view, see *SVF*, index, *s.v.* "ἔλεος"). Moreover, ἔλεος is a conventional topic of "justice" (*Rhet. Her.* 3.3.4), and as such it is frequently encountered in Hellenistic philosophical and rhetorical discussions of law and judgment.

While I maintain that there is clearly an emotional appeal to mercy in James 2.12–13, with Bultmann, I find that here the exhortation to ποιεῖν ἔλεος is much more. We should not forget that the letter of James is thoroughly theocentric, and this fact underlies everything that is said here. Beginning with the commonplaces or *topoi* in the *exordium* and *narratio*, and running through the whole discourse, God is held to be thoroughly just (James

1.5–8, 13–18, 19–27). Moreover, God is πολύσπλαγχνός καὶ οἰκτίρμων (5.11), and his σοφία, unlike the world's, is μεστὴ ἐλέους καὶ καρπῶν ἀγαθῶν (3.17). And equally apparent is the fact that the text presumes a oneness between the Lord Jesus Christ and God's justice, compassion, and mercy (1.1; 2.1). James 2.1–13 shares in and develops this view of God. Accordingly, in working out the thesis that προσωπολημψίαι are incompatible with Jesus' faith (2.1), the text elaborates "acts of partiality" in several very telling ways. Most important for our purpose here are the following: building on the suggestion in 2.1 that "acts of partiality" are dishonorable, James 2.4 reformulates such behavior as "unjust judgments," which is essentially what they are in Leviticus 19.15. This perversion of justice is specifically related to the community's treatment of the poor neighbor (2.2–3; 2.6a; 2.8–11); and the whole argument is focused on the "communal relations" among the beloved brothers and sisters, directly (2.1, 5) and indirectly (2.6b–7). The whole law of God's kingdom is summarized in the commandment to love one's neighbor as one's self (2.8), and "acts of partiality" are held to be a violation of this commandment in particular (2.9). Thus προσωπολημπτεῖν is dishonorable (2.1, 6a), a perversion of justice (2.2–4), and a failure to love one's neighbor (2.8–9). Moreover, one who is guilty of showing partiality is guilty of all the law (2.10–11). This fact and the certainty that the community is to be judged διὰ νόμου ἐλευθερίας, that is, by the very law that is fulfilled in the love-command, is a very good argument that one should not show partiality (2.12–13). Rather, one should "speak and do" what the law requires: one should love the poor neighbor as one's self.

The relationship made between "love of neighbor" and "showing mercy" in James' argument is probably an example of the argument from the topic of "genus" to the topic of "species." In other words, for James a concrete instance of "love of neighbor" is an "act of mercy toward the poor neighbor." The opposite is "showing partiality to the wealthy and dishonoring the poor" (James 2.2–4, 6a, 6b–7), which, again, is a concrete instance of "not loving the poor neighbor as one's self." It follows that for James, whoever is guilty of "showing partiality" is guilty of "not showing mercy." If this is so, then, there is a profoundly logical relationship between love and mercy in James. To paraphrase Aristotle (*Top.* 2.4.26–28), the species (acts of mercy) must necessarily reflect the qualities of the genus (love of neighbor).

Finally, it should be observed that James 2.13 also functions as a *transitio*. That is, it briefly recapitulates what has been said in a way that introduces what is about to be said (*Rhet. Her.* 4.26.35; cf. Lausberg, 1973, vol. I, section 849; and vol. II, section 1244, *s.v.* "*transitio*"). As the conclusion of our unit, the argument in James 2.12–13 holds that one should "show mercy to the poor neighbor." While it recalls God's action toward the poor (2.5) and the summary of God's law in the love-command (2.8), the appeal to "mercy" succinctly introduces a motif that plays large in the elaboration in 2.14–26. In the latter unit it is argued that a living faith must concretize itself in "acts of mercy." Note, that unit begins by employing the topic of advantage (Τί τὸ ὄφελος, ἀδελφοί μου, 2.15) and then uses a social example that features "the pitiable." The poor in 2.15, as in 2.2–3, are unmistakable; also the dishonorable, unjust, incompassionate, and merciless behavior seen in 2.3–4 reappears in another form in 2.16–17. In 2.14–26, as in 2.1–13, there is recollection of the statement that concludes the *narratio* of the letter. There, in James 1.27, "religion that is pure and undefiled *before God*" is introduced in terms of compassionate and merciful action toward the pitiable poor. Thus, the rhetoric of the text itself suggests that the appeal to mercy in James 2.13 is emotionally, logically, religiously, theologically, and socially a vital element of the elaboration in James 2.1–13.

Conclusions

Numerous appraisals of the rhetoric in and of James 2.1–13 have already been made in the foregoing analysis. Here by way of summary we shall focus on several of the most important.

First of all, this unit is a particular manifestation of an elaboration of a theme as it was taught in the *progymnasmata* and the rhetorical handbooks of the Greco-Roman world. The theme to be argued is presented in the form of apotreptic advice (2.1), and then in a well-orchestrated series of steps it is established and worked out. A social example functions as the rationale for the argument (2.2–4); a paradigm grounds the theme in history (2.5), and an argument from the opposite (2.6a), supported with a second social example, expands the exigence and relates it to the broader arenas of the community's life (2.6b–7). Then the whole issue is amplified in a four-part argument from judgment based on the written law: "Love your neighbor as yourself," a maxim from the written law

(2.8), is introduced with its contrary (2.9); this is followed by the rationale for judgment based on the law (2.10) and its confirmation using written testimony (2.11). The elaboration concludes by recapitulating the theme in an exhortation to action (2.12) and by making an emotional appeal that not only paraphrases the theme in terms of the "kind of actions" that should characterize the audience, but also sets the stage for the next unit (2.14–26).

The proofs and the manner in which they are employed make a very straightforward dissuasion from "acts of partiality"; concomitantly they persuade toward acts of love and mercy for the poor neighbor. Such persuasion and dissuasion is typical of deliberative discourse. Also customary for deliberative discourse are the use of paradigm (2.5) and social example (2.2–4; 6b–7), and marshaling epideictic (2.6a; 2.6b–7; 2.12–13) and judicial (2.8–11) elements to buttress a flatly symbouleutic statement (2.1).

Pathos is introduced with the very first words (ἀδελφοί μου) in the unit; and "kinship," one of the topics of "friendship," permeates the whole (2.5). Moreover, *pathos* is present in the pitiable poor (2.2–3; 2.5; the πλησίον, 2.8), as well as in the remarks that characterize the rich and recall the community's experiences at their hands (2.6b–7). The appeal for "acts of mercy" toward the poor, coupled with mention of judgment by the law of God (2.12–13), are also emotionally laden arguments.

Ethos is prominent in topics like the honorable, the just, the lawful, love, and mercy. All of these topics, as well as the ways in which these are related to the topics of "advantage/disadvantage," combine with the epistolary preface (1.1) to suggest the author as a person of good character and good will. The *ethos* of the author combines with the unit's numerous sententious maxims, its frankness of speech, the subject it discusses, and the concerns it develops to support the obvious; namely, the author evinced here is an authoritative figure and would expect his words to be received accordingly.

Concerning matters of style, I reiterate that as far as the NT is concerned, the Greek in James is among the best. Moreover, the unit in hand is polished. The only real grammatical problem appears to be the concatenation of genitives in 2.1; and even this difficulty has been overstated. There are several *hapax legomena* in our unit; and we have seen that rhetorical figures of speech and thought are abundant and adroitly employed.

Finally, and of no little significance, the whole unit shows a definite progression of thought. While the pattern of elaboration is common, it is skillfully handled; not one proof seems illogical. Rational arguments in the form of "first form of conclusion" arguments, enthymemes, and epicheiremes, and the adept play with the topics, especially in the way the text reasons from contraries – all of this would suggest that the author thought much better than we have grown accustomed to hearing that he did.

The topic, "acts of partiality," is never lost sight of in the course of the elaboration. The text weaves a particular communal concern, "dishonorable treatment of the poor (neighbor) community member," together with general statements to make an argument that is pointedly specific in what it intends to accomplish. More than a quarter of the entire letter treats of the conflicts between the rich and the poor and the accompanying opposition to the world as a system of values opposed to God. Our unit plays this out in a tersely aphoristic form. Whatever else the letter says, it clearly says here, and in good rhetorical fashion, that "acts of partiality" are not compatible with Jesus' faith because they are incompatible with God's law. The text clearly seeks to persuade the audience that God's law and Jesus' faith call for acts of love, mercy, and justice toward the elect poor. I conclude that James 2.1–13 is a very persuasive rhetorical argument against "acts of partiality" among "the twelve tribes in the diaspora."

4

THE INTERTEXTURE OF JAMES 2.1–13

Introduction

This chapter concerns the intertexture of James 2.1–13, and, most particularly, it focuses on the intertexture of James 2.5, an apparent allusion to a well-known saying of Jesus. Since the stated purpose of this inquiry is to ascertain the socio-rhetorical function of James 2.5, it is helpful to clarify why and how the intertexture of the unit is integral to my goal.

Intertextual analysis is important for socio-rhetorical criticism because it takes very seriously the point that all language is a social possession (Halliday, 1978, pp. 1–35) and bases itself on the notion that all texts are constructed on the foundations of antecedent texts (see the essays in Draisma, 1989; Vorster, 1989, pp. 19–20; Kristeva, 1969, p. 52). Following Robert Alter's (1989, p. 112) definition of allusion as "the evocation in one text of an antecedent . . . text," whether oral or written, and recalling that allusion is a fundamental aspect of rhetorical invention, it is rather obvious that the intertextual conception of a text as a mosaic of many earlier textual fragments is of primary rhetorical interest.[1] Moreover, as a facet of socio-rhetorical criticism, intertextual study does not only call attention to the ways in which the rhetor appears to activate previous texts; it also addresses the rhetorical subject of the potential effects that allusions have as new figurations in the

---

[1] For the discussion of "allusion" as an aspect of rhetorical "invention," see chapter 1 (pp. 18–20), above. While heartily agreeing with Alter (1989, p. 112; see pp. 111–40) that there is a difference between the common conception and the literary sense of "allusion," namely, "the question of authorial intention," I depart from his emphasis on written texts, because in a traditional rhetorical culture – the kind of culture from which James emanates – oral and written texts are closely connected; see Robbins (1991b, pp. 157–86).

rhetor's strategy of persuasion.[2] Likewise, taking "intertextuality" to refer to "the whole complex of relationships between texts within the general 'text of culture', "[3] we can see that it coincides with the socio-rhetorical interest in the cultural codes and conventions of thought that manifest themselves in a given text (Mack and Robbins, 1989, p. 38). Put differently, the intertextual understanding of a text as a "network of traces" or references to other texts joins with the socio-rhetorical view of a text as both the transmission and maintenance of culture.[4] Finally, because in any given text numerous, previous, socio-ideologically located voices speak (Bakhtin, 1981, pp. 293–94; cited in Robbins, 1992, p. 1161), a socio-rhetorical understanding of the intertexture of James 2.1–13 can help us hear the earlier voices that now speak in the socio-ideologically located voice of James.

The present discussion of the intertexture of James 2.1–13 is a limited one; in other words, I do not propose to follow up every allusion to an earlier text in our unit. Indeed even if such a task were possible, it would be beyond the scope of this investigation. In addition, since all the allusions to previous literature within our unit are not equally important (see Vorster, 1989, p. 26; and Alter, 1989, p. 124), I shall confine the discussion to just those rhetorical allusions that appear to be crucial to the persuasive strategy of the elaboration. Put differently, though I shall ask about the possible sources of key allusions in the unit, and perhaps discover something of their influence upon the author of James, the primary goal is to discuss key allusions as "rhetorical performances" of antecedent texts (on the relation of intertextuality to source hunting and influence chasing, see Vorster, 1989, pp. 15–16; and Hays, 1989, p. 17). Therefore, I shall look at the allusions in James 2.1–13 primarily from the vantage point of the way that students were taught in the *progymnasmata* to exploit earlier texts for their rhetorical purposes. In the process I shall also continue to incorporate insights from modern literary and rhetorical studies, as these may aid our discussion.

[2] See Eagelton (1983, p. 205); on the "effects" of allusions as "new figurations," see Hays (1989, pp. 17–19).

[3] Van Wolde (1989, p. 45; based on Foucault, 1966); cited in Robbins (1992, p. 1161).

[4] For the phrase, "network of traces," see Vorster (1989, p. 21) and Derrida (1979, p. 84). For the understanding of a text as a transmission and maintenance of culture, see Mack and Robbins (1989, pp. 31–67, 195–208); Robbins (1988a); and Halliday (1978, pp. 27, 36, 101, 114).

Both the *progymnasmata* and the ancient rhetorical handbooks show that students were taught to elaborate a given theme by first introducing it in the most appealing manner possible (Bonner, 1977, pp. 250–76; D. L. Clark, 1957, pp. 177–212; Hock and O'Neil, 1986, pp. 9–22; Mack and Robbins, 1989, pp. 33–35; and esp. Butts, 1987). In other words, to work out a given theme and to persuade a given audience to adhere to it in their thought and action, students learned to color the language of their proposals with as much conventional, that is, commonly accepted, material as possible. Consequently, the artful activation of an antecedent text was a common ploy in rendering a given proposal more readily acceptable to an audience. Also, to confirm their proposals students learned to introduce supporting "proofs" that once again exploited commonly accepted social conventions of thought and action. The rhetorical goal was to transfer the audience's adherence from commonly accepted social thought and behavior to the particular thoughts and actions proposed by the rhetor in elaborating the theme (see esp. Perelman, 1982, pp. 21–32). The significance of all this for the intertexture of our unit is that we should necessarily expect references to previous texts in James 2.1–13. Furthermore, while allusions can occur anywhere in an elaboration, we may anticipate their occurrence in the "*probatio*," since allusions are most often used to prove something. In our unit, the "confirmation" is found in verses 5–11. Thus we shall discuss the intertexture of this section first, beginning with the most explicit intertextual reference in it. Then, we shall look at the conclusion of the unit (James 2.12–13). In the process of examining those sections, we shall have the opportunity to address other key allusions, particularly those in the introductory sections (2.1–4).[5] The intertexture of James 2.5, the primary concern, we shall deal with last.

An intertextual analysis of James 2.1–13

In the letter of James there are five explicit references to earlier texts; which is to say, there are five occasions in which a citational formula directly signals an intertextual reference (James 2.8, 11, 23; 4.5 and 6). I am counting the two scriptures in 2.11 as a single instance; others, e.g., Dean B. Deppe (1989, pp. 31, 35–36),

---

[5] Alter (1989, p. 118) notes that "allusions often radiate out to contiguous allusions, and it is also fairly characteristic that one allusion should be superimposed on another."

separate the references in 2.11 and find six citations in James. Four
of these are regularly identified as allusions to texts in the LXX
(Swete, 1968, pp. 381–405): James 2.8 refers to Leviticus 19.18;
James 2.23 to Genesis 15.6 (cf. Rom. 4.3; Gal. 3.6); James 4.5 to
Proverbs 3.34 (cf. 1 Pet. 5.5); and James 4.5, most scholars treat as
a reference to an as yet unidentified "scripture" (on which see Seitz,
1944). Two of the latter occur in our unit, in James 2.8 and 11,
respectively. Because James 2.8 and 11 are crucial elements in a
four-part argument from judgment based on the written law
(2.8–11), and because scholars have detected other possible, though
less explicit, allusions in 2.9–10, we shall discuss the intertexture of
these verses together.

The first and fundamental use of a citational formula in the letter
of James occurs in James 2.8. Moreover, both the form and
language of the allusion mark it as an intertextual reference. The
introductory formula employed here is κατὰ τὴν γραφήν, "according to the scripture." On the one hand, the formula may be
regarded as unusual, since it appears nowhere else in the NT.[6] On
the other hand, it is highly significant that every time James
employs the term γραφή (here, in 2.23, and 4.5) it signals an
intertextual reference. The language of the "scripture" introduced
by this formula is found in the LXX in Leviticus 19.18. There it is
part of the written law, and we refer to it as the love-commandment: ἀγαπήσεις τὸν πλησίον σου ὡς σεαυτόν. When it occurs in
James 2.8 as the first statement of a four-part argument from
judgment based on the written law, the intertextual reference
functions as a proposition from an authoritative text, "a true
assessment" based on ancient testimony in the written law. And, as
I determined from the analysis of the inner texture of 2.1–13, it
supports the theme in verse 1 that "acts of partiality" are incompatible with "the faith of our glorious Lord Jesus Christ."

A careful probe of the respective contexts of the "love-commandment intertext" reveals the following information. First of all the
love-commandment in Leviticus 19.18 is speech attributed to the
Lord in a context where the Lord tells Moses what he should say to
the people of Israel (Lev. 19.1–2). Leviticus connects the whole
corpus of the holiness code with the covenant established between
God and Israel at Sinai (Lev. 1.1; 8–9; 27.34); thus the holiness

[6] This expression is found frequently in the LXX (Deut. 10.4; 1 Chr. 15.15; 2 Chr.
30.5; 35.4; 1 Esdr. 1.4; 2 Esdr. 6.18) and is similar to κατὰ τὰς γραφάς in 1 Cor.
15.3–5), but as a citation formula in the NT it occurs only in James 2.8.

code and the decalogue together define the relationship between God and Israel in the Torah. Besides that, like the decalogue (Exod. 20.1), the laws of the holiness code are presented as the words of the Lord God which he spoke to Moses (Lev. 17.1; 19.1; 26.46); the recurrent statement, "I am the Lord your God" (Lev. 18.2, 30; 26.13), appears throughout the corpus and evokes the Sinai covenant (Exod. 20.2; 6.2 and Lev. 26.45; see Childs, 1979, pp. 173–74, 180–89; cf. James 2.11).

Second, the love-commandment is one statement in a series of assertions that elaborates the meaning of the proposition and rationale (thus, the enthymeme) that the people "shall be holy, because I the Lord your God am holy" (19.2).[7] Third, the elaboration takes the form of a series of restatements of the proposition and rationale (Lev. 19.1–2) which applies the reasoning to specific contexts in daily life. Fourth, the elaboration reconfigures certain commandments from the decalogue in terms of "holiness" that is grounded in God's being, as this is expressed in the opening enthymematic statement (19.1–2). By so grounding its laws (19.2) and holding Israel to be God's elect (19.36b–37), the holiness code, like the decalogue, asserts that Israel's obedience to these commandments reflects her status as God's holy nation (see Childs, 1979, p. 185; Sellin and Fohrer, 1968, pp. 137–143; and Eissfeldt, 1965, pp. 233–39). Fifth, the elaboration features a repetitive technique of closing units with "I am the Lord your God/I am the Lord," which, as the unit shows, are elliptical forms of the premise, "I the Lord your God am holy," in the opening enthymeme ("I the Lord your God am holy," Lev. 19.2; "I am the Lord your God," 19.3, 4, 10, 25, 31, 34, 36; and "I am the Lord," 19.12, 14, 16, 18, 28, 30, 32, 37).

The specific function of the love-commandment in Leviticus 19 occurs in the juxtaposition of positive and negative assertions in the elaboration. For example, the series opens with a positive assertion about honoring mother and father and keeping sabbaths which is followed by an argument from the opposite: "Do not turn to idols or make cast images for yourselves" (NRSV Lev. 19.3–4). The next unit directs that a sacrifice be offered "in such a way that it is acceptable on your behalf," with positive assertions (Lev. 19.5–6)

---

[7] The enthymeme in Lev. 19.2 may be reformulated: (unstated Major premise): "You shall be as I the Lord your God am." (stated Minor premise): "I the Lord your God am holy" (Lev. 19.2c). (stated Conclusion): "You shall be holy" (Lev. 19.2b).

followed by arguments from the opposite (Lev. 19.7–8). This continues with an application of the enthymeme (Lev. 19.2) to reaping the harvests (19.9–10), to stealing, to dealing falsely and lying, and to swearing falsely by, and profaning the name of, God (Lev. 19.11–12), and so forth through 19.13–18.

Leviticus 19.9–10 reverses the pattern of positive statements followed by argument from the contrary, with the result that contrary statements lead the unit. This produces a series of positive statements at the end of the units, preceded by "I am the Lord your God" leading up to the love-commandment: (a) "you shall leave them [fallen grapes] for the poor and alien" (19.10); (b) "you shall fear your God" (19.14); and (c) "you shall love your neighbor as yourself" (19.18).

After this sequence, the last half of the elaboration is framed by "You shall keep my statutes" (19.19), and it amplifies assertions that appear in the first half of the elaboration: (a) "You shall keep my sabbaths and reverence my sanctuary" (19.30); (b) "you shall rise . . . and fear God" (19.32). This leads to a closing enthymeme (19.33–34) about accepting aliens, because "you were aliens," and a conclusion: "you shall keep *all* my statutes" (19.37).[8]

The pattern suggests that the love-commandment (19.18) occurs as the climactic positive statement at the end of the first half of the elaboration of "You shall be holy, for I the Lord your God am holy" (19.1–18). Thus, Leviticus 19.18 is the bridge that leads to the last half of the elaboration, which, as 19.19 and 19.37 make clear, emphasizes obedience to "all" God's statutes and ordinances. Moreover, the command to love the alien as yourself recalls the love-commandment in 19.18. Therefore, because the commandments in Leviticus 19 are focused on the interpersonal or "communal" relations of God's chosen people, the possibility that the love-commandment – which occupies such a key position in the elaboration – could be taken as a summarizing statement for "all God's statutes and ordinances" (Lev. 19.37) should not be overlooked (see James Muhlinberg, *IDB* iv.622). Indeed, the author of

---

[8] In Lev. 19.33–34, "you shall love the alien [who resides with you in your land] as yourself" is the climactic, functional equivalent of "you shall not oppress the alien [who resides with you in your land]," and also of "[the alien who resides with you in your land] shall be to you as the citizen among you." The enthymematic reasoning played out 19.33–34 is something like this. (Major premise): You loved yourself when you sojourned in Egypt. (Minor premise): The stranger who sojourns with you in your land is as you were when you sojourned in Egypt. (Conclusion): The stranger who sojourns with you in your land you shall love as yourself.

James 2.1–13 appears to have appropriated the love-commandment in this way.

Focusing more narrowly on Leviticus 19.18, we find that it translates holiness in the realm of human relations as love.

> καὶ οὐκ ἐκδικᾶταί σου ἡ χείρ, καὶ οὐ μηνιεῖς τοῖς υἱοῖς τοῦ λαοῦ σου καὶ ἀγαπήσεις τὸν πλησίον σου ὡς σεαυτόν· ἐγώ εἰμι κύριος.

> Your hand shall not avenge or declare anger against any of the sons of your people, but you shall love your neighbor as yourself: I am the Lord.

Note that "love" is here the attribute of actions toward one's neighbor; in particular, it is characterized as the contrary of "taking vengeance" and "showing anger" toward one's neighbor.

A comparison of this verse with James 2.8 reveals that the latter text exploits seven of the twenty-four words in Leviticus 19.18. Put differently, of the four clauses in Leviticus 19.18, James 2.8 uses only the third clause, marks it with a citation formula as an authoritative text (γραφή), and recites it verbatim as a subordinate clause of direct discourse in the form of a maxim. Technically speaking, then, James 2.8 is an "abbreviation" (συστέλλειν) of Leviticus 19.18; and the Jamesian performance of the love-commandment is properly a rhetorical "recitation" (ἀπαγγελία) of an ancient authority (see Theon, III, 139–42 in Butts, 1987, pp. 204–05).

The identification of this allusion as a rhetorical "recitation" is based on the fact that the letter of James emanates from a "traditional rhetorical culture," that is, a culture in which "oral and written speech interact closely with one another" (Robbins, 1991b, pp. 160–62). Within such a culture, as Vernon Robbins reminds us, the "repetition of words and phrases in a written document regularly is the result of 'recitation composition' rather than 'copying'" (p. 162). This is what Theon teaches us: he says that in the progymnastic exercise of "recitation" "we try to the best of our ability to report [that is, 'to write'] the assigned chreia very clearly in the same words or in others as well" (Theon, III, 143–45; Butts, 1987, pp. 204–05; 162; Hock and O'Neil, 1986, p. 95). Which is to say, when performing recitations of antecedent texts students learn to write their texts with as much or as little verbatim reproduction as they deem necessary; and the literature unquestionably shows that ancient authors "continually recast the material by adding to it, subtracting from it, rearranging it, and rewording it" (Robbins, 1991b, p. 164). Theon's list of the exercises that students learned in writing a chreia or maxim include "recitation, inflection, comment, critique, expansion, abbreviation, refutation, and confirmation (Theon, III, 139–42; see the discussion in Mack and Robbins, 1989, pp. 36–41). Therefore, James' exploitation of Leviticus 19.18 is appropriately designated as a recitation performance.

One of the most difficult questions about the allusion in James 2.8 concerns the relationship between "the royal law" and the love-commandment. I have agreed with Ropes and Dibelius that "the royal law" is best taken as a Jamesian reference to "the whole law" (2.10), the law of God's kingdom (2.5). Since the love-commandment is – as it is in Leviticus 19 – one precept among the many that make up the whole law, it is obviously not all the law. Thus Ropes (1916, p. 198) and Dibelius (1975, p. 142) are also probably correct in saying that the royal law is "not identical" to the love-commandment. Moreover, as I noted in the previous chapter, the reference to the law as "royal" is best understood as a reference to the source and status of the whole law as the law of God's kingdom (James 2.5). Consequently, it is unlikely that the epithet "royal" means that the love-commandment is the primary or preeminent commandment in the whole law. Indeed, the emphasis of the four-part argument in James 2.8–11 is on fulfilling the *whole* law, and to fail in one part of the whole law is to be guilty of all the law.

On the other hand, when Dibelius (1975, p. 142) asserts that the love-commandment is merely presented as "only a part" of the royal law, I think he understates its significance for our author. In other words, he fails to recognize that James' performance of the love-commandment is a "new figuration"; for in our unit it is not "only a part" of the law, but also our author's basic expression for or summary of the whole law (Ward, 1966b, pp. 138–42; W. D. Davies, 1964, p. 401 note 2; Lachs, 1987, p. 107; and Fuller, 1978).

There is more than enough evidence from both Jewish and Christian sources to corroborate the use of Leviticus 19.18 as a summary of the whole law (R. Hillel in *b. šabb.* 31a; R. Aquiba in *Gen. Rab.* 24.7; see Str-B. 1.356–58; and Matt. 5.43; 19.19; Mark 12.31 // Matt. 22.39 // Luke 10.27; Rom. 13.9; Gal. 5.14; *Did.* 1.2; *Barn.* 19.5; cited in Betz, 1979, p. 276 note 34). Moreover, "the evidence," as Hans Dieter Betz (1985a, p. 37) correctly observes, "indicates that early Christianity was historically united on the fact that Jesus taught the fulfillment of the Torah in the love-commandment" (also Davies, 1964, pp. 405–13). Further, as scholars like Luke Johnson (1986, p. 457; cf. Peter Davids, 1982, p. 114) have argued, it is probable that the author of James ("a servant of the Lord Jesus Christ," 1.1), appropriates "*all* of Torah" in relation to the teachings of Jesus. Indeed, in the context of an argument that is addressed to Christian Jews and that conspicuously concerns "the faith of our glorious Lord Jesus Christ" it is hard to imagine that judgments connecting the poor, the promised kingdom, the royal law, and the love-commandment could have been heard without thinking of Jesus' words and deeds. Though we shall discuss this probability more thoroughly when we examine James 2.5 as an allusion to a saying of Jesus, I wish to suggest here that the reference to Jesus' faith in 2.1 functions as a "global allusion" (Alter, 1989, pp. 123–24), that is, it evokes the whole of what our author perceives Jesus to have believed, said, and done.[9] This suggestion is certainly supported by the logic of the elaboration in 2.1–13, for I have already shown that the argument in 2.8–9 not only corroborates the theme that Jesus' faith is antithetical to acts of partiality (2.1) but also intimates an inherent connection between holding Jesus' faith and fulfilling the whole law. Accordingly, the rhetoric in our unit argues that the love-commandment – which the Lord Jesus Christ *and* his servant James appropriate as the summary of the whole law – is transgressed when one shows partiality.

Drawing on the fact that James 2.8 features a verbatim correspondence to one clause in Leviticus 19.18, some scholars have plausibly argued that the language in James 2.9 is also caused by our author's dependence on the "holiness code" in Leviticus (in particular, see Luke T. Johnson, 1982). For, in close proximity to verse 18, Leviticus 19.15 refers to partiality:

> οὐ ποιήσετε ἄδικον ἐν κρίσει· οὐ λήμψῃ πρόσωπον πτωχοῦ οὐδὲ θαυμάσεις πρόσωπον δυνάστου, ἐν δικαιοσύνῃ κρινεῖς τὸν πλησίον σου.

> You shall not render an unjust judgment; you shall not be partial to the poor or defer to the great: with justice you shall judge your neighbor (NRSV).

[9] "Rather than allusions proper," global allusions are "invocations of a whole corpus, and a world" (Alter, 1989, p. 124). So, from an intertextual perspective, we may say that James 2.1 appears to set "acts of partiality" over against what the Lord Jesus Christ believed, taught, and did.

The principal signal that James 2.9 possibly alludes to Leviticus 19.15 is the compound verb προσωπολημπτεῖν, "to show partiality, or favoritism." Both this term and the abstract compound noun προσωπολημψία in 2.1 reflect the sense of πρόσωπον λαμβάνειν (Lev 19.15), the LXX translation of the Hebrew *naśa panîm*, "to favor, to be partial" (see Thackeray, 1909, pp. 43–44). Observing that Leviticus holds "acts of partiality" to be a perversion of justice also lends support to the suggestion that James 2.9 alludes to Leviticus 19.15. For already we have seen that James reformulates "acts of partiality" (2.1) as "unjust judgments" (2.4), and that verses 2–3 and 6b–7 exemplify "unjust judgments" in the conflicting relations between the rich and the poor.[10] Moreover, Leviticus 19.15 is also similarly concerned with the poor and the mighty. While the contrast in Leviticus 19.15 uses the terms πτωχός and δυνάστης, James' contrast between πτωχός and πλούσιος echoes an equivalent concern for justice in social relations between the powerless and powerful (cf. Deut. 16.19; E. Bammel, *TDNT* VI.888). Further, there are sixteen diferent words in LXX Leviticus 19.15 and ten of them appear in our unit: the verbs: κρίνειν (James 2.12); ποιεῖν (2.8, 12, 13); a noun: κρίσις (2.13 [2x]); adjectives (used as substantives): πλησίος (2.8); πτωχός (2.2, 3, 5, 6); and the definite article, τόν (2.3, 6, 8, 10); an adverb: οὐ (2.4, 5, 6, 7, 11); pronoun: σου (2.8); and the preposition: ἐν (2.1, 2 [2x], 4, 5, 6). While the verb λαμβάνειν occurs in James six times and the noun πρόσωπον occurs twice, they appear in our unit only as compounds: in the verb προσωπολημπτεῖν (2.9) and in the noun προσωπολημψία (2.1). Indeed there are only four terms in Leviticus 19.18 that do not occur in the known vocabulary of the letter of James. These include the verb θαυμάζειν, the noun δυνάστης, the adjective ἄδικος, and the adverb οὐδέ. But even in Leviticus 19.18 we note that θαυμάζειν πρόσωπον is synonymous with πρόσωπον λαμβάνειν and therefore functionally equivalent to προσωπολημπ-

---

[10] I shall probe verses 2–3 and 6b–7 more closely in the next chapter, when I focus on the social and cultural texture of our unit. Here, I simply note that the descriptive aspects of the *ratio* (2.2–3) and the argument from a social example (2.6b–7) speak to the listeners and reader of James' time by invoking typical social relations and values presupposed in the culture from which the epistle emanates. That such an invocation of the social world has an intertextual function within the general "text of culture" should be rather obvious: "Even the behavior and manners of men can be explained not only by their membership in a certain group, but also by the period or the regime to which they belong" (Perelman and Olbrechts-Tyteca, 1971, p. 327; see pp. 327–30; and also 293–305).

τεῖν in James 2.9; similarly, δυνάστης (Lev. 19.15) is reflected in James' use of πλούσιος (James 2.6; cf. 5.1–6). As for ἄδικος in Leviticus 19.18, see ἀδιάκριτος in James 3.17 and ἀδικία in James 3.6. Finally, that there are in James several other passages in which an allusive reference to Leviticus has been hypothesized certainly makes the possibility that James is drawing on Leviticus 19 all the more attractive (cf. Laws, 1982, pp. 108–10).

On the other hand, the allusion in James 2.9 shows a much greater degree of variation than the allusion in 2.8. Not only is there no citation formula in James 2.9, there is no verbatim correspondence to Leviticus 19.15. Comparing James 2.9 with Leviticus 19.15, I find that apart from the play on πρόσωπον λαμβάνειν in προσωπολημπτεῖν, these two verses are different in both their content and form. Leviticus 19.18 comprises nineteen words which are deployed in four parallel clauses. The first three clauses are negative commandments: clauses two and three concretize the meaning of "an unjust judgment" which is introduced in clause one. The fourth clause is a positive commandment, and, standing in antithetical relationship to the previous three clauses, it calls for "just judgment"; that is, it calls for the opposite of the behavior that is prohibited in the previous three clauses. In contrast, James 2.9, with eleven words that comprise three clauses, is a maxim in the form of a present simple conditional sentence. In addition, although both James and Leviticus understand "acts of partiality" as "unjust judgments," Roy B. Ward (1966b, pp. 138–41) has shown that the history of the usage of the partiality-prohibition disallows an *a priori* determination of how an author might employ it. Nevertheless, none of these differences disproves the hypothesis that James 2.9 draws on Leviticus 19.15. They do suggest, however, that if the author is alluding to that scripture, what we have in James 2.9 is a very fine example of "recitation composition" that rearranges and rewords the antecedent wording. The author appears to reformulate the language of Leviticus 19.15 in James 2.9, and thereby to manufacture a rhetorical judgment that suits the purposes of his own argument. In the *Progymnasmata* of Aelius Theon (III, 139–291; Butts, 1987, pp. 202–222) there is ample explanation of references to antecedent texts that display precious little verbatim correspondence (see the discussion in Robbins, 1991b). Consequetly, the greater degree of variation between the apparent allusion in 2.9 and the one in 2.8 is correctly appropriated as emerging evidence for an author who is rather adept in adapting previous literature to his own persuasive purpose.

Already we have seen that James 2.9 is in form and function what Theon calls a "syllogism," a "first form of conclusion argument," and that juxtaposed to 2.8 it trenchantly addresses a behavior that is the opposite of loving one's neighbor as oneself. In consonance with Leviticus 19, the love-commandment and the partiality-prohibition are single precepts in the whole law. But in dissonance with Leviticus 19.18, James 2.8 coheres with the Jesus tradition and appropriates the love-commandment as the summary of the whole law. Further, because James 2.9 strategically recasts the reference to "acts of partiality" (Lev. 19.15) as a premise in an enthymeme, we have a new argument. Thus while our unit agrees with Leviticus 19.15 that "acts of partiality" are "unjust judgments," the rhetoric in James refigures the partiality-prohibition in Leviticus 19.15. Now the latter is not simply a precept from the written law but a rhetorical judgment that is based on the scripture recited in James 2.8, the written summary of the whole law. Hence the injunction against partiality in Leviticus 19.15 is effectively reinterpreted by our author as the opposite of "loving one's neighbor as oneself." Put differently, the Levitical partiality-prohibition is recontextualized and strategically transformed in James' rhetoric; now "acts of partiality," as ἁμαρτία ("sin"), are a failure to fulfill the whole law (James 2.9–11).

James 2.10 and 11 are the final two elements in a four-part argument from judgment based on the written law. Here also there are unmistakable intertextual references to the social codes, the conventions of thought, and the literature of the milieu that produced our argument (as we shall see).

In the analysis of the inner structure of our unit, I found that James 2.10 is, like verses 8 and 9, a rhetorical judgment expressed in the form of a syllogistic maxim, a first form of conclusion argument. Furthermore, I argued that this statement has enormous significance for the elaboration of the theme introduced in James 2.1. That is, verse 10 introduces a broad, general rule that functions as the rationale of the argument of 2.8–11, an argument that corroborates James 2.1. Actually, this verse does double duty in the strategy of persuasion in 2.1–13. It serves as the major premise of two logical deductions: first, in the enthymeme it forms with verse 9; and second, in the epicheireme it creates with verse 11.

Intertextually speaking, the rationale introduced in James 2.10 is

very interesting. In asserting that one becomes guilty of the whole
law when one fails in one point of the law, it voices the well-known
hermeneutical rule that the law in all its parts is one law.[11] There
are numerous conceptual parallels to this principle in both Jewish
and Christian literature (cf. Deut. 27.26; 4 Macc. 5.20; *T. Asher*
2.2–10; 1QS 8.16–17; *b. šabb.* 70b; *m. 'Abot* 2.1; 4.2; Philo *Leg.
Alleg.* 3.241; Gal. 5.3; see Dibelius, 1975, pp. 144–46; Laws, 1982,
pp. 111–12; and the commentaries). And as scholars both ancient
and modern have correctly recognized, the idea of the "oneness of
God's law" is also analogous to Stoicism's notion of the "oneness
of the virtues."[12] Further, the latter conception of virtue is variously exploited in the theory and use of rhetorical *topoi* in the
Greco-Roman moralists and philosophers. For example, concerning the topic of the "honorable," Cicero says, "everything in
this class is embraced in one meaning and under one name, virtue
. . . Therefore when we have become acquainted with all its parts
(wisdom, courage, justice, temperance) we shall have considered the
full scope of honor, pure and simple" (*Inv. Rhet.* 2.53.159). It
appears, therefore, that the conception reformulated in James 2.10
is something of a social convention in the culture that produced
James.

One of the most interesting conceptual parallels to James 2.10
occurs in the pre-Matthean Sermon on the Mount (Q[Matt] 5.19).[13]
Like the letter of James, the SM itself is, as George Kennedy (1984,
pp. 48–49, 39–72) has shown, a splendid example of deliberative
rhetoric; and he has further argued that the "basic proposition" of
the SM is found in Q[Matt] 5.17–20. This coheres with Hans Dieter
Betz's (1985a, p. 39) earlier argument that the latter verses are
presented within the SM as the four "hermeneutical principles
which guided Jesus in his interpretation of the Torah." And, since I
agree both with Helmut Koester (1990, p. 171) that "the author of
this epistle [James] and the redactor of Q who produced the
Sermon on the Mount belong to the same Jewish-Christian milieu,"
and also with Luke Johnson (1986, p. 457; 1982b, esp. pp. 400–01)

[11] For James the integrity of the law is derived from the presupposition that there
is one God, one law-giver; this presupposition is expressed periphrastically in the
citation formula in 2.11, and is explicit in 2.19b and 4.12a–b. Cf. Lev. 19.37.
[12] Cf. Ropes (1916, p. 200), who, in noting that Augustine (*Epistula 167 ad
Hieronymum*) drew this parallel, says: "This doctrine has plainly nothing to do with
that of James." See Dibelius (1975, p. 145).
[13] For the view that Matt. 5–7 is a pre-Matthean composition, an *epitome* of
Jesus' teachings, see Betz (1985a); also Koester (1990, pp. 166–71).

that James' appropriation of dominical sayings colors his understanding of "*all*" of Torah," that the SM and James respectively
adapt this well-known hermeneutical principle (the "oneness of
God's law") becomes a genuinely significant issue. Likewise,
because the principle in question is strategic to James 2.1–13, which
coincidentally is the Jamesian argument that says more about the
law than any other in the letter, and also because there is in the unit
an unmistakable connection between Jesus' faith (James 2.1) and
fulfilling the whole law (2.8, 10), the gravity of this parallel
conception in the SM and James is only enhanced. Finally, we
should not forget that many scholars – including Dibelius – have
observed numerous possible intertextual references to the SM in
James, among which certain ones emphasize themes that are
principal issues for both of those discourses. In particular, both the
SM and James exploit the theme that the kingdom is promised to
the poor, and they do so in terms of the traditional Jewish piety of
the poor (see esp. Dibelius, 1975, pp. 39–45). Nor should we
disregard the similarity in the tone and aphoristic quality of their
respective sayings. To these issues we will return, shortly.

The second instance in our unit that explicitly signals an intertextual reference is in James 2.11. Here, the citation formulas
(ὁ εἰπών, εἶπεν καί) introduce two commandments from the
decalogue, indicating that this verse is also a judgment based on the
written law. The commandments recited are the injunctions against
adultery and murder:

> οὐ μοιχεύσεις (LXX Exod. 20.13; Deut. 5.17).

> You shall not commit adultery (NRSV).

> οὐ φονεύσεις (LXX Exod. 20.15; Deut. 5.18).

> You shall not murder.

While the rhetorical recitation in James 2.8 precisely excerpts and
abbreviates Leviticus 19.18, the Jamesian performances here are
not verbatim recitations. The LXX renders "categorical injunctions
and prohibitions" with οὐ and the future indicative (BDF section
362). In the Hebrew Bible simple prohibitions or negative commands are expressed by the negative with the imperfect; in particular, *lō* with the imperfect is "especially used in enforcing the
divine commands" (Gesenius section 107), and this is their form in
Exodus 20.13, 15 and Deuteronomy 5.17, 18. This also is their form

in Matthew 5.21, 27; 19.18; and Romans 13.9. In James 2.11a–d, however, their form is μή with aorist subjunctive;[14] likewise in Luke 18.20. Besides these formal differences, James 2.11 presents these two prohibitions in an order that diverges from the Masoretic Text. There the decalogue lists the prohibitions against murder and adultery as the sixth and seventh commandments, respectively (Exod. 20.13, 14; Deut. 5.17, 18). The same sequence (murder, adultery) is attested in the NT and by Josephus (see Mark 10.19, which varies in the manuscript tradition; Matt. 19.18; 5.21, 27; and Joseph. *Ant.* 3.91). In contrast, James reverses that sequence, and thus agrees with the LXX and some manuscripts of the MT, as well as with the writings of Philo, Luke, and Paul.[15]

It is noteworthy that in the pre-Matthean SM, immediately following the central proposition of the discourse (5.17–20), the first two commandments of the Torah that are addressed by Jesus are the injunctions against "murder" (5.21–26) and "adultery" (5.27–30). While the order of their occurrence and the form of their presentation is that of the MT, what is of intertextual significance for James 2.10–11 is that James, just like the pre-Matthean SM, follows a reformulation of the hermeneutical principle of "the oneness of the law" (2.10) with a pointed reference to the same two injunctions (on "adultery" and "murder," 2.11). While this might seem coincidental, when it is weighed with the "cumulative effect of the parallels" that James shares with Q^{Matt} 5–7 (see Davies, 1964, p. 403, and on James' parallels to the pre-Matthean SM, see below) it only increases the likelihood that the rhetoric of the pre-Matthean SM is functioning within the milieu that originated the letter of James. In other words, just as James 2.8–9 appears to play off the rhetoric of Leviticus 19.18, 15, the reformulation of the hermeneutical principle on "the oneness of the law" followed by an invocation of the injunctions against "adultery" and "murder" in James 2.10–11 seems to echo the pragmatic dimensions of the rhetoric in Matthew 5.19, 27, 21. Moreover, viewing the pre-Matthean SM as an "epitome" of Jesus' teachings and recognizing

---

[14] Also in Mark 10.19 (variants in the MSS tradition), we find μή + aor. subj.

[15] The LXX sequence in Exod. 20.13, 15 is adultery (stealing, v. 14), murder; in Deut. 5.17, 18 it is adultery, murder (stealing, v. 19). The Nash Papyrus agrees with the LXX Exod. 20.13, 15. Philo has the sequence in LXX Deut. 5.17, 18 (*Decal.* 51, 121, 132, 168–171; *Spec.* 3.8, 83). Cf. Luke 18.20; Rom. 13.9; *Barn.* 20.1; Theoph., *Ad Autol.* 2.34; 3.9; Clem. Alex., *Strom.* 6.146.3; 6.147.2; *Quis div. salv.* 4; Justin, *Dial.* 93. On this, see Dibelius (1975, p. 147 note 122).

that it "is ultimately doctrine about the understanding and implementation of the Torah" (Betz, 1985a, pp. 6, 1–16), that James 2.8–11 is a four-part argument based on the written Torah which occurs within a unit that is headed by a reference to "Jesus' faith" (2.1) and colored by Jesus' language (2.5) makes it all the more reasonable to believe that the rhetoric of the pre-Matthean SM is intertextually significant for the author of James.

In explaining the form and order of the injunctions in James 2.11, scholars have suggested that our author is simply following a written source other than the LXX or MT, or that he is perhaps reiterating common oral church-teaching (Laws, 1982, pp. 115–16; Davids, 1982, p. 117). All such suggestions, however, are based on the notion that James' performances of previous texts are in the main "scribal reproductions." The latter "consisted of making copies of extant texts, transcribing messages and letters from dictation, and reproducing stock documents like receipts. A person received training in these skills during the elementary and grammatical phases of education" (Robbins, 1991b, p. 161). To the contrary, I suggest that James' activations of earlier literature, here and elsewhere in our unit, are not "scribal reproductions," but "progymnastic compositions." This kind of composition, "in contrast to scribal reproduction, consisted of writing traditional materials clearly and persuasively rather than in the oral or written form it came to the writer" (Robbins, p. 161). On this basis, Vernon Robbins recommends "the phrase 'progymnastic rhetoric' to refer to the phenomenon and the phrase 'progymnastic composition' to refer to the writing activities associated with [the *Progymnasmata*]"; and he reminds us that "the full spectrum of progymnastic composition is outlined and discussed" in those "Elementary Exercises" (p. 161). Therefore, whatever the source(s) of the author of James may be, he is "reciting" the words of the law in the form he chooses. For already the analysis of the intertexture of the allusions to LXX texts in verses 8, 9, and 11 makes clear that when James wants to recite a previous text verbatim, he is quite capable of doing so (2.8). Yet it also reveals that (as 2.9 and 11 show) he can adapt a previous saying to his style (2.9) or thoroughly reformulate it, writing the text "clearly and persuasively" according to his own rhetorical purpose (2.11).

It is noteworthy that James 2.8 and 11, like the traditions to which our author is heir, bring together in one argument commandments from both the "holiness code" and the "decalogue." But within the context of James 2.1–13, commandments from the written law are ratified by and subsumed under a reference to "Jesus' faith." Indeed in the rhetoric of the unit these written commandments function as supporting "proofs" for the theme in 2.1.

Specifically about 2.11, we note that the decalogue commandments serve as the minor premise in an epicheireme manufactured by verses 2.10 and 11. As such it confirms the hermeneutical principle in verse 10, the rationale for judgment based on the written law. Thus as the final statement in the four-part argument based on the law (2.8–11) and as the final proof in the confirmation proper (2.5–11) it makes clear certain facts. Namely, just as the violation of the law by committing adultery or murder (2.11) is a failure to fulfill the whole law as summarized in the love-commandment (2.8), even so acts of partiality, whether within the community (2.2–4, 6a) or outside it (2.6b–7), are sinful acts that render one guilty of the whole law (2.9–10). As transgressions of God's law, acts of partiality are therefore incompatible with Jesus' faith – that is, what Jesus believed, said, and did – and should be avoided (2.1).

In the conclusion of the elaboration, verses 12–13, there are other intertextual references that cry out for explication. One of these is the reference to the law as νόμου ἐλευθερίας ("the law of liberty," 2.12). As I have mentioned, this is the second and last time the letter refers to law in this way. The first occurrence of "the law of liberty" suggests that it is synonymous with "the perfect law" (νόμον τέλειον τὸν ἐλευθερίας, 1.25), and we have argued that both of the latter are, like "the royal law" (2.8), Jamesian epithets for "the whole law" (2.10), the law of God's kingdom (2.8; cf. 2.5). What can we determine about the intertextuality of these two references to the law?

Though we lack precise linguistic parallels for "the perfect law" and "the law of freedom" (Ward, 1966b, pp. 108–34. The phrase ḥarût ḥōq in 1QS 10.6–8 probably means "engraved law"; see Dibelius, 1975, p. 118 note 49) these Jamesian expressions echo conventional understandings in the culture. Not only is it a common notion in Jewish literature that God's law is perfect, but similar conceptions are numerous in Hellenistic philosophy. Thus, Spitta (1896, p. 54) says that by "the perfect law," James means "ein besseres nicht denkbar ist" ("a better one is inconceivable"; also Ropes, 1916, p. 177). Similar, too, is the Stoic conception of law in Cic. Nat. D. 2.6.16. And see Philo, Mos. 2.3, where God's law (the laws of Moses) is "most excellent" and "omit(s) nothing that is needful"; and with the latter reference, compare James 1.4, where "perfect" means ὁλόκληροι ἐν μηδενὶ λειπόμενοι (Ward, 1966b, pp. 109–12). In the OT and Jewish thought – and the letter of James – the law is perfect, precisely as it is one, because it comes from God (Deut. 28.1,15; Ps. 1.1–2; 19.7–11; 119.32, 45, 97; *Arist.* 31; cf. 4 Macc. 5.20, 24–26; Philo, *Mos.* 2.48; *Op.* 170–72; *Decal.* 64–65; Joseph. *AJ* 3.89–91; 4.200; also Clem. Al., *Strom.* 1.29; Ward, 1966b, p. 110; and Ropes, 1916, p. 178). So there is little reason to doubt that ὁ τέλειος νόμος is "a non-LXX Greek expression for the OT description of the law as perfect" (Ward, p. 110). While the LXX does not directly associate the Torah with ἐλευθερία (Ward, pp. 112–27), Jewish tradition – and the letter of James – relate them directly and positively. For example, *m.* '*Abot* 3.5, 8; 6.2; and cf. 4 Maccabees 14.2 (see Ropes, 1916, p. 178). Moreover, the positive correlation of "law" and "freedom" is commonplace in Cynic and Stoic philosophy, as it is in Philo, who finds not only the substance of the moral law but also "freedom" in the Law of Moses (Philo, *Mos.* 2.48; *Omn. prob. lib.* 45; cf. Xen. *Mem.* 4.5.2; Diog. Laert. "Diogenes" 6.71; "Zeno" 7.121; Cic. *Parad.* 34; Seneca *De vita beata*, 15.7; Epict. *Diss.* 1.4.32; 4.1.54, 152, 158; M. Ant. 7.9.2).

Thus I conclude that the similarity of these expressions to Hellenistic philosophical conceptions suggests them to be our author's inventive appropriations of the broader culture.[16] And this suggestion is fortified by what we have already seen of the author's handling of rhetorical *topoi*, for there is an unmistakable correspondence between the use and function of the *topoi* in James 2.1–13 and their use and function in Hellenistic paideia and philosophy. This is not to say that the specific content of these values ("freedom," "perfection") in the Hellenistic moralists or philosophers is precisely the same in James. It is to say that for James "freedom" and "perfection" are both moral and theological values, and to a diaspora audience (James 1.1) they would certainly have the "aura of Greek values" (see Mack, 1990, p. 47; and his discussion of rhetorical *topoi*, pp. 37–41). Consequently, it is not surprising that James appropriates and adapts "complex"

---

[16] "A tacit claim that the Greek philosopher's ideal of freedom characterises the Jewish and Christian law may possibly underlie the language of James' (Ropes, 1916, p. 180; cf. Dibelius, 1975, pp. 116–17).

Hellenistic values like τέλειος and ἐλευθερία in characterizing the law.[17] In so doing, he very adeptly represents his appropriation of the law as the way to "perfection" and "freedom."

There were in other sectors of early Christianity very different assessments of the law. In particular, Paul and his followers certainly shared a different opinion: "Christ is the end of the law" (Rom. 10.4). It is apparent from James 2.1–13, and also from the pre-Matthean SM, that the authors of those texts would not have agreed with Paul's assessment of the law. Commenting on James' provocative epithets for the law, especially, "the law of freedom" (1.25; 2.12), Betz (1985b, p. 38; cf. 1978, p. 174 note 106; p. 299 note 65) correctly says: "Paul, on the other hand, finds it possible to bring together such concepts as 'freedom' and 'law' only in the form of an involved and complicated definition (Rom. 8.2)." It is simply beyond the scope of the present investigation to pursue this further. I have mentioned it because it is possible that our author was aware of views similar to Paul's, and if so, then it is also possible that James' epithets are voiced in conscious opposition to such views. But whether the author of James knew of such opinions, his use of conventional values to describe the law resonates with the "text of culture" from which his epistle emanates.

Similarly, in looking at the intertexture of James 2.13 which invokes the themes of judgment and mercy, we find that most commentators agree that the conception expressed in this verse is conventionl in Jewish thought and literature from the prophets to the rabbis (see Sir. 29.1; *T. Zeb.* 5.1; cf. Tob. 4.10–11; cited in Dibelius, 1975, pp. 147–48). For example, Ropes (1916, p. 201) notes that its performance in "Jer. Baba q. viii, 10, 'Every time that thou art merciful, God will be merciful to thee; and if thou art not merciful, God will not show mercy to thee,'" is very close to the performance in James 2.13. Moreover, and especially significant,

[17] For a brief overview, references, and discussion of τέλειος and related terms, see G. Delling, *TDNT* 8.49–87; esp. pp. 67–78; for ἐλευθερία, see *EDNT* I.431–34; and also H. Schlier, *TDNT* II.487–502. As rhetorical topics, τέλειος and ἐλευθερία are "complex" values. On the one hand, they have intrinsic worth; that is, they are perceived as desirable in and of themselves, for they are virtuous (Cic. *Inv.* 2.53.159). On the other hand, they are commonly perceived as values that promote one's "security" and "welfare"; thus they are "advantageous" (Cic. *Inv.* 2.55.166; 56.168). That the author characterizes the law as "the perfect law of freedom" and proclaims the fulfillment of that law in the love-command ("the law of God's kingdom") shows where he locates "perfection" and "freedom." James' "decorative epithets" to the law thoroughly correspond to the persuasive intent of the discourse.

are the similar conceptions attributed to Jesus in the pre-Matthean SM: Q[Matt] 5.7; 6.14; 7.1 (see also Matt. 18.23–35; cited in Ropes, p. 201).

It will be remembered, however, that Dibelius and others have found only a superficial "catchword" connection between verses 12 and 13 (Dibelius, 1975, pp. 147–48; and Laws, 1980, pp. 116–18). I agree that Dibelius is probably correct in judging verse 13 to be an isolated or free-floating saying, but, when he argues that it offers no particular support for the preceding elaboration Dibelius is simply wrong. The primary issue is not that the author employs a "free-floating saying," but how he exploits it, as well as how and for what purpose he makes it function within his discourse.

In the previous chapter I showed that James 2.12–13 forms an epicheireme, a logical deduction, which produces an excellent rhetorical conclusion for the elaboration in 2.1–11. That is, while being a completely logical argument in its own right, it also provides an adequate transition to the next elaboration in 2.14–26, and it does so by summarizing the whole preceding argument as a call for a particular kind of behavior toward the poor neighbor. Thus, it concludes the elaboration by arguing that those who hold Jesus' faith are not to "unjustly judge" their poor neighbors by showing partiality to the rich but to love the poor as they love themselves by showing them mercy. And I reiterate that the rhetoric in 2.12–13 relates "love of neighbor" and "showing mercy" as a rhetorical argument from "genus" (love) to "species" (mercy; Arist. *Top*. 2.4.26–28). Moreover, there is intertextual evidence to corroborate this.

While the appeal to "mercy" is both proper and conventional in *adfectus* and certainly draws on the emotional connotations of mercy in the broader culture, it is more than an "emotion" in James 2.13. On the one hand, "mercy" is here, as it is particularly in Jewish and Christian literature, an attribute of God. For example, Eur. *Or*. 333; Menand. *Epit*., 490; Lib. *Or*. 64.112; *Corp. Herm*. 13.3; 7; 8; 10 (cited in Bultmann, *TDNT* ii.478). Plutarch associates Zeus and mercy (*De cohibenda ira*, 9.458B; cited in Betz, 1975a, p. 188; see Exod. 34.5–6; Deut. 4.31; Ps. 102.8; 3 Macc. 6.9). Specifically, it is an attribute of action, something that God does (Exod. 33.19; 34.5–6; Deut. 4.31; Isa. 30.18; 2 Esdr. 1.25; Tob. 13.2, 5, 9; Jdt. 16.15; Luke 1.50, 54; Eph. 2.4; 1 Tim. 1.2; 2 Tim. 1.2; Tit. 3.5; Heb. 4.16; 2 John 3). Moreover, when Jewish and Christian literature refers to God "showing mercy" what is usually in view is an act of love (Bultmann, *TDNT* ii.480–81). On the other hand, in the LXX ἔλεος is demanded by God of those to whom God shows love (Micah 6.8; Zech. 7.9–10; LXX Jer. 9.23; Hos. 12.7; cf. Dan. 4.27; Sir. 3.30; 40.17; and Tob. 4.9–11. Matt. 5.7; 9.13; 12.7; 18.29, 34; 25.45–46; Mark 5.19; Luke 10.36–37; Rom. 9.23; Col. 3.12; *2 Clem.* 4.3). Ward (1966b, p. 156) notes that ποιεῖν ἔλεος "stands for the obligation given to the covenant people, expected especially toward the poor" (Ps. 37.26; Hos. 14.4; cf. James 1.27), and that later it is "expressly connected with the command to love the neighbor" (*T. Iss* 5.1–2; cf. also 7.6–7; and *T. Zeb* 5.1. See Hollander and De Jonge, 1985, pp. 242–43). What James voices in 2.12–13 had been voiced before. Thus, while the confirmation (James 2.5–11) works out the theme introduced in 2.1, the conclusion (2.11–12) summarizes the elaboration by exploiting well-known attributes of God. This is done, on the one hand, as a means of correcting a particular kind of behavior that the author, because of the written law, judges to be incompatible with Jesus' faith, a behavior that will ultimately, unless avoided, prove fatal to the community he addresses. On the other, it calls the audience to love the poor neighbor by showing him mercy.

So far, the analysis of the intertexture of James 2.1–13 has focused on activations of antecedent texts from the LXX that are interspersed with and colored by allusions to conventional ideas and values that permeated the culture from which our text emanates. And, based on the analysis of the inner texture of the unit, which showed the whole composition to be a thoroughly logical progymnastic elaboration, I have suggested that its intertexture likewise reflects the influence of progymnastic rhetoric.

Further, the logic and content of James 2.1–13 reveals that the interpersonal "actions" of the audience are viewed qualitatively in relation to Jesus' faith, God's actions, God's law, and judgment under God's law. Indeed throughout the unit the rhetoric plays the topic of προσωπολημψία in relation to Jesus' faith, God's actions, law, and judgment, on the one hand; and, on the other hand, in relation to the addressees' behavior in words and deeds toward the poor neighbor. The interpersonal relations ("actions") of the elect poor are the central issue in the letter of James (Ward, 1966b) and throughout the discourse this issue is played by a servant of God and of the Lord Jesus Christ (1.1). The letter-prescript is recalled in the pointed reference to Jesus' faith in 2.1, and the latter verse is the first statement in the first and fundamental argument in the letter-

confirmatio (2.1–5.6). Likewise, "the law" and "judgment," which are integral to this first argumentative unit, show themselves to be dominant concerns throughout the letter, too. For example: κριτής, James 2.4 (elsewhere in 4.11, 12; 5.9); κριτήριον, 2.6; κρίνω, 2.12 (elsewhere 4.11 [3x], 12; 5.9); κρίσις, twice in 2.13 (elsewhere 5.12); and νόμος, 2.8, 9, 10, 11, 12 (elswhere 1.25; 4.11 [4x]).[18]

Of fundamental significance for our purposes is the way the logic of the rhetoric subsumes the references to God's action, law, and judgment under a reference to Jesus' faith and argues that holding Jesus' faith and fulfilling God's law are counterparts. Moreover, James 2.5, the first supporting proof of the theme that is elaborated in James 2.1–13, colors the reference to Jesus' faith (2.1) and the proofs that follow (2.6–13) with language that, intertextually speaking, resonates with the language of a well-known and widely circulated saying of Jesus. It would seem, therefore, that there is very good reason to agree with Koester (1990, p. 171) that for the author of James "the followers of Jesus belong to law-abiding Israel and that fulfillment of the law, though without any emphasis upon circumcision and ritual law, is the appropriate interpretation of the teachings of Jesus."[19] And it is on this basis that I turn now to my central concern, the intertextuality of the statement in James 2.5.

In chapter 1 I introduced the widely-held view that the letter of James exploits a tradition of Jesus' sayings as part of its discourse (Davids, 1985; Luke Johnson, 1986, pp. 457–58, 459–60; and Deppe, 1989). And, in the course of this investigation, I have reiterated this hypothesis as it has suggested itself to the discussion. Now, in looking at James 2.5 as an instance of intertextual reference, we need to keep before us certain salient facts.

First, while almost all commentators hear echoes of Jesus' sayings in James, they are quick to note that the text does not once quote Jesus (Deppe, 1989, pp. 55–149, 167–88, 219–30; and Popkes, 1986, pp. 156–76). Nevertheless, based on previous

[18] On the linear development of rhetorical discourse, see esp. G. A. Kennedy (1984, pp. 5–6, 146, 147); and on rhetorical "liaison," see Perelman (1982, pp. x, xiv, 49, 50, 81, 89–101).

[19] Whatever the author may or may not have thought about the so-called cultic ordinances of the law, matters like circumcision and dietary ordinances, we do not know: "He simply passes over them in silence" (Seitz, 1964, p. 485). To put it differently but fairly, he mentions the cross, the resurrection, and the gospel almost as frequently as he does circumcision; that is, not at all.

research which has demonstrated that in James there are certain sayings that reflect a widespread terminological, material, and religio-historical appropriation of a tradition of Jesus' sayings, the prevailing conclusion among scholars is that the text definitely alludes to sayings that in other literature are directly attributed to Jesus (Dibelius, 1975, pp. 28–29).

Second, about James' not quoting Jesus, we must not overlook the significance of the fact that all the "wise sayings" in the epistle are attributed sayings; that is, they are presented as the words of "James" (1.1). The scholarly consensus is that the Epistle of James is intimately connected with the wisdom tradition, and it is frequently characterized as a type of sapiential discourse (Dibelius, 1975, esp. pp. 1–57; Halson, 1968; Hoppe, 1977; and Baasland, 1982, pp. 123–25, esp. p. 124). This attribution raises a most important rhetorical issue, namely the *ethos* of the author that the letter evokes. Apparently, it evokes the *ethos* of James the Lord's brother. By the letter prescript, the *ethos* of the author constrains the whole discourse. From a rhetorical perspective the *ethos* of the author includes not only the reputation which the author brings to his or her discourse. It also involves the author's characterizations of himself or herself in the discourse; and this includes the style and kinds of arguments employed in the discourse itself (Bitzer, 1968, p. 8; cf. Arist. *Rhet.* 3.19.1; 1.9.1–41). Whether James the Just actually wrote this letter is not our concern here. As I have mentioned, what is important is that this letter seemingly wishes to be heard as a discourse from that James (see Kümmel, 1965, p. 412). In addition to the author's name, which is mentioned but once (1.1), the text identifies him as "a servant/slave (δοῦλος) of God and of the Lord Jesus Christ" (1.1a), and as a "teacher" (διδάσκαλος) and "brother" (ἀδελφός) of his addressees (3.1).

Though the title, "a slave (δοῦλος) of God," has an obvious and important religious meaning, I am just as interested in the social and rhetorical significance it would have had in the Greco-Roman world. In that milieu the "slave" metaphor was similarly employed by persons who desired to present themselves as spokespersons and representatives of their master or patron. This view is confirmed by the excellent study of Dale B. Martin, (1990, pp. 54–58): "One does not, in the end, relativize the authority of Peter, James, Jude, or Paul by thinking of them as slave agents of Christ. Rather, one ties what they say more firmly to the unquestioned authority of the founder whom they represent" (p. 58; see esp. pp. 1–116, 136–49).

Therefore, the epistolary prescript (1.1) makes a bold claim for the author as a leader and authority for the community addressed. It claims for the writer the status of a client; his patrons, those for whom he speaks, are God and the Lord Jesus Messiah. There are other clear indications of patronal language and ideology in James, as we shall see (on the influence of patronal language and ideology in the Greco-Roman world, see esp. Saller, 1982, pp. 7–39).

That he is a "teacher" (διδάσκαλος) likewise suggests an elevated and honored status of leadership within the community; and the tone of the discourse coheres with this. For, judged by the ancient standards of Demetrius, the tone is not that of a friendly letter but that of an *ex cathedra* address (*Eloc.* 231b–232; see above in chapter 1, p. 7). The sententious maxims and aphoristic style in our unit, the topics that are used and the ways in which they are employed, only strengthen the image of a wise and moral teacher who identifies with and is sincerely concerned for his audience (ἀδελφοί; on the use and *ethos* of maxims, see Arist. *Rhet.* 2.21.9–16). The use of ἀδελφός ("brother"), which evokes "companionship, intimacy, and kinship and similar relations," belongs to the *topos* of "friendship" (Arist. *Rhet.* 2.4.28) and it undergirds the "communal concern" of the discourse. Concerning the rhetorical *topos* of "friendship," Aristotle says, "a friend is one who loves and is loved in return, and those who think their relationship is of this character consider themselves friends" (*Rhet.* 2.4.2; see 2.4.1–29). And, as I showed in the last chapter, the pattern of argumentation by which the author elaborates the theme in 2.1 further suggests the influence of the school and the *Progymnasmata*, and that influence has again shown itself in the way our author activates antecedent texts as part of his persuasive purpose. It should also be noted that the influence of the school and progymnastic rhetoric goes a long way in explaining the so-called "diatribal features" that Ropes (1916, pp. 3, 10–18) and Dibelius (1975, p. 2 note 6, and pp. 38, 124–25) have underscored in the letter.

Third, while there is no consensus among scholars about the particular traditions or sources from which our author "invented" his allusions to Jesus tradition, the predominant view is that our author is not dependent upon the canonical Gospels. Rather, he appears to appropriate Jesus tradition from sources very similar to those employed by the canonical Gospels, sources perhaps like the Synoptic Sayings Source (Dibelius, pp. 28–29). Moreover, the surest instances of intertextual reference to Jesus' sayings belong for the most part to the pre-Matthean SM, "specifically to Matthew 5" (Koester, 1990, p. 171). I am chiefly interested in what James appears to do with Jesus tradition in 2.5, and how this functions in the rhetoric of our unit.

The prevailing hypothesis among Jamesian scholars is that James 2.5 alludes to a saying of Jesus that is performed in four other early Christian texts: Matt 5.3; Luke 6.20b; *Gos. Thom.* 54; and Pol. *Phil.* 2.3. These five texts read as follows:

(1) James 2.5

Ἀκούσατε, ἀδελφοί μου ἀγαπητοί· οὐχ ὁ θεὸς ἐξελέξατο τοὺς πτωχοὺς τῷ κόσμῳ πλουσίους ἐν πίστει καὶ κληρονό-μους τῆς βασιλείας ἧς ἐπηγγείλατο τοῖς ἀγαπῶσιν αὐτόν;

Listen, my beloved brothers (and sisters): Has not God chosen the poor before the world to be rich in faith and heirs of the kingdom which he promised to those who love him?

(2) Matthew 5.3

Μακάριοι οἱ πτωχοὶ τῷ πνεύματι, ὅτι αὐτῶν ἐστιν ἡ βασιλεία τῶν οὐρανῶν.

Blessed are the poor in spirit, for theirs is the kingdom of heavens.

(3) Luke 6.20b

Μακάριοι οἱ πτωχοί, ὅτι ὑμετέρα ἐστὶν βασιλεία τοῦ Θεοῦ.

Blessed are the poor, for yours is the kingdom of God.

(4) *Gos. Thom.* 54

Peje Iēsous je henmakarios ne *nhēke* je tōten te *tmentero* nempēue.

Jesus said, "Blessed are the poor, for yours is the kingdom of heavens."

(5) Pol. *Phil.* 2.3

Μακάριοι οἱ πτωχοὶ καὶ οἱ διωκόμενοι ἕνεκεν δικαι-σούνης, ὅτι αὐτῶν ἐστιν βασιλεία τοῦ θεοῦ.

Blessed are the poor, and they who are persecuted for righteousness' sake, for theirs is the kingdom of God.

A comparison of the content of these sayings shows that all five of them share οἱ πτωχοί and ἡ βασιλεία.[20] Matthew, Luke, Polycarp, and the *Gospel of Thomas* share μακάριοι οἱ πτωχοί, ὅτι, ἐστιν, and ἡ βασιλεία. With Luke and Polycarp, James shares οἱ πτωχοί, ἡ βασιλεία, ὁ θεός; and with Matthew and the *Gospel of Thomas*, οἱ πτωχοί and ἡ βασιλεία.

Matthew and the *Gospel of Thomas* refer to "the kingdom of heaven(s)," which is lacking in the versions of Luke, Polycarp, and James. Scholarship agrees, however, that "the kingdom of heaven(s)" is the functional equivalent to Luke's and Polycarp's reference to "the kingdom of God." And there is no question that James' use of "the kingdom" is also a reference to "God's kingdom" as the reward which God "promised to those who love him."

Furthermore, while the four performances of the language in James 2.5 are expressly marked, either contextually (Q[Matt] 5.3, Q[Luke] 6.20b, Pol. *Phil.* 2.3; cf. Matt. 5.1–2; Luke 6.12, 17, 20a; and Pol. *Phil.* 3.2a) or directly (*Gos. Thom.* 54), as sayings of Jesus, a distinctive signal that James 2.5 is an allusion to a saying attributed to Jesus is the fact that the common denominator in all these texts is the idea that "*the kingdom*" is promised to "the poor." And this fact marks the proximity of James 2.5 to the mention of Jesus in 2.1 as an additional signal for an allusion. Although it is true that the OT and Jewish literature reflect the notion that God has a special concern for the poor, and that James 2.5 evokes "the traditional piety of the poor,"[21] Deppe (1989, p. 90) reminds us that "there are no references in the OT, intertestamental literature, or the Talmud specifically saying that God is giving *the kingdom* to the poor" (*emphasis mine*). And he rightly concludes that "this fact makes it unlikely that a Jewish source rather than a saying of Jesus was in the James' mind." Additional support

> for the presence of a saying of Jesus lies in the fact that the word "kingdom" is not Jamesian vocabulary; James 2.5 is the only occurrence of this term in the epistle. Certainly the employment of a term particularly associated with the

[20] The saying in *Gos. Thom.* 54 is extant only in Coptic. Since the other four sayings are all in Greek, and the Coptic version of the *Gospel of Thomas* was translated from Greek, I shall use the Greek terms. According to Koester (in Layton, 1989, p. 38), the *Gospel of Thomas* "is known to have existed in Egypt before the beginning of the third century."

[21] See Koester (1990, p. 74, based on Dibelius, 1975, pp. 39–45); and Betz (1985a, p. 34).

preaching of Jesus is evidence that James is alluding to the same saying quoted in Mt. 5.3 and Lk. 6.20. This is confirmed by the fact that even critical exegetes like Dibelius and Laws admit the probability that James is consciously referring to a logion previously spoken by Jesus.

(Deppe, 1989, p. 91; see Dibelius, 1975, p. 132;
and Laws, 1980, pp. 103–04)

All the sayings except James 2.5 feature the word "blessed." On the other hand, that term occurs twice in the epistle (James 1.12, 25), and both instances are linearly and pragmatically related to James 2.5. The first occurrence of μακάριος is found in the central *propositio* of the epistle (James 1.12), and James 2.5 pointedly recalls the *propositio* with a verbatim repetition of its last clause (ὅν/ἧς ἐπηγγείλατο τοῖς ἀγαπῶσιν αὐτόν). The proposition of the epistle pronounces "supreme bliss" upon the person who successfully endures trial, for, having done so, he/she will receive "the crown of life which is promised (by God) to those who love him" (1.12). The second occurrence of μακάριος (James 1.25) is linearly related to the latter proposition (1.12), and pronounces "supreme bliss" upon the person who "perseveres" (in the midst of trials; cf. James 5.10). Furthermore, James 1.25 characterizes "the blessed person" as one who perseveres by doing what "the perfect law, the law of liberty" commands. And we have already seen how the inner texture of that verse connects the "law of liberty" in James 2.12 with 2.1 and 5. Thus I conclude that the reference to the kingdom in James 2.5 certainly connotes the conception of μακάριος that is found in 1.12 and 1.25. In addition, that connotation is marked with specificity: it concerns God's elect "poor" who, if they are "rich in faith" now, (are indeed "blessed" for they) will in the future receive "God's kingdom," the reward "God promised to those who love him."

On the form of Matthew 5.3, Luke 6.20b, *Gos. Thom.* 54, and Pol. *Phil.* 2.3, each is a macarism or beatitude, a literary form that was well known in both Jewish and Greek literature and culture.[22] Matthew 5.3 has twelve words and Luke 6.20b has ten, and both

---

[22] For a discussion of the history of tradition about the types and uses of macarisms, as well as interesting parallels that inform us about the construction of Q^{Matt} 5.3 and Q^{Luke} 6.20b, see esp. Betz (1985a, esp. pp. 26–32); also F. Hauck and G. Bertram, *TDNT* iv.362–70; Str.-B. 1.189; and cf. Strecker (1988, pp. 28–34).

sayings feature two clauses. *Gos. Thom.* 54 has eleven words, while Pol. *Phil.* 2.3 has fifteen, and each has three clauses. James 2.5, in contrast, is an interrogative sentence consisting of twenty-four words which are deployed in five clauses. Further, the four parallels to James 2.5 are well-aimed, apt, and attributed to Jesus (cf. Theon, III,1–21; Butts, 1987, pp. 186–89, 224–29; Robbins, 1988a, pp. 2–4; Hock and O'Neil, 1986, pp. 23–27, 56–57). In contrast, James 2.5 is a rhetorical example attributed to James.

Recent investigations of the Synoptic Sayings Source (Q) have uncovered intertextual relations among these texts that are highly significant for James 2.5. For example, Q scholars believe that the saying of Jesus in Q^{Matt} 5.3 and Q^{Luke} 6.20b belonged to the initial formative stage in the development of the Synoptic Sayings Source.[23] That particular stratum of Q was apparently composed mainly of wisdom sayings, many of which are also found in the *Gospel of Thomas*. Koester (1990, p. 87), for instance, finds that forty-six of the seventy-nine sayings shared by the *Gospel of Thomas* and the Synoptic Gospels are Q sayings (see his list and discussion, pp. 86–95). A number of scholars now suggest that the latter document, like Q, also predates the canonical Gospels (Kloppenborg, Meyer, Patterson, and Steinhauser, 1990, p. 103).[24] In particular, it is suggested that the source of *Gos. Thom.* 54 – a performance that is very similar to Luke 6.20b – was not Q itself, but most likely a cluster of sayings that also belonged to the initial stratum of Q. That same cluster of sayings, according to Koester (1990, p. 137), was known by Paul and also by the author of *1 Clement* (chapter 13). For our purposes, the primary significance of the previous sentence is that Polycarp *Phil.* 2.3 appears to be intertextually related to *1 Clem.* 13.2 (and probably also to the Gospels of Matthew and Luke).[25] If these scholarly hypotheses

---

[23] See Kloppenborg (1987a, pp. 171–73, 174–245). The sayings in this stratum (Q 6.20b–49; 9.57–62 + 10.2–16, 21–24; 11.2–4, 9–13; 12.2–12; 12.22–34; 13.24–30) comprise "clusters or 'speeches'" that are governed by "sapiential themes and devices" (p. 171). Thus, Kloppenborg classifies Q 6.20b as a "wisdom saying." Koester (1990, pp. 136–38, 149–71), on the other hand, classifies it as a "prophetic saying" (cf. Kloppenborg, 1987a, pp. 34–37). The reader will note that the present research presupposes that Q went through several redactional stages (see Kloppenborg, pp. 89–262, 317–28; and Koester, 1990, pp. 133–71).

[24] That the *Gospel of Thomas* may be as early as the late first century, I do not doubt. And while I agree that it draws on early sources, I am not convinced that it predates the canonical Gospels.

[25] Koester (1990, pp. 19–20; and 1957, pp. 114–20). Also see Schoedel (1967, p. 12).

about the development of the Jesus tradition are correct, then the saying of Jesus alluded to in James 2.5 is indeed a very early, widely known and exploited saying.

Fundamental also is the fact that most of the parallels to Q in the *Gospel of Thomas* belong to the pre-Matthean SM (Q^{Matt} 5–7) and to Q's inaugural sermon (Q^{Luke} 6.20b–49).[26] Concerning the Jamesian parallels to this material, whether we think about "the twenty-five most frequently mentioned parallels"[27] or limit the number to the eight instances that Dean B. Deppe has suggested as the surest instances of "conscious allusion," most of them belong to the pre-Matthean SM.[28] This fact coheres with the similar tone, quality, and theological perspective of James and the pre-Matthean SM, and it supports the hypothesis that the author of our letter and the author of Q^{Matt} 5–7 belong to the same Jewish-Christian milieu (Koester, 1990, p. 171).

The Epistle of James does not reflect a knowledge of the canonical Gospels but of the traditions and/or the sources of these Gospels, and "it is quite possible that some of these sayings and

[26] I agree with Betz and Koester that the form of Q used by the author of the SM (Q^{Matt} 5.3–7.27) was different than that used by the author of the SP (Q^{Luke} 6.20b–49). See Betz (1985a, pp. 17–22, 33–36, 55–56, 89–95, 125–57) and Koester (1990, p. 133).

[27] Following Deppe's (1989, pp. 237–38) list of "the twenty-five most frequently mentioned parallels" in James to sayings of Jesus, we find that seventeen parallels are found in the SM: (1) James 5.12 // Q^{Matt} 5.33–37; (2) James 1.22–25 // Q^{Matt} 7.24–26 // Q^{Luke} 6.47–49; (3) James 1.5 // Q^{Matt} 7.7 // Q^{Luke} 11.9; (4) James 2.5 // Q^{Matt} 5.3 // Q^{Luke} 6.20b; (5) James 5.2 // Q^{Matt} 6.19–20 // Q^{Luke} 12.33b; (6) James 2.13 // Q^{Matt} 5.7 // Q^{Luke} 6.36; (7) James 3.18 // Q^{Matt} 5.9 // Q^{Luke} 6.43; (8) James 4.11–12 // Q^{Matt} 7.1–2a // Q^{Luke} 6.37; (9) James 3.12 // Q^{Matt} 7.16 // Q^{Luke} 6.44; (10) James 4.4 // Q^{Matt} 6.24 // Q^{Luke} 16.13; (11) James 1.19b–20 // Q^{Matt} 5.22a; (12) James 1.2 // Q^{Matt} 5.11–12a // Q^{Luke} 6.22–23a; (13) James 4.2–3 // Q^{Matt} 7.7 // Q^{Luke} 11.9; (14) James 5.10–11a // Q^{Matt} 5.11, 12b // Q^{Luke} 6.22, 23b; (15) James 1.4 // Q^{Matt} 5.48; (16) James 1.17 // Q^{Matt} 7.11 // Q^{Luke} 11.13; (17) James 4.13–14 // Q^{Matt} 6.34 // Q^{Luke} 12.16–21. There are ten parallels between James and the SP: numbers 2, 4, 6, 7, 8, 9, 12, 14 in the preceding list, and also (18) James 4.9 // Q^{Luke}, and (19) James 5.1 // Q^{Luke} 6.24, 25b. One of the remaining six parallels is also a Q saying: (20) James 4.10 // Q^{Matt} 23.12 // Q^{Luke} 14.11; 18.14b.

[28] According to Deppe (1989, pp. 219–20, 222–23); and also Koester (1990, pp. 71–75) there are eight instances in James that are "conscious allusions" to sayings of Jesus. Six of these are found in the pre-Matthean SM. (1) James 1.5 // Q^{Matt} 7.7 // Q^{Luke} 11.9 // *Gos. Thom.* 92, 94; (2) James 4.2c–3 // Q^{Matt} 7.7 // Q^{Luke} 11.9 // *Gos. Thom.* 92, 94); (3) James 2.5 // Q^{Matt} 5.3 // Q^{Luke} 6.20b // *Gos. Thom.* 54; (4) James 4.9 // Q^{Matt} 5.4 // Q^{Luke} 6.21b // *Gos. Thom.* 69b; (5) James 5.2–3a // Q^{Matt} 6.20 // Q^{Luke} 12.33b // *Gos. Thom.* 76b; (6) James 5.12 // Q^{Matt} 5.24–37. The remaining two are also Q sayings: (7) James 4.10 // Q^{Matt} 23.12 // Q^{Luke} 14.11; (8) James 5.1 // Q^{Luke} 6.24–25. Note that only three of the eight instances occur in the SP: numbers 3, 4, and 8.

injunctions were known to James as sayings of Jesus" (Koester, p. 75). It is my opinion that the rhetoric of the pre-Matthean SM, or a collection of sayings very like it, is firmly set and functioning in the environment from which the letter of James originates. Let us look more closely at the functions of James 2.5 and its parallels.

In Q^{Matt} 5.3 the first clause, the macarism, "Blessed are the poor in spirit," is an "anti-macarism" (see Betz, 1985a, p. 30; based upon Gladigow, 1967, pp. 404–33). It is a wisdom statement; that is, it grows out of the wise person's critique of conventional values, such as "Blessed are the rich" (Betz, pp. 30–31). The second clause, "for theirs is the kingdom of heavens," is, as the causal particle (ὅτι) suggests, the reason or rationale for the macarism. This clause is also an eschatological statement and refers proleptically to the last judgment (p. 26). So, as W. D. Davies and D. Allison (1988, p. 445) suggest, "the meaning is neither that the poor [in spirit] now possess the kingdom (it is God's possession) nor that the kingdom consists of the poor [in spirit]; rather are we to think, 'To the poor [in spirit] will be given the kingdom of heaven.'"

Note, too, that Q^{Matt} 5.3 is a rhetorical syllogism, an enthymeme, as are all the beatitudes in Q^{Matt} 5.3–11 (G. A. Kennedy, 1984, p. 49; Robbins, 1985b, pp. 46–51). The rhetorical conclusion is the macarism; the ὅτι clause is the minor premise. As is typical of enthymemes, one of the premises is unstated and tacitly assumed. In this case it is the major premise, something like: "Blessed are they to whom the kingdom of heavens will be given." Further, the enthymeme assumes that the audience would have regarded "the kingdom of heavens" as desirable and advantageous.

In discussing the function of Q^{Matt} 5.3 I should also emphasize that whatever "the poor in spirit" means, it is in this beatitude a quality characterized by actions that one must possess to enter "the kingdom of heavens" (see Strecker, 1988, pp. 33–34; and for a different view, see Guelich, 1982, pp. 109–11). In other words, it characterizes an achieved status, one that marks the achiever as blessed (Robbins, 1985b, pp. 46–51). This is a most important point, for, as Hans Dieter Betz and others have rightly argued, salvation in this discourse depends on hearing and doing the law of God as it is interpreted by Jesus (Betz, 1985a, pp. 34–35; 95, 114, 127, 155; and Strecker, 1988, pp. 30–35, 164–68). Speaking rhetorically, George Kennedy (1984, pp. 46–47) concurs with this assessment and argues that the stasis of the pre-Matthean SM is one of fact; that is, it concerns the question of actions in thought, word, and deed.

Therefore, the argument in Q^{Matt} 5.3 is plainly deliberative rhetoric; that is, it contains advice for the audience's present behavior in the light of a future or eschatological reward that is positively desirable and advantageous. While the macarism itself (Q^{Matt} 5.3a) is an epideictic statement, it functions as the conclusion of a deliberative deduction. Moreover, the pre-Matthean SM is a very clearly focused and well-orchestrated deliberative discourse (G. A. Kennedy, 1984, pp. 39–63).

Q^{Luke} 6.20 is certainly similar to Q^{Matt} 5.3, but there are marked differences in the formal aspects, the reasoning, and the function of the two sayings. Concerning their formal details, the first clause, "Blessed are the poor," is, like Q^{Matt} 5.3a, an anti-macarism. It repeats the first three words (μακάριοι οἱ πτωχοί) of Q^{Matt} 5.3a, but lacks the latter's qualification of the poor ("in spirit"). The second clause: "for yours (ὑμετέρα) is the kingdom of God (τοῦ θεοῦ)" is also like Q^{Matt} 5.3b, a ὅτι clause that invokes an eschatological verdict as the rationale for its macarism. On the other hand, besides having "of God" rather than "of the heavens," it is fundamentally different from Q^{Matt} 5.3b, since it is formulated in the second, rather than in the third, person. Whether this form is earlier than that of Q^{Matt} 5.3 remains undecided (Kloppenborg, 1987a, p. 173).

Like Q^{Matt} 5.3, Q^{Luke} 6.20b is also an enthymeme, a rhetorical syllogism. The macarism is the rhetorical conclusion and the ὅτι clause is the minor premise; the major premise, as in Q^{Matt} 5.3, is tacitly assumed. Here, however, it is something like, "You to whom the kingdom of God belongs are blessed." Because of the use of the second person plural in the stated minor premise, the syllogism is not in typical form, and reformulating the enthymeme is more difficult than is the case with the syllogism in Q^{Matt} 5.3 (see Robbins, 1985b, p. 50). Moreover, as Vernon Robbins (pp. 53–55) has shown, the reasoning in this syllogism inverts the reasoning in Q^{Matt} 5.3. Whereas the reasoning in the latter statement is typical of syllogistic reasoning, since it reasons from the general (unstated Major premise: "Blessed are those to whom the kingdom of God will be given") to the specific (Conclusion: "Blessed are the poor in spirit"), Q^{Luke} 6.20b reasons from the specific (unstated Major premise: "You to whom the kingdom of heaven belongs are blessed") to the general (Conclusion: "Blessed are the poor"). In other words, the use of the second person plural in the minor premise (Q^{Luke} 6.20c) to support the general conclusion (Q^{Luke} 6.20b) suggests that "the reasoning in the Lukan version begins with a conviction that the people spoken to possess the kingdom of God" (p. 56).

Besides the differences in the formal aspects and reasoning of Q^{Matt} 5.3 and Q^{Luke} 6.20, there is a difference in function. Though both statements occur in their respective discourses as the first statement of a rhetorical proem, Q^{Matt} 5.3 pronounces a blessing on people of an achieved status ("the poor in spirit") but Q^{Luke} 6.20b addresses people in the ascribed state of social and economic poverty ("the poor"; see Robbins, 1985b, pp. 51–56; and Kloppenborg, 1987b, p. 173). The Lukan statement is thoroughly epideictic in character; indeed it is a straightforward blessing. Q^{Matt} 5.3 is different; though it contains a macarism, it is a deliberative argument. The contrast is stated well by Koester: Q^{Luke} 6.20b "blesses the situation in which those to whom his [Jesus'] message comes happen to be" (1990, p. 156). Thus "you the poor" are "blessed" because "yours is the kingdom of God."

That Q^{Luke} 6.20b is indeed a straightforward blessing is also manifest in the antithetical structure of the formal proem to Q's inaugural sermon: four statements of praise (Q^{Luke} 6.20b–23) are balanced by four statements of blame or woe (Q^{Luke} 6.24–26). While Q^{Luke} 6.20b–26 lends itself to a deliberative purpose, that purpose appears in the proem only in Q^{Luke} 6.22–23. The latter verses are the only ones in the proem that pronounce a blessing on people of achieved status: people whose actions "on account of the Son of Man" result in religious suffering.[29] Furthermore, G. A. Kennedy (1984, p. 66) argues that the deliberative focus of Q's inaugural sermon is much less than that of the pre-Matthean SM. "Only verses 27–28 really contain advice for the future. The rest is predominantly praise and blame, that is to say, epideictic, and nowhere does the sermon present the great promise of the kingdom of God as an incentive to action." Though the Sermon on the Plain (= SP) is according to classical standards a deliberative discourse,

---

[29] The deliberative intent of the proem to Q's inaugural sermon is evinced in the pragmatic relations of the sayings; that is, in the combination of sayings that pronounce blessings on people in both ascribed and achieved states. To be specific, we find blessings and woes pronounced upon people in the ascribed states of poverty (Q^{Luke} 6.20b–21) and wealth (Q^{Luke} 6.24–25), and these are pragmatically related to blessings that are pronounced on people whose actions "on account of the Son of Man" result in their being "hated, excluded and reviled" by their own (Q^{Luke} 6.22–23).

in comparison to the pre-Matthean SM it is rhetorically a poorer speech (pp. 66–67).

The form of the anti-macarism in *Gos. Thom.* 54 is like that in Q^{Luke} 6.20b ("Blessed are the poor, for yours is the kingdom of . . ."), except for its qualification of the kingdom ("of heavens") which agrees with Q^{Matt} 5.3. Also like Q^{Luke} 6.20b, *Gos. Thom.* 54 differs from Q^{Matt} 5.3 in the rhetorical syllogism it forms; that is, it states its minor premise (like Q^{Luke} 6.20b) with the second person and thus presupposes the conviction that the kingdom of heaven belongs to people in an "ascribed" state of socio-economic poverty. Thus the reasoning in *Gos. Thom.* 54 also results in a general conclusion, "Blessed are the poor." Therefore, it has a thoroughly epideictic function like Q^{Luke} 6.20b. In sum, the form, reasoning, and function of *Gos. Thom.* 54 is similar to Q^{Luke} 6.20b, not Q^{Matt} 5.3.

Further, all the sayings of Jesus in the *Gospel of Thomas* find their significance in making the kingdom or reign of God a present reality for the understanding hearer/reader; that is to say, for the one who understands the meaning of the sayings, the kingdom is not "a future event" but a present reality (S. J. Patterson, in Kloppenborg, Meyer, Patterson, and Steinhauser, 1990, p. 115). Again, this diverges from Q^{Matt} 5.3 and James 2.5 for both of the latter view the kingdom as the future reward of those who obey the Torah.

It is significant that within Q's inaugural sermon (1) the kingdom is never exploited as an incentive for behavior; (2) there is no mention of the law in Q's inaugural sermon, nor in the earliest stratum of Q; and (3) there is no mention of "righteousness" in the SP. Yet, in the SM and in the Epistle of James all three of the latter are of cardinal importance.[30]

Present scholarship holds that the arrangement of the various sayings in the *Gospel of Thomas* is without "rhyme or reason" (Koester, 1990, p. 81). The "mode of composition" is judged to be similar to that of wisdom books (p. 80). Thus it is suggested that the meaning of each saying must be deciphered from the saying itself (p. 82). *Gos. Thom.* 54 is regarded as a "solitary" beatitude; it is sandwiched between a saying on "true circumcision" (p. 53) and a saying about hating one's family (p. 55). There are ten beatitudes

---

[30] On the law and Q, see John S. Kloppenborg (1990). I wish to thank Professor Kloppenborg for graciously sharing an earlier draft of this paper with me.

in the *Gospel of Thomas*, and, while three of them occur in series (*Gos. Thom.* 68–69), seven are "solitary" (*Gos. Thom.* 7, 49, 103, 18, 19, 54, 58; see Davies and Allison, 1988, p. 441). So, while Q^Matt 5.3, Q^Luke 6.20b, James 2.5, and (as we shall shortly see) Pol. *Phil.* 2.3 depend on their pragmatic relations for their meaning and interpretation, *Gos. Thom.* 54 apparently does not.[31]

The form of the macarism in Polycarp, *Phil.* 2.3 is different from the latter sayings primarily because it appears to combine two Jesus-beatitudes into one. It repeats verbatim the first three words ("Blessed are the poor") of the macarism in Q^Matt 5.3, Q^Luke 6.20b, and *Gos. Thom.* 54, but it coordinates them with the macarism in Q^Matt 5.10; though it has διωκόμενοι ("persecuted") rather than δεδιωγμένοι (Q^Matt 5.10; cf. 1 Pet. 3.14). The latter beatitude is the counterpart of Q^Matt 5.3 in the pre-Matthean SM, where it repeats the promise of God's kingdom in its second clause. While Pol. *Phil.* 2.3 agrees with Q^Luke 6.20c in referring to the "kingdom of (God)," it is formulated in the third person like Q^Matt 5.3. Thus the enthymeme it makes is similar to the latter in its reasoning from the general to the specific. On the other hand, because it pronounces a "blessing" upon people in the ascribed state of "poverty" and upon those of an achieved status ("persecuted for righteousness' sake") it reflects pragmatic dimensions that are analogous to those in the proem to Q's inaugural sermon, not those of the proem to the pre-Matthean SM.

"Persecution for *righteousness'* sake," however, is characteristic not of the SP, but of the SM; the term "righteousness" (δικαιοσύνη), as I have mentioned, does not occur in the SP. While the terminology "persecuted for righteousness' sake" in Pol. *Phil.* 2.3 shares that of Matthew 5.10, "righteousness" is understood differently in Polycarp than it is in the pre-Matthean SM. In the SM "righteousness" is an attribute of God that designates the achieved status of those who obey the law as Jesus interpreted it. In Polycarp, however, "righteousness" is nuanced by "the wisdom of the blessed and glorious Paul" (3.2); that is, by the wisdom and teaching that "by grace you have been saved, not of works" (1.3). Furthermore, Polycarp's understanding of "salvation" is different from that in Q's inaugural sermon, the pre-Matthean SM, and the Epistle of James. In Q's inaugural sermon (*not as Luke domesticates*

---

[31] It is possible, however, that future investigations into the the *Gospel of Thomas* may disclose a more thoughtful arrangement of and pragmatic relationships among the various sayings it contains.

it!) salvation is achieved by obeying Jesus' words (6.46–49). In the pre-Matthean SM salvation is achieved by obeying the Torah as Jesus interprets it (5.17–20; 7.24–28); this is suggested in the exordium (Q^{Matt} 5.3–16), indicated in the central proposition (Q^{Matt} 5.17–20), elaborated in the confirmation (Q^{Matt} 5.21–7.20), and recapitulated in the conclusion (Q^{Matt} 7.21–28). In the Epistle of James salvation (James 1.21 and 5.19–20) is achieved by obeying the Torah (2.10; 2.9, 11), and the Torah is summarized in the love-commandment (2.8; cf. 2.12–13). We recall Betz's observation (1985b, pp. 37–39) that early Christianity understood that Jesus taught the fulfillment of the law in obedience to the love commandment. And we conclude that, in a derived sense, one may say that in James, too, Jesus' understanding and interpretation of the Torah finds yet another voice.

In the SM, the various categories of the people "blessed" are all categories of achieved status; that is, all the qualities and states of existence in Q^{Matt} 5.3–12 are those that are related to "righteous" behavior, the fulfillment of the Torah as Jesus interpreted it. Consequently, the pragmatic dimensions of Pol. *Phil.* 2.3 are closer to Q's inaugural sermon than to the SM.

Whereas Q^{Matt} 5.3 and Q^{Luke} 6.20b are the first statements in the discourses they introduce, Pol. *Phil.* 2.3 occurs last among several other sayings of Jesus. Further, all the sayings of Jesus in Pol. *Phil.* 2.3 stand in an antithetical relationship to a list of vices (actions) in 2.2. Thus the rhetoric of Pol. *Phil.* 2.1–3, including the macarism in question, has a deliberative function, advising the Philippians to pursue certain actions and avoid others. Moroever, the combination of "poverty" and "persecution for righteousness' sake" coheres with the recurrent warning against "love of money" (2.2; 4.1, 3; 5.2; 11.1, 2), which is "of central importance in the letter as a whole" (see Schoedel, 1967, pp. 12, 16–17). If this is so, then it seems that Polycarp's beatitude owes its form not primarily to its source, but to its rhetorical and theological function. The deliberative rhetorical function of Pol. *Phil.* 2.3 is therefore analogous to Q^{Matt} 5.3.

How does all this relate to the form and function of James 2.5? To reiterate the obvious: James 2.5 shares two key terms (οἱ πτωχοί and ἡ βασιλεία) with Q^{Matt} 5.3, Q^{Luke} 6.20b, *Gos. Thom.* 54, and Pol. *Phil.* 2.3. Moreover, the fact that all five of these sayings exploit their common terms to produce a sentence that features the same common denominator – "God's kingdom" being promised to "the poor" – strongly suggests that James 2.5 is an allusion to an early and widely transmitted saying of Jesus. And if Deppe is correct that it is only in sayings of Jesus that "God's *kingdom*" is promised to "the poor," then we may be virtually certain that James 2.5 is indeed a Jamesian performance of a saying of Jesus.

Close at hand are the obvious differences in the form and attribution of these sayings. Q^{Matt} 5.3, Q^{Luke} 6.20b, *Gos. Thom.* 54, and Pol. *Phil.* 2.3 are beatitudes attributed to Jesus. In contrast, as was mentioned, the saying in James 2.5 is a rhetorical example attributed to James. The question naturally arises: why is James 2.5 not a beatitude, and why is it not attributed directly to Jesus, as are its parallels?

There are several reasons, the chief of which is that James 2.5 is formulated and attributed to perform a particular function within a particular discourse. It is important to remember that the four parallels to James 2.5 are sayings attributed to Jesus. Theon (III, 1–138; Butts, 1987, pp. 187–204, 224–37) reminds us that such sayings are a particular kind of reminiscence, and that they may be variously attributed.[32] In fact, the "attribution" of a saying is itself a means of rhetorical proof; indeed it is *the* crucial matter (Robbins, 1988a, p. 4).

On the one hand, an attributed saying or act necessarily says something about the person to whom it is attributed; that is, it reveals particular information about the character, the thought, and the action of the speaker or actor. On the other hand, it necessarily connects the speaker or actor with attitudes, values, and concepts that have fundamental significance for the social and cultural situation into which the saying is introduced. Consequently, Q^{Matt} 5.3, Q^{Luke} 6.20b, *Gos. Thom.* 54, and Pol. *Phil.* 2.3 all say something about Jesus' attitude and actions toward the poor. James 2.5, on the other hand, says something about God's attitude and actions toward the poor, and it also says something about the "James" to whom it is attributed. And in all these texts the message concerns "the poor" and "God's kingdom."

The precise content and function of that message, however, is very much determined by the rhetorical and pragmatic dimensions

---

[32] The various exercises performed on and with the chreia, an attributed saying or act, enabled a speaker/writer to exploit it for rhetorical purpose; see Theon, III, 139–291 (Butts, 1987, pp. 204–23, 237–54). Moreover, the literature shows the numerous and different ways that chreiai were attributed and used; see the discussion in Robbins (1991b, pp. 172–77).

of the particular discourse within which we find these sayings, except, *perhaps*, for *Gos. Thom.* 54.[33] Q^{Matt} 5.3, Q^{Luke} 6.20b, and Pol. *Phil.* 2.3 occur within deliberative discourses that are centered on Jesus. James 2.5, however, is part of a deliberative epistle that is predominantly theocentric. How surprising is it, really, that James 2.5, the first fundamental and supporting proof in the first and fundamental argumentative unit of a Christian theocentric document, should mention an action of God to buttress its theme? On the other hand, what is unmistakable about James 2.5 is the fact that, while it speaks of God's action with reference to "the poor," the language of the sentence resonates with the texture of a well-known saying of Jesus in which the poor are promised God's kingdom. Moreover, James 2.5 achieves its meaning and function as a rhetorical example in an elaboration that recalls Jesus' faith (2.1). In other words, the language of Jesus is here reformulated into a statement about God, and it is marked by, subsumed under, and intimately connected to Jesus' faith. Indeed, as I showed in the last chapter, the rhetoric of James 2.5 depends upon that connection. If, as I suggested above, the reference to Jesus' faith is intended to evoke what Jesus himself believed, said, and did, then the implication in James 2.5 is that Jesus' faith is thoroughly consonant with God's words and deeds toward the poor.

This implication only reiterates what the inscription of the letter obviously presupposes. That is, when the text introduces the author, via the δοῦλος metaphor (James 1.1), as a spokesperson for God *and* the Lord Jesus Christ, it informs the audience that the discourse presupposes a complete consonance of will and purpose between God and Jesus (a fact so obvious that it hardly needs mentioning). Consequently, when James 2.5 reformulates the language of an early and well-known saying of Jesus as a historical example that discloses God's attitude and action toward the poor, it functions as a precedent that not only reminds the audience of the unity of will and purpose between God and Jesus toward the poor; it also very effectively makes an indirect claim for the authority of what Jesus said and did toward the poor.

Furthermore, because the technique of allusion generally assumes a commonly held literary tradition between the speaker/writer and the audience (see Perelman and Olbrechts-Tyteca, 1971,

---

[33] The saying in *Gos. Thom.* 54, according to Koester (1990, p. 82), "has meaning in itself," and thus it apparently does not depend on the other sayings in its context for its meaning.

pp. 170, 177; and *The Princeton Encyclopedia of Poetry and Poetics*, p. 18), it is reasonable to believe that the author assumes that the Christians he addresses knew (in some form or other) the saying of Jesus he exploits in James 2.5. This appears to be the case, for the way James introduces and performs this statement indicates that he is appealing to something that is already known by his Christian audience. If this is true, the allusion is a very effective ploy to render the theme of the argument all the more acceptable.

There is another very important aspect to the allusion in James 2.5, and it has to do with the fact that this performance of a saying of Jesus is attributed (apparently) to James the Lord's brother. Modern rhetoricians remind us that one of the primary effects of allusion is an increase in the prestige of the speaker (Perelman and Olbrechts-Tyteca, 1971, pp. 177, 305). Therefore, whoever wrote this letter made a huge claim for James the Just. For to an audience who knew the language in James 2.5 as that of Jesus, the author, "a servant of God *and* the Lord Jesus Christ," comes across as one who, like Jesus, spoke and taught the wisdom of God.

In whatever form, whether oral or written, the author knew this saying of Jesus, both the differences and similarities it shares with its parallels, as well as the particular function it performs in the elaboration, suggest that James 2.5 is a progymnastic composition. Which is to say that the author appears to have recast and recited a saying of Jesus just as easily as he recited the essence of Leviticus 19.15 in James 2.9. Thus, whether he activates an antecedent text from the LXX, as in James 2.8, 9, and 11, or a religious and social convention within the culture (2.10), or a well-known saying of Jesus (2.5), he uses as much or as little verbatim performance as suits his purpose (see Robbins, 1991b). All these performances suggest a manner of composition that is not scribal but progymnastic. James 2.5 is thoroughly explicable as a rhetorical recitation of a saying attributed to Jesus.

Conclusions

Before we turn to the social and cultural texture of James 2.1–13, there are several specific intertextual features of James 2.5 that we should keep in mind. From what we have seen thus far, the intertexture of James 2.1–13, with its concern for the law, judgment, and what God (and Jesus) said and did, appears to be closer to the pre-Matthean SM than to Q's inaugural sermon, the *Gospel of Thomas*, and Polycarp's *Philippians*. Likewise, the intertextuality of James 2.5 reflects more closely the saying in Q^{Matt} 5.3 than the sayings in Q^{Luke} 6.20b, *Gos. Thom.* 54, and Pol. *Phil.* 2.3. For James 2.5 and Q^{Matt} 5.3 achieve their meanings and functions as key elements in deliberative discourses that are fundamentally concerned with actions, and those actions are intimately connected with the law, judgment, and sayings of Jesus. Thus, in my opinion, there is an unmistakable difference in the perspectives of Q^{Luke} 6.20b, *Gos. Thom.* 54, and Pol. *Phil.* 2.3, and the perspective of Q^{Matt} 5.3 and James 2.5. To put it pointedly, there is an intertextual relationship not just in the terminology of Q^{Matt} 5.3 and James 2.5 but also in their reasoning, their focus, and their rhetorical and theological functions.

Of particular significance is the manner in which both of these sayings similarly exploit the traditional piety of the poor. Hans Dieter Betz (1985b, p. 34) has argued that the phrase "the poor in spirit" in Q^{Matt} 5.3 has "two principal aspects": (1) "it represents a correction of the notion that those who are economically poor are to be called blessed"; and, (2) being connected with "the promise of the kingdom of heaven," it discloses that the "poor in spirit" belong "to those who measure up to the required righteousness here and now." Further, and rightly, he says: "the first macarism is unfolded and variously developed in the following macarisms (Matt. 5.4–12). Together they constitute the self-consciousness of the community . . . The rest of the SM is nothing else than the concretization and elucidation of the first macarism [Matt. 5.3]" (p. 35).

In the previous chapter, I argued that the rhetoric of James 2.1–13 plays on the fact that its audience is for the most part socio-economically impoverished ("the poor before the world"); but James 2.5 manipulates their socio-economic impoverishment from the perspective of the Jewish piety of the poor. Some scholars (e.g., Davids 1988, p. 3639), suggest that the opposition between the rich and poor in James may mean that James is closer to Q^{Luke} 6.20b–49 than to Q^{Matt} 5–7. It is true that James and Q^{Luke} share the terms "rich" and "poor," while the pre-Matthean SM does not mention "the rich." But as I have shown, "rich" and "poor" in James are references to achieved states; in the SP they are references to ascribed states. Further, while James and the SM understand "poor" as (an achieved state) based on one's obedience to the Torah as interpreted by Jesus, the SP has no mention of the Torah or "righteousness." In James, unlike the SP, the "rich" are the powerful outsiders and enemies of the "elect poor" (James 5.1–6). They have achieved their status, not because they have wealth ("rich" and "poor" in James are not mere socio-economic designations), but because they identify with and live according to the world and its system of values (4.4). They are the enemies of the "pious poor" – the "righteous"; indeed, they kill the "righteous" (5.6). The opposition between the rich and poor in James is essentially an opposition between the righteous (= the pious poor who obey the law, 2.5, 8, 10–13; cf. 1.9) and the unrighteous (= the rich, 2.6b–7; 4.13–5.6; cf. 1.10. Compare *1 Enoch* 99.11–16). The woes on "the rich" in the SP are based not on their actions toward the poor (as in James; and also in *1 Enoch* 99.13, 15) but on their present, ascribed state of wealth: "Woe to you who are rich, for you have ['now,' Q^{Luke} 6.25, 26] received your consolation," Q^{Luke} 6.24. While James and the SP share the terms, poor and rich, they have diffrent conceptions of who those people are. The thought in James concerning "the poor" is far closer to the pre-Matthean SM than to Q's inaugural sermon. Hence, the construction of James 2.5 makes it very clear that whatever God's reason for choosing the poor the promise of the kingdom cannot be interpreted as a reward for their earthly poverty. For like the "in spirit" qualification of "the poor" in Q^{Matt} 5.3, James 2.5 positively qualifies "the poor" whom God has chosen as the "rich in faith." And, also like "the poor in spirit" (Q^{Matt} 5.3), "the poor" who are "rich in faith" (James 2.5) refers to an achieved status; moreover, in James 2.5 "rich in faith" is synonymous with "loving God," and both are functionally equivalent to fulfilling the law of God. I conclude, therefore, that "the rich in faith" and "those who love God" are Jamesian references to "the poor in spirit": "the Pious Poor" who fulfill the Torah, as interpreted by Jesus and summarized in the love-commandment. The socio-ideologically located voice in Q^{Matt} 5.3 is echoed anew in the voice of the one who speaks in James 2.5. We shall probe this more thoroughly in the next chapter.

5

THE SOCIAL AND CULTURAL TEXTURE OF JAMES 2.1–13

Introduction

The purpose of this chapter is to probe the social and cultural implications of the language in James 2.1–13 in order to determine the social function of the rhetoric in the unit. In particular, I want to determine the socio-rhetorical function of the allusion to a saying of Jesus in James 2.5.

Recalling the discussion of James as rhetorical discourse in chapter 1, I wish to reiterate several presuppositions that are integral to the purpose at hand. First and fundamental is the fact that rhetoric is social discourse that intends to evoke a social response in the thinking and/or behavior of the audience it addresses. Put differently, and with respect to the discourse of the letter of James, the epistle emerged within its culture as a social product and it functioned as a social tool. As rhetorical discourse the letter was inevitably concerned with interpersonal relations, and it intended to influence them. The Epistle of James was designed to have a social function.

Thus I emphasize again a conventional but fundamental rhetorical perspective; namely, that rhetorical discourse is always situational and always functional. It is situational because it is a response to the particular *rhetorical* situation that elicits and determines it; it is functional because it exists to alter the rhetorical situation it addresses "through the mediation of thought and action" (Bitzer, 1968, p. 4; see pp. 3–6). Consequently, rhetorical discourse is always pragmatic discourse. It does not exist for itself, nor is it an instrument of reflection. To the contrary, rhetorical discourse is generated to change reality and is fundamentally a socially motivated mode of action (p. 4).

Rhetorical criticism, as Wuellner (1987, p. 449) has argued, takes us to "the social aspect of language which is an instrument of communication and influence on others." Because the language employed in a rhetorical discourse is a social possession that is fundamentally related to its rhetorical situation (see Perelman and Olbrechts-Tyteca, 1971, p. 513) and because that situaton is a social context, the language of rhetorical discourse has a "texture" that offers clues to the social environment or the location of the thought that stands behind and within it. The context in view here is, as Wuellner (1987, p. 450, following Sloan, 1947, pp. 798–99, 802–03) puts it, the "attitudinizing conventions, precepts that condition (both the writer's *and* the reader's) stance toward experience, knowledge, tradition, language, and other people."[1] Consequently, and with respect to James 2.1–13, this means that as the rhetorical dimensions of this unit appear, the cultural and social dimensions of its language also suggest themselves.

Within the social context (the rhetorical situation) of a rhetorical discourse, the language of the rhetor seeks to constrain the thought and action (words and/or deeds) of the addressees. Thus to get inside the discourse of James 2.1–13, to probe the social implications of the situation it evokes, should provide significant clues both to the social location of its thought and also to its intended social function within its argumentative situation.

Because rhetorical discourse is intertextual discourse – a social possession that is founded on previous texts – inevitably, there is within it a dialogue among different voices. Already we have seen that by hearing the different performances of Jesus tradition in Matthew 5.3, Luke 6.20b, Pol. *Phil.* 2.3, *Gos. Thom.* 54, and James 2.5 – which deal with the theme of "the poor being promised the kingdom [of God]" – as performances in discourses that speak from and within various sectors of early Christianity, we can not only hear the nuanced concerns of different social contexts in nascent Christianity, but we can gain clues about the socio-ideologically located voice that speaks in James 2.5. And these social and cultural clues can help us understand the socio-rhetorical function of that saying.

Therefore, in order to probe the social and cultural implications of James 2.1–13, I shall establish the rhetorical situation, the question, stasis, and the species of its rhetoric. Then, because the exigence evoked by this unit (as we shall see) is fundamentally related to the conflict between "poor and rich," a theme that

---

[1] See the discussion in chapter 1, above, pp. 21–22.

comprises almost a quarter of the entire text of the letter, I shall explore the way this theme is played in the unit (via the rhetorical constraints) in the light of certain, key, cultural codes or scripts that permeated the culture from which James originates. Thus I shall identify some of the social dynamics at play in the language of the unit. Then, focusing on the social dynamics of the rhetoric in our unit, I shall ask about the kind of cultural rhetoric that James is. Finally, I shall look at James 2.5 in the light of our findings, and, based on the inner texture and the intertexture of the unit, I shall ask about the socio-ideologically located voice in that saying. It is within the social context (the rhetorical situation) evoked by the rhetoric in James 2.1–13, that we shall locate the socio-rhetorical function of James 2.5.

The rhetorical situation

As I introduced it in chapter 1, the concept of the rhetorical situation that is operative in this study was proposed by Lloyd Bitzer (1968). According to Bitzer (pp. 7–8), the rhetorical situation has three essential constituents. First is the "exigence" which is a problem or "an imperfection marked by urgency; it is a defect, an obstacle, something waiting to be done, a thing which is other than it should be" (p. 6). This problem "specifies the audience to be addressed and the change to be effected" (p. 7). Within a given context, there are a number of exigencies, some of which may not be rhetorical; "an exigence is rhetorical when it is capable of positive modification and when positive modification requires discourse or can be assisted by discourse" (p. 7). Second, rhetorical discourse requires an audience, which "must be distinguished from a body of mere hearers or readers: properly speaking, a rhetorical audience consists only of those persons who are capable of being influenced by discourse and of being mediators of change" (p. 8). The third essential is the constraints that are operative in the situation, including those that are introduced by the rhetor to persuade the audience. These are "made up of persons, events, objects, and relations which are parts of the situation because they have the power to constrain decision and action needed to modify the exigence (p. 8).

The rhetorical exigence

The rhetorical exigence in James 2.1–13 appears in the first admonition (2.1): προσωπολημψίαι, "acts of partiality." The plural form of the abstract substantive προσωπολημψία reflects classical Greek usage, and refers to the "kinds, cases, occasions, [and] manifestations of the idea" the substantive expresses (Smyth, 1956, section 1000; cf. Moulton, ii.27–28; BDF section 142). Thus, Ropes (1916, p. 185) correctly translates ἐν προσωπολημψίαις "with acts of partiality." That the whole unit concerns "actions" is supported in the summarizing maxim in 2.12, Οὕτως λαλεῖτε καὶ οὕτως ποιεῖτε. The exigence is exemplified in the preferential treatment that the community's judicial assembly gives to the wealthy brother (2.2–3).

The compound term προσωπολημψία is found only in Christian texts. It occurs in the NT but four times: Romans 4.11; Ephesians 6.9; Colossians 3.25; and James 2.1. Cf. (λαμβάνειν πρόσωπον) *Barn.* 19.4; *Did.* 4.3; (προσωπολημψία) Pol. *Phil.* 6.1; (ἀπροσω-πολήμπτως) 1 Peter 1.17; *1 Clem.* 1.3; *Barn.* 4.12 (see BAGD, *s.v.*; and Eduard Lohse, *TDNT* vi.768–80; esp. pp. 779–80). As already mentioned, it has the sense of πρόσωπον λαμβάνειν, the LXX translation of the Hebrew *naśa panîm*, "to favor, to be partial" (Thackeray, 1909, pp. 43–44). While the Hebrew phrase is used both positively and negatively, it is primarily related to the bias of a judge in a judicial context. For example, in Malachi 1.8, 9 (along with the synonymous form, ἐξιλάσκειν πρόσωπον, in Mal. 1.9a; cf. also αἱρετίζειν πρόσωπον, in 1 Sam. 25.35) it is used positively and in Leviticus 19.15; LXX Psalm 81.2, negatively. Accordingly, "to show partiality" is an act of injustice (Lev 19.15). Further, as Roy Bowen Ward (1966b, pp. 41–77; esp. p. 77) has shown, even when the term is employed outside the context of a courtroom, "judgmental overtones" are customarily associated with it.

We have observed that the unit characterizes "acts of partiality" in several important and interrelated ways. Here it is enough to note that "showing partiality" is viewed by the author as a "sin" (the verb προσωπολημπτεῖν is *hapax legomenon*, occurring in the NT only in James 2.9; cf. Pol. *Phil.* 6.1; see MM, *s.v.*, p. 553). That particular characterization of "acts of partiality" shows how the exigence in James 2.1–13 is related to what appears to be the primary rhetorical problem of the letter.

George Kennedy (1984, esp. pp. 33–36) reminds us that when a rhetorical analysis concerns a unit that is but one part of a larger discourse, an awareness of the rhetorical situation that generated the whole may prove helpful in understanding the rhetoric of the particular part.[2] The rhetorical situation that apparently occasioned the letter of James is played out in the theme of "various trials," especially as trials concern "the test of faith" (James 1.2–4). As is often the case with letters, James reveals its exigence in the *exordium* (1.2–12).[3]

Like the wisdom writers, James seems to mean by such "trials" the general afflictions of everyday life in the world. The trials do not appear to be those of a particular persecution, as in 1 Peter; nor are they eschatological tribulations, as in Paul. Rather they are the perennial experience of life in the world, as in Ben Sira and others in the wisdom tradition (Laws, 1980, 50–53; Halson, 1968, pp. 308–14; and see esp. Hoppe, 1977). While the text does not precisely define these afflictions, it does suggest that in them one experiences the testing of one's faith (1.2). As the letter unfolds, moving forward "linearly" and by "liaison" (see G. A. Kennedy 1984, pp. 5–6, 146–47; and Perelman, 1982, p. 183), this fact gives structure to the whole discourse, and we find that the various trials are always addressed with respect to the overriding concern of "communal relations."

For example, in the letter's *exordium* (James 1.2–12) and *narratio* (1.13–27) we learn that the testing of one's faith may have either a positive or negative result. The *exordium* rehearses the positive aspects and results of such trials (1.3–4, 12). The positive outcome is emphatically stated: the test of faith may perfect one's endurance (1.3), and this leads not only to the achievement of a perfect and complete character (1.4), but also to a future reward, "the crown of life," which is promised to those who love God (1.12; "the kingdom," 2.5). The *narratio* defines the negative dimension as a "temptation with evil" which, if not endured or resisted, gives birth to sin and culminates in death (1.14–15). Whatever role, if any, God is perceived to have in the testing of one's faith, a fundamental fact for James is that temptation with evil does not come from God; indeed, God himself is said to be incapable of being tempted

---

[2] For further discussion, see G. A. Kennedy (1984) on "rhetorical situation," "rhetorical problem," and "rhetorical question."

[3] See Davids (1982, pp. 35–38); Fry (1978, pp. 427–35); Hartin (1991, pp. 26–34); Hoppe (1977, pp. 1–43, 119–48; 1989, pp. 19–29); and cf. Luck (1967; 1971, pp. 163–64).

with evil (1.13, 17–18). For James the mainspring of temptation with evil is located in the addressees' own desires for pleasure (1.14). And, for this reason, a fundamental issue in the letter is the necessity of an undivided heart: an unswerving commitment to God and his purposes (cf. James 4.8b; on this see L. T. Johnson, 1985; Seitz, 1947; 1957; 1959).

The *confirmatio* of the letter (James 2.1–5.6) further embellishes this view, arguing that human desires which produce sin are informed by a wisdom that is "earthly, unspiritual, and devilish" (3.15). Associated with "the world" (4.4) and "the devil" (4.7), this wisdom is contrary to "the wisdom from above," God's wisdom (3.17; cf. 1.2). According to James, then, temptation toward evil comes from within and from without. It springs from human desires for the pleasures of the world (4.2–3), and it is inspired by the wisdom from below (3.14–16). In typical rhetorical fashion, the topics "desire" and "pleasure" are played out in connection with values that rhetorical theory specifies as being vitally connected with a deliberative cause, namely, the achievement of advantage or benefit (Arist. *Rhet*. 1.3.5; Cic. *Inv. Rhet*. 2.51.159–56.169; *Rhet. Her*. 3.2.3). The yield is disorder, wickedness of every kind, and death (James 3.16); in other words, it produces neither righteousness nor life (cf. James 1.19–27; 5.20).

There is no suggestion in James that the various trials in which one's faith is tested can be removed. On the other hand, the text passionately maintains that this exigence can be modified. To put it another way, given the quality of trials of faith, the fundamental rhetorical stasis in the letter of James is one of fact. "What shall we do?"[4] From beginning to end the letter answers this question by seeking to persuade its hearers to endure their various trials of faith (James 1.2–5), to resist evil and honor God (4.7–10). Indeed, the whole letter turns on the central *propositio* (1.12): those who faithfully endure trials of faith are those who really love God, and it is they who will receive the promised reward and supreme joy (1.12, 25; 2.5, 26; 3.13, 18; 5.11, 19–20).

Keeping in mind that rhetorical discourse develops linearly and by liaison, and that the repetition of certain motifs and themes

---

[4] See Nadeau (1964, "Hermogenes' *On Stases*"). In judicial rhetoric, which refers to past time, the issue would be: "What was done?" In deliberative rhetoric, which refers to future action, the issue is: "What shall be done?" See G. A. Kennedy (1984, pp. 18–19, 46–47).

creates trains of thought that amplify the discourse, the qualitative characterization of "acts of partiality" as "sin" recalls the primary exigence of the whole letter. Thus, our unit confronts the problem of partialities as the negative consequent of the (negative) trial of faith; that is, it treats a particular manifestation of the temptation toward evil (1.14–15a) in terms of its negative consequent: sinful actions that are incompatible with the faith of Jesus Christ (2.1). Thus by clarifying and correcting the thoughts and actions of the audience, James tries to dissuade them from sin and death; by defining and proving what is honorable and thus beneficial, the rhetoric seeks to persuade the audience to endure their trials; to faithfully obey the perfect law, which is the word of truth and life (1.25; 5.19–20); to humble themselves before the Lord (4.10); to establish their hearts (5.8); and to hold to, and return wanderers from, the truth (5.19–20). Further, as the analyses of the inner texture and the intertexture of James 2.1–13 have shown, the rhetoric reveals that faithfully obeying the perfect law is intimately connected with the quality of Jesus' own faith (2.1). Qualitatively, from the perspective of James, such obedience is perhaps synonymous with holding the faith of Jesus Christ (2.1).

We further note that "acts of partiality" are not simply the sins of an individual; they are confronted as a social problem for the elect community, (2.2–4, 6a, 6b–7, 9). For the author of James, this behavior is a social evil that can not only kill the sinner but destroy the community. In James 2.1–13 προσωπολημψίαι are a socio-rhetorical problem. And the rhetoric of the unit is intended to modify this exigence.

The rhetorical audience

The second constituent in the rhetorical situation of James 2.1–13 is the audience that it evokes. The rhetorical audience is composed of those persons who, through their thought and action, can modify the exigence and thus alter the reality of their situation (2.6a). In other words, the audience elicited here are persons who are capable of becoming mediators of change by not "showing partiality" (2.1, 9; 2.8, 13).

Hermogenes suggests that an examination of the terms the author uses in addressing and referring to an audience can reveal those that are most capable of rhetorical development and interpretation. He delineates seven classes or ranks into which references to persons in a rhetorical discourse may be divided. A brief examination of the letter of James using the first four of Hermogenes' seven categories sets the stage (see Hermogenes' *On Stases*, Rabe, vol. vi, p. 30). Hermogenes recognized that any term may fit into more than one category or rank; thus, I have included "the rich" in three categories; "the poor" in two.

It is intriguing that nowhere in James do we find persons in the audience addressed by name (which is Hermogenes' first category). This fact coheres with the lack of specificity in the prescript (1.1) and with the general nature of the material in the letter.[5] But above all, it suggests that the concerns of the audience are treated on a communal level.

That "communal relations" are the overriding concern in James 2.1–13 and throughout the letter is suggested by Hermogenes' second category of references; namely, those that indicate a relation of one person to another.[6] First in this category are brothers (2.1; 2.5). The term ἀδελφός occurs twice in our unit: 2.1, 5. In the letter it occurs nineteen times, in the following seven forms: Ἀδελφοί μου (8x): 1.2; 2.1, 14; 3.1, 10, 12; 5.12, 19; ἀδελφοί μου ἀγαπητοί (3x): 1.16, 19; 2.5; ἀδελφοί (4x): 4.11a; 5.7, 9, 10; ὁ ἀδελφός (1x): 1.19; ἀδελφός (1x): 2.15; ἀδελφοῦ (1x): 4.11b; τὸν ἀδελφὸν αὐτοῦ (1x): 4.11b. Second are the poor (2.2, 3, 5, 6). The term πτωχός is a technical term in James; see below. Third, the rich (2.5, 6). ὁ πλούσιος is also a technical term. The adjective (πλούσιος) occurs in 1.10, 11; 2.5, 6, 5.1; cf. also ὁ πλοῦτος ("wealth") in 5.2. Following Hermogenes (see his fifth and sixth categories for ranking and scrutinizing persons, *On Stases*, Rabe, vol. vi, p. 30) and listing the descriptions and attributes of actions by which the author characterizes "the rich," we find the following: the rich oppress [the beloved brothers] (2.6b); the rich drag [the beloved brothers] into court (2.7); the rich blaspheme the honorable name which was invoked over [the beloved brothers] (2.7); the rich man will pass (1.10) and fade away in all his doings (1.11); the rich will find that their riches have rotted and their garments are moth-eaten (5.2), and the rust of their gold and silver will testify against them

---

[5] The general nature of the epistle is treated below, in the discussion of the letter prescript.

[6] The following relational terms may also be appropriated as "rhetorical constraints," the third constituent of the rhetorical situation (see below). As such, they properly belong under the topics of "justice/injustice" (*Rhet. Her.* 3.3.4) and the "praiseworthy/blameworthy" (*Rhet. Her.* 3.4.7).

in judgment and eat their flesh with fire (5.3a); the rich have laid up treasure for the last days (5.3b); they have defrauded the laborers/ harvesters who mowed their fields (5.4); they have lived on earth in luxury and pleasure (5.5a); they have fattened their hearts in a day of slaughter (5.5b); and they have condemned and killed the right-eous man (5.5c). Fourth are judges (2.4); then heirs (2.5); the neighbor (2.8; 4.12); and also the synagogue (a "judicial assembly," 2.2). Elsewhere in the letter and belonging to the category indi-cating a relation of one person to another are the terms: tribes (1.1), sister (2.15), widows (1.27), orphans (1.27), friend (2.23; 4.4), teachers (3.1), elders (5.14), and assembly (5.14).

Further, Hermogenes' category of references that carry connota-tions of blame is exploited by James in addressing problems faced by the audience in their communal relations: judges with evil thoughts (2.4); the rich who oppress (2.6b–7); those who dishonor the poor (2.6); one who shows partiality (2.9; cf. 2.1); one who commits sin (2.9; 4.8; 5.20); the transgressor (2.9, 11); one who fails in one point of the law (2.10); one who commits adultery or murder (2.10; cf. 4.4; 5.6); and the one who has shown no mercy (2.13). Other references in the letter that carry connotations of blame are: the double-minded person (1.8; 4.8); the wrathful person (1.20); "O foolish person!" (2.20); "Unfaithful creatures!" (4.4); a friend of the world (4.4); an enemy of God (4.4); and the proud (4.6).

Fourth, other references suggesting character and marking values that are important for the rhetorical audience are: the gold-fingered man, dressed in fine clothes (2.2, 3); the poor man in shabby clothing (2.2, 3); the poor (2.5–6); the "rich in faith" (2.5); those who inherit the kingdom (2.5); those who love God (2.5); those who fulfill the whole/royal law (2.8, 10); those who love their neighbors as themselves (2.8); those who are judged under the law (2.12); one who shows mercy (2.13). Elsewhere in James and belonging to this category of references are: the blessed or supre-mely happy person (μακάριος, 1.12, 25; μακαρίζειν in 5.11; also see χαρά, 1.2; 4.9; and εὐθυμεῖν, 5.13.). Included here also are the humble person (1.9; 4.6), harvesters or field workers (5.4), the rich (4.13–5.6), those who buy and sell (presumably merchants, 4.13–17), the farmer (5.7), the patient person (5.7, 8), and the suffering person (5.10, 13). Cf. the verbs κακοπαθεῖν (5.13); ἀσθενεῖν (5.14); κάμνειν (5.15); πειράζειν (1.13 [3x], 14); and also the nouns: πειρασμός (1.2,12); and θλῖψις (1.27). These are some of the more important references to people by which the author develops his picture of the audience; on this basis, he exhorts them toward the identity and behavior he wishes them to pursue.

The audience presupposed in this argument is the same one evoked by the letter prescript (1.1); that is, probably an unspecified community (or communities) of Christian Jews in the dispersion. James 1.1 is typical of ancient letter prescripts found from the third century BCE to the third century CE. It contains the three elements: the superscription or sender in the nominative case; the adscription or addressee in the dative case, and the salutation, an imperatival infinitive. Both the superscription (Ἰάκωβος θεοῦ καὶ κυρίου Ἰησοῦ Χριστοῦ δοῦλος) and the adscription (ταῖς δώδεκα φυλαῖς ταῖς ἐν τῇ διασπορᾷ) are amplified, as is customary for letters in both the NT and early Greco-Roman literature. The simple salutation (χαίρειν), though conventional in Greek letters, occurs in the NT only here and in the two embedded encyclicals in Acts 15.23 and 23.26 (see Aune, 1987, p. 184). While the letter prescript is the fundamental element in epistolary form, it is not a technical feature in rhetorical arrangement. Nonetheless, as G. A. Kennedy (1984, p. 24) and D. F. Watson (1988, pp. 40–43; 95–96) have pointed out, the prescript has an undeniable rhetorical function which is like that of the *exordium*. It joins with the *exordium* (1.2–12) to prepare the audience for the discourse that follows. Together the prescript and *exordium* introduce the author and the audience, help to establish the *ethos*, *pathos*, and *logos* of the letter, and prepare for the topics that are used in developing the discourse. The artful connection between the prescript and exordium (χαίρειν ... χαράν) is deliberate and unmistakable. On the one hand, it shows that, as the text itself reveals, there is no justifiable reason for the claim that the prescript is a later interpolation (see Dibelius, 1975, pp. 18, 20, 67–68). On the other hand, it emphasizes the topic of "joy" (χαρά) which is fundamental to the theme presented in the author's first admonition, 1.2), that an ambiguous fact of human existence, "trials" (πειρασμοῖ), can serve to their "advantage" and "well-being."

Excursus. Christian Jews in the dispersion

The adscript (1.1b) identifies the audience as ταῖς δώδεκα φυλαῖς ταῖς ἐν τῇ διασπορᾷ. Is this to be interpreted literally or metaphorically? By itself and taken literally, the phrase ταῖς δώδεκα φυλαῖς connotes Israel, the Jews (Exod 24.4; 28.21; 39.14; Josh. 4.5; Sir.

44.23; *As. Mos.* 2.4–5; *2 Apoc. Bar.* 1.2; 62.5; 63.3; 64.5; 77.2; 78.1, 4; 84.3; *T. Benj.* 9.2; Acts 26.7; see Ropes, 1916, pp. 120–25; and K. H. Rengstorf, *TDNT* ii.321–28; Maurer, *TDNT* ix.245–50).

The tribal structure of Israel was destroyed with the exile (of the northern kingdom in 722 BCE, and of the southern kingdom in 587 BCE). The Jews who returned to Judea were organized differently, as clans (Ezra 2; Neh. 7). The memory of "the twelve tribes" lived on (cf. Ezra 8.35), however, and continued to function even in the rabbinic period as a social and theological symbol of Israel's integrity and unity as God's chosen people (Cohen, 1987, pp. 104–23, esp. 115–16). Burton Mack (1988, p. 127) argues that "each of the early Jesus movements drew upon a conception of 'Israel' in order to imagine its place in the scheme of things. These conceptions determined the stance each took in relation to some form of Judaism encountered directly in its particular environment."

Qualified by the phrase ταῖς ἐν τῇ διασπορᾷ, which in and of itself refers to the scattering of the Jews, the whole expression seems to refer to the Jews outside Palestine (Deut. 30.4; Neh. 1.9).[7] On the other hand, taking the adscript metaphorically, it may refer to the Christian church scattered in the world, and thus dispersed from its real commonwealth which is in heaven (Ropes, 1916, pp. 124–25).

The latter interpretation is readily acceptable, for quite early the Christian church came to see itself as the new Israel, the new "twelve tribes"; and since heaven was understood to be the true home of the new Israel, wherever in this world the new Israel may have been, it was in the dispersion. Although the metaphorical interpretation is enticing, and despite the fact that it became and remains today the customary interpretation in both the church and the academy, Peter Davids (1982, p. 64; also B. S. Childs, 1984, p. 435) is correct, in my opinion, when he says that it leaps too quickly over the literal sense and primary meaning of the adscript.

Whether we understand this phrase literally or metaphorically, however, we must take into consideration that the whole adscript is fundamentally qualified by the superscript. To put it another way, the adscript does not stand on its own; but rather, like the whole

---

[7] The noun διασπορά occurs 3x in the NT: James 1.1; 1 Pet. 1.1; John 7.35. The verb, διασπείρω, also appears 3x: Acts 8.1, 4; 11.19. See Schmidt (*TDNT* ii.98–104); Foakes-Jackson and Lake (1920, 2.137–68); and Swete (1968, pp. 1–3).

letter, it is attributed to one Ἰάκωβος θεοῦ καὶ κυρίου Ἰησοῦ Χριστοῦ δοῦλος (1.1a). Thus we search for the meaning of the adscript in the light of the superscript. How would a reader in the first century have heard the prescript of James?

The predominant scholarly opinion holds that in early Christianity there was but one James who could have addressed a discourse in this manner and expected it to be well received. That was James, the Lord's brother (Gal. 1.19; 2.9, 12; Matt. 13.55; Mark 6.3; Acts 12.17; 15.13; 21.18; 1 Cor. 15.7; cf. Jude 1). As I mentioned earlier, whether he actually wrote our letter is not the issue before us; the question is whose identity and authority does the superscription presuppose and intend to convey (Bitzer, 1968, p. 8). The letter apparently *wishes* to be taken as a discourse by James the brother of Jesus (Kümmel, 1975, p. 412) and "more than any other person in the early church," James the Just "was the representative figure of Jewish Christianity" (Childs, 1984, p. 435).

If, then, the letter wishes to be heard as a discourse from that James, it seems plausible that the prescript wishes to evoke as the primary audience an unspecified community or communities of Christian Jews probably residing outside Palestine (Davids, 1982, pp. 63–64; Mußner, 1987, pp. 2–23, 60–61). That the author of James would have regarded as the "the twelve tribes" those Jews who embraced Jesus as Messiah is certain (1.1; 2.1). And this is strengthened by the fact that among some early Christians there was a firm belief that a part of Messiah's work was the restoration of "the twelve tribes" (see Schürer, 2.530–31; *Sib. Or.* 2.171; 3.249; Acts 26.7; also Horsley, 1987, pp. 199–208; Mayor, 1892 [1990], p. 30; and cf. E. P. Sanders, 1985, p. 106; cf. pp. 91–119). Moreover, that such an audience is in view is buttressed by the thoroughly Jewish-Christian character of the document itself. The overwhelming majority of scholars have long recognized that James is a decidedly Jewish-Christian document (Bartlett, 1979; B. A. Pearson, 1989, p. 376; and Rendall, 1927). Laws (1980, pp. 3–6; 36–38), however, is less convinced.

Where ἐν τῇ διασπορᾷ the audience was located is not stated. A "circular" or "encyclical" like James would have found applicability in a number of geographical locations. Concerning the realm of authority envisioned by the traditions of Christian Jews associated with James the Just, Koester (1982, vol. ii, p. 156) suggests that in Palestine and Syria this realm may have "included several organized local communities. One can assume that these churches were kept together not only through the sending of messengers on certain occasions, but also through writings in which the order of life for these congregations was set forth." In any case, determining the geographical location or historical situation of the letter and determining its *rhetorical situation* are not the same thing. Our purpose here is not to rehearse the various theories about the historical identity of the audience James exhorts; though, concerning such, the hypotheses by Ropes (1916, pp. 39–43) and Davids (1982, pp. 28–34) are as good as any, and better than most. Here, our primary concern is the rhetorical situation of James.

Of the various communal problems addressed by the author, the chief one is perhaps the conflict between the poor and the rich. For the most part the addressees appear to be materially poor. On the other hand, some members of the community are evidently wealthy (2.2–3; 6b–7). Further, the text suggests that the community is busily involved with living in the world (4.13–5.7). That the author views the world as a system of values opposed to God (James 4.4) in no way means that he exhorts the audience to withdraw from life in the world; it does mean that the audience is exhorted to live out its peculiar identity in the world (1.1–27; 2.1, 5, 7, 8, 13; 3.10, 16–18; 4.1–4, 13–17; 5.7–18; see L. T. Johnson, 1985).

James 2.1–13, which is the first and primary argument in the letter-*confirmatio*, begins with the direct address, Ἀδελφοί μου (2.1). This is the same form of address featured in the first admonition of the *exordium* (1.2), and there is nothing in the text to suggest a different audience in 2.1. In only two instances does a sentence in James *begin* with the words Ἀδελφοί μου: here in 2.1 and in 5.19. This is no accident. As the *first* and fundamentally emphatic elements in a Greek sentence, these words *begin* the *first* sentence (2.1) in the *first* argument (2.1–13) of the *confirmatio* or *probatio* (2.1–5.6), that is, the core section of the whole; and they *begin* the *last* sentence in James (5.19–20). The whole appeal to endure various trials of faith, an appeal that is introduced and laid out in the *exordium*, flatly stated in the letter's *propositio*, clarified in the *narratio*, and invoked with urgency in the *conclusio*, is argued out from *probatio* through *adfectus* under the frame of an authoritarian fraternal concern: Ἀδελφοί μου! In James 1.1 the author identifies himself as a Christian, and in 2.1 he attributes that designation to his audience, for he marks his second and last mention of the name Jesus with the possessive reference, "*our* (ἡμῶν) glorious Lord Jesus Christ."[8]

Of fundamental significance to our unit is the fact that the audience is viewed, at least by the author, as God's chosen poor. For example, the use of ὁ πτωχός in James 2.5–7, as well as the way in which the author handles the motifs of rich and poor throughout the letter, gives the impression that these Christian Jews are perceived in the tradition of *ʿanawim* piety as "the elect poor," the people of God.[9] This perception coheres nicely with the election terminology, "to the twelve tribes," in the prescript (1.1), as it also does with the reference to "the humble brother," in the *exordium* (1.9).

Some, however, find an apparent problem with the use of ὁ πτωχός in these verses. Because it is customarily argued that the two men in James 2.2 are strangers or visitors, and therefore outsiders, some have argued that the use of πτωχός in James 2.2 for an outsider is inconsistent with its usage in 2.5–7, where it seems to identify the community as "the elect poor." The question naturally arises: why, if indeed James' addressees are "the poor," does the author use the term πτωχός to refer to an outsider, someone who is not a member of the community?

Are the two men in James 2.2–3 strangers or members of the community? The question in 2.4, "have *you* not discriminated *among yourselves*?" (οὐ διεκρίθητε ἐν ἑαυτοῖς), suggests that both the shabbily dressed man and the gold-fingered man are community members. On the other hand, allowing the gold-fingered man as a member of the community seems to contradict the opinion that throughout the epistle "the rich" appear not as members but as outsiders and enemies to the elect poor (2.6b–7; cf. the indictments of the rich [merchants] in James 4.13–17, and of the rich [landowners] in 5.1–6). How then can the gold-fingered man be a member of the community when οἱ πλούσιοι, as a group, stand outside the community James addresses?

Ward (1966b, pp. 78–98; and 1969) has shown that the

---

[8] This is the first of only three occurrences of ἡμῶν in James; cf. also 2.21 (Ἀβραὰμ ὁ πατὴρ ἡμῶν), and 3.6 (ἡ γλῶσσα καθίσταται ἐν τοῖς μέλεσιν ἡμῶν). The genitive singular form (μου) occurs 13x: 11x it functions in a direct address to the audience, ἀδελφοί μου (1.2, 16, 19; 2.1, 5, 14; 3.1, 10, 12; 5.12, 19). The two remaining usages (2.3, 18) are in direct discourse that is attributed to persons in the audience, whether hypothetical or real.

[9] See chapter 4, pp. 127, 139–40, 153.

difficulties here are more apparent than real. They disappear when the συναγωγή in 2.2 is viewed not as a worshiping community but as a judicial assembly. This is the only occurrence of the term συναγωγή in James, and, according to Davids (1982, p. 108), this appears to be the only use of the term in the NT to refer to a Christian meeting. James features the customary NT term ἐκκλησία but once (5.14), where it occurs within the context of liturgical language and refers to a Christian worship-assembly. In the LXX, the term συναγωγή frequently translates ʿedāh ("assembly, meeting"; Exod. 12.19; Lev. 19.2; LXX Ps. 110.1); the term ἐκκλησία usually appears for qāhāl ("convocation, congregation"; Deut. 4.10; 2 Esdr. 2.64; 1 Macc. 2.56; see Schürer, vol. ii, pp. 423–62, esp. pp. 429–431). "Synagogue" has a variety of usages; for example, it refers to "the place of assembly": (1) of Jews (Joseph. *Ant.* 19.300, 305; *BJ* 2.285–89; 7.44; Philo, *Quod omn. prob.* 81, referring to the Essenes; Matt. 4.23; Mark 3.1; Luke 6.6; John 18.20; Acts 17.17; see Schürer, vol. ii, pp. 439–47, esp. p. 439 note 60). (2) Of Christians (*Herm. Man.* 11.14; *Epiph. Haer.* 30.18, referring to the Ebionites); and of "the meeting-house of the Marcionists" (from an inscription discovered at Lebaba near Damascus [= *OGIS* 608]; see MM, p. 601). It also refers to the "congregation or assembled group" (1) of Jews (Acts 6.9, 9.2; Rev. 2.9; 3.9; see Schürer, vol. ii, p. 429 note 12). (2) Of Christians (*Herm. Man.* 11.9, 13; Ign. *Pol.* 4.2; *Trall.* 3; see *LPGL*, *s.v.* συναγωγή; also W. Schrage, *TDNT* 7.840–41). And the term can also designate the "occasion or type of gathering," as distinct from the place and group (Acts 13.43; the *Testament of Epicteta*, from Thera [= *IG* XII 3, no. 33], as cited in Schürer, vol. ii, p. 430 note 13; Pl. *Tht.* 150a; D.L. 2.129; see LSJ, *s.v.*; and BAGD, *s.v.*). Drawing on early Tannaitic rabbinic texts that treat of judicial procedures, Ward (1966b, pp. 78–107) suggests that the example reflects a judicial assembly or church court. The descriptions of partiality in Jewish courts are extremely similar to the example in James 2.2–3; e.g., with reference to the differences in the litigants' clothing, see esp. *b. šebu.* 31a; and concerning the differences in the litigants' standing or sitting, see *b. šebu.* 30a. In the NT there is ample evidence to suggest that courts were held within the synagogues (Matt. 10.17; 23.34; Mark 13.9; Luke 12.11; 21.12; Acts 22.19; 26.11; see BAGD, p. 782.d). Furthermore, that Christian ἐκκλησίαι would have drawn upon Jewish judicial procedures in dealing with legal grievances in their communities is not unlikely; cf. esp. 1

Corinthians 6.1–11. For a full discussion of the latter text, with particular emphasis on Greek legal procedures and systems, see Alan C. Mitchell (1986).

If both men are litigants in the community's court, then "the natural assumption would be that both are members of the community" (Ward, 1966b, p. 97). The customary view that they are strangers or visitors is based on their being directed where to stand or sit (2.3). In a judicial setting, however, such directions are naturally understood as "court instructions" (p. 97). The verb εἰσέρχεσθαι, which occurs three times in James (2.2, twice; cf. 5.4), is also applicable to a judicial setting (Ward, 1966b, pp. 85–86, 93–94; see εἰσέρχομαι in LSJ, "as a law term"; MM, *s.v.*; BAGD, *s.v.*; and J. Schneider, *TDNT* iii.666–84). Further, note that the gold-fingered man is not referred to as ὁ πλούσιος. Instead, he is described by a rhetorical periphrasis, as "a gold-fingered man in bright clothes" (ἀνὴρ χρυσοδακτύλιος ἐν ἐσθῆτι λαμπρᾷ).[10]

While that description plainly indicates that he has status and wealth (Davids, 1982, p. 108; Betz, 1961, pp. 197–98), it also avoids using the term ὁ πλούσιος, which, in James, consistently characterizes a group that stands outside the community and is aligned with the "world." The term πτωχός in James 2.2b stands antithetically parallel to ἀνὴρ χρυσοδακτύλιος in 2.2a; and in 2.3e it is antithetically parallel to τὸν φοροῦντα in 2.3d (cf. Ward, 1966b, pp. 106–07). Thus there is no contradiction in the use of the terms πτωχός and πλούσιος in our unit; both the gold-fingered man and the poor man are members of the same community, and that community is envisioned and addressed by the author as "the elect poor." Ward (p. 105), therefore, concludes that in James "the πτωχοί are not a group among the elect; they are the elect" (cf. Dibelius, 1975, p. 44; and Keck, 1965, pp. 116–17).

We have also observed that scholarship is virtually unanimous in arguing that "the elect poor" whom James addresses are materially, relatively impoverished. Dibelius (1975, pp. 45–47) and Davids (1982, p. 45) are representative of the majority opinion, which

---

[10] The compound adjective χρυσοδακτύλιος is a *hapax legomenon*; cf. Epict. 1.22.18, and the references cited in Mayor (1892 [1990], p. 82). The noun ἀνήρ occurs 6x in James: 1.8, 12, 20, 23; 2.2; 3.2; ἐσθής occurs in 2.2 [2x], 3, and only 5x elsewhere in the NT: Luke 23.11, ἐσθῆτα λαμπράν; 24.4; Acts 1.10; 10.30, ἐν ἐσθῆτι λαμπρᾷ; 12.21, ἐσθῆτα βασιλικήν. See BAGD and LSJ. The adjective λαμπρός occurs 9x in the NT: in Rev. 15.6; 18.14; 19.8; 22.1,16; Luke 23.11; Acts 10.30; James 2.2, 3. In the latter four instances it is used of garments (cf. Philo, *Jos.* 105; *Herm. Vis.* 1.2.2); see Oepke (*TDNT* iv.16–28).

Ropes (1916, p. 133) succinctly expresses: "They [the addressees] appear to be largely poor and struggling people, subject to the hardships of the poor, cf. 1^{10} 2^1 ff. 6. Note the prevalent eagerness to have, implied in 4^{1-3}." This view of the audience is maintained throughout the letter, and in our unit it is of central importance. Thus we find the rhetorical "constraints" associated with "security" and "well-being" (James 2.2–3; 6b–7), and, as we shall see, the emotions traditionally evoked by such topics, principally "desire" (2.4), bubble to the surface.

The rhetorical constraints

The rhetorical constraints, what Aristotle calls "extrinsic" and "intrinsic" proofs (*Rhet.* 1.2.2) represent the third essential constituent of the rhetorical situation. Among the "standard sources" of constraints are "beliefs, attitudes, documents, facts, traditions, images, interests, motives, and the like," that the author employs to persuade the audience (Bitzer, 1968, p. 8).

In our unit, as in the whole letter, a fundamental constraint is the *ethos* of the author that the letter evokes; apparently, James the Lord's brother (see chapter 2, above). By the letter prescript (James 1.1), the *ethos* of the author constrains the whole discourse. From a rhetorical perspective this embraces not only the reputation which the author brings to his or her discourse. It also involves the author's characterizations of himself or herself in the discourse and it includes the style and kinds of arguments employed in the discourse itself (Bitzer, 1968, p. 8; cf. Arist. *Rhet.* 3.19.1; 1.9.1–41). We have already suggested that, via the δοῦλος-metaphor, the author, a διδάσκαλος and ἀδελφός of his addressees (3.1), is introduced as an authoritative spokesperson for God and for the Lord Jesus Christ (1.1a). And we have likewise noted that the tone and style of the discourse coheres with that of an honored and authoritative figure. All this undergirds our unit.

Other key constraints, which have already been treated in the analyses of the inner texture and the intertexture of the unit, are: the faith of the (honorable) Lord Jesus Christ (2.1); the *ethos* and *pathos* of the audience as God's "elect poor" (2.5); God (2.5, 11); the rich and their unjust, shameful behavior (2.6–7); an allusion to a saying of Jesus (2.5); scripture (2.7); the topics of "honor/shame" (2.1, 5, 6a), which include as subtopics such things as "justice" (2.4), the "law" (2.8–11), "love" (2.8), and "mercy" (2.13); the topics associated with "security" or "fortune" (2.2–3), promises and rewards (2.5, 12–13), judgment (2.12); and again, "love" (2.8) and "mercy" (2.13). Here, intentionally, I twice mention "love" and "mercy." The reader should remember that both of the latter are viewed as "complex" topics by the rhetoricians, that is, they are subtopics of both "honor" and "security" (Cic. *Inv. Rhet.* 2.53.159–56.169). One of the areas in which James has been grossly misunderstood is in his use of *topoi*. The argument that the thought in James jumps illogically from one topic to another holds little weight in the light of the elementary exercises in composition (the *progymnasmata*) and the rhetorical handbooks. Those historical sources provide insightful information about the *topoi*: how they were understood; how they were logically interrelated; and how they were to be chosen and developed. I think that a failure to consider properly these rudimentary matters has resulted in a badly skewed understanding of James. All the latter are rhetorical in nature; that is, they have the persuasive power to constrain the audience to accept the argument and to reconcile their behavior to it.

The question and stasis of the unit, and its species of rhetoric

Here our purpose is to determine first the fundamental question and stasis of the argument in James 2.1–13, and then the species of the rhetoric to which the unit belongs. The means by which we do this is systematically spelled out in "stasis theory," which, in ancient education, was the doctrine that helped students to locate the key issues in a case (Quint. 3.6.1–83, 91–104).[11] So, an argument arises from a conflict of opinions on a given subject. That conflict of opinions is the stasis or issue of the argument, and it takes the form of a question that focuses the contrary views of proponents and opponents (Nadeau, 1964, pp. 369, 375).

Stasis theory holds that there are four basic questions, each of which gives rise to a corresponding form of stasis. (1) There is the stasis of "fact," a conjectural issue that concerns the question of whether or not a thing exists, whether or not a thing has been done, and whether or not a thing should be done and by whom (Nadeau, 1964, p. 370; G. A. Kennedy, 1984, pp. 18–19, 46–47). (2) The

---

[11] On "stasis theory," see G. A. Kennedy (1984; 1963, pp. 306–14); Lausberg (vol. i, sections 79–138); J. Martin (1974, pp. 28–52); and Volkmann ([1885] 1987, pp. 38–108). For a systematic treatment, see Hermogenes, *Peri Staseon* (in Rabe, vol. vi, pp. 28–92), and the English translation by Nadeau (1964).

stasis of "definition" arises from the question of "what a thing is through its essence or essential qualities" (Nadeau p. 370). Thus, "if the facts are admitted, but there is a disagreement about the definition of the terms," then we have the question of definition (Kennedy, pp. 18–19). (3) The stasis of "quality" has to do with the nonessential attributes or "extenuating circumstances, etc." (Nadeau, p. 370). When the "facts and definitions are admitted by all parties, but the action is justified on other grounds," then the question is one of "quality" (Kennedy, p. 19). (4) The stasis of "objection" or "jurisdiction" basically concerns procedural arguments (Nadeau, p. 370); for example, "a speaker rejects the right of a tribunal to make a judgment" (Kennedy, p. 19). In any given case, there may be more than one question and stasis; yet there is usually only one that predominates, and it functions as the controlling issue in the discourse or argument (Kennedy, p. 18).

The question and stasis of the unit

The question that gives rise to the principal stasis (conflict) elaborated in James 2.1–13 appears to be one of definition, and it concerns the essence of προσωπολημψίαι. The question, then, is: "What are προσωπολημψίαι?" This conclusion is reached by dividing the case in our unit according to the stasis theory of Hermogenes (Nadeau, 1964, p. 368). The process of dividing the case "could be viewed as one of elimination" (G. A. Kennedy, 1963, p. 308). As Quintilian puts it: one moved through the list of stases "until the parties ceased to agree"; at that point "the question arose" (Quint. 7.1.6). Let us rehearse this.

First, we find that the "fact" of προσωπολημψίαι is not doubted but considered obvious; their reality is taken for granted (2.1), and exemplified (2.2–3). Therefore, the question and stasis do not appear to be ones of "fact" (Nadeau, 1964, pp. 382, 393, 396–404; Kennedy, 1963, p. 309). Likewise, we may eliminate the stasis of "jurisprudence," since nowhere in the text is there any evidence that suggests an objection to the right of the community's judicial assembly to hear a case involving community members, nor is there any objection based on "the legal technicalities of written documents" (Nadeau, 1964, pp. 382, 413–19; Kennedy, 1963, pp. 312–13). This leaves us with the stases of "definition" and "quality."

Given the obviously preferential treatment of the wealthy brother by the judicial assembly, if the conflict of opinions reflected in James 2.1–13 turns on a denial that the preferential treatment shown to the wealthy brother is an instance of προσωποληψίαι, then the stasis is one of definition (quite possibly the addressees would have preferred to define their behavior toward both men as culturally correct expressions of τιμή; see Cic. *Inv. Rhet.* 1.10; 2.53; Quint. 3.6.56; Nadeau, 1964, pp. 382, 404–06; Kennedy, 1963, pp. 307–09). On the other hand, if the question that focuses the argument here is one of quality, then the debate presupposes not only an admission by the community that the behavior of the court toward the gold-fingered man was indeed προσωποληψία; it also presupposes an attempt by the community to justify their behavior (perhaps by arguing that προσωπολημψίαι are not forbidden, or by alleging that deferring to the wealthier and more powerful man would more than likely result in his benefaction of the community, or some similar appeal based on mitigating circumstance; Quint. 3.5.14; 3.6.56; Cic. *Inv. Rhet.* 1.10; Nadeau, 1964 pp. 375, 382–83, 406–13; Kennedy, 1963, pp. 309–11).

The fact that the rhetoric plays προσωπολημψίαι in the light of its qualitative attributes, that is, in the light of such topics as advantage (2.4), honor (2.6a), and the lawful (2.8–11), might incline the interpreter to argue, too quickly, that the stasis is one of quality. There is no doubt that the rhetoric rehearses the nature of this behavior. But a closer look at the unit suggests, in my opinion, that the fundamental question and stasis of the unit is really one of definition. And, if this is so, then the essential qualities of προσω-πολημψίαι serve to amplify the definition the author presupposes for that behavior, as well as to buttress his (presupposed) charge: "You have shown προσωπολημψίαι to the wealthy brother."

How does the rhetoric define προσωπολημψίαι? Already we have seen that James activates an antecedent text, Leviticus 19.15, and holds that προσωπολημψίαι are essentially "unjust judgments," as the rhetorical question in 2.4 makes clear: "Have you not become unjust judges with evil motives?" Playing off Leviticus 19.15, then, προσωπολημψίαι are manifestations of "unrighteousness/injustice" (ἀδικία); they are the opposite of "ἐν δικαιοσύνῃ κρινεῖς τὸν πλησίον σου," LXX Leviticus 19.15d. Further, we have seen that this understanding of acts of partiality is not limited to Jewish and Jewish-Christian subcultures in the Hellenistic-Roman world. For even in that world, the dominant culture within which James functions, such behavior is defined as a perversion of justice. For example, Menander Rhetor (in Russell and Wilson, 1981, pp. 166–67) says: "under justice, you should include (ἐν δὲ τῇ δικαιοσύῃ) . . . freedom from partiality (τὸ μὴ πρὸς χάριν) and from prejudice in giving judicial decisions (μηδὲ πρὸς ἀπέχθειαν κρίνειν τὰς δίκας), equal treatment of rich and poor (τὸ μὴ προτιμᾶν τοὺς εὐπόρους τῶν ἀδυνάτων)."

Therefore, when the author begins the letter-*confirmatio* (James 2.1–5.6) with an admonition against προσωπολημψίαι, he brings into view something that Jews, Christians, Greeks, and Romans would readily understand as a perversion of justice. That the admonition presupposes such behavior to be incompatible with Jesus' faith would hardly surprise Jewish Christians who knew of and judged Jesus' faith as that which promoted his "honorable reputation" (τῆς δόξης). But having said these things, things to which a Jewish-Christian audience "in the dispersion" could and would give ready assent, the author then proceeds to pin the label προσωπολημψίαι on a behavior that, even though it conflicted with the common understanding of "justice," was apparently a public custom within the patron–client culture of the Hellenistic-Roman world. Indeed, as a cultural script, that is, a conventional code of behavior, the patron–client system presupposed that deference be shown to the wealthy and powerful; moreover, that system labeled such behavior as "honorable" and "just."

If the author can make the label stick, and he does, then the qualitative issue, though clearly present, remains secondary to the primary stasis of definition. Put differently, the author's definition and elaboration of his charge against the community allows no viable recourse to "a plea of justification" (the qualitative stasis). Rather, it allows debate concerning the essence of προσωπολημ-ψίαι. Thus, stasis theory suggests that the question that gives rise to the argument in James 2.1–13 arises from the stasis of definition: the charge (κατάφασις) of the author is that the elect community is guilty of προσωπολημψίαι, which is defined as "unjust judgments" (James 2.4) and "sin" (James 2.9a). Likewise, stasis theory presupposes the audience's answer (ἀπόφασις), a denial: "Deferring to the wealthy brother was not an act of partiality; it was an act of honor."

The question, therefore, is a "rational" issue; it focuses on "actions" and "involves nothing more than the consideration of the nature" of προσωπολημψίαι (Quint. 3.6.86).[12] Further, since the

[12] A rational case concerns acts, while a legal case debates written documents. Further, a rational case concerns a stasis of fact, or definition, or quality (Quint. 3.6.66–67; D. F. Watson, 1988, p. 12).

persons involved in the presentation of the case (James 2.2–3) are unnamed, stasis theory labels the question "indefinite." And as such, it is a much "more comprehensive" question than a "definite" issue (Quint. 3.5.8).[13]

The species of rhetoric in the unit

Considering the species of rhetoric in the unit, we find that the advice given is characterized by persuasion and dissuasion (προ-τροπὴ καὶ ἀποτροπή; Arist. *Rhet.* 1.3.1), and it refers mainly to the attributes of future-actions (*Rhet.* 1.3.4) that should characterize the community's interpersonal relations, though it also applies to present-actions (*Rhet.* 1.6.1; 1.8.7). The focused aim of the advice is the expedient or beneficial.

Frequently in deliberative rhetoric, the topic of the expedient or "advantageous" (τὸ σύμφερον) was studied and elaborated primarily with a view toward "security." For example, Aristotle held that the positive end of deliberative discourse was "advantage," and that all other considerations ("justice/injustice," "honor/shame") are subjugated to this end (*Rhet.* 1.3.5). Cicero (*Part. Or.* 24.83) – perhaps because of Stoic influence – says that while "the whole procedure in giving advice and pronouncing an opinion is directed" toward "advantage," this must be done in such a manner that one never loses sight of the "primary considerations" of what is "possible" and what is "necessary." And here "necessity" is defined "as something that is an indispensable condition of our security or freedom." Thus he argues that these concerns "must take precedence in public policy of all the remaining considerations, alike of honor and of profit [= advantage]." While the Stoics held that "honor" and "security" never conflict (Cic. *Off.* 3.3.11), there were those who disagreed (*De Or.* 2.82.334–35). See the material and discussion cited in the Loeb edition of *Rhetorica ad Herennium*, p. 161 (notes). In Cic. *Inv. Rhet.* 2.56.169, security is defined as "a reasoned and unbroken maintenance of safety"; and in *Rhet. Her.* 3.2.3, "to consider Security is to provide some plan or other for ensuring the avoidance of a present or imminent danger."

---

[13] The categories "definite"/"special" and "indefinite"/"general" are determined here just as they are in categorizing a "chreia" or "maxim" (see Butts, 1987, pp. 187–90, 225–26; Walz, vol. i, p. 202; cf. vol. i, p. 235). For example, Quintilian says: "The question 'Should a man marry?' is *indefinite*; the question, 'Should Cato marry?' is *definite*" (3.6.8). See the discussion in Robbins (1985a, pp. 33–45).

"Security" is a primary topic in the elaboration of "advantage" in James 2.1–13.

In the *Rhetorica ad Herennium* and Cicero's *De Inventione Rhetorica* "the advantageous" is discussed under two heads, "security" and "honor." The topic of "security" (τὸ χρήσιμον) has two divisions: (1) "power" or "might," and (2) "craft" or "strategy," and these divisions are developed by such topics as "status" (e.g., the clothing of the two men, James 2.2–3; cf. James 1.9–11; 2.14–16; 4.1–4; 4.13–5.6); "wealth" (e.g., πλούσιος, 2.5, 6; cf. πλοῦτος, 5.2; and πτωχός, 2.2, 3, 5, 6; cf. 1.9–11; 2.14–16; 4.13–5.6), "promises" (e.g., ἐπαγγέλλεσθαι, James 2.5; 1.12) and the like.

"Honor" (τὸ καλόν) also has two divisions (*Rhet. Her.* 3.2.3; Cic. *Rhet. Inv.* 2.51.159–56.169): (1) "the right," which comprises topics like wisdom,[14] justice,[15] courage (a subtopic of which is endurance),[16] and temperance;[17] and (2) "the praiseworthy," which comprises those things that are praised by recognized authorities, like the gods,[18] allies, fellow citizens, and descendants.[19]

[14] "We shall be using the topics of Wisdom in our discourse if we compare advantages and disadvantages, counselling the pursuit of the one and the avoidance of the other"; and when "we recommend some policy in a matter whose history we can recall either from direct experience or hearsay" (*Rhet. Her.* 3.3.4). See James 2.6b–7, "Is it not the rich who . . . ?" See also 1.5–8; 3.13–18; 4.14, 17.

[15] On the "topics of Justice," see *Rhet. Her.* 2.3.4. In our unit, see esp. James 2.4 (κριτής; cf. 4.11,12; 5.9); James 2.6 (κριτήριον); James 2.12 (κρίνειν; cf. 4.11 [3x], 12; 5.9); and also James 2.12 (κρίσις; cf. 5.12). Also, the term νόμος (2.8, 9, 10, 11, 12; cf. 1.25; 4.11 [4x]); W. Gutbrod, *TDNT* iv.1080–82, 1089.

[16] *Rhet. Her.* 3.2.3; 3.3.6; 4.25.35; Cic. *Inv. Rhet.* 2.54.163. Patience, perseverance, confidence, and highmindedness are subtopics of courage (Cic. *Inv. Rhet.* 2.54.163). On the topic of perseverance or endurance, see also Ps. Arist. *VV.* 4.4. In our unit the topic of "endurance" is presupposed in connection with the primary exigence of the letter, as was mentioned above, pp.70; 158–60. Connected with "endurance" and "patience" are the uses of τελεῖν (James 2.8) and τηρεῖν (2.10; cf. 1.27). Both of the latter concern "the law" (and cf. παραμένειν in connection with "the perfect law, the law of liberty," 1.25).

[17] "We shall be using the topics of Temperance if we censure the inordinate desire for office, money, or the like"; when "we show how much is enough in each case, advise against going too far, and set the due limit to every matter" (*Rhet. Her.* 3.3.5). See also *Rhet. Her.* 3.2.3; Cic. *Inv. Rhet.* 2.53.159; 2.54.164; and cf. Plutarch, *De virt. mor.* 2.441A. Very closely connected with the topics "poor," "rich," and "acts of partiality" are the topics λείπειν (James 1.4, 5; 2.15) and ἐπιθυμία (1.14–15; cf. also ἐπιθυμεῖν, 4.2). The latter are accompaniments of "sobriety of mind" or temperance. These topics run through the whole of James (see 1.19–21, 26; 3.1, 2, 6, 9–12, 14, 16–17; 4.1–4, 11, 13–17; and 5.5–6).

[18] The term θεός occurs in James 2.5; cf. 1.1, 5, 13 (2x), 20, 27; 2.19, 23 (2x); 3.9; 4.4 (2x), 6, 7, 8; κύριος and Ἰησοῦς Χριστός (2.1; cf. 1.1).

[19] "Allies," "fellow citizens," and "descendants," and their opposites (e.g., "an

The conflict of opinions which unfolds before us is a debate about two kinds of honorable behavior: one is what is "honorable" "before the world" (τῷ κόσμῳ, James 2.5), as a system of values; the other is what is "honorable" "before God" (τῷ Θεῷ καὶ πατρί, 1.27).[20] At the same time, the debate involves "advantageous" behavior: while the rhetoric takes for granted the wealth and status of the gold-fingered man and presupposes the advantages of "fortune," it pointedly juxtaposes the advantage of a different type of "action": πλουσίους ἐν πίστει[21] – which is synonymous with "loving God" – and it champions its "benefit": ἡ βασιλεία ἧς [ὁ Θεὸς] ἐπηγγείλατο (2.5). Judging James 2.1–13 by these classical rhetorical standards, and also in the light of what we have already learned about the species of rhetoric in this argument, what we have before us is undeniably symbouleutic or deliberative rhetoric.

The social and cultural rhetoric of the unit

Dibelius (1975, p. 48) argued that the most accentuated train of thought in James is "the *piety of the Poor*, and the accompanying opposition to the rich and to the world." This is plainly evident in James 2.1–13, the first and fundamental argumentative unit in the letter-*confirmatio* (2.1–5.6).[22] In the analysis of the pattern of argumentation in the unit, we discovered two social examples that reflect this train of thought, and both are concerned with the socio-rhetorical problem that gave rise to the unit; namely, "acts of partiality" or unjust judgments in the social relations among the elect poor, within (2.2–4) and without (2.6b–7) the community.

In looking at these social examples it is important to keep in mind the research of social and cultural anthropologists into the type of culture that existed in the first-century Mediterranean

enemy of God," "a friend of the world," James 4.4) are relational terms and reflect the letter's interest in proper "communal concerns."

[20] See the discussion in chapter 3, above, pp. 82–85.

[21] "Rich in faith" is an attribute of existence only because it is first and foremost an attribute of action. The fundamental stasis of the letter of James is "fact"; the fundamental question is: "What shall we do?" The whole discourse reverberates the elaboration of faith in the first two argumentative units of the letter-*confirmatio* (2.1–13; 2.14–26): faith is something that one does; indeed, "faith apart from works is dead" (2.26).

[22] This theme is introduced in the *exordium* (1.10–11), and is broached in the final statement of the *narratio* (1.26–27). It appears in the first and final units of the *confirmatio* (2.1–13; 4.13–5.6). The theme has special significance in the letter of James, for in the author's view, the addressees are God's elect poor (2.5–7).

world. That research suggests that certain cultural codes or scripts informed the behavior and self-understanding of the people in view here. In other words, cultural codes or scripts are socially shared meanings by which people view and define themselves and their relationships with others. As such, they are especially significant in the social formation, construction, and maintenance of communities in the ancient milieu. In James 2.1–13 the three cultural scripts of "honor," the idea of "limited good," and "patron–client relations" inform the social and cultural dynamics at play in the rhetoric.

The cultural scripts of honor, limited good, and patron–client relations

Symbolically speaking, honor concerns one's social standing; it involves both how a person views and values himself or herself, as well as a profound sensitivity to the way that person is viewed and valued by others. Honor, then, is essentially a claim to worth, and it necessarily involves "proper attitudes and behavior," according to the prescribed cultural cues of the society. It may be "ascribed" in the sense that it comes to one passively, as a gift of fortune; that is, through birth, family, and connections to others who are powerful and of honored status. Or, it may be "acquired" in that one actively pursues and achieves it, usually at the expense of others as part of the social contest of challenge and response (Malina, 1981, pp. 47–48). As an anthropological category, "shame" concerns a person's sensitivity to the way that he or she is perceived by others. As a rhetorical topic, "honor" necessarily presupposes a sensitivity to others' perceptions of a person's social worth. As the contrary of honor, "shame" (αἰσχύνη) implies the "consciousness of some guilt or impropriety" (see Arist. *Rhet.* 2.6.2). Further, just as there is individual honor, there is, whether in natural or voluntary groups of people, corporate honor.

Recalling the list, above, of the rhetorical constraints that function in James 2.1–13, the dominance of the values honor and shame is obvious. These two constraints were also "the prime focus and pivotal values" in the social interaction of the patron–client culture (Malina, 1981, p. 84; see pp. 25–50; 80–93; 142; Garnsey and Saller, 1987, pp. 148–51, and p. 229). For example, in the theme (James 2.1) honor is emphatically connected to the faith of the Lord Jesus Christ. In the *ratio* (2.2–4), there is an effort to arouse shame by labelling the social behavior it depicts as dishonorable (= evil, πονηρός, 2.4). In the first proof of the *probatio*, the example (2.5), honor is reflected in God's choice and promise to the elect poor. In 2.6a shame is bluntly attributed to the elect poor, and in 2.6b–7 it is attributed to the rich outsiders. In 2.8 the law of God is thoroughly honorable; and in 2.9 "acts of partiality," a violation of God's law, are thoroughly dishonorable and shameful. Again, in 2.10–11, fulfilling the whole law is honorable, while keeping the whole law but failing in one point of it is shameful behavior. In the *conclusio* (2.12–13) it is argued that an honorable judgment under the honorable law belongs to the one who has loved the poor neighbor by showing him mercy, but to the one who has shown partiality to the rich, thereby dishonoring and not loving the poor neighbor with merciful actions, belongs a (merciless) judgment: a judgment without honor.

The social implications of the appeal to "mercy" (James 2.13) are, as the analyses of the inner texture and intertexture have already shown, very appropriate to the elaboration in 2.1–12. First, Aristotle defines the "emotion" ἔλεος as "a kind of pain [λύπη] excited by the sight of evil [κακῷ], deadly or painful, which befalls one who does not deserve it" (*Rhet.* 2.8.2). Second, among the "evils" that excite "pity" he lists "all evils of which fortune is the cause" (2.8.9), and a conventional subtopic of the latter is "poverty." (The topic "fortune" includes "noble birth, wealth, power, *and their contraries* [emphasis mine; *Rhet.* 2.12.2; cf. 1.5.1–18]). Third, he notes that ἔλεος is aroused by people and sufferings that are close by (2.8.13–14); for example, a πλησίος (2.8.2; cf. James 2.8) or others like us (2.8.13; cf. James 2.2, 3, 5, 6a). In *Rhet.* 2.8.2, he says, "pity" is easily aroused among "friends"; and the broad topic of "friendship" includes, as species, companionship, intimacy, kinship, and similar relations (Arist. *Rhet.* 2.4.28). The topic of "friendship" is treated as a sub-category of "justice," "honor," and "advantage," and it plays large in James, especially in the category of "kinship" (ἀδελφός, 19 times; see G. Stählin, *TDNT* ix.113–71; esp. pp. 146–71). Fourth, Aristotle holds that the rhetor can arouse mercy especially in situations where there are "signs," "actions," and "words" that are pitiable. As an example of the latter, he specifically refers to "the dress [ἐσθῆτας]" of the sufferer (*Rhet.* 2.8.16; cf. James 2.2–3). Another such situation is when "some evil comes to pass from a quarter whence one might have reasonably expected something good"

(2.8.11). An example of the latter in James are the "partialities" and "unjust judgments" in the "elect community's court" (James 2.2–4). Thus the social texture of the appeal to mercy in the *adfectus* (2.13) is very appropriate for a rhetorical elaboration in which the "pitiable poor" are so prominent.

The idea of "limited good" is apparently a common notion in a peasant economy, the kind of economy that James reflects (Moxnes, 1988, esp. p. 174; Garnsey and Saller, 1987; Malina, 1981). This is the notion that "all of the desired things in life such as land, wealth, health, friendship, and love, manliness and honor, respect and status, power and influence, security and safety" are limited goods, existing in fixed quantities and without the possibility of being increased (Foster, 1965, p. 296 as cited in Moxnes, 1988, p. 77; see T. F. Carney, 1975, pp. 198–99). Further, it is understood and accepted that certain people will have and get more of these benefits than others. The idea of limited good, however, promotes a defensive posture, as one seeks to preserve his/her goods; it also creates struggle and suspicion in a peasant economy, for, if anyone attains more than he or she appears to need and/or deserve, it is commonly viewed as costing the other members of the community. While there appears to be in a limited-good society the notion that "all should share equally," it is quite significant that the "sharing of wealth in order to gain status is a way to solve the problem of inequality within a society with high demands for solidarity" (Moxnes, 1988, pp. 78, 79).

In ancient Mediterranean culture the patron–client system was in one sense a way of dealing with limited goods.[23] A patron–client relationship is an interpersonal relationship between individuals or networks of individuals that are "characterized by inequality and asymmetry in power and status"; the partners were not social equals and made no pretense to equality. Further, it presupposed "mutual solidarity and obligations: for example, landlord–tenant, ruler–servants" (Moxnes, 1988, p. 174). It was, then, a sort of unwritten contract, initiated by a positive challenge, a gift or benefit. It was based on the reciprocal exchange of a whole range of goods and services, and because the partners were not equal the

---

[23] These characteristics are based on the conventional features of patron–client societies in Eisenstadt and Roniger, 1984, pp. 48–49; and the discussions in Moxnes (1988, pp. 22–47), and Saller (1982, pp. 7–78). Also see Malina (1981, pp. 71–93); and D. B. Martin (1990, esp. pp. 22–30, 68).

goods and services exchanged were different. Usually, in a peasant economy, the things exchanged were those that were not normally available within the village or community, goods and services that were badly needed. For example, a patron might give money or food to a client; the client, then, would publicly honor the patron and show him loyalty. Other chief characteristics of patron–client relations that are important are the following. (1) Not infrequently they subverted traditional values and undermined the (horizontal relations) or solidarity of a kinship group. (2) Generally speaking, patron–client relationships were begun deliberately, maintained for some duration, and could be terminated voluntarily. And (3) of special significance is that patron–client relations were based on "favoritism" in which the exchange of goods and services, whether as benefactions or requitals, was fundamentally linked to personal honor (see Saller, 1982, pp. 17–21; Garnsey and Saller, 1987, pp. 148–49; and Malina, 1988, pp. 25–50).

How do the idea of "limited good" and the "patron–client system" play in the social examples in James 2.2–4 and 6b–7? The inner dynamics of the rhetoric in James 2.1–4 shows that 2.1 forms with 2.4 an enthymematic structure that uses a social example (the *ratio*, 2.2–4, the basis for the proposition adduced in 2.1) to define προσωπολημψίαι in terms of action, thought, and quality. The example (2.2–4), which grounds the theme (2.1) in the social sphere of the elect poor, plays the definition in two antithetic comparisons. The first is the comparison of two social types, both of whom are members of the elect poor (2.2). One, the gold-fingered man, is wealthy and powerful; the other man is the social opposite of the first, being poor and powerless. The second comparison concerns the antithetic treatments these two litigants receive at the hands of the elect poor's judicial assembly (2.3). While honor is shown to the brother with wealth and status, the treatment shown to the poor brother, the social inferior of the wealthy brother, is what Aristotle calls "slight" (ἡ ὀλιγωρία): "an actualization of opinion in regard to something which appears valueless" (*Rhet.* 2.2.3). According to Aristotle, there are three kinds of "slight": "disdain, spitefulness, and insult" (*Rhet.* 2.2.3; see 2.1.1–8). In particular, based on the statement in James 2.6a, the particular kind of "slight" in view is "insult" (ὕβρις), for "dishonour is characteristic of insult; and one who dishonours another slights him" (*Rhet.* 2.2.6).

The thought (διαλογισμός) that guides the προσωπολημψίαι of the judicial assembly is mirrored in their "looking upon"

(ἐπιβλέπειν) the attire of the wealthy brother. It is his conspicuous
possession of limited goods that prompts the judges "to honor"
him and "to slight" the poor brother. Likewise, the quality of their
thought and actions surfaces in their being labeled "judges with *evil*
(πονηρῶν) motives." That remark (James 2.4) and the further
definition of προσωπολημψίαι as "sin" (2.9) recall the first mention
of "sin" in 1.15. The latter statement connects "sin" to "desire"
which "entices," "lures," and "tempts" a person (1.14) with "evil"
(κακῶν, 1.13). These statements enhance the social behavior in
2.2–4 and suggest that the wealth, power, and status of the wealthy
brother are limited goods that the elect poor value and desire.
Furthermore, the actions of the judges toward the powerful brother
are easily appropriated, in the light of the patron–client system, as
positive challenges toward someone who could possibly become, or
perhaps already was, a patron of the community. And the term
διαλογισμῶν ("motives, calculations") is most appropriately used,
for within a patron–client system such calculated gestures toward a
powerful litigant within a judicial assembly would more than likely
have been reciprocated in his benefactions to the assembly (Malina,
1981, pp. 30–32).

There is another aspect of this social example that is pertinent to
the conflict between the poor and rich in James. For, while there is
in James a conspicuous antagonism in the social relations of the
elect poor and the rich outsiders (cf. 2.6b–7; 4.13–17; 5.1–6), the
social example in 2.2–4 suggests that the conflict between the
powerful and the powerless is not merely between insiders and
outsiders. It is being replicated in the interpersonal relations of the
elect community itself. This is so individually and corporately.

At the individual level, we note first that the gold-fingered, finely
arrayed man is like the rich outsiders in that he reflects social status
and power. Yet this man is not an outsider but one of the "elect
poor," as the text makes sufficiently clear (ἀδελφοί μου . . .
συναγωγὴν ὑμῶν; James 2.1 and 2). Likewise, when in 4.13–17 and
5.1–6 the author stringently rebukes the "merchants" and "the
rich" (probably landowners or landlords), he is not speaking to
outsiders but to community members who have means; he warns
them against the greedy, selfish, and violent behavior that characterizes the typical rich who are outsiders. Perhaps, as in Psalms
35.11–16; 55.12–15, what we have here (cf. also James 4.4;
5.19–20) are "small-group complaints . . . over friends who turn
away from the suffering individual, thus betraying the duty to live

in solidarity with one another" (Gerstenberger, 1988, p. 31). It is also possible that when the author speaks in 2.6b of the typical behavior of "the rich" (= the powerful), namely, that they "oppress" the (elect) poor (= the powerless) and "drag" them into court, he is talking about the gold-fingered man's oppression of the poor brother (2.2–4). This suggestion finds support in scholarly investigations (e.g. D. B. Martin, 1990, pp. 22–30) which suggest that within a judicial assembly in a patron–client society, the kind evoked in 2.2–4, the powerful individual would be the one more likely to take another (less powerful) individual to court. Thus the patron–client structure gives depth to the social implications of the language in 2.2–4, and it pointedly suggests that a member of the elect poor who has status and power is behaving as the typically rich behaved (cf. Arist. *Rhet*. 2.16.1–17.6 for a traditional appraisal of wealth and its effect on the character of a person).

At the corporate or community level (in συναγωγὴν ὑμῶν, 2.2), the "elect poor" – being represented by those who judge the case – also behave like οἱ πλούσιοι in their treatment of the litigants. For in their legal proceedings they show favoritism toward the brother who has wealth and status. Again the patron–client structure of the Greco-Roman world suggests that this was typical behavior for the powerful and privileged (D. B. Martin, 1990, pp. 22–30; Garnsey and Saller, 1987, pp. 107–26, 148–59; Saller, 1982, p. 220). Moreover, recalling our remarks about the "motives" that guide the legal proceedings in 2.2–4, we note here that that reference also quite likely evokes "the prevailing mentality" of the patron–client culture; namely, "acquisition" (Moxnes, 1988, p. 32; based on Finley, 1973, p. 144). The patronal system presupposed the acquisition of benefits based on favoritism (Saller, 1982, pp. 7–39, 217, 221). Indeed, the principle that runs through the culture is "*do ut des*": "I give so that you may give." The powerful man, in a patron–client relationship, would have been honor-bound to reciprocate. And in such a culture the one who possessed the greater honor could and would most probably have received preferential treatment.

Although this kind of favoritism runs rough-shod over the common, accepted understanding of justice, apparently it was not atypical within a patron–client system. That "honor" (including its subtopic, "justice") could conflict with "expediency" was common knowledge (Cic. *De Or*. 2.82.335–37). And, as we have noted, unwritten contracts not infrequently conflicted with written laws, and subverted the horizontal relations of a kinship group ("my brothers [and sisters] . . . you have made distinctions among yourselves," James 2.1, 4).

As I showed earlier, the social example in 2.6b–7 is the second element in a two-part argument from the opposite. James 2.6a, the first element, is the statement of the opposite. It effectively restates the indictment, "Have you not become judges with evil calculations?" (2.4), in terms of the cultural script of "honor": "You have dishonored the poor man." At the same time, 2.6a functions directly and antithetically to the rhetorical example in James 2.5; thus it clarifies the theme that προσωπολημψίαι are incompatible with Jesus' faith (2.1) with respect to the social behavior within the elect community. The rhetorical questions in verses 6b–7 embellish the statement in 2.6a with a social example about the rich (= the powerful) outsiders and their shameful treatment of the elect poor. Thus the inner dynamics of the rhetoric suggest that this social example also functions as a typical, supporting proof for the deliberative theme in James 2.1. Therefore, it qualitatively expands the definition of προσωπολημψίαι as "unjust judgments" (2.1–4) by relating it to the socio-economic and religious arenas of the social context outside the community.

The appeal in this social example is to what the audience knows about the rich from experience.[24] It is a wisdom argument (*Rhet. Her.* 3.3.4). That is, it argues that experiential wisdom should make it obvious to the elect community that the rich, and the system of values within and by which they function, are inimical to the advantage and well-being of the pious poor.

The verb καταδυναστεύειν, "to oppress, exploit, dominate," is often used in the LXX "of outrages against the poor, widows, and orphans" (Amos 4.1; 8.4; Ezek. 18.12; 22.7, 29).[25] This is the sense in which it is used in James 2.6b, and there is no indication that this oppression or their being "hauled into courts" is motivated by the fact that they are Christians.[26] The religious dimension of the social context, however, is clearly in view in 2.7b, for the "honorable

---

[24] For experience as the source or subsidiary cause of wisdom and knowledge, see Job 8.4; 21.6; Eccles. 1.13, 16–17; and Ps.-Aristotle *VV*. 4.1–2.

[25] See BAGD, p. 410. Καταδυναστεύειν appears in the NT only twice: here in reference to the oppression of the poor by the rich (cf. 1 Cor. 11.22; see *Diogn.* 10.5), and in Acts 10.38 where it concerns the work of the devil (cf. Plut. *Is. et Os.* 41.367D; and *Herm. Mand.* 12.5.1–2).

[26] The term ἕλκειν occurs only here in James. It is elsewhere in the NT 7x: John 6.44; 12.32; 18.10; 21.6, 11; Acts 16.19; 21.30. Κριτήριον ("a court of judgment") appears 3x: in James 2.6, and 1 Cor. 6.2, 4.

name" probably refers to "Jesus," and this coheres with the emphatic reference to "the faith of our honorable [τῆς δόξης] Lord Jesus Christ" (2.1). Though the reasons why the rich "slander" (βλασφημεῖν; cf. BAGD, p. 142) the "honorable name" are not disclosed, Dibelius draws on other texts to suggest several good possibilities. For example, as in Acts 19.23–27 and 1 Corinthians 12.1–3, it could be that the Christians adversely affect "the economic interests of the rich" (Dibelius, 1975, p. 140). In any case, all three accusations against the rich are easily appropriated as the views of the exploited poor within a patron–client society. Within James 2.1–13, the social example in 2.6b–7 has a genuine socio-rhetorical significance for God's elect poor. On the one hand, by focusing on the conflict between the elect poor and the rich out-siders it calls for the elect community to recognize and honor their solidarity as God's chosen poor; on the other hand, it calls for the community to change its behavior. As I mentioned above, the accusation in 2.6a is interrelated to the incriminating question in 2.4; the two social examples (2.2–4; 6b–7) are also interrelated. Together, and especially when viewed according to the social relations of a "limited good" society and patron–client structure, they imply that the elect community replicates in its own fraternal relations the dominant mentality of the broader culture: acquisi-tion. Thus the motives, values, and behavior that typify the social arenas outside the elect community (2.6b–7) are social scripts within the elect community, too (2.2–3). Following the example (2.5) and the statement from the opposite (2.6a), the social example in 2.6b–7 argues indirectly that the behavior of the worldly-advantaged rich is inappropriate among God's elect poor.[27]

The social nature of the rhetoric in the unit

The social examples in James 2.2–4 and 2.6b–7 are, like the whole deliberative unit (2.1–13), community-oriented rhetoric. And I think this is also true of the letter as a whole. Thus, I agree with

---

[27] With respect to the latter point, and the previous paragraph, the author is not merely addressing the character of the community's enemies. Rather he is in very good rhetorical fashion obliquely refuting the community's self-destructive behavior, for all three of the accusations against the rich outsiders have already been implicated of the pious poor (2.2–4, 5–6a). In similar fashion, the railings against the rich in James 4.13–5.6 are indirect admonitions to the members of the commu-nity who have wealth, status, and power to treat the elect poor mercifully. See Stowers (1986a, p. 128).

Roy Ward that the letter of James reveals an "urgent concern that the members of the community look out for their fellows"; and it exhorts its audience to an "ethical concern . . . positively centered on the intra-fraternal affairs of" the elect community.[28] Likewise, I concur with Ward (1966b, pp. 200–01) in his disagreement with Dibelius that the emphasis of the letter is on proper communal relations and not on "personal holiness"; that is, the letter "goes beyond mere personal piety . . . to a concern for proper, well-ordered fraternal relations."

Therefore, in focusing on "the social aspect of [the] language [in James 2.1–13] which is an instrument of communication and influence on others" (Wuellner, 1987, p. 449), I suggest that the kind of social rhetoric in view here is "communitarian social rhetoric."[29] Accordingly, the "communitarian argumentation" in James 2.1–13 seeks to create an ideal community, one that the author envisions and addresses as "the elect poor" (2.5–7). It displays a "conversionist" mentality, one that seeks to change the attitudes of the audience (2.1, 5, 8); and a "reformist" attitude to the procedures and practices of the community in its interpersonal relations (2.2–4, 6–7, 9–13). Based on the question and stasis of definition, the social rhetoric focuses on the nature of προσωπολημ-ψίαι which the author defines as "unjust judgments" (2.4) and "sin" (2.9) to produce a community without favoritism. The author addresses the attitudes of the people (2.2–4, 6b–7) in order to convert them to a different view of themselves and each other (2.5, 6b). Thus he seeks to reform the procedures by which and the structures within which they deal with one another (2.8–13).

The "communitarian" view is a localized utopian conception, focusing straight away on the sect it addresses. Thus Dibelius (1975, p. 49), in my opinion, was correct to refer to the ethic of James as a "conventicle-ethic." Though, I hasten to reiterate that the predominant concern in James is not the individual but the community as a whole (Ward, 1966b, pp. 200, 202). Consequently, I think Dibelius (p. 49) misjudges James 2.1–13 as a "sub-Christian" argument. As "communitarian social rhetoric" the

[28] Ward, 1966b, pp. 201–02 (see page v in the "Summary" that precedes his dissertation).

[29] The terms "communitarian," "conversionist," and "reformist," as well as their being types or kinds of "social rhetoric" (e.g., "conversionist social rhetoric") are derived from B. R. Wilson (in R. Robertson, 1969, pp. 361–83, as applied in Wolde, 1978, pp. 47–67). I am deeply indebted also to Professor Vernon Robbins who shared and discussed this material with me.

persuasion is fundamentally an argument of and about social formation. Put differently, the rhetoric of James is a "world-building" discourse (see P. Berger, 1969, pp. 3–28; and on the "interpersonal function" of language, see Halliday, 1978). That is, it seeks to effect a particular kind of community by remolding the thought and behavior of its addressees to conform with a particular understanding of God's truth (James 1.21; 5.19–20; 1.25; 2.1, 8).

The "conversionist" mentality that evinces itself holds that the outside world (4.4), the system of values championed by "the powerful" (= the rich, 2.6b–7; 4.13–5.6) is corrupted. It is informed by a wisdom that understands the world to be corrupted because individuals are corrupted (2.4, 6a, 9; cf. 1.13–15; 3.1–2; 4.1–4); nevertheless, it holds that individuals, communities, and the world itself are responsible for their own actions (2.1; cf. 2.14–26; 3.1–12, 13–18; 4.11–5.20).

On the other hand, the rhetoric evinces a clear mandate for social reform within the community's own institutions. An example of the latter is the indictment of the community's judicial assembly (2.2–4). Moreover, the rhetoric argues that there are this-worldly, as well as other-wordly, benefits to be derived from corporate reform (2.13, 5; 1.25, 12).

To be sure, there is no call for a systematic social reform of the community; rather, the rhetoric presses for the solidarity of the whole community, including both its wealthy (powerful) members and its (powerless) poor members (2.2–4; 1.26–27; 2.15–17; 4.11–12; 5.12–20). Still there is no escaping the fact that when the text asserts that God's whole law is to be kept (2.8–12; 1.19–25) it implies a thoroughgoing means of institutional reform for all sectors of the community's life. One does not invoke the law as James does unless the function of the law is being presupposed for the community's identity and way of life. To put it bluntly and more specifically the rhetoric of James, along the lines of traditional Jewish *'anawim* piety, suggests that the addressees are and should be "*the* elect Poor," those who humbly depend upon and love God, by obeying God's law.

I have agreed with Luke Johnson (1985, p. 172) that this does not mean that James advocates that the elect community withdraw from the world. The text reflects a community whose members are busily involved with making a living in the world; some of the members are apparently doing this quite successfully (hence the invectives in 4.13–5.8). This is never condemned. What James does advocate is that the community wisely live out its peculiar God-given identity, assuming its rightful place in the world but without being contaminated by the world's God-less values and wisdom (4.4). The community is expected to live in association with "the rich" but it must not live as "the rich" live.

While the rhetoric of James also envisions a reversal of the powers and values that dominate the world, there is no suggestion that like some revolutionary social rhetorics James condones a violent attitude and behavior toward the world on the part of the elect. To the contrary, the advice to endure worldly trials (1.12, 25), wisely (1.5–11; 3.13–18), avoiding wrath (1.19–20), and patiently waiting for the Lord (5.7–12), suggests an insider's view of the community as God's elect who must faithfully and humbly wait on God to reverse the worldly system. Yet it is equally clear that the community does not wait for God to reform its own behavior; the rhetoric calls for an immediate correction of the community's interpersonal relations in thought, words, and deeds in the light of God's truth, "the perfect law of liberty" (1.21, 25; 2.8–13; 5.19–20).

The "communitarian social rhetoric of James" faces an enormous task in confronting certain aspects of a society that presupposes the cultural scripts of "limited good" and the "patron–client system." It also is apparent that in challenging these cultural scripts the debate turns on the "pivotal values" of the patron–client culture: "honor and shame." In defining προσωπολημψίαι as "unjust judgments," and therefore as dishonorable and shameful behavior the rhetoric runs against what appears to be a common practice in the culture. Aristotle expresses the perspective that undergirds the practice: "Now men think that they have a right to be highly esteemed by those who are inferior to them in birth, power, and virtue, and generally, in whatever similar respect a man is far superior to another; for example, the rich man to the poor man in the matter of money" (*Rhet.* 2.5.7). To take this a bit further, if the example refers to a particular incident known to the author, it could be that a failure on the part of the community to show favoritism to an actual or potential patron would have resulted in a failure to receive his benefaction. Aristotle notes that "men are angry at slights from those by whom they think they have a right to be well treated; such are those on whom they have conferred or are conferring benefits" (*Rhet.* 2.2.8). It is this kind of behavior, its causes, accompaniments, and results that the author attacks. This takes us to the last sub-section of our discussion.

The cultural nature of the rhetoric in the unit

The "framework for exploring different kinds of cultural rhetoric" that is employed here is based on Vernon Robbins' (1993) article, "Rhetoric and Culture: Exploring Types of Cultural Rhetoric in a Text." Drawing on the cultural research of anthropologists and sociologists, Robbins introduces "four major terms" by which to analyze and interpret "cultural rhetorics": "(a) dominant culture rhetoric; (b) subculture rhetoric; (c) contraculture rhetoric; and (d) counterculture rhetoric." The term "culture" is used by Robbins "in the most neutral way possible"; thus it "means 'interaction of body–mind–culture' that goes back millions of years – that which . . . makes humans human" (based on Geertz, 1973, pp. 33–54).

Thus far, our analysis of the rhetoric in James 2.1–13 suggests that there are two basic cultures in view: Hellenistic-Roman culture and Jewish culture. The rhetoric in our unit, as well as in the whole letter, is bi-cultural rhetoric; which is to say that both of those cultures are contributors to the rhetorical environment from which James speaks. Further, our analysis indicates that the dominant culture is the Hellenistic-Roman culture. As an encyclical written to Jewish Christians in the dispersion (1.1), the letter of James reflects the "system of attitudes, values, dispositions, and norms supported by social structures vested with power to impose itself on people in a significantly bounded territorial region" (this is Robbins' definition of "a dominant culture," p. 4). Likewise, the analysis of James' rhetoric shows that it is feeding off Jewish culture and adopts a subcultural position to Jewish tradition which it uses counterculturally[30] to the dominant Greco-Roman culture.[31]

---

[30] "A counterculture . . . arises from a dominant culture and/or subculture and is 'concerned with the rejection of *explicit* and *mutable* characteristics of the culture from which it arises'" (Robbins, 1993, pp. 9–10, quoting K. A. Roberts, 1978, p. 114). A "contraculture" is not a "subculture"; rather it comprises "groups that do not involve more than one generation, which do not elaborate a set of institutions that allow the group to be relatively autonomous and self-sufficient, and which do not sustain an individual over an entire life span" (K. A. Roberts, 1978, p. 113, as cited in Robbins, 1993, p. 8).

[31] "Subcultural rhetoric," of course, is the use of language, which is marked by the social aspects of a "subculture" to constrain the thoughts and actions of people. Robbins (1993, p. 4; K. A. Roberts, 1978, p. 112) defines "subcultures" as "wholistic entities which affect all of life over a long span of time. '[The term subculture] stand[s] for the cultural patterns of a subsociety which contains both sexes, all ages, and family groups, and which parallels the larger society in that it provides for a network of groups and institutions extending throughout the individual's entire life cycle'" (p. 4).

In suggesting that the cultural rhetoric of James is subcultural to Jewish culture, I hold that it is a discourse that is at pains to affirm "the fundamental value orientation" of Jewish tradition (Roberts, 1978, p. 12; cited in Robbins, 1993, p. 11). Asserting that the cultural rhetoric of James is countercultural to Hellenistic-Roman culture, I maintain that in telling ways it "rejects the norms and values which unite the dominant culture" (Roberts, 1978, p. 13; quoted in Robbins, 1993, p. 11). And I propose that "the value conflict" that James has with Hellenistic-Roman culture is "one which is central, uncompromising, and wrenching to the fabric of the culture"; thus, "the concept of counterculture also implies a differentiation *between* the two cultures which is more distinct than the areas of *overlap*" (Roberts, 1978, p. 121; quoted in Robbins, 1993, p. 11). The thoroughly Jewish-Christian character of James is generally recognized by the vast majority of New Testament scholars. There is nothing in the text that suggests an institutional conflict, competition, or hostility to Jewish tradition. Moreover, the central and fundamental significance of the Torah as "the perfect law of freedom" (James 1.25) attests to the close relation that James bears to Jewish religion. The fact that James holds Jesus to be Messiah and Lord (1.1; 2.1) is best understood as an intramural disagreement within a Jewish subculture. As Jewish-Christian rhetoric James is subcultural within Jewish culture.

On the other hand, while James adroitly exploits the traditional *topoi* of Hellenistic-Roman culture and plays them with relative ease, much in the manner of the moralists and some philosophers, we have seen in the social rhetoric of James 2.1–13 an obvious conflict with the cultural scripts of limited good and the patron–client system. While it is true that the common understanding of justice in the Hellenistic-Roman culture also conflicted with those cultural scripts, the way in which James disagrees with them and seeks to constrain the attitudes and actions of its audience is informed by Jewish cultural rhetoric.

In particular, James offers its audience an alternative cultural script to that of the patron–client script of the dominant culture. And it provides a rationale for the behavior it champions. As I noted in chapter 3, James is well aware that "honor" is a variously defined value, and we have seen how Jewish culture informs James' countercultural attack on the typical honor/shame conventions of the Hellenistic-Roman world, as that was delineated by Aristotle (*Rhet.* 2.5.7).

Specifically with regard to the rhetorical exigence that evoked James 2.1–13, the problem of προσωποληηψίαι, James draws its definition of that behavior from Leviticus 19.15. Though some in the dominant culture also railed against such perversions of justice as contrary to honor and law, the honor and law they championed were not those of Israel's God. For James there is no other God, no other law (4.12; 2.10–11); and honor is the reputation of those who faithfully depend upon the one God, the one law-giver and judge, and fulfill the whole law (2.8, 10; 1.25).

But that which makes James' cultural rhetoric subcultural to Jewish cultural rhetoric, that which essentially differentiates it from a thorough-going, predominantly Jewish cultural rhetoric, is the fact that James is a Christian version of a Jewish value system. For we have also seen that while James draws its definition of προσωποληημψίαι from Leviticus 19.15 and confirms it – over against the Hellenistic-Roman (popular) scripts of honor/shame, limited good, and the patronal system – with a four-part argument from the written Torah, it exploits Lev 19.18 as a summary of the whole law and postures it in relation to a saying of Jesus (2.5). While Jesus apparently interpreted the fulfillment of the Torah in the love-command, the cultural rhetoric of James subsumes this interpretation under and intimately connects it with Jesus' own faith, and interestingly enough, the whole argument turns on James 2.5.

The implication is clear: holding Jesus' faith (2.1) and fulfilling the Torah (2.10) are synonymous for the author of James. Both find their essence in loving one's neighbor as oneself (2.8). The rationale for this behavior the author of James does not find in the dominant rhetoric of the Hellenistic-Roman culture, nor in some countercultural Cynic rhetoric; rather, it derives from a Christianized view of the behavior he constrains from Leviticus 19.18, 15.

Fundamentally significant for the particular social location of thought evinced in James 2.1–13 is the prominence of the Torah and judgment (2.8–13). As rhetorical constraints, both the Torah and judgment are treated as subtopics of honor, and in unmistakable rhetorical fashion they are qualified in reference to the honorable faith of Jesus (2.1), and also in reference to the faith of the elect poor (2.5).

In the light of the rhetorical situation that gave rise to James 2.1–13 the socio-rhetorical significance of James 2.5 is suggested in

the pattern of the argument. As the first and fundamental supporting proof for the theme that προσωπολημψίαι are incompatible
with Jesus' faith, James 2.5 exemplifies God as the real patron of
the elect poor. In so doing it devalues the world's system of values,
as they are exposed in the social examples that precede it (2.2–4)
and follow it (2.6b–7). Thus it gives countercultural voice to a
"value conflict" that James has with Hellenistic-Roman culture, a
conflict that is "central, uncompromising, and wrenching to the
fabric of the culture." For honor to God, the true patron of the
elect poor, demands love (= merciful actions) toward the poor
neighbor.

Because God is portrayed as the true patron of the elect poor, the
cultural rhetoric of James discloses the only wealth that God
honors: being "rich in faith." For James, being "rich in faith" is an
attribute of actions and synonymous with "loving God." Moreover, the logic and pattern of the rhetoric in the unit divulges that
"rich in faith" is also equivalent to "fulfilling the whole law," as
summarized in the love-commandment (2.8; cf. 2.12–13). Consequently, James 2.5 argues that the elect poor are those who love the
poor neighbor and show him/her mercy.

I conclude that the socio-rhetorical function of James 2.5 is this:
it is a rhetorical judgment that in its own rhetorical situation sets
forth in one sentence the social identity, the way of life, and the goal
of God's chosen poor. It envinces a social location of thought that
is fundamentally theocentric in its view of social life, and, artfully
performed in language that alludes to a well-known and widely
distributed saying of Jesus, it not only buttresses the argument that
Jesus' faith is incompatible with acts of partiality; it recalls the
quality of Jesus' faith and relates that to the way of life it envisions
for the elect poor. As a servant of God and the Lord Jesus Christ,
the author argues that Jesus' faith is ratified in fulfilling the whole
law as it is summarized in the love-commandment.

Thus the social texture of James 2.5 coheres with its intertexture
and the pattern of argumentation within which it functions.
Socially, it provides self-definition and the primary cultural script
for the elect poor in the world. Intertextually, the social location of
thought in James 2.5 is very similar to that in the pre-Matthean
Sermon on the Mount. Indeed the "rich in faith" in James are like
the "poor in spirit" in the pre-Matthean SM: they are the pious
poor who obey God's law. Whereas the author of the pre-
Matthean SM argues in good rhetorical fashion that God's law is

ratified in the words of Jesus and in the obedience of his followers, the author of James 2.1–13 argues in good progymnastic fashion that God's law is ratified in the faith of Jesus and – as the allusion to the saying of Jesus in James 2.5 makes clear – also in the faith of his servants.

6

CONCLUSION

Before I summarize the course of our investigation and suggest something of its possible contribution to New Testament studies, I should like to ask very briefly some general questions about the ideological implications of the rhetoric in James, particularly with reference to James 2.5. By "the ideological implications of the rhetoric," I mean how the "ideology" of the Epistle of James functions as the social use of language that it is; namely, a written instance of deliberative discourse emanating from the first century of the Mediterranean world. And, here, the operative definition of ideology is a "neutral" one, the one employed by John H. Elliott (1981), in *A Home for the Homeless: A Sociological Exegesis of 1 Peter, Its Situation and Strategy*. Accordingly, ideology is " 'an integrated system of beliefs, assumptions and values, not necessarily true or false, which reflects the needs and interests of a group or class at a particular time in history' " (p. 268; quoting D. B. Davis, 1975, p. 14). And I presume (following Elliott) that the ideological character of James is such that there is within it "an interrelation and inseparability of social and religious frames of reference, meaning and function" (p. 268).

We have discussed some of the ways in which the rhetoric of James 2.1–13 exploits the "beliefs, assumptions and values" of the author, the audience, and the broader culture in an effort to persuade the audience that acts of partiality are incompatible with Jesus' faith. Here, the questions before us involve the "needs and interests" of the people evoked in the rhetoric of this text. How are the self-interests of the author and the community functioning in this rhetoric? In other words, if the strategies of the author's rhetoric are successful what benefits are achieved and for whom are these benefits achieved? Could it be that if successful people would rally around the socio-ideologically located thought and voice in this unit particular benefits would fall to people of low estate? What might be the situation in the overall context?

We have argued that the cultural rhetoric in James is subcultural to Jewish culture. And there is no evidence that the religious community of James is in competition with another religious group, as, for example, there is Matthew's rhetoric. Rather, it appears that the people whom James addresses are surrounded by people within a Greco-Roman value structure, and they are trying to find their way in an environment that is dominated by those values.

The broader community apparently follows the ordinary conventional procedures within the culture. The letter of James seems to envision and to establish the authority of its author within the community it addresses, around a rhetoric that uses Christian rhetoric that is subcultural to Jewish culture and countercultural to Greco-Roman culture. In other words, the rhetoric establishes boundaries for acceptable behavior. The rhetoric of James is essentially a "communitarian social rhetoric." It envisions a particular self-understanding or identity for a community (or communities) of Jewish Christians in the dispersion, and it establishes boundaries for behavior that conforms to the community's self-identity that it envisions. Those who conform to this behavior are honorable; those who will not conform are dishonorable and are warned that their behavior will result in their destruction. The big question is, what is at stake in the rhetoric of the text?

Our investigation suggests that the socio-rhetorical function of the saying in James 2.5 is that it sets forth the identity of James' community, their way of life, and their ultimate reward. Accordingly, the community is envisioned as the Pious Poor, along the lines of the traditional Jewish piety of the poor. The way of life, "rich in faith," is a Jamesian expression for humble dependence on God and faithful obedience to the Torah, as this was interpreted by Jesus (1.1; 2.1). The reward that awaits those who live "rich in faith" is the kingdom of God. Further, we argued that James understands the Torah to be summarized in the love-commandment (2.8), and the elaboration holds that the whole law is fulfilled in obeying this commandment (2.8–11). The structure of the rhetorical example in James 2.5 makes it clear that fulfilling the love-commandment means being "rich in faith," and that is synonymous with "loving God." It is very significant that the author of this text believes that one loves God by loving one's neighbor. But what does all this mean for the social relations of the religious community envisioned in James?

There are clearly material benefits at stake. While some within this community have wealth and possessions, the overall impression is that the larger community is materially disadvantaged. Thus when James 2.13 invokes "mercy" as the species of love (2.8) that the shabbily dressed man (2.2) needs most, and the text launches into an elaboration (2.14–26) that defines "faith" by the attributes of merciful actions toward those who need clothing, food (2.15–16) and shelter (2.25), the rhetoric seems to suggest that the author expects the community members who have wealth and possessions to employ those "goods" with respect to the needs of their fellow community members, just as God employs good gifts (1.17) with respect to them. Likewise, the reminder concerning traditional Jewish covenantal obligations toward the widows and orphans (1.27), and the exhortation concerning the suffering and the sick (5.13) – all these concerns seem to indicate that if the rhetoric of James is successful, then those community members who have material needs could expect material benefits from those who possess them.

There are likewise social status benefits in view. James 2.5 is the rhetorical example that discloses the author's basis for differentiating the elect poor from the rich outsiders. It calls for the community to remember their God-honored identity and status; thus it promotes the collective honor of the elect poor over against the rich and powerful, and the way of life they exemplify. This, coupled with the social comparison in 2.2–4 which demands justice for community members without regard for worldly advantage, certainly endorses the social status of the lowly as thoroughly honorable.

On the other hand, recognizing that the concepts "poor" and "rich" are not mere economic terms and that the elect poor includes some members who are materially wealthy, what are the status benefits of this rhetoric for those who have plenty? Like the patron–client relation, the concept of limited good is instinctual to the culture in view. Consequently, the community member who had an abundance of limited goods, more than he or she apparently needed, would have been suspected of having disadvantaged another. Does this mean, then, that if James' rhetoric is successful the wealthier members of the elect would have been placed under even greater suspicion?

Or could it be that James' rhetoric opens the door for those with plenty to assume an even more honorable status within the elect community? For if the mutual solidarity that James 2.5 envisions for the community becomes actual, given the patron–client relation, would not those with plenty be honor-bound to become patrons for the community? We may recall, from the previous chapter, the anthropological insight that within a patron–client system the "sharing of wealth in order to gain status is a way to solve the problem of inequality within a society with high demands for solidarity" (Moxnes, 1988, pp. 78, 79). Is this the benefit that James holds out for the wealthy community members? That they, like God, the giver of "every good and perfect gift" (1.17), are to become the honored patrons of their more impoverished community members?

If this is so, however, does it not also presuppose that the community is being dissuaded from the dominant mentality of the larger patron–client culture, the mentality of "acquisition"? And in a world that views all goods as limited, does this not mean that James envisions a different kind of world? Because I have found the rhetoric of the pre-Matthean SM, or something very like it, to be at play in James' rhetoric about "the kingdom which he [God] promised to those who love him" (2.5), I wonder if perhaps it is possible that within the ideology of James the ideology of Q^{Matt} 6.33 finds a new voice. Does not Q^{Matt} 6.24–34 seem to reflect a sapiential understanding of the world that coheres with the sapiential understanding of God and humankind in James 1.9–18? And the latter is simply another aspect of the sapiential view in James 3.13–5.18.

In any case, it does appear that James offers material and status benefits to both the poor and wealthy members of the elect poor. Further, the boundaries it draws gives no space within the elect community for a member, whether with plenty or little, to judge the worth of another brother or sister on the basis of his or her material and/or social benefits (4.11–12).

Earlier I said that the fundamental constraint in the rhetoric of James is the ethos of the implied author. And I have argued that the text wishes to be heard as one from James, the Lord's brother. Likewise, we have seen how the text presupposes the patron–client relation as the basis upon which the evoked author presents himself

to the community as the (client) of God and the Lord Jesus Christ
(1.1). The posture of the author with respect to the community is
that of a broker. Is it possible that the text is here setting up James
of Jerusalem as the broker for God and Jesus, and the benefits they
espoused (wisdom, justice, social status, self-status)? To an audience that functioned according to the patron–client script of the
Mediterranean culture in the first century, the author would have
come across as an authoritative patron who offers his patrons'
benefits to the audience. The patron–client relation then seems to
support the text's strong move to establish James, the Lord's
brother, as the patron of Jewish Christians ("the twelve tribes") in
the dispersion.

Finally, the author appears to engage in a head-on confrontation
with the honor/shame structure. By demanding that social superiors
and subordinates treat each other with "justice," that is, as equals
(2.4, 9; 4.6–10, 11–12), the rhetoric runs counter to certain
prescribed cultural cues of the society. The letter of James is, in a
very real sense, brutal rhetoric; it belongs to a subcultural group
struggling to survive amid the trials of life in a hostile world.

In chapter 1, I introduced the thesis that the Epistle of James is a
written instance of deliberative rhetoric that exploits a tradition of
Jesus' sayings in an effort to constrain the thoughts and actions of
its addressees. And I argued that the composition was intended to
function as a literary letter, an encyclical, to Jewish Christians in
the dispersion. The elasticity of the ancient letter genre not only
permits such a classification, it presumes it. And the dominance of
rhetorical composition, as the culture of context for written persuasion in the milieu from which James originates, allowed us the
room for wondering if perhaps James' discourse reflects this. Not
only has our investigation uncovered nothing that disqualifies this
proposal, it has, happily, endorsed it.

In chapter 2, in order to ask the scholarly community's permis-
sion to look at James according to the canons of classical rhetoric,
we first showed that there has long been, and there still remains, a
great deal of uncertainty about how to classify, appropriate, and
understand the letter of James. And we found that the rhetorical
qualities of James were not infrequently noticed but were seldom
emphasized. Then, we took a detailed look at what has been the
predominant classification and understanding of James for the last
seventy years, the view of Martin Dibelius that James is best
understood and interpreted as a representative of the so-called

"genre," paraenesis. We traced this understanding through the secondary sources on which it was based all the way back to the primary sources it claimed to explicate. We found that there is no such thing; paraenesis is not a literary genre but the positive mode of deliberative rhetoric. So, we decided to cast our lot not with Dibelius but with the ancients; that is, with Aristotle, Quintilian, and Cicero, and the teachers of elementary rhetorics, Theon and Hermogenes. Then, following the lead of other New Testament scholars who have returned to ancient rhetoric in an attempt to understand writings like James, we turned to James 2.1–13, which, according to Dibelius and the scholarly majority, is one of the three most important units in the letter. It is also the unit in which James 2.5 makes its case.

In chapter 3, we asked James 2.1–13 if it could perform as a progymnastic elaboration, in the manner of those presented in the rhetorical handbooks and the *progymnasmata*. We found that it could, and it did, and it did so easily and well. So far as I know, no one has pursued and analyzed the "internal dynamics" of the argumentation in the way that we have done.[1]

In chapter 4, we probed the intertextuality of our unit. We found that James exploits other texts in progymnastic fashion. The text activates antecedent texts from the LXX, common conceptions and *topoi* in the broader culture, and also sayings in the Jesus tradition. We compared James 2.5 with its four known parallels, Q^{Matt} 5.3, Q^{Luke} 6.20b, *Gos. Thom.* 54, and Pol. *Phil.* 2.3, and we found that it is very close to Q^{Matt} 5.3. And, following Hans Dieter Betz's thesis that Q^{Matt} 5–7 is a very early pre-Matthean composition, and Helmut Koester's thesis that the author of James and the author of the SM come from the same milieu, we have argued that the pre-Matthean SM, or something like it, has an intimate intertextual connection with the rhetorical language in James 2.1–13. And we have concluded that James 2.5, in the manner of a progymnastic recitation, is a Jamesian performance of the saying of Jesus in Q^{Matt} 5.3.

In chapter 5, we examined the social and cultural texture of our unit and of the saying in James 2.5. We determined that our unit, like the letter of James itself, is deliberative discourse. It is essentially "communitarian social rhetoric" that envisions its ad-

[1] I am pleased that D. F. Watson (1993) agrees with me that James 2.1–13 is a rhetorical elaboration of a theme. I wish to thank Professor Watson for sharing with me a copy of his very fine paper.

dressees as "God's elect poor," and it seeks to constrain the thought and actions of its addressees in such a way that they live this identity in the world. We discovered that James' rhetoric is subcultural to Jewish cultural rhetoric and countercultural to Greco-Roman cultural rhetoric. It constrains its Jewish sources around a Christian rhetoric that, informed by Jesus' interpretation of the law as summarized in the love-commandment, opposes certain aspects of the cultural scripts that constrain the thought and behavior of the dominant Greco-Roman culture. And we determined that the socio-rhetorical function of James 2.5 is that it recalls in the language of Jesus (very like the saying in Q^{Matt} 5.3) a precedent about God's promise of the kingdom to the poor; and that that precedent in essence sets forth the identity, the way of life, and the goal of God's pious poor.

In the present chapter, we have suggested that if the strategies of James' rhetoric are successful, there are very positive and life-enhancing material and status benefits to be obtained for the struggling Christians that it addresses. But we have also discovered that the way of life which this text sets forth presupposes a radical willingness on the part of its audience to live in but not of the world.

One of the dominant benefits to be obtained if this rhetoric is successful is that its author will be viewed and honored as a spokesperson for God and the Lord Jesus Christ. Which means, as the rhetoric in the light of its culture shows, that the author will be perceived as a patron who offers to his community the "goods" or "benefits" that God and Jesus offer. The rhetoric very much envisions its author as the authoritative patron of God and Christ for the twelve tribes in the dispersion. Moreover, because this letter wishes to be taken as a letter of James, the Lord's brother, written to Jewish Christians in the dispersion, it also seems to confront us with the possibility that within the first century there was someone, or some group, who believed or wanted to believe that James the Just could have spoken this way. Is it not rather interesting that the very first and primary argumentative unit in the whole discourse, James 2.1–13, uses the first and primary saying (Q^{Matt} 5.3) in a Jewish *epitome* of the teachings of Jesus (Q^{Matt} 5–7) as its first and primary proof that acts of partiality are incompatible with Jesus' faith? Is it only coincidence that the first and primary argument in a letter that wishes to be heard from James the Just is about "justice"? Is it only coincidence that Jesus' faith and the whole law are shown to be, in quite good rhetorical fashion, interrelated and inseparable; that holding Jesus' faith and fulfilling the whole law mean fulfilling the love-commandment? Is it only coincidence that James the Just is made to speak the same wisdom that Jesus spoke?

I have argued that James is pseudonymous, and I am still inclined to believe this is so. But being pseudonymous, it may well be the result of an exercise in προσωποποιΐα, "a speech-in-character" (Theon, VIII, 1–10). In my opinion, the letter of James is an early text, written before the fall of Jerusalem (70 CE). It shows no dependence on the written Gospels, but clearly draws on something like the pre-Matthean SM for key statements in its development. In James, as Koester has rightly argued, we find the same view that we find in the pre-Matthean SM; the Christians who are addressed are viewed as "belong[ing] to law-abiding Israel, and the fulfillment of the law, though without any emphasis upon circumcision and ritual law, is the appropriate interpretation of the teachings of Jesus' (Koester, 1990, p. 171). While some scholars seem to believe that James the Just could not speak for five minutes without addressing the subject of circumcision or food laws, there were evidently some in the ancient world who believed he could. Perhaps he did. The Epistle of James wants to suggest itself as evidence for this; and Robert M. Grant (1963, p. 221) is correct in saying that the materials in this letter may well "go back to the early days of the Jerusalem church." Socio-rhetorical criticism, as we have engaged in it here, suggests among other things that the use of the sayings of Jesus in early Christian literature was not necessarily marked by scribal reproduction. And it argues on solid grounds that variant performances of Jesus' sayings are not necessarily the result of oral tradition. It appears that some of the earlier writings that make up the New Testament (the Epistle of James being one of them) were written by authors who were quite capable of, and had no hesitation in, performing Jesus' sayings in ways that justified their own views of how their communities should appropriate Jesus' interpretation of the Torah. James 2.1–13 is a very fine rhetorical elaboration that demonstrates this phenmenon; and James 2.5 is an artful performance of the principal beatitude in the pre-Matthean Sermon on the Mount.

BIBLIOGRAPHY

Adams, C. (1905) *Lysias: Selected Speeches XII, XVI, XIX, XXII, XXIV, XXV, XXXII, XXXIV*, with introduction, notes, and appendices, foreword by H. L. Levy, New York: American Book Company; repr. Norman, OK: University of Oklahoma Press (1950).

Adamson, J. B. (1976) *The Epistle of James*, NICNT, Grand Rapids: William B. Eerdmans.

(1989) *James: The Man & His Message*, Grand Rapids: William B. Eerdmans.

Aland, K. (1944) "Der Herrenbruder Jakobus und der Jakobusbrief," *TLZ*, pp. 97–104.

(1976) *Synopsis Quattuor Evangeliorum*, Stuttgart: Deutsche Bibelstiftung.

Aland, K. and B. Aland (eds.) (1987) *The Text of the New Testament. An Introduction to the Critical Editions and to the Theory and Practice of Modern Textual Criticism*, trans. E. Rhodes, Grand Rapids: William B. Eerdmans; Leiden: E. J. Brill.

Allen, W., *et al.* (1972–73) "'Horace's first book of *Epistles* as letters," *CJ* 68,2, pp. 119–33.

Alonso-Schoekel, L. (1973) "'James 5:2 (=5:6) and 4:6," *Bib* 54, pp. 73–76.

Alter, R. (1989) *The Pleasures of Reading in an Ideological Age*, A Touchstone Book, New York: Simon & Schuster.

Aristotle. *The 'Art' of Rhetoric*, trans. J. H. Freese, LCL, Cambridge: Harvard University Press; London: William Heinemann (1926).

Nicomachean Ethics, trans. H. Rackham, LCL, Cambridge: Harvard University Press; London: William Heinemann (1932).

Posterior Analytics, trans. H. Tredennick, LCL, Cambridge: Harvard University Press; London: William Heinemann (1926).

Topica, trans. E. S. Forster, LCL, Cambridge: Harvard University Press, London: William Heinemann (1926).

Arnim, J. von (ed.) *Stoicorum Veterum Fragmenta*, 4 vols., Leipzig: Teubner (1903–24); repr. 4 vols. in 2, New York: Irvington Publishers (1986).

Arrighetti, G. (1973) *Epicuro. Opere: Introduzione, testo critico, traduzione e note*, 3rd edn., Florence: Einaudi.

Atkins, J. W. H. (1934) *Literary Criticism in Antiquity: A Sketch of its Development*, 2 vols., Cambridge: Cambridge University Press; repr. Gloucester, MA: Peter Smith (1961).

Attridge, H. W. (1976) *First-Century Cynicism in the Epistles of Heraclitus*, Missoula, MT: Scholars Press.

Augustine *On Christian Doctrine*, trans. D. W. Robertson Jr., The Library of Liberal Arts 80, Indianapolis: Bobbs-Merrill (1958).

Aune, D. E. (1987) *The New Testament in Its Literary Environment*, Library of Early Christianity, vol. VIII, ed. W. A. Meeks, Philadelphia: Westminster Press.

  (ed.) (1988) *Greco-Roman Literature and the New Testament: Selected Forms and Genres*, SBLSBS 21, Atlanta: Scholars Press.

Baasland, E. (1982) "Der Jakobusbrief als neutestamentliche Weisheits-schrift," *ST* 36, pp. 119–39.

  (1988) "Literarische Form, Thematik und geschichtliche Einordnung des Jakobusbriefes," in *ANRW* II.II, 25.5, Berlin and New York: De Gruyter, pp. 3646–84.

Bakhtin, M. M. (1981) *The Dialogic Imagination: Four Essays*, ed. M. Holquist, trans. C. Emerson, Austin: University of Texas Press.

Baldwin, C. S. (1924) *Ancient Rhetoric and Poetic*, New York: Macmillan Press; repr. Gloucester, MA: Peter Smith (1959).

  (1928) *Medieval Rhetoric and Poetic*, New York: Macmillan Press; repr. Gloucester, MA: Peter Smith (1959).

Bammel, E. (1968) "πτωχός, κτλ.," *TDNT* VI, pp. 885–915.

Banks, R. (1975) *Jesus and the Law in the Synoptic Tradition*, Cambridge: Cambridge University Press.

Barnard, L. W. (1967) "The Early Roman Church, Judaism, and Jewish Christianity," *ATR* 49, pp. 371–84.

Barnett, A. E. (1962) "James, Letter of," *IDB* 2, pp. 794–99.

Barth, M. (1969) "The Faith of the Messiah," *HeyJ* 10, pp. 363–70.

Bartlett, D. L. (1979) "The Epistle of James as a Jewish-Christian Document," in SBLSP 2, ed. P. Achtemeier, Missoula, MT: Scholars Press, pp. 73–86.

Bauckham, R. (1988) "Pseudo-Apostolic Letters," *JBL* 107,3, pp. 469–94.

Bauer, W. F. *A Greek-English Lexicon of the New Testament and Other Early Christian Literature*, 2nd edn., trans., rev., and augm., W. F. Arndt, F. W. Gingrich, and F. W. Danker, Chicago: The University of Chicago Press (1979).

Baur, F. C. (1845) *Paulus, der Apostel Jesu Christi, sein Leben und Wirken, seine Briefe und seine Lehre. Ein Beitrag zu einer kritischen Geschichte des Urchristentums*, Stuttgart: Becker & Müller.

  (1878) *The Church History of the First Three Centuries*, trans. A. Menzies, London: Williams & Norgate.

Beck, D. L. (1973) "The Composition of the Epistle of James," Ph.D. diss., Princeton University; Ann Arbor, MI: University Microfilms.

Beker, J. C. (1950) *The Church Faces the World: Late New Testament Writings*, Philadelphia: Westminster Press.

Bellinzoni, A. J. (1967) *The Sayings of Jesus in the Writings of Justin Martyr*, Leiden: E. J. Brill.

Bengel, J. A. (1877) *Bengel's New Testament Commentary*, trans. C. Lewis and M. Vincent, 2 vols., Grand Rapids: Kregel Publications (1981).

Bergauer, P. (1962) *Der Jakobusbrief bei Augustinus und die damit verbundenen Probleme der Rechtfertigungslehre*, Vienna: Herder.

Berger, K. (1980) "Der Impliziten Gegner. Zur Methode des Erschliessens von 'Gegnern' in neutestamentlichen Texten," in Lührmann and Strecker (1980), pp. 373–400.

(1984a) *Formgeschichte des Neuen Testament*. Heidelberg: Quelle & Meyer.

(1984b) "Der Jakobusbrief," in *Bibelkunde des Alten und Neuen Testaments, II Neues Testament*, 2nd edn., Heidelberg: Quelle & Meyer, pp. 456–61.

(1984c) "Hellenistische Gattungen im Neuen Testament," in *ANRW* II, 25,2, Berlin and New York: De Gruyter, pp. 1031–423, 1831–85.

Berger, P. (1969) *The Sacred Canopy: Elements of a Sociological Theory of Religion*, Anchor Books, New York: Doubleday & Company.

Berger, P. and T. Luckman (1960) *The Social Construction of Reality: A Treatise on the Sociology of Knowledge*, Anchor Books, New York: Doubleday & Company.

Bertram, G. (1974) "φρήν, κτλ," *TDNT* IX, pp. 220–35.

Betz, H. D. (1961) *Lukian von Somosata und das Neue Testament, TU 76, Berlin: Akademie-Verlag.*

(1967) *Nachfolge und Nachahmung Jesu Christi im Neuen Testament*, Tübingen: J. C. B. Mohr (P. Siebeck).

(1972) *Der Apostel Paulus und die sokratische Tradition. Eine exegetische Untersuchung zu seiner "Apologie" 2 Korinther 10–13*, BHTh 45, Tübingen: J. C. B. Mohr.

(ed.) (1975a) *Plutarch's Theological Writings and Early Christian Literature*, SCHNT 3, Leiden: E. J. Brill.

(1975b) "The Literary Composition and Function of Paul's Letter to the Galatians," *NTS* 21, pp. 353–79.

(ed.) (1978) *Plutarch's Ethical Writings and Early Christian Literature*, SCHNT 4, Leiden: E. J. Brill.

(1979) *Galatians: A Commentary on Paul's Letter to the Churches in Galatia*, Hermeneia, Philadelphia: Fortress Press.

(1985a) *Essays on the Sermon on the Mount*, Philadelphia: Fortress Press.

(1985b) "Eschatology in the Sermon on the Mount and the Sermon on the Plain," in SBLSP, Atlanta: Scholars Press, pp. 343–50.

(1986) "The Problem of Rhetoric and Theology according to the Apostle Paul," in A. Vanhoye (1986), pp. 16–48.

Beyer, H. W. (1968) "ἐπισκέπτομαι, κτλ.," *TDNT* VI, pp. 599–622.

Beyer, K. (1962) *Semitische Syntax im Neuen Testament*, Göttingen: Vandenhoeck & Ruprecht.

Beyschlag, W. (1874) "Der Jakobusbrief als urchritstliches Denkmal," *TSK* 1, pp. 105–65.

(1886) *Handbuch über den Brief des Jacobus*, 6th edn., Gttingen: Vandenhoeck.

Bieder, W. (1945) "Christliche Existenz nach dem Zeugnis des Jakobusbriefes," *TZ* 5, pp. 93–113.

Bihlmeyer, K. (1970) *Die Apostolische Väter*, 3rd edn., Tübingen: J. C. B. Mohr (P. Siebeck).

Bitzer, L. F. (1968) "The Rhetorical Situation," Philosophy and Rhetoric 1, pp. 1–14.

Blass, F., A. Debrunner, and R. W. Funk (1961) *A Greek Grammar of the New Testament and Other Early Christian Literature*, Chicago: The University of Chicago Press.

Blenkinsopp, J. (1983) *Wisdom and Law in the Old Testament: The Ordering of Life in Israel and Early Judaism*, Oxford: Oxford University Press.

Boethius's De topicis differentiis, trans. E. Stump, with notes and essays on the text, Ithaca and London: Cornell University Press, 1978.

Boggan, C. W. (1982) "Wealth in the Epistle of James," Ph.D. diss., The Southern Baptist Theological Seminary; Ann Arbor, MI: University Microfilms.

Bonner, S. F. (1977) *Education in Ancient Rome: From the Elder Cato to the Younger Pliny*, Berkeley and Los Angeles: University of California Press.

Borg, M. J. (1984) *Conflict, Holiness and Politics in the Teaching of Jesus*, New York and Toronto: Edwin Mellen Press.

Boring, M. E. (1982) *Sayings of the Risen Christ*, Cambridge: Cambridge University Press.

(1986) "Criteria of Authenticity: The Lucan Beatitudes as a Test Case," *Forum* 1,4, pp. 3–38.

Botterweck, G. J. and H. Ringgren (eds.) (1974–) *Theological Dictionary of the Old Testament*, Grand Rapids: William B. Eerdmans.

Bradley, K. R. (1987) *Slaves and Masters in the Roman Empire: A Study in Social Control*, New York and Oxford: Oxford University Press.

Brand, W. J. (1970) *The Rhetoric of Argumentation*, New York: Bobbs-Merrill.

Braun, H. (1968) "ποιέω, κτλ.," *TDNT* vi, pp. 458–84.

Brinktrine, J. (1954) "Zu Jak, 2,1," *Bib* 3, pp. 40–42.

Britton, A. (1981) "Situation in the Theory of Rhetoric," *Philosophy and Rhetoric* 14, pp. 234–48.

Brockington, L. H. (1955) "The Septuagintal Background to the New Testament Use of *doxa*," in *Studies in the Gospels* (For R. H. Lightfoot), ed. D. Nineham, Oxford: B. Blackwell, pp. 1–8.

Brown, F., S. R. Driver, and C. A. Briggs *A Hebrew and English Lexicon of the Old Testament*, Oxford: Clarendon Press (1952).

Bryant, D. C. (ed.) (1958) *The Rhetorical Idiom*, Ithaca: Cornell University Press.

(1973) *Rhetorical Dimensions in Criticism*, Baton Rouge: Louisiana State University Press.

Bultmann, R. (1910) *Der Stil der paulinischen Predigt und die kynisch-stoische Diatribe*, Göttingen: Vandenhoeck & Ruprecht.

(1957) *Theology of the New Testament*, trans. K. Grobel, New York: Charles Scribner's Sons.

(1963) *History of the Synoptic Tradition*, trans. from 2nd German edn. by J. Marsh, Oxford: Basil Blackwell.

(1964) "ἔλεος, κτλ.," *TDNT* ii, pp. 477–87.

Burchard, C. (1980) "Gemeinde der strohernen Epistel. Mutmaßungen über Jakobus," in Lührmann and Strecker (1980), pp. 315–28.

Burger, K. H. (1895) *Die Briefe des Jacobus, Petrus, und Judas*, 2nd edn., Munich: C. H. Beck.

Burgess, T. (1902) "Epideictic Literature," *University of Chicago Studies in Classical Philology* 3, pp. 89–248.

Burke, K. (1970) *The Rhetoric of Religion: Studies in Logography*, Berkeley and Los Angeles: University of California Press.

(1978) "Methodological Repression and/or Strategies of Containment," *Critical Inquiry* 5, pp. 401–16.

Burkert, W. (1985) *Greek Religion*, trans. J. Raffin, Oxford: Basil Blackwell.

Burkitt, F. C. (1924) *Christian Beginnings*, London: University of London Press.

Butts, J. R. (1987) "The *Progymnasmata* of Theon: A New Text with Translation and Commentary," Ph.D. diss., Claremont Graduate School; Ann Arbor, MI: University Microfilms.

Cadbury, H. J. (1920) *The Style and Literary Method of Luke*, Cambridge: Harvard University Press.

(1954) "The Single Eye," *HTR* 47, pp. 69–74.

Cameron, R. D. (1983) "Sayings Traditions in the Apocryphon of James," Ph.D. diss., Harvard University.

Campenhausen, H. F. von (1963) "Polykarp von Smyrna und die Pastoral- briefe," in *Aus der Frühzeit des Christentums: Studien zur Kirchen- geschichte des ersten und zweiten Jahrhunderts*, Tübingen: J. C. B. Mohr (P. Siebeck), pp. 197–252.

(1972) *The Formation of the Christian Bible*, trans. J. A. Baker, Philadel- phia: Fortress Press.

Canik, H. (1967) *Untersüchungen zu Senecas epistulae morales*, Spudas- mata, Studien zur klassischen Philologie und ihren Grenzgebieten 18, ed. H. Hommel and E. Zin, Hildesheim: Greg Olms.

Cantinat, J. C. M. (1973) Les Epîtres de Saint Jacques et de Saint Jude, Sources bibliques, Paris: J. Gabalda.

Carney, T. F. (1975) *The Shape of the Past: Models in Antiquity*, Kansas: Coronada Press.

Carrington, P. (1940) *The Primitive Christian Catechism: A Study in the Epistles*, Cambridge: Cambridge University Press.

Chadwick, H. (1961) "Justification by Faith and Hospitality," TU 79, p. 281.

Chaine, J. (1927) *L'Epîtres de Saint Jacques*, Ebib 20, Paris.

Charles, R. H. (1908) *The Greek Versions of the Testaments of the Twelve Patriarchs*, Oxford: Clarendon Press.

Charlesworth, J. H. (ed.) (1983) *The Old Testament Pseudepigrapha*, 2 vols., New York: Doubleday & Company.

Chase, J. R. (1961) "The Classical Conception of Epideictic," Ph.D. diss., Cornell University; Ann Arbor, MI: University Microfilms.

Childs, B. S. (1979) *Introduction to the Old Testament as Scripture*, Philadelphia: Fortress Press.

(1984) *The New Testament as Canon: An Introduction*, Philadelphia: Fortress Press.

Church, F. F. (1978) "Rhetorical Structure and Design in Paul's Letter to Philemon," *HTR* 71, pp. 17–33.

Cicero *De Inventione, De Optimo Genere Oratorum, Topica*, trans. H. M. Hubbell, LCL, Cambridge: Harvard University Press; London: William Heinemann (1949).

  De Oratore, Books I–II, trans. E. W. Sutton and H. Rackham, LCL, Cambridge: Harvard University Press; London: William Heinemann (1942).

  De Oratore, Book III and *De Partitione Oratoria*, trans. H. Rackham, LCL, Cambridge: Harvard University Press; London: William Heinemann (1942).

  The Letters to His Friends, 2 vols., trans. W. G. Williams, LCL, Cambridge: Harvard University Press; London: William Heinemann (1943, 1954).

  Orator, trans. H. M. Hubbell, LCL, Cambridge: Harvard University Press; London: William Heinemann (1939).

Cladder, H. J. (1904a) "Die Anlage des Jakobusbriefes," *ZKT* 28, pp. 37–57.

  (1904b) "Der formale Aufbau des Jakobusbriefes," *ZKT* 28, pp. 295–330.

Clark, D. L. (1957) *Rhetoric in Greco-Roman Education*, New York: Columbia University Press.

Clarke, M. L. (1971) *Higher Education in the Ancient World*, London: Routledge & Kegan Paul.

Clement of Alexandria, trans. G. W. Butterworth, LCL, Cambridge: Harvard University Press; London: William Heinemann (1919).

Cohen, S. J. D. (1987) *From Maccabees to the Mishnah*, The Library of Early Christianity, vol. 7, ed. W. A. Meeks, Philadelphia: Westminster Press.

Coleman, R. (1974) "The Artful Moralist: A Study of Seneca's Epistolary Style," *CQ* n.s. 24, pp. 276–89.

Collins, J. J. (1983) *Between Athens and Jerusalem: Jewish Identity in the Diaspora*, New York: Crossroad.

Colson, F. H. (1919) "Phaedrus and Quintilian, 1.9.2," *Classical Review* 33, pp. 59–61.

  (1921) "Quintilian I.9 and the 'Chria' in Ancient Education," *Classical Review* 35, pp. 150–54.

Colson, F. H. and G. H. Whitaker (eds.) *The Complete Works of Philo*, 10 vols. and 2 suppl. vols., LCL, Cambridge: Harvard University Press; London: William Heinemann (1981).

Conley, T. M. (1979) "Ancient Rhetoric and Modern Genre Criticism," *Communication Quarterly*, Fall, pp. 47–53.

  (1984) "The Enthymeme in Perspective," *Quarterly Journal of Speech* 70, pp. 168–87.

  (1987) *Philo's Rhetoric: Studies in Style, Composition and Exegesis*, Center for Hermeneutical Studies in Hellenistic and Modern Culture, Monograph 1, Berkeley, CA: Center for Hermeneutical Studies.

Conzelmann, H. and A. Lindemann (1988) *Interpreting the New Testament: An Introduction to the Principles and Methods of N.T. Exegesis*, trans. S. Schatzmann (from the 8th rev. German edn.), Peabody, MA: Hendrickson.

Corbett, E. P. J. (1969) *Rhetorical Analysis of Literary Works*, New York: Oxford University Press.

(1971) *Classical Rhetoric for the Modern Student*, New York: Oxford University Press.

Countryman, L. W. (1980) *The Rich Christian in the Church of the Early Roman Empire: Contradictions and Accommodations*, Texts and Studies in Religion, New York and Toronto: Edwin Mellen.

Cranfield, C. E. B. (1965) "The Message of James," *Scottish Journal of Theology* 18, pp. 182–93.

Crossan, J. D. (1983) *In Fragments: The Aphorisms of Jesus*, San Francisco: Harper & Row.

(1986) *Sayings Parallels: A Workbook for the Jesus Tradition*, Foundations and Facets, Philadelphia: Fortress Press.

Dahl, N. (1976) "Letter," in *IDBSup*, ed. K. Crim, Nashville: Abingdon Press, pp. 538–40.

Dana, G. N. T. and J. R. Mantey (1927) *A Manual Grammar of the Greek New Testament*, Toronto: Macmillan.

Danby, H. (1933) *The Mishnah. Translated from the Hebrew with Introduction and Brief Explanatory Notes*, Oxford: Oxford University Press.

Davids, P. H. (1978) "Tradition and Citation in the Epistle of James," in *Scripture, Tradition and Interpretation. Essays Presented to Everett F. Harrison by His Students and Colleagues in Honor of His Seventy-fifth Birthday*, ed. W. Gasque and W. LaSor, Grand Rapids: William B. Eerdmans, pp. 113–26.

(1982) *The Epistle of James. A Commentary on the Greek Text*, NIGTC, Grand Rapids: William. B. Eerdmans.

(1985) "James and Jesus," in *Gospel Perspectives: The Jesus Tradition Outside the Gospels, Vol. 5*, ed. D. Wenham, Sheffield: JSOT Press, pp. 63–84.

(1988) "The Epistle of James in Modern Discussion," in *ANRW* II, 25,5, Berlin and New York: De Gruyter, pp. 3622–45.

Davies, S. L. (1983) *The Gospel of Thomas and Christian Wisdom*, New York: Seabury Press.

Davies, W. D. (1948) *Paul and Rabbinic Judaism*, 4th edn., Philadelphia: Fortress Press.

(1964) *The Setting of the Sermon on the Mount*, Cambridge: Cambridge University Press.

(1984) *Jewish and Pauline Studies*, Philadelphia: Fortress Press.

Davies, W. D. and D. C. Allison, Jr. (1988) *A Critical and Exegetical Commentary on The Gospel According to Saint Matthew*, ICC, Edinburgh: T. & T. Clark.

Davis, D. B. (1975) *The Problem of Slavery in the Age of Revolution 1770–1823*, Ithaca and London: Cornell University Press.

Deissmann, A. (1901) *Bible Studies*, trans. A. Grieve, Edinburgh: T. & T. Clark.

(1927) *Light From the Ancient East*, trans. L. Strachan, London: Hodder & Stoughton.

Delling, G. (1972) "τέλος, κτλ.," *TDNT* VIII, pp. 49–87.

Delobel, J. (ed.) (1982) *Logia. Les Paroles de Jésus – The Sayings of Jesus* (Memorial to Joseph Coppens), Leuven: University Press/Peeters.

Demetrius *De elocutione (On Style)*, ed. and trans. W. R. Roberts, LCL, rev. edn., Cambridge: Harvard University Press; London: William Heinemann (1953).

Denniston, J. D. (1952) *Greek Prose Style*, Oxford: Clarendon Press; repr. Westport, CT: Greenwood Press (1979).

Deppe, D. B. (1989) *The Sayings of Jesus in the Epistle of James*, Chelsea, MI: Bookcrafters.

Derrida, J. (1979) "Living On: Border Lines," trans. J. Holbert, in H. Bloom, *et al.*, *Deconstruction and Criticism*, New York: Seabury Press.

de Wette, W. M. L. (1826) *Lehrbuch der historisch-kritischen Einleitung in die kanonischen Bücher des Neuen Testaments*, Berlin: Reimer.

(1847) *Kurze Erklärung der Briefe des Petrus, Judas und Jakobus*, Leipzig: Weidmann.

Dibelius, M. (1935) *From Tradition to Gospel*, trans. B. L. Wolf from the rev. 2nd edn. of *Die Formsgeschichte des Evangeliums*, The Library of Theological Translations, ed. W. Barclay, Cambridge: James Clarke & Co. (1971).

(1936) *A Fresh Approach to the New Testament and Early Christian Literature*, London: Ivor Nicholson and Watson; repr. Westport, CT: Greenwood Press, Inc. (1979).

(1975) *James: A Commentary on the Epistle of James*, 11th edn., rev. H. Greeven, trans. M. A. Williams, ed. H. Koester, Hermeneia, Philadelphia: Fortress Press.

Dibelius, M. and H. Greeven, (1984) *Der Brief des Jakobus*, Exegetischer Kommentar über das Neue Testament begründet von Heinrich August Wilhelm Meyer, Fünfzehnte Abteilung, 12 Auflage, Göttingen: Vandenhoeck & Ruprecht.

Dihle, A. (1962) *Die goldene Regel: Eine Einfuehrung in die Geschichte der antiken und fruehchristlichen Vulgaerethik*, Göttingen: Vandenhoeck & Ruprecht.

(1973) "Posidonius' System of Moral Philosophy," *JHS* 93, pp. 50–57.

Dijk, T. A. Van (1977) *Text and Context. Explorations in the Semantics and Pragmatics of Discourse*, New York: Longman; reprint (1980).

Dill, S. (1905) *Roman Society from Nero to Marcus Aurelius*, New York: Macmillan.

Dillon, J. (1977) *The Middle Platonists: 80 B.C. to A.D. 220*, Ithaca, NY: Cornell University Press.

Dio Chrysostom *Discourses*, vols. 1–5, trans. J. W. Cohoon and H. L. Crosby, LCL, Cambridge: Harvard University Press; London: William Heinemann (1932, 1939, 1940, 1946, 1951).

Diogenes Laertius *Lives of Eminent Philosophers*, 2 vols., trans. R. D. Hicks, LCL, Cambridge: Harvard University Press; London: William Heinemann (1972).

Dobschütz, E. von (1902) *Die urchristlichen Gemeinden: Sittengeschichtliche Bilder*, Leipzig: J. C. Heinrichs.

Donelson, L. R. (1986) *Pseudepigraphy and Ethical Argument in the Pastoral Epistles*, *HUT* 22, Tübingen: J. C. B. Mohr (P. Siebeck).

Donfried, K. P. (1974) *The Setting of Second Clement in Early Christianity*, *NovTSup* 38, Leiden: E. J. Brill.

(1991) *The Romans Debate: Revised and Expanded Edition*, Peabody, MA: Hendrickson Publishers.

Doty, W. G. (1969) "The Classification of Epistolary Literature," *CBQ* 31, pp. 183–99.

(1973) *Letters in Primitive Christianity*, Philadelphia: Fortress Press.

Draisma, S. (ed.) (1989) *Intertextuality in Biblical Writings: Essays in honour of Bas van Iersel*, Kampen: J. H. Kok.

Dungan, D. L. (1971) *The Sayings of Jesus in the Churches of Paul. The Use of the Synoptic Tradition in the Regulation of Early Church Life*, Oxford: Basil Blackwell; Philadelphia: Fortress Press.

Dupont, J. (1958) *Les Béatitudes: Le problème littéraire. Les deux versions du Sermon sur la Montagne et des Béatitudes*, vol. I, 2nd edn., Louvain: E. Nauwelaerts.

(1961) "Les Pauvres en esprit," in *À la rencontre de Dieu* (For A. Gelin), Paris: Le Puy, pp. 265–72.

(1969) *Les Béatitudes: La Bonne Nouvelle*, vol. II, Paris: J. Gabalda.

(1973) *Les Béatitudes: Les Évangélistes*, vol. III, Paris: J. Gabalda.

Eagelton, T. (1983) *Literary Theory: An Introduction*, Minneapolis: University of Minnesota Press.

Easton, B. S. (1932) "New Testament Ethical Lists," *JBL* 51, pp. 1–12.

(1957) "The Epistle of James," in *IB*, New York: Abingdon Press, vol. XII, pp. 3–74.

Edelstein, L. and I. F. Kidd (eds.) (1972) *Posidonius: The Fragments*, Cambridge: Cambridge University Press.

Eichholz, G. (1953) *Jakobus und Paulus*, ThExh n.s. 39, Munich: Kaiser.

(1961) *Glaube und Werke bei Paulus und Jakobus*, ThExh n.s. 88, Munich: Kaiser.

Eisenstadt, S. N. and L. Roniger (1984) *Patrons, Clients, and Friends*, Cambridge: Cambridge University Press.

Eissfeldt, O. (1965) *The Old Testament: An Introduction*, trans. P. Ackroyd, New York and Evanston: Harper & Row.

Eleder, F. (1966) "Jakobusbrief und Bergpredigt," Ph.D. diss., Vienna.

Elliger, K. and W. Rudolph (eds.) *Biblica hebraica stuttgartensia*, Stuttgart: Deutsche Bibelstiftung (1977).

Elliott, J. H. (1981) *Home for the Homeless: A Sociological Exegesis of 1 Peter, Its Situation and Strategy*, Philadelphia: Fortress Press.

(ed.) (1986) *Social-Scientific Criticism of the New Testament*, Semeia 35, pp. 1–194.

Elliott-Binns, L. E. (1953) "James 1:18: Creation or Redemption?," *NTS* 3, pp. 148–61.

(1956) *Galilean Christianity*, Chicago: Alec R. Allenson, Inc.

Emmerton, J. A. (1962) "τὸ αἷμά μου τῆς διαθήκς; The Evidence of the Syriac Versions," *JTS* 13, pp. 111–17.

Epictetus *Discourses*, trans. W. A. Oldfather, 2 vols., LCL, Cambridge: Harvard University Press; London: William Heinemann (1925, 1928).

Epp, E. J. and G. W. MacRae, S.J. (eds.) (1989) *The New Testament and*

Its Modern Interpreters, Philadelphia: Fortress Press; Atlanta: Scholars Press.

Erasmus, Desiderius (1516) *Opera omnia*, vol. VI, Leiden: Vander (1705); repr. London: Gregg (1962).

Ericson, J. M. (1983) "Rhetorical Criticism: How to Evaluate a Speech," in *Demosthenes' ON THE CROWN. A Critical Case Study of a Masterpiece of Ancient Oratory*, ed. J. Murphy, newly trans. J. Keaney, Davis, CA: Hermagoras Press, pp. 127–36.

Exegetical Dictionary of the New Testament. (1990) ed. H. Balz and G. Schneider, trans. V. P. Howard and J. W. Thompson, Grand Rapids: William B. Eerdmans.

Exler, F. X. J. (1923) *The Form of the Ancient Greek Letter*, Washington, DC: Catholic University of America.

Farmer, W. R. (1986) "The Sermon on the Mount: A Form-Critical and Redactional Analysis of Matt 5:1–7:29," in SBLSP, Atlanta: Scholars Press, pp. 56–87.

Feine, P. (1893) *Der Jakobusbrief*, Eisenach: M. Wilkens.

Felder, C. H. (1982) "Wisdom, Law, and Social Conflict in the Epistle of James," Ph.D. diss., Columbia University; Ann Arbor, MI: University Microfilms.

Felten, J. (ed.) (1913) *Nicolai Progymnasmata*, Rhetores Graeci XI, Leipzig: Teubner.

Fenton, J. C. (1955) "Pseudonymity in the New Testament," *Theology* 58, pp. 51–56.

Ferguson, J. (1958) *Moral Values in the Ancient World*, London: Methuen.
   (1970) *The Religions of the Roman Empire*, New York: Cornell University Press.

Festugière, A.-J. (1955) *Epicurus and His Gods*, Oxford: Basil Blackwell.

Finley, M. I. (1973) *The Ancient Economy*, Sather Classical Lectures 43, Berkeley: University of California Press.

Fiore, B. (1986) *The Function of Personal Example in the Socratic and Pastoral Epistles*, AnBib 105, Rome: Biblical Institute Press.

Fitzmyer, J. A. (1971) "The Oxyrhynchus Logoi of Jesus and the Coptic Gospel according to Thomas," in *Essays on the Semitic Background of the New Testament*, London: Chapman, and SBLSBS 5, Missoula, MT: Scholars Press (1974).
   (1981; 1985) *The Gospel According to Luke*, 2 vols. AB 28–28a, New York: Doubleday & Company.

Foakes-Jackson, F. J. and K. Lake (eds.) (1920) *The Beginnings of Christianity Part I The Acts of the Apostles*, Vol. I Prolegomena I: The Jewish, Gentile and Christian Backgrounds, London: Macmillan & Co.

Foerster, W. (1971) "εὐσεβής, κτλ.," *TDNT* VII, pp. 175–85.

Foerster, W. and J. Hermann (1965) "κλῆρος, κτλ.," *TDNT* III, pp. 758–85.

Fontaine, C. R. (1982) *Traditional Sayings in the Old Testament*, Sheffield: Almond Press.

Forbes, P. B. R. (1972) "The Structure of the Epistle of James," *EvQ* 44, pp. 147–53.

Forester, R. (ed.) (1927) *Labanii Opera*, vol. IX, Leipzig: B. G. Teubner.

Foster, G. (1965) "Peasant Society and the Image of Limited Good," *American Anthropologist* 67, pp. 293–315.

Foucault, M. (1966) *Les mots et les choses*, Paris: Gallimard.

Francis, F. O. (1970) "The Form and Function of the Opening and Closing Paragraphs of James and 1 John," *ZNW* 61, pp. 110–26.

Friederiksen, M. W. (1975) "Theory, Evidence, and the Ancient Economy," *Journal of Roman Studies* 65, pp. 164–71.

Frischer, B. (1982) *The Sculpted Word: Epicureanism and Philosophical Recruitment in Ancient Greece*, Berkeley: University of California Press.

Fry, E. (1978) "The Testing of Faith. A Study of the Structure of the Book of James," *BT* 29, pp. 427–35.

Fuller, R. and I. Fuller (eds.) (1978) *Essays on the Love Command*, Philadelphia: Fortress Press.

Funk, R. W. (1973) *A Beginning-Intermediate Grammar of Hellenistic Greek*, 3 vols., 2nd corrected edn., SBLSBS 2, Missoula, MT: Scholars Press.

(1986) "The Beatitudes and Turn the Other Cheek," *Forum* 2.3 pp. 103–28.

Furnish, V. P. (1964–65) "The Jesus–Paul Debate: From Baur to Bultmann," *BJRL* 47, pp. 342–81.

(1968) *Theology and Ethics in Paul*, Nashville: Abingdon Press.

(1972) *The Love Command in the New Testament*, Nashville: Abingdon Press:.

Gager, J. G. (1975) *Kingdom and Community: The Social World of Early Christianity*, Englewood Cliffs: Prentice-Hall.

Gaiser, K. (1959) *Protreptic und Paraenese bei Platon. Untersuchungen zur Form des Platonischen Dialogs*, TBA 40, Stuttgart: W. Kohlhammer Verlag.

Garnsey, P. and R. P. Saller (1987) *The Roman Empire: Economy, Society, and Culture*, London: Gerald Duckworth & Company.

Geertz, C. (1973) *The Interpretation of Cultures. Selected Essays*, Harper Torchbooks, New York: Basic Books.

Geffcken, J. (1909) *Kynika und Verwandtes*, Heidelberg: Carl Winters Universitätsbuchhandlung.

Gehardsson, B. (1961) *Memory and Manuscript: Oral Tradition and Written Transmission in Rabbinic Judaism and Early Christianity*, ASNU 22, Uppsala: Almqvist & Wiksell.

Gerstenberger, E. S. (1988) *Psalms, Part 1; with an Introduction to Cultic Poetry*, FOTL 14, ed. R. Knierim and G. M. Tucker, Grand Rapids: William B. Eerdmans.

Gertner, M. (1962)) "Midrashim in the New Testament," *JSS* 7, pp. 267–92.

Gesenius, W. and E. Kautzsch *Gesenius' Hebrew Grammar*, trans. A. E. Cowley, 2nd edn., Oxford: Clarendon Press (1910); repr. (1980).

Geyser, A. S. (1975) "The Letter of James and the Social Condition of his Addressees," *Neot* 9, pp. 25–33.

Gilmore, D. (1982) "Anthropology of the Mediterranean Area," *Annual Review of Anthropology* 11, pp. 175–205.

Gladigow, B. (1967) "Der Markarismus des Weisen," *Hermas* 95, pp. 404–33.

Goldstein, J. A. (1968) *The Letters of Demosthenes*, New York and London: Columbia University Press.

(1976) *I Maccabees*, AB 41, New York: Doubleday & Company.

(1983) *II Maccabees*, AB 41a, New York: Doubleday & Company.

Goodenough, E. R. (1928) "The Political Philosophy of Hellenistic Kingship," *Yale Classical Studies* 1, pp. 55–102.

Goodspeed, E. J. (1937a) *An Introduction to the New Testament*, Chicago: University of Chicago Press.

(1937b) "Pseudonymity and Pseudepigraphy in Early Christian Literature," in *New Chapters in New Testament Study*, New York: Macmillan Co., pp. 169–88.

Goodwin, W. W. (1894) *A Greek Grammar*, new edn., London: Macmillan and Co.; repr. n.p., St Martin's Press (1981).

Goppelt, L. (1972) "τύπος, κτλ.," *TDNT* VIII, pp. 246–59.

Gowan, D. E. (1987) "Wealth and Poverty in the Old Testament: The Case of the Widow, the Orphan, and the Sojourner," *Int* 41,4, pp. 341–53.

Grafe, E. (1904) *Die Stellung und Bedeutung des Jakobusbriefes in der Entwicklung des Urchristentums*, Tübingen and Leipzig: J. C. B. Mohr (P. Siebeck).

Grant R. M. (1963) *A Historical Introduction to the New Testament*, San Francisco: Harper & Row; repr. New York: Simon and Schuster, A Touchstone Book.

(1965) *The Formation of the New Testament*, New York: Harper & Row.

(1977) *Early Christianity and Society*, San Francisco: Harper & Row.

(1978) "The Sermon on the Mount in Early Christianity," *Semeia* 12, pp. 215–31.

Grube, G. M. A. (1965) *The Greek and Roman Critics*, Toronto: The University of Toronto Press.

Grundmann, W. (1972) "ταπεινός, κτλ.," *TDNT* VIII, pp. 1–26.

Guelich, R. A. (1976) "The Matthean Beatitudes: 'Entrance-Requirements' or Eschatological Blessings?," *JBL* 95, pp. 415–34.

(1982) *The Sermon on the Mount. A Foundation for Understanding*, Waco, TX: Word Books Publisher.

Gutbrod, W. (1967) "νόμος, κτλ.," *TDNT* IV, pp. 1036–91.

Hack, R. K. (1916) "The Doctrine of Literary Forms," *HSCP* 27, pp. 1–65.

Hackforth, R. and B. R. Rees (1970) "Letters, Greek," in *OCD*, pp. 598–99.

Hadidian, D. E. (1951–52) "Palestinian Pictures in the Epistle of James," *ExpT* 63, pp. 227–28.

Halliday, M. A. K. (1978) *Language as Social Semiotic. The Social Interpretation of Language and Meaning*, London: Arnold.

Halm, K. (ed.) (1863) *Rhetores Latini Minores*, Leipzig: Teubner; repr. Dubuque, IA: Brown, n.d.

Halson, B. R. (1968) "The Epistle of James: 'Christian Wisdom'?," *SE* 4, pp. 308–14.

Hammond, N. G. L. and H. H. Scullard (eds.) *The Oxford Classical Dictionary*, 2d edn., Oxford: Clarendon Press (1970).

Hands, A. R. (1968) *Charities and Social Aid in Greece and Rome*, London: Thames & Hudson.

Hanse, H. (1964) "ἔχω, κτλ.," *TDNT* II, pp. 816–32.

Hanson, A. (1979) "Seminar Report: Report on the Working Group on 'The Use of the Old Testament in the Epistle of James' held during the Seminar on 'The Use of the Old Testament in the New' at Tübingen in 1977 and Chatenay-Malabry in 1978," *NTS* 25, pp. 526–27.

Harnack, A. von (1897) *Geschichte der altchristlichen Litteratur bis Eusebeius*, I.2., Leipzig: J. C. Hinrichs.

(1908) *The Sayings of Jesus: The Second Source of St. Matthew and St. Luke*, *NTS* 3, trans. J. R. Wilkinson (from the 1907 edn.), London: Williams & Norgate; New York: G. P. Putnam's Sons.

Hartin, P. J. (1991) *James and the Q Sayings of Jesus*, JSNTSup 47, Sheffield: JSOT Press.

Hartlich, P. (1889) "De exhortationum a Graecis Romanisque scriptarum historia et indole," *Leipziger Studien* 11, pp. 207–336.

Hartmann, G. (1942) "Der Aufbau des Jakobusbriefes," *ZKT* 66, pp. 63–70.

Hauck, F. (1957) *Der Briefe des Jakobus, Petrus, Judas und Johannes*, NTD 10, 8th edn., Göttingen: Vandenhoeck & Ruprecht.

(1968) "πένης, κτλ.," *TDNT* VI, pp. 37–40.

Hauck, F. and G. Bertram (1967) "μακάριος, κτλ.," *TDNT* IV, pp. 362–70.

Hauck, F. and W. Kasch (1968) "πλοῦτος, κτλ.," *TDNT* VI, pp. 318–32.

Hays, R. B. (1983) *The Faith of Jesus Christ. An Investigation of the Narrative Substructure of Galatians 3:1–4:11*, SBLDS 56, Chico, CA: Scholars Press.

(1989) *Echoes of Scripture in the Letters of Paul*, New Haven and London: Yale University Press.

Hegermann, H. (1990) "δόξα, ης, ἡ," *EDNT* I, pp. 344–49.

Heilbroner, R. L. (1972) *The Making of the Ancient Economy*, Englewood Cliffs: Prentice-Hall.

Heinrici, C. F. G. (1908) *Der literarische Charakter der neutestamentlichen Schriften*, Leipzig: Duerr.

Hellholm, D. (ed.) (1983) *Apocalypticism in the Mediterranean World and the New East*, Tübingen: J. C. B. Mohr (P. Siebeck).

Hengel, M. (1974a) *Judaism and Hellenism*, trans. J. Bowden, Philadelphia: Fortress Press.

(1974b) *Property and Riches in the Early Church: Aspects of a Social History of Early Christianity*, trans. J. Bowden, Philadelphia: Fortress Press.

Hennecke, E. and W. Schneemelcher (eds.) *New Testament Apocrypha*, trans. R. McL. Wilson (ed.), 2 vols., Philadelphia: Westminster Press (1963–65).

Herder, J. G. (1884) "Briefe zweener Jesus in unserem Kanon," in *Herder's Sämmtliche Werke*, ed. B. Suphan, Berlin: Weidmann, VII, pp. 471–573.

Hermogenes (1913a) *Peri Staseon*, in *Hermogenes Opera*, ed. H. Rabe, Rhetores Graeci VI, Leipzig: Teubner, pp. 28–92.

(1913b) *Progymnasmata*, in *Hermogenes Opera*, ed. H. Rabe, Rhetores Graeci VI, Leipzig: Teubner, pp. 1–27.

Hershbell, J. P. (1978) "De virtute morali (*Moralia* 440D-452D)," in Betz (1978), pp. 135–69.

Hiebert, D. E. (1978) "The Unifying Theme of the Epistle of James," *BSac* 135, pp. 221–31.

Hijmans, B. L., Jr. (1959) *ASKESIS: Notes on Epictetus' Educational System*, Assen: Van Gorcum.

Hirsh, E. D. (1967) *Validity in Interpretation*, New Haven: Yale University Press.

Hock, R. F. and E. N. O'Neil (eds.) (1986) *The Chreia in Ancient Rhetoric. Volume I: The Progymnasmata*, SBLTT 27, Atlanta: Scholars Press.

Hollander, H. W. and M. de Jonge (1985) *The Testaments of the Twelve Patriarchs. A Commentary*, SVTP 8, Leiden: E. J. Brill.

Hollenbach, P. (1987) "Defining Rich and Poor Using Social Sciences," in SBLSP, Atlanta: Scholars Press, pp. 50–63.

Hoppe, R. (1977) *Der theologische Hintergrund des Jakobusbriefes*, FB 28, Würzburg: Echter Verlag.

(1989) *Jakobusbrief*, SKKNT 15, Stuttgart: Katholisches Bibelwerk.

Horna, K. (1935) "Gnome, Gnomendichtung, Gnomologien," PW, vol. VI, Stuttgart: J. B. Metzler.

Horsley, R. A. (1987) *Jesus and the Spiral of Violence. Popular Jewish Resistance in Roman Palestine*, San Francisco: Harper & Row.

Horsley, R. A. and J. S. Hanson (1985) *Bandits, Prophets, and Messiahs. Popular Movements at the Time of Jesus*, New Voices in Biblical Studies, ed. A. Y. Collins and J. J. Collins, Minneapolis, MN: Winston Press.

van der Horst, P. W. (1978) *The Sentences of Pseudo-Phocylides. With Introduction and Commentary*, Leiden: E. J. Brill.

Hort, F. J. A. (1909) *The Epistle of St. James: The Greek Text with Introduction, Commentary as far as chapter IV, verse 7, and Additional Notes*, London: Macmillan.

Howard, G. (1967) "On the 'Faith of Christ'," *HTR* 60, pp. 459–65.

(1974) "The Faith of Christ," *ExpT* 85, pp. 212–15.

Howes, R. F. (ed.) (1961) *Historical Studies of Rhetoric and Rhetoricians*, Ithaca: Cornell University Press, pp. 3–15.

Hudson, H. H. (1923) "The Field of Rhetoric," *Quarterly Journal of Speech Education* 9, pp. 167–80.

Hurley, P. J. (1985) *A Concise Introduction to Logic*, 2nd edn., Belmont, CA: Wadsworth Publishing Company.

Iser, W. (1975) *The Implied Reader: Patterns of Communication from Bunyan to Beckett*, Baltimore and London: The Johns Hopkins University Press.

(1978) *The Act of Reading: A Theory of Aesthetic Response*, Baltimore and London: The Johns Hopkins University Press.

Isocrates. 3 vols., trans. G. Norlin (vols. I–II), L. Van Hook (vol. III), LCL, Cambridge: Harvard University Press; London: William Heinemann (1928, 1929, 1945).

Jackson, J. J. and M. Kessler (eds.) (1974) *Rhetorical Criticism*, Essays in honor of J. Muilenburg, PTMS 1, Pittsburg: Pickwick Press.

Jacobs, I. (1976) "The Midrashic Background for James II:21–3," *NTS* 22, pp. 475–64.

Jacobson, A. D. (1978) "Wisdom Christology in Q," Ph.D. diss., Claremont Graduate School.

Jaeger, W. (1939) *Paideia: The Ideals of Greek Culture*, trans. G. Highet, 3 vols., New York: Oxford University Press.

(1948) *Aristotle: Fundamentals of the History of His Development*, trans. with the author's corrections and additions by R. Robinson, 2nd edn., Oxford: Oxford University Press.

(1961) *Early Christianity and Greek Paideia*, Cambridge, MA and London: The Belknap Press of Harvard University Press.

Jamestrow, M. *A Dictionary of the Targumim, The Talmud Babli and Yerushalmi, and the Midrashic Literature*, London: Luzac (1886–1900); repr. New York: Judaica Press (1985).

Jeremias, J. (1971) *Theology of the New Testament*, trans. J. Bowden, New York: Charles Scribners' Sons.

Jewett, R. (1982) "Romans as an Ambassadorial Letter," *Int* 36, pp. 5–20.

Johanson, B. (1973) "The Definition of Pure Religion in James 1:27," *ExpT* 84, pp. 118–19.

Johnson, L. T. (1979) *The Literary Function of Possessions in Luke-Acts*, SBLDS 39, Missoula, MT: Scholars Press.

(1981) *Sharing Possessions: Mandate and Symbol of Faith*, OBT 9, Philadelphia: Fortress Press.

(1982a) "Rom 3:21–26 and the Faith of Jesus," *CBQ* 44, pp.77–90.

(1982b) "The Use of Leviticus 19 in the Letter of James," *JBL* 101, pp. 391–401.

(1983) "James 3:13–4:10 and the Topos ΠΕΡΙ ΦΘΟΝΟΥ," *NovT* 25, pp. 327–47.

(1985) "Friendship with the World/Friendship with God: A Study of Discipleship in James," in *Discipleship in the New Testament*, ed. F. Segovia, Philadelphia: Fortress Press, pp. 166–83.

(1986) *The Writings of the New Testament: An Interpretation*, Philadelphia: Fortress Press.

(1988) "JAMES," in *Harper's Bible Dictionary*, ed. J. L. Mays, San Francisco: Harper & Row.

(1995) *The Letter of James*, AB 37A, Garden City: Doubleday.

Judge, E. A. (1960) *The Social Pattern of Christian Groups in the First Century*, London: Tyndale.

(1960–61) "The Early Christians as a Scholastic Community," *JRH* 1, pp. 4–15, 125–37.

Kamlah, E. (1964) *Die Form der katalogischen Paraenese im Neuen Testament*, WUNT 7, ed. J. Jeremias and O Michel, Tübingen: J. C. Mohr (P. Siebeck).

Karris, R. A. (1971) "The Function and Sitz-im-Leben of the Paraenetic Elements in the Pastoral Epistles," Ph.D. diss., Harvard University.

Kawerau, G. (1889) "Die Schicksale des Jakobusbriefes in 16. Jahrhundert," *ZKWKL* 10, pp. 539–70.

Kea, P. (1986) "The Sermon on the Mount: Ethics and Eschatological Time," in SBLSP, Atlanta: Scholars Press, pp. 88–98.

Keck, L. E. (1965) "The Poor Among the Saints of the New Testament," *ZNW* 56, pp. 100–29.

(1966) "The Poor among the Saints in Jewish Christianity and Qumran," *ZWL* 57, pp. 54–78.

(1974) "On the Ethos of Early Christianity," *JAAR* 42, pp. 435–52.

(1984) "Ethics in the Gospel According to Matthew," *Iliffe Review* 41, pp. 39–56.

Kelber, W. H. (1983) *The Oral and the Written Gospel*, Philadelphia: Fortress Press.

Kelly, F. X. (1973) "Poor and Rich in the Epistle of James," Ph.D. diss., Temple University; Ann Arbor, MI: University Microfilms.

Kennedy, G. A. (1963) *The Art of Persuasion in Greece*, Princeton: Princeton University Press.

(1972) *The Art of Rhetoric in the Roman World*, Princeton: Princeton University Press.

(1980) *Classical Rhetoric and Its Christian and Secular Tradition from Ancient to Modern Times*, Chapel Hill and London: The University of North Carolina Press.

(1983) *Greek Rhetoric Under Christian Emperors*, Princeton: Princeton University Press.

(1984) *New Testament Interpretation Through Rhetorical Criticism*, Chapel Hill and London: The University of North Carolina Press.

(1991) *Aristotle "On Rhetoric": A Theory of Civic Discourse*, New York and Oxford: Oxford University Press.

Kennedy, H. A. A. (1911) "The Hellenistic Atmosphere of the Epistle of James," *Exp* 8,2, pp. 37–52.

Kern, H. (1835) "Der Character und Ursprung des Briefes Jakobi," *Tübinger Zeitschrift für Theologie* 8, pp. 1–73.

(1838) *Der Brief des Jakobus untersucht und erklärt*, Tübingen.

Kilpatrick, G. D. (1967) "Übertreter des Gesetzes," *TZ* 23, p. 433.

Kim, C.-H. (1972) *The Familiar Letter of Recommendation*, Missoula, MT: Scholars Press.

King, K. (1987) "Kingdom in the Gospel of Thomas," *Forum* 3,1, pp. 48–97.

Kinneavy, J. L. (1987) *Greek Rhetorical Origins of Christian Faith: An Inquiry*, New York and Oxford: Oxford University Press.

Kirk, J. A. (1969) "The Meaning of Wisdom in James: Examination of a Hypothesis," *NTS* 16, pp. 24–38.

Kittel, G. (1942) "Der geschichtliche Ort des Jakobusbriefes," *ZNW* 41, pp. 71–105.

(1950/1) "Der Jakobusbrief und die apostolischen Väter," *ZNW* 43, pp. 54–112.

Kittel G. and G. von Rad (1964) "δοκέω, δόξα, κτλ.," *TDNT* ii, pp. 232–55.

Kittel, G. and K. Friedrich (eds.) (1964–76) *Theological Dictionary of the New Testament*, trans. G. W. Bromiley, 10 vols, Grand Rapids: William B. Eerdmans.

Kline, L. L. (1975) *The Sayings of Jesus in the Pseudo-Clementine Homilies*, SBLDS 14, Missoula, MT: Scholars Press.

Kloppenborg, J. S. (1978) "Wisdom Christology in Q," *LTP* 34, pp. 129–47.

(1984) "Tradition and Redaction in the Synoptic Sayings Source," *CBQ* 46, pp. 34–62.

(1986a) "Blessing and Marginality. The Persecution Beatitude in Q, Thomas, & Early Christianity," *Forum* 2,3, pp. 36–56.

(1986b) "The Function of Apocalyptic Language in Q," in SBLSP, Atlanta: Scholars Press, pp. 224–35.

(1987) *The Formation of Q: Trajectories in Ancient Wisdom Collection,* Studies in Antiquity and Christianity, Philadelphia: Fortress Press.

(1988) *Q Parallels: Synopsis, Critical Notes, and Concordance,* Sonoma, CA: Polebridge Press.

(1990) "Nomos and Ethos in Q," in *Gospel Origins and Christian Beginnings,* ed. J. Goehring, *et al.,* Sonoma, CA: Polebridge Press.

Kloppenborg, J. S., M. W. Meyer, S. J. Patterson, and M. G. Steinhauser (1990) *Q-Thomas Reader,* Sonoma, CA: Polebridge Press.

Knowling, R. J. (1904) *The Epistle of James,* London: Methuen & Company.

Knox, W. L. (1945) "The Epistle of James," *JTS* 46, pp. 10–17.

Koester, H. (1957a) "Die ausserkanonischen Herrenworte als Produkte der christlichen Gemeinde," *ZNW* 48, pp. 220–37.

(1957b) *Synoptische überlieferung bei den apostolischen Vätern,* TU 65, Berlin: Akademie.

(1979) "I Thessalonians – Experiment in Christian Writing," in *Continuity and Discontinuity in Church History. Essays Presented to George Huntston Williams on His 65th Birthday,* ed. F. Church and T. George, Leiden: E. J. Brill, pp. 33–44.

(1982) *Introduction to the New Testament.* Vol. I: *History, Culture, and Religion of the Hellenistic Age,* and vol. II: *History and Literature of Early Christianity.* Hermeneia, Foundations and Facets, Philadelphia: Fortress Press.

(1990) *Ancient Christian Gospels: Their History and Development,* London: SCM; Philadelphia: Trinity Press International.

Koskenniemi, H. (1956) *Studien zur Idee und Phraseologie des griechischen Briefes bis 400 n. Chr.,* *AASF* ser. B, 102,2, Helsinki: Finnischen Akademie der Wissenschaften.

Kozy, J., Jr. (1970) "Review of Ch. Perelman and L. Olbrechts-Tyteca, *The New Rhetoric: A Treatise on Argumentation,* The University of Notre Dame Press, 1969," *Philosophy and Rhetoric* 3,4, pp. 249–54.

Kristeva, J. (1960) Σημειοτική, *Recherches pour une sémanalyse,* Paris: Seuil.

Kroll, W. (1924) *Studien zum Verständnis der römischen Literatur,* Stuttgart: J. B. Metzler.

Küchler, C. G. (1818) *Commentatio de rhetorica epistolae Jacobi indole,* Leipzig.

Kümmel, W. (1965) "Martin Dibelius als Theologe," in *Heilsgeschehen und Geschichte,* *MaTS* 3, Marburg: Lahn, pp. 192–206.

(1972) *The New Testament: The History of the Investigation of its Problems,* trans. S. M. Gilmour and H. C. Kee, Nashville: Abingdon.

(1975) *Introduction to the New Testament*, trans. H. C. Kee, rev. edn., Nashville: Abingdon.

Kürzdörfer, K. (1966) "Der Character des Jakobusbriefes. Eine Auseindersetzung mit den Thesen von A. Meyer und M. Dibelius," Diss., Tübingen.

Kuhn, K. G. (1952) "πειρασμός – ἁμαρτία – σάρξ im NT und die damit zusammenhängenden Vorstellungen," *ZThK* 49, pp. 200–22.

(ed.) *Konkordanz zu den Qumrantexten*, Göttingen: Vandenhoeck & Ruprecht (1960).

Lachmann, M. (1949) *Sola fide. Eine exegetische Studie über Jak. 2*, BFCT 2,50, Gütersloh: C. Bertelsmann.

Lachs, S. T. (1987) *A Rabbinic Commentary on the New Testament*, New York: KTAV Publishing House.

Lake, K. *The Apostolic Fathers*, LCL, 2 vols., Cambridge: Harvard University Press; London: William Heinemann (1912).

Lampe, G. W. H. (ed.) *A Patristic Greek Lexicon*, Oxford: Clarendon Press (1961).

Lausberg, H. (1967) *Elemente der Literarischen Rhetorik*, 3rd rev. edn., Munich: Max Hueber Verlag.

(1973) *Handbuch der literarischen Rhetorik*, 2 vols., Munich: Max Hueber Verlag.

Laws, S. (Marshall) (1969) "Δίψυχος: a local term?," *SE* 6, pp. 348–51.

(1973) "The Doctrinal Basis for the Ethics of James," *SE* 7, pp. 293–305.

(1974) "Does Scripture Speak in Vain?: A Reconsideration of James 4:5," *NTS* 20, pp. 210–15.

(1980) *The Epistle of James*, HNTC, San Francisco: Harper & Row.

Layton, B. (1987) *The Gnostic Scriptures*, New York: Doubleday & Company.

(ed.) (1989) *Nag Hammadi Codex II,2–7. Together with XIII,2, Brit. Lib. Or. 4926(1), and P. Oxy. 1, 654, 655*, NHS 20, vol. I, Leiden and New York: E. J. Brill.

Lebram, J. C. H. (1983) "The Piety of Jewish Apocalyptists," in Hellholm (1983), pp. 171–210.

Levens, R. G. C. (1970) "Letters, Latin," in *OCD*, p. 599.

Liddell, H. G. and R. Scott *A Greek–English Lexicon: A New Edition Revised and Augmented throughout*, ed. H. S. Jones, 9th edn., Oxford: Clarendon Press (1940; repr. 1985).

Lohse, E. (1957) "Glaube und Werke," *ZNW* 48, pp. 1–22.

(1968) "πρόσωπον, κτλ.," *TDNT* VI, pp. 768–80.

Longinus "On the Sublime," trans. W. H. Fyfe, LCL, Cambridge: Harvard University Press; London: William Heinemann (1932).

Louw, J. and E. A. Nida (eds.) *Greek–English Lexicon of the New Testament Based on Semantic Domains*, 2 vols., New York: United Bible Societies (1988).

Luck, U. (1967) "Weisheit und Leiden. Zum Problem Paulus und Jakobus," *TLZ* 92, cols. 253–58.2.

(1968) *Die Vollkommenheitsforderung der Bergpredigt*, ThExh 150, Munich: Chr. Kaiser Verlag.

(1971) "Der Jakobusbrief und die Theologie des Paulus," *Theologie und Glaube* 61, pp. 161–79.

(1984) "Der Theologie des Jakobusbriefes," *ZTK* 81, pp. 1–30.

Lüdemann, G. (1989) *Opposition to Paul in Jewish Christianity*, trans. M. E. Boring, Minneapolis: Fortress Press.

Lührmann, D. (1969) *Die Redaktion der Logienquelle*, WMANT 33, Neukirchen und Vluyn: Neukirchener Verlag.

Lührmann, D. and G. Strecker (eds.) (1980) *Kirche. Festschrift für Gunther Bornkamm*, Tübingen: J. C. B. Mohr (P. Siebeck), 1980.

Luther, M. *Luther's Works*, American edn., ed. J. Pelikan and H. Lehmann, 55 vols., St. Louis, MO: Concordia; Philadelphia: Fortress Press, 1955– .

Lutz, C. (1947) "Musonius Rufus: 'The Roman Socrates,' " *Yale Classical Studies* 10, pp. 3–147.

Luz, U. (1983) "Sermon on the Mount/Plain: Reconstruction of QMt and QLk," in SBLSP, Chico, CA: Scholars Press, pp. 473–79.

(1989) *Matthew 1–7*, trans. W. Linss, Minneapolis: Augsburg.

McCall, M. H., Jr. (1969) *Ancient Rhetorical Theories of Simile and Comparison*, Cambridge: Harvard University Press.

MacDonald, D. R. (1987) *There is No Male and Female: The Fate of a Dominical Saying in Paul and Gnosticism*, Philadelphia: Fortress Press.

McGuire, M. (1982) "The Structural Study of Speech," in *Explorations in Rhetoric* (D. Ehninger Festschrift), ed. R. Mckerrow, Glenview, IL: Scott, Foresman & Co., pp. 1–22.

Mack, B. L. (1984) "Decoding the Scriptures: Philo and the Rules of Rhetoric," in *Nourished with Peace: Studies in Hellenistic Judaism in Memory of Samuel Sandmel*, ed. F. E. Greenspahn *et al.*, Denver: University of Denver (Colorado Seminary), pp. 81–115.

(1988) *A Myth of Innocence. Mark and Christian Origins*, Philadelphia: Fortress Press.

(1990) *Rhetoric in the New Testament*, Guides to Biblical Scholarship/NT Series, Minneapolis: Fortress Press.

Mack, B. L. and V. K. Robbins (1989) *Patterns of Persuasion in the Gospels*, Sonoma, CA: Polebridge Press.

MacMullen, R. (1974) *Roman Social Relations, 50 B.C. to A.D. 284*, New Haven: Yale University Press.

(1981) *Paganism in the Roman Empire*, New Haven and London: Yale University Press.

(1984) *Christianizing the Roman Empire*, New Haven and London: Yale University Press.

McKane, W. (1970) *Proverbs*, The Old Testament Library, London: SCM.

Maier, G. (1980) *Reich und arm. Der Beitrag des Jakobusbriefes*, Giessen: Basel.

Malherbe, A. J. (1970) " 'Gentle as a Nurse': The Cynic Backgound to I Thess ii," *NovT* 12 pp. 203–17.

(1972) "I Thessalonians as a Paraenetic Letter," unpublished SBLSP; references to a (Yale Divinity School Library) typescript graciously provided by Professor Malherbe.

(1977) *Social Aspects of Early Christianity*, Baton Rouge: Louisiana State University Press.

(1983) "Exhortation in First Thessalonians," *NovT* 25, pp. 238–56.

(1986) *Moral Exhortation: A Greco-Roman Sourcebook*, The Library of Early Christianity, vol. 4, ed. W. A. Meeks, Philadelphia: Westminster Press.

(1987) *Paul and the Thessalonians*, Philadelphia: Fortress Press.

(1988) *Ancient Epistolary Theorists*, SBLSBS 19, Atlanta: Scholars Press.

(1989a) "Greco-Roman Religion and Philosophy and the New Testament," in Epp and MacRae (1989), pp. 3–26.

(1989b) *Paul and the Popular Philosophers*, Minneapolis: Fortress Press.

(1992) "Hellenistic Moralists and the New Testament," *ANRW* II, 26,1, Berlin and New York: De Gruyter, pp. 267–333.

Malina, B. (1978) "The Social World Implied in the Letters of the Christian Bishop-Martyr (Named Ignatius of Antioch)," in SBLSP, 2, Missoula, MT: Scholars Press, pp. 71–119.

(1981) *The New Testament World: Insights from Cultural Anthropology*, Atlanta: John Knox.

(1986a) *Christian Origins and Cultural Anthropology: Practical Models for Biblical Interpretation*, Atlanta: John Knox.

(1986b) "Interpreting the Bible with Anthropology: The Case of the Poor and the Rich," *Listening* 21,2, pp. 148–59.

(1987) "Wealth and Poverty in the New Testament and Its World," *Int* 41,4, pp. 354–67.

Manson, T. W. (1937) *The Sayings of Jesus*, London: SCM; repr. (1949).

Marcus, J. (1982) "The Evil Inclination in the Epistle of James," *CBQ* 44, pp. 606–21.

Marrou, H. I. (1956) *A History of Education in Antiquity*, trans. G. Lamb, London and New York: Sheed and Ward, Inc.

Marshall, I. H. (1978) *Commentary on Luke*, Grand Rapids: William B. Eerdmans.

Martin, D. B. (1990) *Slavery as Salvation: The Metaphor of Slavery in Pauline Christianity*, New Haven: Yale University Press.

Martin, J. (1974) *Antike Rhetorik. Technik und Methode*, Handbuch der Altertumswissenschaft 2,3, Munich: C. H. Beck.

Martin, R. P. (1978) "The Life-Setting of the Epistle of James in the Light of Jewish History," in *Biblical and Near Eastern Studies* (For W. S. LaSor), ed. G. Tuttle, Grand Rapids: William B. Eerdmans, pp. 97–103.

Marty, J. (1935) *L'Épître de Jacques*, Paris: F. Alcan.

Marxsen, W. (1968) *Introduction to the New Testament*, trans. G. Buswell, Philadelphia: Fortress Press.

Massebieau, L. (1895) "L'épître de Jacques est-elle l'oeuvre d'un chrétien," *RHR* 32, pp. 249–85.

Maurer, C. (1974) "φυλή," *TDNT* IX, pp. 245–50.

Maynard-Reid, P. U. (1987) *Poverty and Wealth in James*, Maryknoll, NY: Orbis Books.

Mayor J. B. (1892) *The Epistle of James*, London: Macmillan & Company; repr. of 3rd edn., Grand Rapids: Kregel Publications (1990).

Meeks, W. A. (1983) *The First Urban Christians: The Social World of the Apostle Paul*, New Haven: Yale University Press.

(1986) *The Moral World of the First Christians*, The Library of Early Christianity, vol. 6, Philadelphia: Westminster Press.

Metzger, B. M. (1971) *A Textual Commentary on the Greek New Testament*, London and New York: United Bible Societies.

(1987) *The Canon of the New Testament: Its Origin, Development, and Significance*, Oxford: Clarendon Press.

Meyer, A. (1930) *Das Rätsel des Jacobusbriefes*, BZNW 10, Giessen: Töpelmann.

Minear, P. (1971) " 'Yes and No': The Demand for Honesty in the Early Church," *NovT* 13, pp. 1–13.

Mitchell, A. C. (1986) "I Corinthians 6:1–11: Group Boundaries and the Courts of Corinth," Ph.D. diss., Yale University.

Mitton, C. L. (1966) *The Epistle of James*, London: Marshall, Morgan & Scott.

Moffatt, J. (1928) *The General Epistles*, London: Hodder & Stoughton.

Morris. K. F. (1957) "An Investigation of Several Linguistic Affinities between the Epistle of James and the Book of Isaiah," Ph.D. diss., Union Theological Seminary in Virginia.

Moule, C. F. D. (1979) *An Idiom-book of New Testament Greek*, 2nd edn., Cambridge: Cambridge University Press.

Moulton, J. H. (1907) "The Epistle of James and the Sayings of Jesus," *Exp* ser. 7,4, pp. 45–55.

Moulton, J. H., F. W. Howard, and N. Turner *A Grammar of New Testament Greek*, 4 vols., Edinburgh: T. & T. Clark; vol. I, *Prolegomena*, 3rd edn., with corrections and additions, 1949; vol. II, *Accidence and Word Formation*, with an Appendix on Semitisms in the New Testament, 1979; vol. III, *Syntax*, 1963; vol. IV, *Style*, 1976.

Moulton, J. H. and G. Milligan (1957) *The Vocabulary of the Greek Testament, Illustrated from the Papyri and Other Non-Literary Sources*, 2nd edn., London: Hodder & Stoughton.

Moxnes, H. (1988) *The Economy of the Kingdom: Social Conflict and Economic Relations in Luke's Gospel*, Philadelphia: Fortress Press.

Muhlinberg, J. (1962) "Holiness," *IDB* 4, pp. 616–25.

Murphy, J. (ed.) (1983) *Demosthenes' On the Crown*, Davis, CA: Hermagoras Press.

Mussies, G. (1972) *Dio Chrysostom and the New Testament*, Studia ad Corpus Hellenisticum 2, Leiden: E. J. Brill.

Mußner, F. (1987) *Der Jakobusbrief*, 5th edn., *HTKNT* 13,1, Freiburg, Basel, and Vienna: Herder & Herder.

Nadeau, R. (1952) "The Progymnasmata of Aphthonius," *Speech Monographs* 19, pp. 264–85.

(1964) "Hermogenes' *On Stases*: A Translation with an Introduction and Notes," *Speech Monographs* 31, pp. 361–424.

Neirynck, F. (1986) "Paul and the Sayings of Jesus," in A. Vanhoye (1986), pp. 265–321.

Nestle, E. and K. Aland *Novum Testamentum Graece*, 26th edn., Stuttgart: Deutsche Bibelstiftung (1979).

Neusner, J. (1984) *Judaism in the Beginning of Christianity*, Philadelphia: Fortress Press.
Nickelsburg, G. W. E. (1977) "The Apocalyptic Message of 1 Enoch 92–105," *CBQ* 3, pp. 309–28.
(1978–79) "Riches, The Rich, and God's Judgment in 1 Enoch 92–105 and the Gospel According to Luke," *NTS* 25, pp. 324–44.
(1983) "Social Aspects of Palestinian Jewish Apocalypticism," in Hellholm (1983), pp. 641–54.
Niederwimmer, K. (1990) "ἐλευθερία, ας, ἡ," *EDNT* ι, pp. 431–34.
Nock, A. D. (1933) *Conversion: The Old and the New in Religion from Alexander to Augustine of Hippo*, Oxford: Clarendon Press.
(1972) *Essays on Religion and the Ancient World*, 2 vols., Oxford: Clarendon Press.
Norden, E. (1898) *Die antike Kunstprosa vom VI. Jahrhundert v. Chr. bis in die Zeit der Renaissance I–II*, 9th edn., Leipzig; repr. Stuttgart: Teubner (1983).
Oepke, A. (1964) "ἄσπιλος," *TDNT* ι, p. 502.
(1967) "λάμπω, κτλ.," *TDNT* νι, pp. 16–28.
Oesterley, W. E. (1910) "The General Epistle of James," *The Expositor's Greek Testament*, vol. ιν, London: Hodder & Stoughton.
O'Neil, E. (ed.) (1977) *Teles (The Cynic Teacher)*, SBLTT 11, Missoula, MT: Scholars Press.
Osiek, C. (1983) *Rich and Poor in the Shepherd of Hermas: An Exegetical-Social Investigation*, ed. B. Vawter, CBQMS 15, Washington, DC: The Catholic Bible Association of America.
Pardee, D. (1982) *Handbook of Ancient Hebrew Letters*, Chico, CA: Scholars Press.
Parker, D. H. (1972) "Rhetoric, Ethics, and Manipulation," *Philosophy and Rhetoric* 5,2, pp. 69–87.
Parry, R. St. J. (1903) *A Discussion of the General Epistle of St. James*, London: Clay.
Pearson, B. A. (1989) "Jas, 1–2 Peter, Jude," in Epp and MacRae (1989), pp. 371–406.
Pearson, L. (1981) *The Art of Demosthenes*, American Philological Association Special Publications 4, Chico, CA: Scholars Press.
Perdue, L. G. (1981) "Paraenesis in the Epistle of James," *ZNW* 72, pp. 241–56.
(1986) "The Wisdom Sayings of Jesus," *Forum* 2,3, pp. 3–35.
(1990) "The Social Character of Paraenesis and Paraenetic Literature," *Semeia* 50, pp. 5–39.
Perdue, L. G. and J. G. Gammie (eds.) (1990) "Paraenesis: Act and Form," *Semeia* 50, 1–271.
Perelman, C. (1963) "The Social Contexts of Argumentation," in *The Idea of Justice and the Problem of Argument*, trans. J. Petrie, London: Routledge & Kegan Paul, pp. 154–60.
(1968) "Rhetoric and Philosophy," *Philosophy and Rhetoric* 1, pp. 15–24.
(1982) *The Realm of Rhetoric*, Notre Dame: Notre Dame University Press.

Perelman, C. and L. Olbrechts-Tyteca (1971) *The New Rhetoric. A Treatise on Argumentation*, Notre Dame and London: Notre Dame University Press.

Petersen, N. R. (1978) *Literary Criticism for New Testament Critics*, Guides to Biblical Scholarship/NT Series, Philadelphia: Fortress Press.

Pfeiffer, E. (1850) "Der Zusammenhang des Jakobusbriefes," *TSK* 23, pp. 163–81.

Plato *Laches. Protagoras. Meno. Euthydemus*, trans. W. R. M. Lamb, LCL, Cambridge: Harvard University Press; London: William Heinemann (1924).

Plutarch *Moralia*, LCL, 16 vols., Cambridge: Harvard University Press; London: William Heinemann (1926–29).

Poehlmann, W. R. (1974) "Addressed Wisdom Teaching in *The Teaching of Silvanus*: A Form Critical Study," Ph.D. diss., Harvard University Press.

Poland, L. M. (1985) *Literary Criticism and Biblical Hermeneutics: A Critique of Formalist Approaches*, AARAS 48, Chico, CA: Scholars Press.

Polanyi, K. (1968) *Primitive, Archaic, and Modern Economics*, ed. G. Dalton, New York: Doubleday & Company.

Popkes, W. (1986) *Adressaten, Situation und Form des Jakobusbriefes*, SBS 125/126, Stuttgart: Katholisches Bibelwerk.

Pratscher, W. (1987) *Der Herrenbruder Jakobus und die Jakobustradition*, FRLANT 139, Göttingen: Vandenhoeck & Ruprecht.

Preminger, A. *et al.* (eds.) (1974) *Princeton Encyclopedia of Poetry and Poetics*, London and Princeton: Princeton University Press.

Quintilian *Institutio Oratia*, trans. H. E. Butler, LCL, 4 vols., Cambridge: Harvard University Press; London: William Heinemann (1920).

Rabe, H. (ed.) (1909) "Aus Rhetoren-Handschriften," *Rheinisches Museum*, N.F., Frankfurt: Sauerländer 64, pp. 284–92.

(1926) *Aphthonii Progymnasmata*, Rhetores Graeci x, Leipzig: B. G. Teubner.

Rad, G. von (1972) *Wisdom in Israel*, Nashville: Abingdon Press.

Ralfs, A. (ed.) *Septuaginta*, 8th edn., Stuttgart: Deutsche Bibelgesellschaft; repr. (1979).

Raymond, J. (1984) "Enthymemes, Examples, and Rhetorical Method," in *Essays on Classical Rhetoric and Modern Discourse*, ed. R. Connors *et al.*, Carbondale and Edwardsville: Southern Illinois University Press, pp. 140–51.

Redditt, P. L. (1983) "The Concept of *Nomos* in Fourth Maccabees," *CBQ* 45, pp. 249–70.

Reese, J. M. (1965) "Plan and Structure in the Book of Wisdom," *CBQ* 27, pp. 391–99.

(1970) *Hellenistic Influence on the Book of Wisdom and its Consequences*, AnBib 41, Rome: Biblical Institute Press.

Reicke, B. (1964) *The Epistles of James, Peter, and Jude*, AB 37, New York: Doubleday & Company.

Rendall, G. H. (1927) *The Epistle of St James and Judaic Christianity*, Cambridge: Cambridge University Press.

Rendtorff, H. (1953) *Hörer und Täter*, Die urchristliche Botschaft 19, Hamburg: Furche.

Rengstorf, K. H. (1964) "δώδεκα, κτλ.," *TDNT* II, pp. 321–28.

Rhetorica ad Alexandrum, trans. H. Rackham, rev. edn., LCL, Cambridge: Harvard University Press; London: William Heinemann, 1965.

Rhetorica ad Herennium, trans. H. Caplan, LCL, Cambridge: Harvard University Press; London: William Heinemann, 1954.

Ricoeur, P. (1977) *The Rule of Metaphor*, trans. R. Czerny, Toronto: University of Toronto Press.

Robbins, V. K. (1981) "Summons and Outline in Mark: Three Step Progression," *NT* 23, pp. 97–114.

(1984) *Jesus the Teacher: A Socio-Rhetorical Interpretation of Mark*, Philadelphia: Fortress Press.

(1985a) "Picking Up the Fragments: From Crossan's Analysis to Rhetorical Analysis," *Forum* 1,2, pp. 31–64.

(1985b) "Pragmatic Relations as a Criterion for Authentic Sayings," *Forum* 1,3, pp. 35–63.

(1987a) "Rhetorical Argument about Lamps and Light in Early Christian Gospels," in *Context. Essays in Honour of Peder Johan Borgen*, ed. P. W. Bockman and R. E. Kristiansen, Relieff 24, University of Trondheim: Tapir, pp. 177–95.

(1987b) "The Woman who Touched Jesus' Garment: Socio-Rhetorical Analysis of the Synoptic Accounts," *NTS* 33, pp. 502–15.

(1988a) "The Chreia," in Aune (1988), pp. 1–23.

(1988b) "Pronouncement Stories from a Rhetorical Perspective," *Forum* 4,2, pp. 3–32.

(1989) *Ancient Quotes and Anecdotes: From Crib to Crypt*, Sonoma, CA: Polebridge Press.

(1991a) "The Social Location of the Implied Author of Luke-Acts," in *The Social World of Luke-Acts*, ed. J. Neyrey, Peabody, MA: Hendrickson Publishers, pp. 305–32.

(1991b) "Writing as a Rhetorical Act in Plutarch and the Gospels," in *Persuasive Artistry: Studies in New Testament Rhetoric in Honor of George A. Kennedy*, ed. D. F. Watson, Sheffield: JSOT Press, pp. 157–86.

(1992) "The Reversed Contextualization of Psalm 22 in the Markan Crucifixion: A Socio-Rhetorical Analysis," in *The Four Gospels: 1992. Festschrift Frans Neirynck*, ed. F. Van Segbroeck, C. M. Tuckett, G. Van Belle, and J. Verheyden, Leuven: Leuven University Press, pp. 1161–83.

(1993) "Rhetoric and Culture: Exploring Types of Cultural Rhetoric in a Text," in *Rhetoric and the New Testament: Essays from the 1992 Heidelberg Conference*, ed. S. E. Porter and T. H. Olbricht, Sheffield: Sheffield Academic Press, pp. 447–67.

(1996a) *Exploring the Texture of Texts: A Guide to Socio-Rhetorical Interpretation*, Valley Forge: Trinity Press International.

(1996b) *The Tapestry of Early Christian Discourse: Rhetoric, Society and Ideology*, London: Routledge.

Robbins, V. K. and J. H. Patton, (1980) "Rhetoric and Biblical Criticism," *The Quarterly Journal of Speech* 66, pp. 327–37.

Roberts, K. A. (1978) "Toward a Generic Concept of Counter-Culture," *Sociological Focus* 11, pp. 111–26.

Roberts, W. R. (ed.) (1902) *Demetrius On Style. The Greek Text of Demetrius* DE ELOCUTIONE *edited after the Paris Manuscript*, with introduction, translation, facsimiles, etc., Cambridge: Cambridge University Press; repr. NY: Arno Press (1979).

(ed.) (1910) *Dionysius On Literary Composition. Being the Greek Text of the* DE COMPOSITIONE VERBORVM, with introduction, translation, notes, glossary, and appendices by W. R. Roberts, London: Macmillan & Co.; repr. New York: AMS Press (1976).

Robertson, A. T. (1923) *A Grammar of the Greek New Testament in the Light of Historical Research*, Nashville: Broadman Press.

Robertson, A. T. and W. H. Davis (1985) *A New Short Grammar of the Greek Testament*, 10th edn., New York: Harper & Row; repr. Grand Rapids: Baker Book House.

Robertson, R. (ed.) (1969) *Sociology of Religion*, Baltimore: Penguin Books.

Robinson, D. W. B. (1970) " 'Faith of Jesus Christ' – A New Testament Debate," *Reformed Theological Review* 29, pp. 71–81.

Robinson, J. M. (1982) "Early Collections of Jesus' Sayings," in *Logia: Les Paroles de Jesus – The Sayings of Jesus*, (Memorial to Joseph Coppens), Leuven: Leuven University Press/Peeters, pp. 389–94.

Robinson, J. M. and H. Koester (1971) *Trajectories through Early Christianity*, Philadelphia: Fortress Press.

Rohrbaugh, R. L. (1987) " 'Social Location of Thought' as a Heuristic Construct in New Testament Study," *JSNT* 30 pp. 103–19.

Ropes, J. H. (1916) *A Critical and Exegetical Commentary on the Epistle of St. James*, ICC 40, Edinburgh: T. & T. Clark.

Ross, A. (1957) *The Epistles of James and John*, Grand Rapids: William B. Eerdmans.

Rountree, C. (1976) "Further Thoughts on the Discourse Structure of James," International Linguistics Center, Dallas, TX.

Russell, D. A. and N. G. Wilson (eds.) (1981) *Menander Rhetor*, with translation and commentary, Oxford: Clarendon Press.

Rustler, M. K. (1952) "Thema und Disposition des Jakobusbriefes. Eine formkritische Studie," Diss., Vienna.

Safrai, S. and M. Stern (eds.) (1974; 1976) *The Jewish People in the First Century*, 2 vols., CRINT I.1,2, Assen: Van Gorcum; Philadelphia: Fortress Press.

Saller, R. (1982) *Personal Patronage Under the Early Empire*, Cambridge and New York: Cambridge University Press.

Sanders, E. P. (1969) *The Tendencies of the Synoptic Tradition*, SNTSMS 9, Cambridge: At the University Press.

(1985) *Jesus and Judaism*, Phildelphia: Fortress Press.

Sanders, J. T. (1983) *Ben Sira and Demotic Wisdom*, SBLMS 28, ed. J. Crenshaw, Chico, CA: Scholars Press.

Scaglione, A. (1972) *The Classical Theory of Composition*, University of

North Carolina Studies in Comparative Literature 53, Chapel Hill: The University of North Carolina Press.

Schammberger, H. (1936) *Die Einheitlichkeit des Jacobusbriefes im anti-gnostischen Kampf*, Gotha: Klotz.

Schille, G. (1977) "Wider die Gespaltenheit des Glaubens. Beobachtungen am Jakobusbrief," in *Theologische Versuche*, ed. P. Waetzel and G. Schille, Berlin (Ost): Evangelische Verlags-Anstalt, pp. 71–89.

Schlatter, A. von (1956) *Der Brief des Jakobus*, 2nd edn., Stuttgart: Calwers Verlag.

(1985) *Der Brief des Jakobus, mit einem Begleitwort von Franz Mußner*, 3rd edn., Stuttgart.

Schlier, H. (1964a) "ἀφίστημι, κτλ.," *TDNT* I, pp. 512–14.

(1964b) "ἐλεύθερος, κτλ.," *TDNT* II, pp. 487–502.

Schmidt, K. L. (1964a) "βασιλεύς, κτλ.," *TDNT* I, pp. 574–93.

(1964b) "διασπορά, κτλ.," *TDNT* II, pp. 98–104.

(1968) "πταίω," *TDNT* VI, pp. 883–84.

Schmidt-Clausing, F. (1969) "Die unterschiedliche Stellung Luthers und Zwinglis zum Jakobusbriefes," *Reformatio* 18, pp. 568–85.

Schneider, J. *(1965)* "ἔρχομαι, κτλ.," *TDNT* III, pp. 666–84.

(1967) "παραβαίνω, κτλ.," *TDNT* V, pp. 740–42.

(1972) "τιμή, κτλ.," *TDNT* VIII, pp. 169–80.

Schniewind, J. and G. Friedrich (1964) "ἐπαγγέλλω, κτλ.," *TDNT* II, pp. 576–86.

Schoedel, W. R. (1967) *The Apostolic Fathers: A New Translation and Commentary*, vol. V, *Polycarp, Martyrdom of Polycarp, Fragments of Papias*, London: Thomas Nelson & Sons.

(1985) *Ignatius of Antioch*, Hermeneia, Philadelphia: Fortress Press.

Schoeps, H. J. (1949) *Theologie und Geschichte des Judenchristentums*, Tübingen: J. C. B. Mohr (P. Siebeck).

Schrage, W. (1971) "συναγωγή, κτλ.," *TDNT* VII, pp. 840–41.

(1988) *The Ethics of the New Testament*, trans. D. E. Green, Philadelphia: Fortress Press.

Schrage, W. and H. Balz (1980) *Die Briefe des Jakobus, Petrus, Johannes und Judas*, NTD 10, Göttingen: Vandenhoeck & Ruprecht.

Schrenk, G. (1967) "ἐκλέγομαι, κτλ.," *TDNT* IV, pp. 144–92;

Schrenk G. and V. Herntrich (1967) "λεῖμμα, κτλ.," *TDNT* IV, pp. 194–214.

Schubert, P. (1939a) *Form and Function of the Pauline Thanksgivings*, BZNW 20, Berlin: Töpelmann.

(1939b) "Form and Function of Pauline Letters," *JR* 19, pp. 365–77.

Schürer, E. (1973–87) *The History of the Jewish People in the Age of Jesus Christ (175 B.C.–A.D. 135)*, rev. and ed. G. Vermes *et al.*, vols. I–III.2, Edinburgh: T. & T. Clark.

Schürmann, H. (1968) *Traditionsgeschichtliche Untersuchungen*, Düsseldorf: Patmos.

Schütz, R. (1922) "Der Jakobusbrief. Kolometrisch übersetzt," *TBl* 1, pp. 24–32.

Schulz, S. (1987) *Neutestamentliche Ethik*, Zürich: Theologischer Verlag.

Schulze, J. D. (1802) *Der Schriftstellerische Werth und Charakter des Petrus-, Judas- und Jacobusbriefes*, Weissenfels.

Schwegler, A. (1846) *Das nachapostolische Zeitalter in den Hauptmomenten seiner Entwicklung*, vol. ɪ, Tübingen: Fues.

Seitz, O. J. F. (1944) "The Relationship of the Shepherd of Hermas to the Letter of James," *JBL* 63, pp. 131–40.

(1947) "Antecedents and Significance of the Term ΔΙΨΥΧΟΣ," *JBL* 66, pp. 211–19.

(1957) "Afterthoughts on the term 'Dipsychos'," *NTS* 4, pp. 327–34.

(1959) "Two Spirits in Man: An Essay in Biblical Exegesis," *NTS* 6, pp. 82–95.

(1964) "James and the Law," *SE* 2, pp. 472–86.

Sellin, E. and G. Fohrer (1968) *Introduction to the Old Testament*, Nashville: Abingdon Press.

Selwyn, E. G. (1947) *The First Epistle of Peter. The Greek Text with Introduction, Notes, and Essays*, 2nd edn., London: Macmillan & Co.; repr. Grand Rapids: Baker Book House (1981).

Seneca *Epistulae Morales*, 3 vols., trans. R. M. Gummere, LCL, Cambridge: Harvard University Press; London: William Heinemann, 1917, 1920, 1925.

Moral Essays, 3 vols., trans. J. W. Basore, Cambridge: Harvard University Press, 1928, 1929, 1935.

Shepherd, M. H. (1956) "The Epistle of James and the Gospel of Matthew," *JBL* 75, pp. 40–51.

Sidebottom, E. M. (1967) *James, Jude, I Peter*, London: Nelson.

Siegert, F. (1980) *Drei hellenistisch-jüdische Predigten*, WUNT 20, Tübingen.

Siker, J. S. (1987) "The Canonical Status of the Catholic Epistles in the Syriac New Testament," *JTS* 38, pp. 311–29.

Sloan, T. O. (1947) "Rhetoric: Rhetoric in Literature," in *The New Encyclopaedia Britannica*, 15th edn, vol. xv, pp. 798–805.

Smallwood, E. M. (1981) *The Jews Under Roman Rule From Pompey to Diocletian: A Study in Political Relations*, Leiden: E. J. Brill.

Smith, J. Z. (1975) "The Social Description of Early Christianity," *RelSRev* 1, pp. 19–21.

Smyth, H. W. (1956) *Greek Grammar*, Cambridge: Harvard University Press.

Soden, H. F. von (1905) *Urchristliche Literaturgeschichte*, Berlin: A. Duncker.

Souček, J. B. (1958) "Zu den Problemen des Jakobusbriefes," *EvT* 18, pp. 460–69.

Spengel, L. (1853–56) *Rhetores Graeci*, 3 vols., Leipzig: Teubner; repr. Frankfurt: Minerva (1966).

Spitta, F. (1896) "Der Brief des Jakobus," in *Zur Geschichte und Literatur des Urchristentums*, vol. ɪɪ, Göttingen: Vandenhoeck & Ruprecht.

Stählin, G. (1975) "φιλέω, κτλ.," *TDNT* ɪx, pp. 113–71.

Stauffer, E. (1952) "Das 'Gesetz der Freiheit' in der Ordensregel von Jericho," *TLZ* 77, cols. 527–32.

Stirewalt, M. L. (1991) "The Form and Function of the Greek Letter-Essay," in Donfried (1991), pp. 147–71.

"A Survey of Uses of Letter-Writing in Hellenistic and Jewish Communities through the New Testament Period" (unpublished essay).

Stone, M. E. (ed.) (1984) *Jewish Writings of the Second Temple Period*, CRINT II,2, Assen: Van Gorcum; Philadelphia: Fortress Press.

Storr, G. C. (1797) "In epistolam Jacobi. Dissertatio exegetica," in *Opuscula academica ad interpretationem Librorum Sacrorum pertinentia*, vol. II, Tübingen, pp. 1–74.

Stowers, S. K. (1981) *The Diatribe and Paul's Letter to the Romans*, SBLDS 57, Ann Arbor: Scholars Press.

(1984) "Social Status, Public Speaking and Private Teaching: The Circumstances of Paul's Preaching Activity," *NovT* 26,1, pp. 59–82.

(1986a) *Letter Writing in Greco-Roman Antiquity*, The Library of Early Christianity, vol. V, ed. W. A. Meeks, Philadelphia: Westminster Press.

(1986b) "The Social Sciences and the Study of Early Christianity," in *Approaches to Ancient Judaism*, vol. V, ed. W. Green, Studies in Judaism and Its Greco-Roman Context, Atlanta: Scholars Press, pp. 148–82.

Strack, H. L. and P. Billerbeck (1965) *Kommentar zum Neuen Testament aus Talmud und Midrasch*, 4th edn., 5 vols., Munich: C. H. Beck.

Strecker, G. (1988) *The Sermon on the Mount*, trans. from the 2nd edn. by O. C. Dean, Jr., Nashville: Abingdon Press.

Stuhlmacher, P. (1965) *Gerechtigkeit Gottes bei Paulus*, FRLANT 87, Göttingen: Vandenhoeck & Ruprecht.

(1979) *Vom Verstehen des Neuen Testaments*, GNT 6, Göttingen: Vandenhoeck & Ruprecht.

Swete, H. B. (1968) *An Introduction to the OT in Greek*, rev. R. R. Ottley, with an appendix containing *The Letter of Aristeas*, ed. H. St. J. Thackeray, New York: KTAV Publishing House.

Tannehill, R. C. (1975) *The Sword of His Mouth*, SBLSS, Philadelphia: Fortress Press; Missoula, MT: Scholars Press.

(1984) "Types and Functions of Apophthegms in the Synoptic Gospels," in *ANRW* II, 25,2, Berlin and New York: De Gruyter, pp. 1792–829.

Tasker, R. V. G. (1957) *The General Epistle of James*, Grand Rapids: William B. Eerdmans.

Thackeray, H. St. J. (1909) *A Grammar of the Old Testament according to the Septuagint*, vol. I, Cambridge: Cambridge University Press.

Thackeray, H. St. J. *et. al.* (eds.) *The Complete Works of Flavius Josephus*, 9 vols., LCL, Cambridge: Harvard University Press; London: William Heinemann (1929–65).

Theissen, G. (1978) *Sociology of Early Palestinian Christianity*, trans. J. Bowden, Philadelphia: Fortress Press.

Theon *Progymnasmata*. (1832) ed. C. Walz, Rhetores Graeci, I, Stuttgart: Cotta.

Thomas, J. (1968) "Anfechtung und Vorfreude," *KD* 14, pp. 183–206.

Thraede, K. (1970) *Grundzüge griechisch-römischer Brieftopik*, Zetemata: Monographien zur klassischen Altertumswissenschaft 48, ed. E. Burk and H. Diller, Munich: C. H. Beck.

Thyen, H. (1956) *Der Stil der jüdisch-hellenistischen Homilie*, FRLANT 47, Göttingen: Vandenhoeck & Ruprecht.

Tielemann, T. (1894) "Versuch einer neuen Auslegung und Anordnung des Jakobusbriefes," *NKZ* 5, pp. 580–611.

Townsend, M. J. (1975) "James 4:1–4: Warning against Zealotry?," *ExpT* 87, pp. 211–13.

Traub, H. W. (1955) "Pliny's Treatment of History in Epistolary Form," *Transactions of the American Philological Association*, 86, pp. 213–32.

Trenkler, F. S. (1894) *Der Brief des heiligen Jakobus*, Freiburg: Herder.

Vanhoye, A. (ed.) (1986) *L'Apôtre Paul: Personalité, style et conception du ministère*, BETL 73, Leuven: Leuven University Press/Peeters.

Verner, D. C. (1983) *The Household of God: The Social World of the Pastoral Epistles*, SBLDS 71, Chico, CA: Scholars Press.

Vetschera, R. (1911–12) *Zur griechischen Paränese*, Smichow/Prague: Rohlicek & Sievers.

Vielhauer, P. (1975) *Geschichte der urchristlichen Literatur: Einleitung in das Neue Testament, die Apokryphen und die apostolischen Väter*, Berlin and New York: De Gruyter.

Volkmann, R. (1885) *Die Rhetorik der Griechen und Römer in systematischer übersicht*, 2nd edn., Leipzig: Teubner; repr. Hildesheim: Georg Olms Verlag (1987).

Vorster, W. S. (1989) "Intertextuality and *Redaktionsgeschichte*," in Draisma (1989).

Vouga, F. (1984) *L'Épître de Saint Jacques*, CNT 13a, Geneva: Labor et Fides.

Wachob, W. H. (1988) "The Relationship Between the Epistle of James and Q," unpublished paper presented to the Southeastern Regional SBL Meeting, Macon, GA.

(1993) "'The Rich in Faith' and 'the Poor in Spirit': The Socio-Rhetorical Function of a Saying of Jesus in the Epistle of James," Ph.D. diss., Emory University; Ann Arbor, MI: University Microfilms.

Walker, R. (1964) "Allein aus Werken. Zur Auslegung von Jakobus 2,14–26," *ZTK* 61, pp. 155–92.

Walz, C. (ed.) *Rhetores Graeci*, 9 vols., Stuttgart: Cotta (1832–36); repr. Osnabrück: Zeller (1968).

Wanke, J. (1977) "Die urchristlichen Lehrer nach dem Zeugnis des Jakobusbriefes," in *Die Kirche des Anfangs* (Festschrift für H. Schürmann zum 65. Geburtstag), ed. R. Schnackenburg *et al.*, ETS 38, Leipzig: St. Benno Verlag, pp. 489–511.

Ward, R. B. (1966a) "A Review: Martin Dibelius, *Die Brief des Jakobusbrief* (MeyerK 15)," *JBL* 85, pp. 255–56.

(1966b) "The Communal Concern of the Epistle of James," Ph.D. diss., Harvard University.

(1968) "The Works of Abraham: James 2:14–26," *HTR* 61, pp. 283–90.

(1969) "Partiality in the Assembly, James 2:2–4," *HTR* 62, pp. 87–97.

(1973) "James of Jerusalem," *ResQ* 16, pp. 174–90.

(1976) "JAMES, LETTER OF," in *IDBSup*, ed. K. Crim, Nashville: Abingdon Press, pp. 469–70.

(1993) "James of Jerusalem in the First Two Centuries," in *ANRW* II, 26,1, Berlin and New York: De Gruyter, pp. 779–812.

Warmuth, G. (1983) "*kābôd*," *TDOT* III, pp. 335–41.

Watson, D. F. (1988) *Invention, Arrangement, and Style: Rhetorical Criticism of Jude and 2 Peter*, SBLDS 104, Atlanta: Scholars Press.

(1989) "1 Corinthians 10:23–11:1 in the light of Greco-Roman Rhetoric," *JBL* 108,2, pp. 301–18.

(1993a) "James 2 In the Light of Greco-Roman Schemes of Argumentation," *NTS* 39, pp. 94–121.

(1993b) "The Rhetoric of James 3:1–12 and a Classic Pattern of Argumentation," *NovT* 35, pp. 48–64.

Watson, W. G. E. (1984) *Classical Hebrew Poetry: A Guide to Its Techniques*, *JSOTSup* 26, Sheffield: JSOT Press.

Weichert, V. (ed.) (1910) *Demetrii et Libanii qui feruntur ΤΥΠΟΙ ΕΠΙΣΤΟΛΙΚΟΙ et ΕΠΙΣΤΟΛΙΜΑΙΟΙ ΧΑΡΑΚΤΗΡΕΣ*, Leipzig: Teubner.

Weiss, B. (1904) *Der Jakobusbrief und die neuere Kritik*, Leipzig: Deichert.

Weiss, J. (1937) *The History of Primitive Christianity*, 2 vols., trans. and ed. F. C. Grant *et al.*, New York: Wilson-Erickson.

Weiss, K. (1976) "Motiv und Ziel der Frömmigkeit des Jakobusbriefes," in *Theologische Versuche*, VII, ed. P. Waetzel and G. Schille, Berlin (Ost): Evangelische Verlags-Anstalt, pp. 107–14.

Welles, C. B. (1934) *Royal Correspondence in the Hellenistic Period*, New Haven: Yale University Press.

Wendland, P. (1895) "Philo und die kynisch-stoisch Diatribe," in Wendland and O. Kern, *Beiträge zur Geschichte der griechischen Philosophie und Religion* (Festschrift für Hermann Diels), Berlin: Georg Reimer.

(1905) "Die Rede an Demonikos," in *Anaximenes vom Lampsakos: Studien zur ältesten Geschichte der Rhetorik*, Berlin: Wiedmann, pp. 81–101.

Wessel, W. (1953) *An Inquiry into the Origin, Literary Character, Historical and Religious Significance of the Epistle of James*, Ph.D. diss., University of Edinburgh.

Westerholm, S. (1978) *Jesus and Scribal Authority*, ConNT 10, Lund: Gleerup.

White, J. L. (1972a) *The Body of the Greek Letter*, SBLDS 2, Missoula, MT: Scholars Press.

(1972b) *The Form and Structure of the Official Petition*, SBLDS 5, Missoula, MT: Scholars Press.

(1981a) "The Ancient Epistolography Group in Retrospect," *Semeia* 22, pp. 1–15.

(1981b) "The Greek Documentary Letter Tradition Third Century B.C.E. to Third Century C.E.," *Semeia* 22, pp. 89–106.

(1983) "Saint Paul and the Apostolic Letter Tradition," *CBQ* 45, pp. 433–44.

(1986) *Light From Ancient Letters*, FFNT, Philadelphia: Fortress Press.

(1988) "Ancient Greek Letters," in Aune (1988), pp. 85–105.

White, J. L. and K. A. Kensinger (1976) "Categories of Greek Papyrus Letters," in SBLSP, Missoula, MT: Scholars Press, pp. 79–91.

Wichelns, H. A. (1925) "The Literary Criticism of Oratory," in *Studies in Rhetoric and Public Speaking in Honor of James Albert Winans*, ed. A. M. Drummond, New York: Century Co.; repr. in Bryant (1958), pp. 5–42.

Wifstrand, A. (1948) "Stylistic Problems in the Epistle of James and Peter," *ST* 1, pp. 170–82.

Wilckens, U. (1971) "σοφία, κτλ.," *TDNT* VII pp. 465–76, 496–528.

Wilder, A. N. (1971) *Early Christian Rhetoric: The Language of the Gospel*, Cambridge: Harvard University Press.

Wilke, C. G. (1843) *Die neutestamentliche Rhetorik. Ein Seitenstueck zur Grammatik des Neutestamentlichen Sprachidioms*, Dresden/Leipzig: Arnold.

Williams, J. G. (1981) *Those Who Ponder Proverbs: Aphoristic Thinking and Biblical Literature*, Sheffield: Almond Press.

Wilson, S. G. (1983) *Luke and the Law*, Cambridge: Cambridge University Press.

Windisch, H. and H. Preisker (1951) *Die Katholischen Briefe*, HNT 15, 3rd edn., Tübingen: J. C. B. Mohr (P. Siebeck).

Wissowa, Georg et al. (eds) (1894–) *Paulys Real-Encyclopedie der classischen Altertumswissenschaft*, Stuttgart: J. B. Metzler.

Wolde, E. van (1989) "Trendy Intertextuality," in Draisma (1989).

Wolverton, W. I. (1956) "The Double-Minded Man in the Light of Essene Psychology," *ATR* 38, pp. 166–75.

Worden, R. D. (1973) "A Philological Analysis of Luke 6:20b-49 and Parallels," Ph.D. diss., Princeton Theological Seminary; Ann Arbor, MI: University Microfilms.

Wuellner, W. H. (1976) "Paul's Rhetoric of Argumentation in Romans: An Alternative to the Donfried-Karris Debate over Romans," *CBQ* 38, pp. 330–51.

(1978a) "Der Jakobusbrief im Licht der Rhetorik und Textpragmatik," *LB* 43, pp. 5–66.

(1978b) "Toposforschung und Torah-interpretation bei Paulus und Jesus," *NTS* 24, pp. 463–83.

(1979) "Greek Rhetoric and Pauline Argumentation," in *Early Christian Literature and the Classical Intellectual Tradition: In Honorem Robert M. Grant*, ed. W. Schoedel and R. Wilson, Théologie historique 53, Paris: Beauchesne, pp. 177–88.

(1986) "Paul as Pastor. The Function of Rhetorical Questions in First Corinthians," in A. Vanhoye (1986), 49–77.

(1987) "Where is Rhetorical Criticism Taking Us?," *CBQ* 49, pp. 448–63.

Xenophon *Memorabilia and Oeconomicus*, trans. E. C. Marchant, LCL, Cambridge: Harvard University Press; London: William Heinemann (1923).

Young, F. W. (1948) "The Relation of 1 Clement to the Epistle of James," *JBL* 67, pp. 339–45.

Zahn, T. von (1909) *Introduction to the New Testament*, trans. J. M. Trout et al., 3 vols., New York: Charles Scribner's Sons.

Zeller, D. (1977) *Die weisheitliche Mahnsprueche in den Synoptikern*, FB 17, Würzburg: Echter Verlag.

Zerwick, M. and M. Grosvenor (1981) *A Grammatical Analysis of the Greek New Testament*, unabridged, rev. edn., Rome: Biblical Institute Press.

Zmijewski, J. (1980) "Christliche 'Vollkommenheit'. Erwägungen zur Theologie des Jakobusbriefes," *SUNT* A,5, pp. 50–78.

INDEX OF SOURCES AND AUTHORS

Mishna (*'Abot*) 6, 82, 126, 131
Moses, Assumption of 164

Nicolaus of Myra 9n.22

Origen 26–27

Philo 97n.78, 126, 128, 130, 131, 168
Plato 45, 46, 48, 49, 50, 168
Plutarch 88n.61, 133, 176n.17
Polycarp 23, 89, 138, 139, 140, 141, 147,
    148, 149, 150, 152, 155, 157, 199
Posidonius 14, 42, 49
Pseudo-Aristotle 76, 176n.16
Pseudo-Demetrius 2n.3, 3, 10, 15,
    43n.24
Pseudo-Isocrates 42, 43, 45, 49, 50
Pseudo-Justin 46
Pseudo-Libanius 2n.3, 3, 4, 8, 10, 15, 16,
    43n.24
Pseudo-Phocylides 76

Quintilian 8, 9n.21, 12n.36, 13, 15, 16,
    18n.52, 19, 20, 21n.61, 50, 56n.40, 73,
    79, 88n.58, 94n.67, 95n.70, 96, 101,
    102n.78, 106, 107n.88, 171, 172, 173,
    174, 175, 199
Qumran 33n.15, 34n.18, 126, 130

Rhetorica ad Alexandrum 12n.36, 15,
    16, 75, 76, 78n.40, 94n.68, 106n.85,
    109
Rhetorica ad Herennium 12n.36, 15,
    18n.52, 21n.61, 50, 61, 62n.10, 63, 64,
    70n.29, 73, 75, 76, 77n.38, 78, 85, 86,
    88, 90n.62, 93n.66, 94n.67, 95n.70,
    105, 106n.85, 107, 109, 111, 159,
    161n.6, 175, 176, 184

Seneca 14, 42, 45, 49
Sibylline Oracles 69n.27, 165
Socrates 48, 74
Stoicorum Veterum Fragmenta 8n.16
Syrianus 15

Talmud 6, 126, 139, 168
Theon 9, 43n.24, 48n.32, 57, 120, 121,
    124, 125, 141, 149, 199, 201
Thomas, Gospel of 23, 138, 139, 140,
    141, 142, 146, 147, 148, 149, 150, 152,
    155, 199
Thucydides 46

Xenophon 131

Zebulon, Testament of 132, 134
Zwingli, U. 31

Modern Authors

Adams, C. 95n.69
Adamson, J. B. 25, 26, 27, 28, 31,
    32n.14, 33n.15, 34, 35n.20,
    36n.21, 59n.1, 60n.2, 66n.15, 83n.49, 84,
    85n.53, 92
Aland, K. 17n.47
Allen, W. 10n.25
Alter, R. 114, 115, ¹16n.5, 122
Arnim, J. von, 8n.16
Arrighetti, G. 7n.15
Attridge, H. W. 8n.16
Aune, D. E. 2, 3, 4, 5, 6, 7n.15, 8,
    13n.38, 16n.46, 41, 60n.2, 163

Baasland, E. 6, 7, 8n.17, 11n.29, 12n.35,
    18n.49, 25, 26, 30, 31, 33, 34, 52, 54,
    55, 56, 59n.1, 136
Bakhtin, M. M. 115
Baldwin, C. S. 9n.22, 19n.56
Bammel, E. 1n.2, 81, 123
Barnard, P. M. 48
Barnett, A. E. 27
Barth, M. 64
Bartlett, D. L. 165
Bauckham, R. 5
Baur, F. C. 34
Beck, D. L. 32, 34
Beker, J. C. 34n.18
Bengel, J. A. 54, 67n.22
Bergauer, P. 28
Berger, K. 5n.9., 6, 7, 8n.16, 12n.35,
    48n.32, 50, 52, 55n.39, 59n.1
Berger, P. 187
Bertram, G. 88n.61
Betz, H. D. 7n.15, 8n.16, 39, 54, 92,
    121, 126, 129, 132, 133, 139n.21,
    140n.22, 142n.26, 143, 148, 152, 169,
    199
Beyer, H. W. 83
Beyer, K. 66n.15
Bitzer, L. F. 21, 22, 136, 154, 156, 165,
    170
Boggan, C. W. 1n.1
Bonner, S. F. 9n.19, 116
Borg, M. J. 2n.2
Braun, H. 108n.89
Brinktrine, J. 67n.21
Britton, A. 21n.62
Bryant, D. C. 2n.5, 3, 11n.27, 21, 22

INDEX OF BIBLICAL REFERENCES

INDEX OF SUBJECTS